An Introduction to Parapsychology

An Introduction to Parapsychology

by

H.J. Irwin

McFarland & Company, Inc., Publishers
Jefferson, North Carolina, and London

British Library Cataloguing-in-Publication data available

Library of Congress Cataloguing-in-Publication Data

Irwin, H.J. (Harvey J.)
An introduction to parapsychology.

  Bibliography: p. 281.
  Includes indexes.
  1. Psychical research. I. Title
BF1031.I79   1989   133.8   88-32593

ISBN 0-89950-396-9 (lib. bdg.; 50# acid-free natural paper)

Manufactured in the United States of America.

McFarland   Box 611   Jefferson NC 28640

Acknowledgments

This book has grown out of my experiences in teaching parapsychology at the University of New England during the past ten years. In this context I benefited by the efforts of my students who provided feedback on the course and who worked hard to educate me. Reliance upon earlier course notes as a framework for my book was enabled by the University's agreement to release copyright.

The content of the book has been influenced by numerous researchers whose parapsychological work I have found a source of inspiration. I have endeavored to acknowledge these contributions through appropriate citations in the text, but I would like specifically to record my intellectual indebtedness to the work of John Beloff, Sue Blackmore, John Palmer, Louisa E. Rhine, and Rex Stanford.

Thanks are due to the following people who graciously read and offered constructive comment upon various sections of the manuscript: Carlos Alvarado, Alan Gauld, Ray Hyman, Jürgen Keil, Gertrude Schmeidler, Sybo Schouten, Michael Thalbourne, and Debra Weiner.

Cases of out-of-body experience from my book *Flight of Mind* are quoted in Chapter 12 by permission of the publisher, Scarecrow Press. The quotation in Chapter 15 from an article in the *Applied Psi Newsletter* by Mishlove and Kautz (1982) is made by courtesy of the authors and the publisher, the Center for Applied Intuition.

Jule Eisenbud, Stanley Krippner, Helmut Schmidt, Ian Stevenson, and Charles Tart provided photographs for reproduction as figures in the book: their generosity here is greatly appreciated. Other figures were supplied by the Foundation for Research on the Nature of Man (FRNM) and by the Mary Evans Picture Library (MEPL). The source of each figure is given in the text. The technical expertise of the University of New England's Media Resources Unit in various photographic tasks and of Ivan Thornton in preparing the line drawings is acknowledged with thanks.

I am greatly indebted to the word-processing skills and forebearance of Ann Matthews in typing and amending sections of the manuscript; the

v

assistance of Edie Liptrot, Gerda van Houtert and the word-processing unit of the University's Department of External Studies also is appreciated.

September 1988   H.J. Irwin
                                           University of New England
                                           Armidale, Australia

Contents

List of Figures

1
Introduction

Parapsychology is the scientific study of experiences which, if they are as they seem to be, are in principle outside the realm of human capabilities as presently conceived by conventional scientists. Thus parapsychological phenomena ostensibly indicate the operation of factors unknown to or unrecognized by orthodox science, so-called *paranormal* factors. Familiar examples of such anomalous phenomena are experiences that seemingly involve extrasensory perception (ESP) and apparitions (e.g., ghosts). The objective of this book is to provide an introductory survey of parapsychologists' efforts to explore the authenticity and bases of these apparently paranormal phenomena.

As a general delineation of the scope of parapsychological research the above paragraph has several features warranting consideration. Most important is the point that in no way is there any presumption here of the existence of "the paranormal," contrary to the approach of many contemporary parapsychologists who actually regard parapsychology as the study of the paranormal. Certainly people report having experiences in which it seemed to them there was, for example, some information acquired without the involvement of the recognized human senses. But when such an "extrasensory" experience is termed *parapsychological* no conclusion has necessarily been reached that there exists a paranormal process by which information can be mediated outside the individual's sensory capacities.

As far as the definition of parapsychological experiences is concerned it is purely a matter of appearances, of how an experience *seems* to be. A fundamental task of researchers then is to investigate the actual bases of these experiences, determining the extent to which the phenomena are explicable within the framework of accepted principles of mainstream science and, if appropriate, defining the respects in which that framework should be extended in order to accommodate empirical findings on the phenomena.

Although parapsychological experiences appear to be paranormal they therefore are not defined to be so; rather, the question of their paranor-

1

mality is a matter for investigation. It is important to appreciate the distinction between *parapsychological experiences* that do occur and underlying *paranormal processes* that are mere hypotheses for scientific investigation. All ESP experiences thus are parapsychological, but we require proof that any of them could be paranormal.

The foregoing representation of parapsychology also highlights the discipline's paradoxical relationship with science. Despite the fact that parapsychological phenomena ostensibly are contrary to conventional scientific wisdom, it is through the methods of science that the phenomena are studied. Sociologically speaking, parapsychology is undertaken as a scientific endeavor regardless of its subject matter, flaws in any of its research procedures, and the skeptical rhetoric of its critics. More specifically, the perspective adopted in this book is that parapsychology is very much allied to psychology, the science of behavior. In other words, parapsychological research rightly is conducted predominantly within the broader context of the scientific investigation of behavior and its phenomena are best understood in the light of an appreciation of the principles of psychology. Thus a feature of modern parapsychology is that investigation of its phenomena is staged in the controlled environment of the psychological laboratory whenever possible. Scientific methodology is emphasized also in field studies of the sort that predominated in the days when such interests were known as *psychical research,* the study of phenomena apparently mediated directly by the mind or "soul."

In part the scientific orientation in parapsychology demands that the design and the conduct of an investigation be as impervious as possible to the beliefs of the research personnel (except of course where such beliefs are the focus of the study). It is as well to note at the outset that a similar approach ideally should be adopted by you as a student of parapsychology. This is no simple achievement, in essence because the subject matter of parapsychology tends to evoke extreme reactions in people, either of uncritical, soft-minded gullibility in the paranormal or of unyielding, closed-minded skepticism. To get the most from your study of parapsychology it will be necessary to set aside such narrow preconceptions of the subject and consciously to strive for a more objective, evenhanded style of weighing up arguments and data on both sides of an issue.

As it is depicted in this text, parapsychology additionally is centered on experiences of *people.* This is not to claim that other animals are devoid of so-called psychic abilities. Indeed there has been some investigation, both in the laboratory and in the field, of parapsychological phenomena associated with animals. But like their counterparts in psychology these studies derive their pertinence largely from their role as simplified and highly controlled models of human behavior and from the comparative or evolutionary perspective they bring to the human context. The quantitative and qualitative data on people's parapsychological experiences also are manifoldly more extensive, detailed and diverse than that for animals; the human focus in parapsychology thereby is apt in relation to its empirical footing and its capacity for theoretical productivity. At the same time, when behavioral scientists seek to address the experiences of people rather than the behavior of animals they appreciate the difficulty of the task. Human cognitive, social, cultural, emotional, motivational, perceptual, neuropsychological, psychodynamic, and other psychological factors are so complex and variable that no individual experience can possibly be understood completely in terms of one basic dimension or process. Although parapsychology's emphasis upon people as the object of its study may make the discipline more personally meaningful, you therefore should not have unduly high expectations of finding simple, comprehensive, scientifically sound answers to questions about the nature of parapsychological experiences.

The scope of the field of parapsychology has drawn comment from both conceptual and pragmatic perspectives. In conceptual terms there has been some unease that parapsychology in essence is defined negatively. That is, a phenomenon is held to lie within the field's boundaries for no other reason than that it is defined not to lie outside them. This is a feature of the widely endorsed alternative notion of parapsychology as the study of the paranormal or of processes as yet undiscovered and unrecognized by science. That approach is founded upon a negative definition because parapsychologists are unable to specify what it is (as opposed to what it is not) that indicates an experience's involvement of the paranormal. It is, for example, thought insufficient to define extrasensory perception (ESP) as direct apprehension of information by the mind, for the reason that "direct apprehension" is specifiable not in any affirmative way but only as something that is *not* via the usual sensory channels and is *not* derived inferentially from previous knowledge. Presumably what would be required here is a means of nominating what this paranormal transfer of information actually is, enabling its discrimination from other, superficially similar experiences that are based on mere delusion and hallucination.

The common notion of parapsychology as the study of the paranormal is not embraced in this book. Rather, parapsychology here is defined as the study of experiences having the appearance of being in principle outside the realm of human capabilities as conceived by conventional scientists. Within the theoretical framework of modern behavioral science, an extrasensory experience, for example, simply could not have occurred as it is reported to have done. But now the task of the parapsychologist is not the study of negatively-defined underlying paranormal factors, but rather it is deemed to entail a systematic exploration of various possible bases and characteristics of experiential reports. Certainly this work will include investigation of the occurrence of extrasensory experience when sensory and inferential sources of information have procedurally been eliminated, but this is quite distinct from a pursuit of the paranormal.

By defining parapsychology in terms of *appearances* the discontent over negative definition should lose some of its potency. It is unnecessary for example, to define extrasensory experience in a way that will distinguish it from delusory or hallucinatory experience, because conceivably "ESP" might one day be shown to be just that. Admittedly, if paranormality is negatively defined then ultimately so too must the "appearance of being paranormal," but at least the latter is not predicated upon the exclusion of any list of scientifically accepted processes.

This raises the possibility that the terms of our adopted definition are temporally relative, that is, a given phenomenon might not be classified as parapsychological forever. Suppose that ESP were shown conclusively to be due to some presently recognized psychological processes and was relabeled with some name less provocative of the paranormal. In time people then might come to view such an experience no longer as incompatible with scientific principles nor as suggestive of a paranormal event, in which case the phenomenon rightly would shift from the parapsychological domain to some other area of psychology. But in that event the phenomenon should at least remain a legitimate issue for psychological research. If on the other hand extrasensory experience was defined explicitly as a *paranormal* phenomenon, a demonstration that this was not so more likely would prompt psychologists to believe the phenomenon had been eliminated as a matter for research. Temporal relativity therefore does not loom as an unacceptable limitation of our definition of parapsychology.

Cultural relativity could be another type of conceptual limitation. Certainly if parapsychology is depicted as the study of the paranormal there is the problem that what people classify as paranormal will vary from one culture to another. In some societies, for example, ESP is regarded as a human skill that falls entirely within the natural order, yet in our society it generally is thought of as paranormal. On the other hand by defining parapsychology in terms of its phenomena's apparent relation to conventional scientific principles, the issue of cultural relativity becomes somewhat less contentious because science is an international and comparatively cross-cultural activity. A phenomenon's status in the framework of conventional science therefore is accorded greater significance than its interpretation by members of individual societies. The definition of parapsychology may still be culturally bound to the extent of its scientific perspective, but in any event that is quite consistent with the view that parapsychology has a claim to being part of the world of science.

The demarcation of parapsychological phenomena in terms of appearances nevertheless encounters a few practical problems. One is that some instances of stage magic, especially mentalism, might be held to have the superficial form of the paranormal and hence have grounds for being classified as parapsychological. Although most researchers properly would reject this categorization it could have merit in some respects. A parapsychologist's knowledge of legerdemain certainly can be advantageous as a guard against fraudulent psychics (Hansen, 1985), and magical tricks can be used in a laboratory setting as a context for exploring the foundations of people's interpretation of events as paranormal (e.g., see Benassi, Singer & Reynolds, 1980). But while the superficial form of stage magic may be that of the paranormal these performances typically are not *perceived* by the audience as actually being paranormal.

By presenting himself or herself as a magician instead of as a medium or psychic, the performer communicates the illusory character of the act and hence people do not see it as involving processes currently unrecognized by conventional science. For that reason a piece of stage magic generally would not be regarded as a parapsychological experience. If magicians do depict themselves as psychic, however, their performance may well be accepted by the audience as paranormal. In that case magic falls in much the same class as fraud. The stance taken here is that if the public is deceived into construing a phenomenon as paranormal then their experience should nonetheless be deemed parapsychological and be the subject of study by parapsychologists. The result of such research of course may be that people become aware of the deception, the phenomenon becomes decreasingly viewed as paranormal, and its study shifts from the predominantly parapsychological domain to that of social psychologists and sociologists.

Again, there may be other phenomena interpreted as paranormal by the general public and yet excluded from study by parapsychologists. The great majority of scientific parapsychologists would not concede as legitimate issues in their field such things as witchcraft, popular astrology, fairies, the Bermuda Triangle, numerology, and Tarot readings, despite the common image of these matters as paranormal in the mind of the public and indeed for many skeptics (e.g., see Frazier, 1981). Parapsychologists' rejection of these topics springs essentially from political motives; to give serious consideration to the above phenomena would severely prejudice parapsychology's already tenuous status as a science in the eyes of the rest of the scientific community. While these motives are understandable and, at least for pragmatists, even laudable it is unsatisfactory to have a definition of parapsychology that requires the rider, "unless it would be inexpedient to categorize a given experience as parapsychological." On the other hand to specify the field purely in terms of a list of admissible phenomena also would lack conceptual force. The wisest option would seem to be simply to acknowledge the existence of limitations in the way the proposed demarcation of parapsychology applies in practice.

Although the inclusion of some particular phenomena in the field is disputed there is broad consensus in the view that traditionally there have been three basic domains of parapsychological research, namely extrasensory perception, psychokinesis, and the survival hypothesis. The nature of each of these will be addressed in turn.

An *extrasensory experience* is one in which it appears that the experient's mind has acquired information directly, that is, seemingly without either the mediation of the recognized human senses or the processes of logical inference. By way of illustration, on a few occasions I have been thinking about some friend and have had my thoughts interrupted by a phone call from that very person. Now, with sufficient knowledge of the context of this type of occurrence it could be possible to explain, or explain away, the experience in "rational" terms that do not appeal to the existence of any paranormal process called ESP. To this extent it is presumptuous to label the experience "extrasensory." But as with other parapsychological phenomena, we are concerned just with appearances, and from that perspective the above example superficially suggests the operation of some paranormal link between my thoughts and those of my friend. The example, no doubt a familiar encounter for many readers, represents a particular type of extrasensory experience that ostensibly entails direct mind-to-mind communication, so-called *telepathy*. In some instances the extrasensory experience relates to information not in another mind but in part of the objective environment. Thus a person's awareness of sensorially inaccessible visual events is termed *clairvoyance,* and ESP of auditory events, *clairaudience;* again, "clairvoyance" commonly is used in a generic fashion to designate extrasensory apprehension of any class of objective events. Sometimes too, ESP apparently is displaced in time. Extrasensory awareness of a future event is known as *precognition,* and that of a past event, *retrocognition.*

Often it can be difficult to determine how an actual extrasensory experience should best be classified. Consider an example. From time to time I find myself thinking I have not heard from one of my professional colleagues for a while, and later the same day I receive a letter from that person. Perhaps this is a coincidence. But perhaps the event may be deemed to entail extrasensory awareness of the letter, in which case my experience would be considered clairvoyant. Or the experience might be construed as apparent awareness of the perceptions of the mail sorter, that is, an instance of telepathic experience. Or again it could be represented as a precognitive experience of the subsequent mail delivery or of my opening the letter, or perhaps even a retrocognitive experience of my correspondent writing the letter some days earlier. In practice therefore, the utility of the proposed categories of ESP may be doubtful. Much the same could be said of their application to the description of laboratory data. Thus it was felt necessary to devise the expression *general extrasensory perception* (GESP) to refer to data that could have reflected unknown components of clairvoyance or telepathy or both (Rhine, 1948, p. 44). In the laboratory context the various terms nevertheless may usefully be employed in conveying the type of experimental procedure followed in an investigation.

In this book one convenient terminological convention is observed as far as possible. The terms extrasensory perception, telepathy, clairvoyance, precognition and the like usually are intended to refer to a hypothetical paranormal process, one that conceivably could account for a given parapsychological phenomenon; of course, the process might or might not actually exist. On the other hand such expressions as extrasensory experience, telepathic experience, clairvoyant experience, and precognitive experience designate events that do occur, experiences that people do have and which on the surface suggest the operation of a paranormal process. It could be said for example that a parapsychologist investigates the nature of extrasensory experience, and in the course of doing so gathers evidence on the existence or otherwise of extrasensory perception. The "extrasensory" in *extrasensory experience* therefore pertains to appearances and not necessarily to reality, whereas the "extrasensory" in *extrasensory perception* refers to the nature of a hypothesised paranormal reality. Occasionally this convention is overlooked, usually in order to avoid the tedium of frequent repetition of a given expression, but the sense should nonetheless be evident; for example, reference may be made to ESP when clearly we are speaking of extrasensory experience.

Extrasensory experience and ESP constitute one of the three basic domains of parapsychological research. A second domain is that of *psychokinesis* (PK), a word that translates literally as "movement by the mind." A PK experience entails an apparent mind-over-matter effect, that is, a case where an individual's thoughts or preferences appear to have had a direct influence upon the structure of the physical environment. The influence seemingly occurs without the mediation of recognized physical energies or mechanisms, particularly those comprising the human motor system. In the popular view PK probably would be most strongly exemplified by the spoon-bending performances of the Israeli psychic Uri Geller or by the apparently paranormal displacement of objects by the Russian psychic Nina Kulagina. Psychokinetic experiences however, need not involve observable movement; the stopping of a clock at the time of a loved one's death, for example, commonly is construed as an event of the mind-over-matter variety.

The labels *extrasensory perception* and *psychokinesis* were devised originally to convey the ostensible nature of the respective phenomena in a vividly descriptive fashion. Today however, they are rather unsatisfactory as technical terms because they are so presumptive of the paranormal processes that hypothetically could underlie the experiences. Even if ESP exists it might well operate by way of some (as yet undiscovered) sort of sensory modality, a "sixth sense," and hence not be "extrasensory." Again, if ESP is truly extrasensory then it might be more akin to ideation than to "perception." Similar objections can be leveled at the term psychokinesis.

Although it is convenient to have graphically descriptive nomenclature for a phenomenon it should also be atheoretical, and unfortunately neither of the two above terms meet this criterion. For that reason *psi phenomena* was promoted by the British parapsychologists Thouless and Wiesner (1948) as a generic term encompassing both ESP and PK. The Greek letter *psi* here is used to denote the unknown and perhaps paranormal element in these experiences in much the same way as the letter x represents the unknown in an algebraic equation until its identity is determined. But in effect psi constitutes more than a blanket term; there has developed a (sometimes tacit) assumption that the paranormal element in ESP is the same as the one in PK, that these two parapsychological domains share a common underlying process or mechanism. Thouless proposed further that the so-called extrasensory facets be known as *psi gamma* and the psychokinetic facets, *psi kappa*. These two terms, unlike that of *psi* itself, have never attracted broad endorsement, and ESP and PK now are so entrenched in the parapsychological and indeed the popular vocabulary that it is unlikely they will be replaced at least until their actual bases become established by researchers and accepted by the public.

Supplementary to the study of psi phenomena a traditional domain of parapsychological research concerns the *survival hypothesis,* the notion that there is some element of human existence that survives death. As we shall see in the next chapter much of the original interest of psychical researchers in the survival hypothesis focused on claims of communication between deceased spirits and mediums during spiritualist seances. Other phenomena also were pursued in this context; thus, evidence for life-after-death was sought in experiences of apparitions, poltergeists, reincarnation, and of one's self being outside the physical body (the out-of-body experience), among others. Modern parapsychologists continue to study these sorts of experience, although more as phenomena in their own right than as avenues for validating the survival hypothesis. Nevertheless these experiences collectively form an important sector of parapsychology; as they usually are differentiated experientially from the fundamental psi phenomena of ESP and PK they have come to be regarded as the third domain of the discipline. Even if the survival hypothesis proves not to provide a legitimate basis for their conceptual integration, each of these experiences *appears* to entail the existence of a nonphysical or spiritual self, and thereby this research domain has coherence beyond that of merely comprising parapsychological phenomena other than the basic psi experiences.

Within each of the domains of parapsychological investigation three central issues arise. These relate respectively to authenticity, underlying processes, and phenomenology. The scope of these three issues now will be considered.

In the opinion of many parapsychologists the principal objective of their research is to determine whether or not the evident paranormal quality of a given class of parapsychological experience is *authentic*. That is, allowing for the instances that can be accommodated by conventional psychological processes, are some parapsychological experiences due to the operation of paranormal factors? Because parapsychology is a scientific discipline there presently is a consensus that this issue properly can be resolved only in the laboratory. Admittedly such an attitude took time to evolve, and as we shall see in Chapter 2 the founders of the discipline sought to authenticate the existence of the paranormal in other ways.

The issue of authenticity nevertheless has always been close to the heart of parapsychological research. In the extrasensory experience, for example, the issue is whether it is really possible for a person to acquire information when all opportunity for rational inference and input from recognized sensory sources have been ruled out. Similarly, in relation to the notion of PK, can a person's thoughts and preferences affect the state of a physical system when all recognized physical energies and mechanisms are excluded as mediators? And is there a nonphysical element of human existence that can separate from the physical body, can survive organic death, can retain its organization as an integral personality after death, can appear before and haunt the living, can be born again in another body, and so on? All of these inquiries entail the issue of authenticity.

Authenticity relates to the question of "whether"; the issue of *underlying processes* concerns the question of "how." So-called *process-oriented* research is designed to ascertain the processes by which parapsychological experiences are enacted. It is one thing to demonstrate that a paranormal phenomenon called ESP does exist; it is quite another thing to establish the ways in which it works. Note, however, that process-oriented research is not predicated upon the authenticity issue. In the first place it is both feasible and valid to conduct investigations of the operating characteristics of a parapsychological phenomenon before that phenomenon is shown to be paranormal. Secondly, it is legitimate, and just as instructive, to undertake such investigations even if the phenomenon eventually proves not to be paranormal; like other behavioral scientists parapsychologists seek to understand the bases of human experience, and even if those bases are found to be entirely compatible with accepted psychological knowledge, that knowledge nonetheless is enriched by the demonstration of its capacity to account for parapsychological as well as other psychological phenomena. Process-oriented research therefore is justified irrespective of the issue of authenticity.

The third major issue in parapsychological research is important but currently rather underrated. It focuses on the description of parapsychological phenomena from the *experient's* point of view; investigators seek to establish the characteristics of the phenomena as actually experienced and the impact such experiences have upon the individual. This approach is known as *phenomenological* research. It too is independent of the authenticity issue; the phenomenology of people's parapsychological experiences can be documented whether or not those experiences have a paranormal basis. On the other hand, the phenomenological issue can be linked with process-oriented research. Although it certainly is possible to study phenomenological characteristics of the experiences without the slightest concern for underlying processes, such study often does suggest ideas about the nature of underlying processes. In other words phenomenological research is useful in generating hypotheses for investigation in process-oriented research.

More generally, the issue of phenomenology has to do with the question of "what" or, to be less elliptical, the discernment of what it is that parapsychology has to explain. There is some tendency among parapsychologists either to be smug over this matter or to ignore it altogether: It commonly is assumed that we know what an extrasensory experience is, what a psychokinetic experience is, what an out-of-body experience is, and so forth, and that the empirical objective is to investigate their paranormality and underlying processes. But there is more to an experience than its definition. Human experience has a range of different dimensions, and there are facets of parapsychological experience other than its ostensible paranormality. For example, investigation of the hypothetical paranormal process ESP might well help us understand the informational origins of extrasensory experience, but there remain to be addressed the bases of the form taken by the experience, its thematic content, its temporal course, its emotional tenor, its social context, and its impact upon the individual, among other things. The purpose of phenomenological research is to establish all such experiential features of parapsychological phenomena.

In many respects therefore, phenomenological research should set the research agenda in parapsychology, because it has the function of specifying the essential characteristics of the phenomena to be explained. The latter role of course is not exclusive to the phenomenological approach. Process-oriented research also throws up empirical relationships requiring further investigation; these would include observed correlations between the occurrence of parapsychological phenomena and features of the experient's personality and beliefs, for example. And the authenticity issue constantly provides items for the research program.

At the same time phenomenology could rightly be deemed the primary issue of parapsychological research in that it has some degree of logical precedence over the other two major issues; as apparent paranormality is itself a phenomenological feature of parapsychological experiences, the phenomenology issue effectively anticipates that of authenticity, and as noted above, the impetus for process-oriented research sometimes comes from phenomenological data. Many parapsychologists probably would feel this to be flagrantly overstating the case, but my central argument remains that phenomenological research is too neglected and depreciated at this still early phase of the development of parapsychological science. For that reason the text gives attention to the issue of phenomenology as well as to those of authenticity and underlying processes.

Before proceeding to consider research on particular parapsychological phenomena, it is appropriate to examine the historical origins of the field. That is the topic of the next chapter.

Key Terms and Concepts

parapsychology
paranormal
psychical research
parapsychological experiences
experient
extrasensory perception (ESP)
extrasensory experience
telepathy
clairvoyance
precognition

retrocognition
general extrasensory perception
   (GESP)
psychokinesis (PK)
psi
psi phenomena
the survival hypothesis
authenticity
process-oriented research
phenomenology

Study Questions

1. Parapsychology commonly is defined as the science of the paranormal. What are the advantages and the disadvantages of that approach?

2. Explain why a phenomenon need not be paranormal in order to be parapsychological. Why then are parapsychologists intent upon investigating the paranormality of such experiences?

3. List some of the phenomena regarded as paranormal by the general public but which you suspect to be disregarded in a science of parapsychology. What are your feelings about the omission of these topics from study?

4. Explore the various facets of the conceptual relationship between parapsychology and science.

5. Many people believe their pets to have psychic abilities. In your view, to what extent should this issue occupy a prominent position in parapsychological research? What might be learned from such research?

6. The subject matter of parapsychology tends to evoke rather extreme reactions in people. Conduct a simple survey of some friends and acquaintances on the issue. What range of reactions is evident? What motives might underlie these reactions?

7. What is the difference between extrasensory perception and extrasensory experience, and what is the significance of the distinction?

8. Recall one of your own extrasensory experiences and try to classify it as telepathic or clairvoyant and as precognitive or contemporaneous or retrocognitive. In light of that exercise what is your impression of the utility of the various categories of extrasensory experience?

9. How apt are the terms extrasensory perception and psychokinesis?

10. Examine a few of your own parapsychological experiences. What interesting hypotheses do these experiences suggest for the respective research issues of authenticity, underlying processes, and phenomenology?

11. To what extent are the three major research issues of authenticity, underlying processes, and phenomenology independent of each other?

12. As objectively as you can, look closely at your own attitudes and beliefs and then specify your preconceptions and prejudices about parapsychological phenomena.

13. Some phenomena other than parapsychological ones are defined negatively. The sudden infant death syndrome (SIDS) or "crib death," for example, is diagnosed by exclusion. That is, a given case is classified as SIDS only when other (positively-defined) causes systematically are ruled out. The negative definition of SIDS evidently has acted as a stimulus for researchers to identify the bases of the condition. Why then are parapsychologists taken to task for defining their phenomena in a negative fashion?

2
Origins of Parapsychological Research

In the reckoning of most writers the discipline of parapsychology is barely more than a hundred years old. The commencement of parapsychology, or psychical research as it then was called, generally is put at February 20, 1882, when the Society for Psychical Research (SPR) was officially constituted in England. The SPR was founded principally on the initiative of some academics at Cambridge University and several other people, all of whom believed that various claims for the existence of paranormal phenomena warranted scientific scrutiny. It may be noted that a number of SPR members in these early days were skeptics; others were philosophers concerned fundamentally with the metaphysical implications of parapsychological experiences if these should prove to be genuinely paranormal. Nevertheless the founders of the SPR were united in their conviction that the objective investigation of parapsychological phenomena was called for, despite the prevailing disinterest in such research among the established divisions of science.

Recorded instances of parapsychological experiences of course may be found among all cultures and in all historic periods. Indeed some cases were documented in much detail: the church's hagiographic records of the lives of the saints provide many such examples. On the other hand the notion of testing the accuracy and authenticity of reported parapsychological experiences emerged very slowly (Inglis, 1977). In the seventeenth century writers such as Henry More and Joseph Glanvill showed themselves alert to the possibility of fraud, delusion, and unreliable observation in such cases. But concern of this sort was sporadic and had little claim to representing the basis of an academic discipline. The basic perspective of More and Glanvill, for example, was religious rather than scientific. They were endeavoring to ascertain the earthly presence of the devil and diabolical forces.

Two main factors can be seen to have led to the foundation of parapsychology in 1882. These were the movements known respectively as Mesmerism and Spiritualism, and we will consider them in turn.

13

Mesmerism

Franz Mesmer was born in Switzerland in 1733 and later studied medicine at the University of Vienna. Mesmer was particularly interested in the influence which physicians can exert over their patients. At the folk level there was a tradition that certain divinely inspired individuals had the power to cure the sick by touch, the so-called "laying on of hands," and some of these healers used magnets to strengthen the healing force that emanated from them. Mesmer believed that a similar sort of energy was involved in the ability of physicians to promote their patients' return to health. Through experimentation he found, for example, that he could influence the rate of blood flow by movements of a magnet. He subsequently discovered a magnet was not necessary: the same effect could be achieved with any object over which he had passed his hands. Mesmer concluded there exists a healing force or "fluid" known as *animal magnetism* (so named to distinguish it from ordinary mineral magnetism).

Mesmer moved to Paris in 1778 and his method of treatment became highly fashionable, much to the annoyance of the medical fraternity; not surprisingly, he frequently was accused of being a charlatan. Of most interest in the present context are some of the by-products of Mesmer's technique. As Mesmer made magnetic "passes" over his patients they would fall into a deep sleep-like state or trance, although their eyes could be open or closed. In this state the "magnetized" individuals would be remarkably compliant with Mesmer's suggestions, reporting for example complete freedom from pain. Today we would designate this state of consciousness a hypnotic trance. There are some differences in the behavior of Mesmer's patients and that of contemporary subjects under hypnosis, but largely these seem to reflect changes in people's expectations of what should happen in such a state.

Other reported by-products of magnetic induction were so-called "higher phenomena" such as the subject's ability to "see" events that were sensorially inaccessible: thus gestures made by the magnetizer in another room might be described accurately. Following these initial observations, disciples of Mesmer endeavored to use the magnetic trance as a means of evoking telepathy, clairvoyance, traveling clairvoyance (the impression of transporting clairvoyant awareness to a distant location), and other parapsychological experiences (see Dingwall, 1967–1968).

Broadly speaking, the parapsychological facet of the mesmeric movement either was ignored by the scientific establishment or was used as evidence of the bogus character of animal magnetism (Leahey & Leahey, 1983, Ch. 5). Further, the movement had no direct effect on the foundation of the SPR. That is to say, when the SPR began its investigations of parapsychological phenomena it looked to hypnotism only as an ancillary research technique. Nevertheless mesmerism can be regarded as a factor in the origins of parapsychological research in two important respects. First, the activities of Mesmer's followers raised the possibility that through careful manipulation of test conditions a researcher might be able to ascertain the authenticity of parapsychological phenomena. Thus an individual might be found to exhibit certain behavior which by virtue of the investigator's control over the situation could be due only to paranormal factors. Second, mesmerism implied that parapsychological phenomena could be examined outside occultist and quasireligious contexts. This was of special significance in light of the fact that the major catalyst for the SPR's establishment was indeed a religious movement, that of Spiritualism.

Spiritualism

Parapsychological research as a coherent discipline was precipitated by the Spiritualist movement which began in America in the middle of the nineteenth century. Although one can point to many philosophical antecedents (see Anderson, 1987; Leahey & Leahey, 1983, pp. 162–164), Spiritualism was brought to popular awareness in 1848 by events in the household of a family named Fox (E. Isaacs, 1983).

In December 1847 a blacksmith, John Fox, his wife, and two of their children, 14-year-old Maggie and 12-year-old Kate, moved into a wooden cottage in Hydesville (near Rochester), New York. The house is said to have had a reputation for being associated with uncanny events, and in March 1848 the family began to hear a variety of strange sounds: rappings, bangs and scrapings as if furniture was being shifted. This outbreak of percussive activity became more insistent until March 31 when the inexplicable noises were particularly intense. John Fox decided to check if the window sashes were being rattled by the wind and gave the window frames a strong shake. Young Kate commented that each time her father shook the windows the noises were heard as if in reply. It occurred to her to snap her fingers to see if that would elicit a similar response. The "ghost," as it was taken to be, responded to this challenge with raps in the pattern of Kate's snapping fingers. Maggie also joined in the game. Mrs. Fox then decided to use the "ghost's" percussive responses to questions as a means of communication. She asked if the noises were being produced by a spirit: "If it is, make two raps." Immediately two raps sounded. In this fashion it is said the Foxes ascertained the communicating spirit to be that of a man who at the age of 31 had been murdered and his body buried in the cellar of the Foxes' house.

Several neighbors were called in and they too witnessed the spirit communications. One neighbor had the idea of facilitating communication by

calling the letters of the alphabet, the spirit being asked to rap when appropriate and thereby spell out whole sentences. By this means further gruesome details of the murder were conveyed. The deceased man allegedly was Charles Rosma, a traveling salesman who had been robbed and murdered by a former occupant of the house. The latter denied this claim and the occurrence of the murder never was verified. An effort to locate the corpse was thwarted by the fact that the ground under the cellar was waterlogged. Many years later a newspaper reported the finding of a skeleton in the cellar when an old wall collapsed, but corroboration of the report is lacking (Prince, 1930, pp. 155–156).

More and more people flocked to the house to witness the communications. Leah, an older married daughter of the Foxes, realized that her sisters could be exploited as a commercial proposition. Soon the girls were traveling about the country giving demonstrations of their contact with the spirit world. In a rented hall typically a lecture would be given on spiritualism and then questions put to the spirits on behalf of members of the paying audience. The activities of the Fox sisters received much attention in the press. Public interest increased further as new phenomena were reported. People at the Foxes' seances felt themselves touched by an invisible hand, objects moved unaccountably, and musical instruments played without human intervention.

Needless to say there were charges that the percussive noises and other effects were produced by fraudulent means. It was suggested that the raps could have been effected by snapping toe joints. In later years both Kate and Maggie used this explanation when they offered confessions of their fraudulent practices (Neher, 1980, pp. 213–214; "Spiritualism exposed," 1888/1985). Some commentators point out that at the time of the confessions the Fox sisters were destitute and hence their statements may have been designed to gain financial advantage and perhaps also to discredit their elder sister Leah with whom they had fallen out. The confessions subsequently were retracted.

For present purposes the authenticity of the Foxes' spirit communications is of peripheral concern. The fact remains that the idea of communicating with deceased persons captured the imagination of the American public. Mediums sprang up in other parts of New York State and within a few years the message of spiritualism had spread throughout America and to Europe. Its growth was soon to accelerate dramatically as people found wanting alternative world-views based solely on an agnostic science or on a Christianity under siege from Darwin's theory of evolution. Spiritualism offered an appealing compromise, for here was a religious movement that claimed direct "scientific proof" of its central tenets.

Opposite: Figure 1. The home of the Fox family c.1850 (photo: MEPL).

Although many mediums were caught out in deception, reports persisted that there were some trustworthy spiritualist mediums who were able to produce ostensibly paranormal phenomena under circumstances thought to preclude trickery. Such assertions were all but ignored by the scientific establishment. Under the contemporary scientific view of the world paranormal events could not happen and hence were bound to be bogus, undeserving of academic attention. Dissension from these assumptions by a few Cambridge intellectuals and others in Britain led to the formation of the Society for Psychical Research in 1882. They felt the implications of parapsychological phenomena were so great that science could not afford to ignore the phenomena or to reject them out of hand. If investigation should indicate that the prevailing scientific world view was incomplete that surely would be worth knowing, they maintained.

Although most mediums incorporated elements of their own style in their seances, the basic features of spiritualist seances were surprisingly uniform. The following outline of the phenomenology of trance mediumship draws on the account by Broad (1962, Ch. 10). For convenience of exposition it is assumed that the medium was a woman, as the considerable majority of spiritualist mediums indeed were; of course, this is not to imply that male mediums did not achieve eminence too.

The medium sat quietly in her chair either in the dark or in very subdued lighting and she closed her eyes. Soon she began to breathe deeply and to be rather restless for a few minutes. On becoming calmer she started to whisper to herself, then to talk audibly in a voice and manner unlike her usual self. It was as if another personality had gained control of the medium's vocal cords. This trance personality usually was the same in each seance conducted by the medium and was known as the *spirit guide* or *control;* it was depicted as the medium's "contact" in the spirit world.

The trance-personality or control would converse with the *sitters,* the people attending the seance, for perhaps an hour or more. Often it would present itself as a child and speak in a childish fashion; other controls would claim to be Red Indian, Hindu or Chinese and talk in a false stereotypic style of broken English. The control's narrative typically was entertaining and sometimes it would make remarks derogatory or embarrassing to the medium. It also would refer to its past life on earth and to the nature of postmortem existence. After a period of general conversation the control would claim to be in communication with the spirit of a deceased relative or friend of one of the sitters. Messages to the sitter and references to the spirit's earthly life would be conveyed through the control as an intermediary. With some mediums the voice of the control would actually be replaced by another voice purporting to be that of the spirit or *communicator* itself; this was called "direct voice" communication.

Usually contact would be made with several communicators during a seance, particularly if more than one sitter was present. In some instances the spirit communication would be a discourse in the form of spiritual teachings or literature; this now has come to be termed *channeling* (Hastings, 1987). At the end of the seance the medium again would show a certain amount of restlessness, groaning and whispering, then resume her normal voice and manner. Having come out of the trance state she generally was ignorant of what had happened during the seance.

What were the phenomena of the seance room that moved people in Britain (and later those in other countries) to call for objective investigation in accordance with the fundamental tenets of science? A useful way to address this issue is to examine the careers of some of the more eminent mediums. As well as illustrating the reported phenomena the review provides a context for exemplifying the development of investigative techniques.

Three Spiritualist Mediums:
Their Careers and Their Investigation

Daniel Dunglas HOME (1833–1886)

Broadly speaking there are two types of mediums. *Mental mediums* provide information to which they evidently do not have access by normal means. For example they may foretell the future, describe distant events of interest to the sitter, name the location of the sitter's lost possessions, give a history of the owner of a particular object presented to them, and communicate with deceased personalities. *Physical mediums* generally have the abilities of mental mediums but additionally appear to have the power to influence the physical state of objects. The seance table may rise from the floor, "spirit" raps may be heard, furniture in the seance room may be displaced, objects and people may be levitated, and so on. At the spirits' behest these physical effects usually occur under conditions of darkness or of subdued lighting.

Daniel Home (pronounced "Hume") was an exponent of physical mediumship and by some accounts one of the best. Home was born in 1833 near Edinburgh, Scotland, and was raised by an aunt, although he remained emotionally close to his mother. At the age of 9 he and his aunt emigrated to Connecticut; his parents also moved to America but Daniel continued to live with his aunt. Home's mother died when he was 17, much to his distress. Shortly afterwards inexplicable noises and movement of furniture began to plague the house. The young Home was familiar with the recent events in the Fox household and he too tried to communicate with the source of the spirit raps. Using an alphabet technique he eventually obtained a message, ostensibly from his deceased mother, reassuring him and declaring that he had a "glorious mission" in life to cure the sick and to convert people to a belief in spiritualism.

Home began to hold seances for the neighbors in his aunt's parlor. Sitters were told where to find long-lost relatives and misplaced possessions. While the participants in these early seances were greatly impressed, Home's aunt was convinced the whole affair was the work of the devil and after just one week she threw him out of the house. Home moved in with friends and became a full-time medium. His talents were reported in the press and his fame spread.

It would appear that Home never accepted money for his seances, a fact which many spiritualists have taken as proof of his honesty. Nevertheless he lived very well for the rest of his life as a houseguest. His personal magnetism, empathy and readiness to display his "gift" made him most welcome in the best of homes.

Some of his mental feats took the form of spirit possession, as in the following instance (Home, 1864/c.1973, pp. 26–27). One day in 1852 the Elmers, a Massachusetts family with whom Home was staying, were visited by a cleric named Brittan. In the middle of a conversation with the visitor Home suddenly fell into a trance. He groaned, then declared "Hannah Brittan is here!" The medium paced the floor, moaning, striking his head and crying "Save them from the pit!" and "There's no light! Where am I?" The Elmer family was mystified but the Reverend Brittan was quite shaken: as far as he was aware no one in Massachusetts knew the story of Hannah Brittan. It emerged that many years earlier a relation named Hannah became insane with worry about hell and eternal torment.

Home suffered from tuberculosis or what the Victorians called consumption, and in the hope of improving his health he sailed for England in the spring of 1855. It is a testimony to his talents and character that having arrived in England virtually penniless and with few contacts Home established himself within a month as a favorite of London's most eminent hostesses.

One of Home's physical phenomena was the appearance of "spirit hands" during his seances. Spiritualists believed that discarnate spirits could become visible to sitters by drawing on *ectoplasm,* a substance allegedly issued from the body of the medium. Sometimes these *materializations* (as they are termed) comprised only parts of a bodily form, and the phenomenon of luminous spirit hands was one relatively common such instance. A spirit hand was observed in an 1855 sitting with the English poets Elizabeth Barrett Browning and Robert Browning. The latter reportedly found spiritualism distasteful and took part in the seance with great reluctance (although that view may in fact have been formulated by

Figure 2. Daniel Dunglas Home (photo: MEPL).

Robert after the event; see Jenkins, 1982, pp. 44–45). His wife Elizabeth on the other hand was mystically inclined and as the evening progressed it became clear that she found Home quite captivating. During the seance a large luminous white hand appeared and at Home's command it made the suitably poetic gesture of crowning Elizabeth with a wreath of clematis that had been decorating the table at which they sat. This infuriated Robert Browning and although he had no proof he charged that the spirit hand was actually Home's foot or some device manipulated by the medium's foot.

This incident was the inspiration for Browning's poem "Mr Sludge the Medium." This vengeful work recounted the fraudulent activities and weak character of a supposedly fictitious spiritualist medium; the latter however, was a thinly disguised caricature of Home. Although Robert decided not to publish "Mr Sludge" until after Elizabeth's death, his intense animosity toward Home was no secret.

Home responded by publishing a vitriolic attack on Browning in a spiritualist magazine. Now, normally this would have been an unforgivable indiscretion, as the Brownings were the darlings of the English social set. Yet far from becoming a social outcast Home found his reputation if anything enhanced by the affair, so strong was his own position becoming in the higher social circles. In any event Home's fame spread to the Continent and for the remainder of his life he toured Europe as an honored guest of the rich and the privileged.

One of Home's most famous feats occurred in December 1868 at the London apartment of Lord Adare. Home traveled and lived with Adare for over a year. During this period Adare recorded all of the psychical manifestations he witnessed, privately publishing his notes in 1869. On the night in question Home conducted a seance in the darkened dining room after dinner. Two sitters other than Adare were present, Lord Lindsay and Adare's cousin Captain Wynne. While in trance Home announced that the spirits would whisk him out of the fourth floor window of an adjacent room and in through the window of the dining room. According to reports from each of the witnesses Home was heard to enter the next room and shortly afterwards appear outside the window of the seance room, floating in mid-air. Home is said to have glided in through the window and sat down at the table.

Many writers have sought to explain how this instance of apparent *levitation* could have been performed by normal means. One of the SPR founders, Frank Podmore (1902), later argued that Home merely crept back past the three sitters in the dark and hopped up on the window sill, making it appear under the poor conditions for observation that he was floating outside the window. It does seem unlikely that none of the seance participants detected Home's passage through the dining room to the window sill, although it should be said that the three sitters firmly believed in Home's powers and thus may have perceived only what they dearly needed to. On similar grounds Wyndham (1937, p. 199) argues the sitters may simply have hallucinated the experience. Others, including the master magician Houdini, have declared that because there was a small balcony outside each window, it was quite possible for Home to have leapt from one to the other if he was reasonably fit and had no fear of heights (Hall, 1984, p. 120). According to Lambert (1976, pp. 311–312) Home could easily have used ropes to swing from one window to the next and into the seance room. There also have been suggestions that the three witnesses were obliged to give testimony in support of Home's levitation because of his homosexual relationship with one or more of them (Hall, 1984). It may be noted there are some discrepancies among the accounts of the three witnesses.

Many people had attended Home's seances in the hope of catching the medium in some fraudulent act but Home's performance never was exposed conclusively as sham. There was one instance of a sitter who claimed to have seen Home's shoulder or body rising and falling in synchrony with the movements of a spirit hand (Jenkins, 1982, pp. 47–48), and of course there were many people like Robert Browning who declared Home a fake on no hard evidence at all. On a few occasions Home did offer himself for testing by skeptical investigators (e.g., Zorab, 1970) and while he came through these tests with his reputation essentially intact it must be said that many of the investigators were ill-qualified for the task they undertook. Indeed techniques for testing mediums were poorly developed at this time. Often the investigator simply observed what the medium did. Even when some simple controls over the medium's movements were imposed they were ones which readily could be circumvented by a skilled conjurer.

One comparatively extensive investigation of Home's seance phenomena was undertaken by the chemist and physicist (later Sir) William Crookes, an eminent figure of the scientific establishment. In the *Quarterly Journal of Science* for July 1870 Crookes announced his intention to determine whether the reported phenomena of spiritualist seances were authentic or bogus. To the extent that other scientists were at all interested in this objective they generally felt assured that the authority of Crookes would do much to dispel the "superstitious attitudes" encouraged among members of the public by the spiritualist movement.

Crookes's work with Home began in 1871. To the astonishment of the scientific community Crookes reported that all of the phenomena associated with Home were genuine! Most of Crookes's conclusions were based on passive observation of the phenomena under conditions which he felt were adequate for the purpose of valid investigation. Thus he noted the occurrence of spirit raps governed by some form of intelligence; the movement of furniture and other objects either in contact with Home or at some distance from the medium; levitation of furniture and of Home himself; *materialization* of spirit hands, faces, and "phantasmic forms" or apparitions; *automatic writing* through the medium's hand or with a planchette; and *apports,* the paranormal transference of objects into the seance room from other locations. Crookes also designed a couple of specific tests of the medium's powers. He set up weights in a chemical balance and asked the medium (or the spirits working through the agency of the medium, as Home would have it) to influence the mass of an item to upset the equilibrium of the balance. He also enclosed one end of a small accordion in a cage of copper wire and asked that the instrument be played. According to Crookes, Home passed each of these tests.

Not unexpectedly the report by Crookes on Home's performance evoked vehement criticism by other scientists, much of it emotionally rather than rationally based and some involving outright misrepresentation. Because seance phenomena were incompatible with accepted scientific principles the phenomena must be shown to be bogus. Hence, it was argued that Crookes's procedures were not sufficiently tight to preclude trickery. Without any supportive evidence it was charged that Home had attached to the accordion a wire or some such device by which he was able to extract a few notes from the instrument, or that he had smuggled into the room another accordion that was used to produce some music (Wyndham, 1937, p. 231).

Whether or not these criticisms were fair, it must be said that the value of Crookes's investigation of Home is questioned by some recent evidence. It seems possible that his report on another medium, Florence Cook, was spurious, in part intended to conceal an affair between Crookes and Cook (Hall, 1962). Although there is no direct indication of any similar collusion between Crookes and Home this evidence, if confirmed, necessarily would undermine the integrity of Crookes and thereby raise doubts about the validity of all of his psychical research including that involving Home.

While it may be true that Home never was detected in fraudulent practices it could be argued that at the time techniques for investigating mediums were poorly developed and that Home was subjected to very few tests by independent, suitably trained researchers of unimpeachable character. In later years as the sophistication of investigative procedures increased, the number of physical mediums fell. Indeed after the 1940s the physical medium almost became an extinct species, with the physical phenomena of the spiritualist era having no major parallels until the Uri Geller episode of the mid 1970s.

Hélène SMITH (1861–1929)

We now turn to a medium who operated at a time when psychical research was better established. Hélène Smith was the pseudonym of Catherine Elise Muller, a nonprofessional medium in Geneva from the early 1890s. Her career is outlined by Flournoy (1900), from whom the following account is drawn. Smith was the daughter of a Hungarian merchant who had settled in Geneva after traveling extensively and acquiring several languages in the process; the father's facility for languages may have some bearing on the nature of Smith's mediumship, as we shall see.

Hélène Smith first heard of spiritualism at the age of 30 when an acquaintance lent her a book on the subject. Her curiosity roused, she joined a spiritualist circle. At the second of the seances she attended (April 1892) there was received a spirit communication announcing that the spirit of Victor Hugo would be her protector and spirit guide or control. In subsequent seances Smith began to experience visual and auditory images said to be evoked by her spirit guide, and to develop the ability of automatic writing. While in the dissociated state of a mediumistic trance she would seemingly become possessed by a discarnate spirit who would force her hand to write messages for the sitters attending the seance.

Smith soon became a strong medium and was very well known among spiritualists. During her seances she is said to have moved objects at a distance, apported flowers and Chinese coins, helped sitters to locate misplaced possessions, predicted future events, seen spirit visitors, clairaudiently heard spirits talking, and elicited spirit raps. "Victor Hugo" remained her spirit guide for approximately six months, when there emerged another control identifying itself as "Leopold" which eventually supplanted the original guide. After a period, "Leopold" claimed to be the deceased spirit of Cagliostro, an Italian-born mystic who frequented the French court during the reign of Louis XVI and Marie Antoinette.

In 1894 Professor Theodore Flournoy, a professor of psychology at the University of Geneva, accepted a colleague's invitation to attend some of Smith's seances. To Flournoy's astonishment she was able to give him accurate information about events which had occurred in his family before he was born. Thus motivated, Flournoy determined to investigate Smith's psychic talents. One of his first tasks was to undertake a character analysis of the spirit guide Leopold/Cagliostro. He judged Leopold's personality to be quite a contrast to that of Smith. Further, when Leopold wrote through the hand of Smith the handwriting differed from Smith's usual script, showing the style of the previous century. When Leopold spoke through Smith (so-called direct voice communication) the voice was a deep bass with a strong easily recognizable Italian accent.

On the other hand there were other facets of Leopold that did not ring true. His handwriting was strikingly dissimilar to that used in some of Cagliostro's letters preserved in French archives. During the seances Leopold evidently did not understand Italian and would ignore anyone who addressed him in that language. Worse still the spirit guide was very vague or evasive about questions concerning his terrestrial existence and did not furnish a single name, date, or precise fact which could be investigated for its authenticity.

At one seance the spirits revealed that Smith was the reincarnation of Marie Antoinette. Later Smith would go into trance and "become" Marie Antoinette, a character which she carried quite naturally. Nevertheless there again were marked discrepancies between the spirit's handwriting

Figure 3. Hélène Smith, a self-portrait with her "guardian angel" (photo: MEPL).

through the hand of Smith and that of the real Marie Antoinette, and Flournoy was able to trap the "Queen" in various malapropisms. Flournoy constructed a psychoanalytic-type interpretation of this phase of Smith's mediumship, arguing that "Leopold" and "Marie Antoinette" were secondary personalities of the medium, reflecting certain unconscious desires and anxieties.

While Flournoy rejected the notion that Smith literally was in contact with a spirit world he was prepared to countenance the possibility that she had paranormal access to information. For example in October 1894 there began another cycle of Smith's mediumship in which she took on the role of an Indian princess of the fifteenth century. In these seances the entranced Smith exhibited a good deal of knowledge about Indian historical events, costumes, and language. Flournoy investigated the accuracy of this material and its accessibility in Geneva. He was forced to conclude that the source of Smith's knowledge of these matters was a "psychological enigma." He did not, however, rule out the possibility of *cryptomnesia,* that is, subconscious memory of material read many years previously.

One of the most fascinating phases of Smith's mediumship began in November 1894 when Smith's own spirit reportedly was transported to the planet Mars in a number of seances. While in trance she would describe the human, animal and floral life of Mars and would also speak and write in the "language" of that planet. Since her spirit guide gave purported translations of the written communications Flournoy was able to examine the Martian language for its structure. He found that the Martian scripts were not random scribblings but indeed exhibited an alphabet which was used consistently across the series of seances. Nevertheless it was clear that the vowels and consonants of Smith's Martian language were those of French (her native tongue) and that the grammar, inflexions and construction also were modeled on French. On this basis Flournoy concluded that the Martian language was an extraordinary elaboration by Smith's unconscious mind. As an intellectual endeavor Smith's Martian communications certainly did not impress him, but as a feat of memory and subconscious creativity the effort was remarkable.

Smith also provided purported descriptions and sketches of the Martian landscape. Of course Flournoy was unaware of the discrepancies between these accounts and details of Martian topography revealed by recent Voyager space probes, but he did comment to Smith on the extraordinarily human-like character of her descriptions of life on Mars. Apparently stung by Flournoy's comments Smith later reported spirit excursions to another planet which had grotesque inhabitants and a language evidently unlike any earthly one.

Whether or not you are persuaded by Flournoy's (1900) analysis it does present an exciting method for investigating mental mediums, and it is unfortunate that similar studies are lacking in the literature. The analysis of the Martian cycle also raises important questions about the creative capacity of the unconscious and serves to caution us that even in those cases of spontaneous parapsychological experiences where fraud and willful deception confidently may be ruled out there still is a possibility that subconscious fantasy may have played a substantial role.

Charles BAILEY (c.1870–1947)

The last of our trio of mediums, Charles Bailey, is of special interest to me because he too was an Australian. Bailey merits consideration here because he generated much interest on the international parapsychological scene and because investigation of his talents illustrates the role of physical constraints in testing physical mediums. His career is documented by Irwin (1987a).

Charles Bailey reportedly was born in Richmond, Victoria, Australia, in about 1870. He had little education, even being described by one biographer as illiterate. Usually he was employed in poorly paid positions, at one time being a boot operative, and possibly for this reason he expected payment by his sitters. His professional mediumship began in 1889 and eventually he gained the patronage of American-born Melbourne millionaire T.W. Stanford.

Now, Stanford was ardently devoted to spiritualism and psychical research for much of his life (Dommeyer, 1975). He was the brother of the founder of Stanford University in California and he made substantial donations to that university for the purpose of encouraging psychical research. Stanford began his studies of seance phenomena in America and continued this work after migrating to Australia, doing much to stimulate psychical research in that country. Although Stanford arranged private sittings with many mediums, his work with Charles Bailey over 12 years represents one of the most detailed and sustained records of mediumship in the history of parapsychology. Between 1902 and 1913 thorough accounts were maintained of each sitting of Bailey's circle in Melbourne and subsequently these were presented as ten bound volumes to Stanford University. In 1903 Stanford published the results of his early observations in a small booklet, and monthly reports of Bailey's seances were printed in an Australian spiritualist magazine, the *Harbinger of Light*.

Bailey's particular speciality was *apportation* of a wide range of objects. While seated in darkness or subdued light, sitters would hear various objects fall on to the seance table. According to spirit communications these apports were conveyed by the spirits with whom Bailey was in contact. Among the apports recorded by Stanford in his 1903 booklet were several live specimens of exotic birds, birds' nests (many containing eggs), live fish, large quantities of seaweed and sand replete with aquatic fauna, a fishing net, a live turtle, exotic plants, ivory, beads and precious stones, a human skull, a leopard skin, and a sizeable piece of tapestry. Most sensational however, were apported clay tablets and cylinders said to bear ancient Babylonian inscriptions some of which were translated by Bailey's spirit controls. Communications from ancient Aztec personages also occurred apparently through the discarnate personality of an American scholar Professor Edward Robinson; the biographical details of Robinson were largely authentic.

Stanford's work with Bailey was purely documentary. No attempt was made to impose constraints upon the medium's activities, although Stanford reassured his readers that he had not observed anything remotely suggestive of deception. Tests of an apparently more stringent character were conducted in Sydney by Dr. Charles MacCarthy, a physician of some note. In the first series of sittings the membership of the circle was chosen by MacCarthy himself. Bailey was not permitted to enter the seance room before the session and he was searched by a number of the sitters (although rarely was he stripped completely), then enclosed in a double-sewn canvas bag with only his arms and head free. The seance room was searched and after Bailey entered the room it was locked for the duration of the sitting. Generally all lights were extinguished before any apports were produced. In seven sessions under these conditions the medium apported 54 objects, including some inscribed cylinders and clay tablets, foreign coins, semiprecious stones, an Arabic newspaper, a hot semibaked "chupatti" cake, live birds, and various marine creatures including a crab and a small, barely alive shark. For the second series of seances Bailey was stripped to his underwear and searched, then placed in a "cage" of mosquito netting. On occasions sitters also were searched and Bailey was required to wear boxing gloves, to change into a new suit, or to be placed in the canvas bag as well as in the cage as additional precautions against conjuring. The usual diversity of tablets and cylinders and other apports again were produced.

After considering several rival hypotheses, MacCarthy felt that the paranormality of Bailey's phenomena was an inescapable conclusion. He did note that the inscriptions and figures on the apported tablets and cylinders looked remarkably sharp and fresh but he was not perturbed by this, believing the impressions to be too difficult to simulate. When photographs of the tablets were submitted to the British Museum by the SPR's Sir Oliver Lodge, however, the supposed antiquities were declared to be forgeries. A tablet obtained by Sir Arthur Conan Doyle (an ardent spiritualist) in a 1920 sitting with Bailey also was referred to the British Museum and found to be an imitation. Conan Doyle nevertheless did not hold this against the medium, arguing that it may have been easier for the discarnate "transporting agency" to locate and handle one of these forgeries than an authentic tablet buried deep in some archaeological site.

Another Australian researcher, A.W. Dobbie, also reported the communications of Bailey's Hindu control to be nonsensical scribblings and a peepul tree ostensibly apported from India to be a cutting from an olive tree. Be that as it may, it was Bailey's actual production of objects in MacCarthy's extended test series that stood as the medium's principal achieve-

Figure 4. Charles Bailey (photo: Harbinger of Light).

ment. MacCarthy's investigations attracted international attention and arrangements were made for the medium to be tested overseas. In 1904 Bailey went to Italy to be scrutinized by a committee of the Milan Society for Psychical Studies. The committee's report was inclined to favor Bailey's apports as being genuinely paranormal phenomena, although it would appear that Bailey was rather more resistant to the researchers' imposition of controls than he is depicted as being in Australian investigations.

In 1910 Bailey traveled to France to be studied in Grenoble by a group led by the eminent French parapsychologist Colonel Albert de Rochas.

Although no sleight-of-hand was detected, evidence was brought forward that Bailey was recognized as a man who two days earlier had purchased some birds similar to those produced during the test. The spirit control had declared the birds to have been apported from India. Bailey denied purchasing the birds and refused to conduct further sittings for the Grenoble committee. Investigations in London during the following year also found Bailey to be uncooperative in certain respects. In one of these sessions Bailey was unable to produce apports when unexpectedly being required to be enclosed in a satinette bag tied at the neck. Two birds were apported under similar test conditions in the following session, but subsequent inspection revealed a hole had been made in one corner of the bag. As a consequence an adverse report was issued.

Bailey's career as a medium suffered further in 1914 when a "spirit" he materialized was seized by a sitter who in turn had the drapery wrenched from his grasp. The seance, held in Sydney, ended in chaos. Bailey's international reputation rapidly deteriorated. He did continue to conduct seances in Sydney and overseas for another thirty years until shortly before his death in 1947, but he was no longer of interest to parapsychologists. Bailey's friends and the faithful members of his circle nevertheless continued to defend his reputation and to reject the reports of the "pseudoscientists."

That sense of mutual antipathy between spiritualists and parapsychologists has persisted to this day. In the main, spiritualists reject the reductionist approach of scientists and now look to personal revelation and faith rather than experimental scrutiny for substantiation of their convictions. Parapsychologists, on the other hand, are determined to emphasize the scientific character of their discipline and therefore they are intent on dissociating parapsychology from anything to do with occultism. They are a little embarrassed by the fact that parapsychology had its roots in spiritualism, or, to be more precise, was inspired by some of the implications of the reported activities of spiritualist mediums. Despite occasional efforts to encourage communication between parapsychologists and spiritualists the gulf between them looms ever large. As we shall see in the section on the survival hypothesis, some parapsychological research does relate to metaphysical matters and in this regard it would be of interest to spiritualists and other religious folk. On the other hand, perhaps parapsychologists can be more objective in such research if they themselves avoid too close an identification with religious movements.

Conclusions

We now have looked at the careers of three mediums, Daniel Home, Hélène Smith, and Charles Bailey. Of course there are many other mediums that could have been discussed, but these three suffice for the present. First, they instance the variety of phenomena that are reported to occur in the seance room and that elicited the interest of the founders of the SPR. Second, they illustrate three broad types of mediumistic performance. Some seance phenomena, like those associated with Bailey, undoubtedly are produced by fraudulent means, even if sitters themselves proclaim their paranormality (Besterman, 1932; Davey & Hodgson, 1887). Others, while not intentionally deceitful, appear to be rooted in subconscious fantasy: Smith's psychic excursions to Mars evidently were of this sort. And in yet other cases there seems to be something going on that we cannot immediately explain, something that warrants further investigation; for example, a few of Home's feats and perhaps also the Indian phase of Smith's mediumship remind us that it is appropriate to keep an open mind about parapsychological phenomena and indeed to explore their authenticity under more scientific conditions. It is as well to remain alert to each of these three possibilities when you ponder the performance of contemporary psychics.

What are the lessons to be learned from past investigations of mediums? One is that if parapsychologists are to investigate the talents of mediums the researcher must be in total control. She or he, rather than the medium, must define the circumstances and objectives of the test. Another is that it must be acknowledged that while spiritualism precipitated psychical research and posed many questions for researchers to pursue, investigation of mediums has failed to authenticate any parapsychological phenomenon. In the view of the majority of contemporary parapsychologists, before the alleged events of the seance room can be assessed it is necessary to undertake laboratory studies of experimental analogs of such events. For example, if it is asserted that mediums can predict the future by paranormal means the parapsychologist must design an "event prediction" task that can be performed in a laboratory setting where potentially confounding variables can be controlled. Questions other than authenticity might similarly be scrutinized. According to some spiritualists the presence of skeptics at a seance can inhibit the occurrence of the phenomena. That suggestion is one that can be examined through appropriate exercises in the laboratory. (The types of tasks used by modern parapsychologists in their investigations will be described in subsequent chapters.) Finally, if the work of Flournoy is any guide, the study of spiritualist mediums may offer a novel avenue of inquiry into the capacities of the subconscious mind. Certainly our present understanding of such capacities is meager and any unexploited research technique such as this does warrant attention.

But such advanced questions were far from the minds of the British group that set about the establishment of the Society for Psychical Research in 1882. Their perspective was much simpler, namely that the phenomena of the seance room did deserve some manner of intellectual scrutiny. On the other hand the scientific community of the time was inclined simply to ignore these phenomena completely. Certainly a few scientists suggested the need for empirical investigation but only with the objective of exposing the reported effects as sham and humbug. The distinguished physicist Michael Faraday (1853) for example, conducted simulated seances with a table fitted with a loose top and showed that when sitters laid their hands on the tabletop they unwittingly exerted lateral pressure on it and made it turn. On this basis he asserted the table-tipping phenomena of seances had a natural explanation; as Inglis (1977, p. 217) notes, however, Faraday's demonstration in no way accommodated the reports of tables moving around the seance room or even rising above the floor. Other intellectuals sought to ridicule spiritualist phenomena. Thus the Orientalist Richard Burton commented, "In case I ever become a spirit, I trust I shall not be summoned into anybody's drawing-room and there made to play the banjo and rap people's heads, in return for a fee of a guinea" (Wyndham, 1937, p. 135). But in the main, intellectuals believed that the cause of scientific rationalism was best served by ignoring the claims of spiritualism. Psychical research was then, very much a protest against the prevailing scientific zeitgeist.

The movements of spiritualism and mesmerism therefore had a significant place in the *origins* of parapsychology. Their influence on the subsequent development of the discipline, however, was rather less substantial.

Key Terms and Concepts

mesmerism
mesmeric trance
animal magnetism
spiritualism
materialization
seance
sitter
reading
ectoplasm
possession
levitation
laying on of hands
table tipping
medium
physical medium/phenomena

mental medium/phenomena
psychometry
spirit hands
Society for Psychical Research
  (SPR)
Daniel Home
Hélène Smith
Charles Bailey
automatism (sensory or motor)
automatic writing
planchette
control, spirit guide
apports
cryptomnesia

Study Questions

1. Interest in paranormal phenomena is as old as history itself. Why then do most commentators maintain that parapsychology has existed for barely one century?

2. In the view of almost all nineteenth century intellectuals the notion of animal magnetism was sheer quackery, yet mesmerism evidently contributed in some way to the foundation of the Society for Psychical Research. How do you account for this?

3. Parapsychologists today would tend to classify the events in the Fox household as an apparent poltergeist outbreak. Similar cases have been documented in many cultures and in many eras. What factors were peculiar to the Hydesville case that led to its inspiration of a religious movement?

4. How can the spiritualist movement be said to have precipitated parapsychology as a discipline?

5. What are the principal differences in the careers of the three spiritualist mediums Home, Smith and Bailey, and what is the significance of these differences?

6. What purported phenomena were associated with spiritualist mediums and how were these investigated?

7. From the parapsychologist's viewpoint is there anything to be learned from the activities of mediums?

3

The Phenomenology
of Extrasensory Perception

A phenomenological approach to extrasensory experience, the study of ESP as actually experienced, emerged very gradually from a tradition of gathering case reports primarily for other purposes. Before reviewing the phenomenological characteristics of ESP the conceptual background of case collection will be outlined.

Approaches to Case Collection in Parapsychology

One of the initial tasks undertaken by the Society for Psychical Research was the development of precise criteria for the collection of reports on spontaneous parapsychological experiences. The SPR's focal objective here was to educe the existence of paranormal phenomena from case reports and hence it was thought necessary to ensure that each accepted report be strongly indicative of the occurrence of something paranormal.

The most basic of the SPR criteria was that the experience must be on record, preferably in writing but at the very least as an oral communication to another person, *before* the content of the experience was substantiated. Suppose, for example, a woman dreamt of her son's death. If she happened to have written an account of her dream in her diary or had described it to her husband before news of the son's death was received, this could qualify as an acceptable case of a parapsychological experience. Investigation of the case then would be undertaken by SPR members. The first piece of evidence that would be called for here would be the original diary entry or a statement from the husband on his recollection of events. Additionally, corroborative material would be sought from diverse sources. If possible, investigators would question other witnesses such as people who had been told of the experience and others who had been present at the son's death. A copy of the death certificate and character references for the principals of the case would be obtained. Ideally statements should be procured and interviews conducted as soon after the incident as possible. In this fashion it was hoped to guarantee the case subject's veracity and to eliminate errors of recall, both deliberate and unintentional. If some authentic examples of paranormal phenomena were excluded by application of these criteria then that was deemed a necessary cost of ensuring that the selected cases were evidentially reliable.

By this means, case collections of parapsychological experiences were compiled by the SPR and by the societies for psychical research that soon were founded in many other countries. The major surveys conducted along these lines include a collection of over 700 cases of telepathic experience by Gurney, Myers and Podmore (1886); Henry Sidgwick's study of telepathic phenomena in the form of an apparition of a person on the verge of death (Sidgwick, Johnson, Myers, Podmore & Sidgwick, 1894); Eleanor Sidgwick's (1888–1889) and Saltmarsh's (1934) collections of precognitive experiences; Eleanor Sidgwick's (1891) study of clairvoyant experiences; Tyrrell's (1942/1963) analysis of apparitional experiences drawn from the SPR files; and Stevenson's (1970) survey of imageless or "intuitive" telepathic impressions, and his series of reports on apparent reincarnation memories (e.g., Stevenson, 1966).

It is clear from the survey reports that the early SPR investigators looked to spontaneous cases very largely as a means of ascertaining the authenticity of parapsychological phenomena, that is, a means of providing evidence that these phenomena stem from the operation of paranormal factors. That orientation is instanced in a most extreme form by a later investigation undertaken by the American psychical researcher Walter Franklin Prince (1928). His study cites parapsychological experiences of scientists, lawyers, clergymen, literary figures and others considered to qualify as unimpeachable witnesses. Like the founders of the SPR, Prince believed that adequately documented case reports from reliable experients could provide sound testimony to the existence of paranormal processes, a view still endorsed by some parapsychologists today (e.g., see Stevenson, 1971, 1987b).

Additionally, some of the SPR investigators began to examine spontaneous case collections for indications of the nature or characteristics of parapsychological experiences. Through content analysis of cases researchers hoped to define, for example, the circumstances under which each different type of parapsychological experience occurred and thereby to gain some insight into the ways in which the supposed paranormal processes could operate. While it must be acknowledged that these early studies primarily were concerned with the issue of authenticity, they therefore exhibited a measure of appreciation for process-oriented research and even a glimmering awareness of the issue of phenomenology.

Subsequently it was realized by the American parapsychologist Louisa

E. Rhine that for *purposes other than authentication,* cases could be collected under criteria far less stringent than those proposed by the SPR, and thus in the 1950s she undertook analyses of all spontaneous cases which seemed both to have been reported in good faith and to be instances of parapsychological experiences. Her argument was that since a given case report will be at least partially reliable, in a sizeable collection of uninvestigated cases (such as her own Duke University collection) the elements of unreliability would be random "noise" against which would stand out the reliable and consistent data on the characteristics and occurrence of parapsychological experiences. While validation of individual reports might be thought necessary for the authentication of the phenomena it was not therefore essential to the pursuit of other issues, she maintained. Specifically, uninvestigated case reports could indicate the nature of the processes underlying parapsychological experiences.

From the outset L.E. Rhine (1951) believed that these indications should be scrutinized further by means of controlled experimental research, although as she pursued her work with case analysis she seems to have become increasingly more confident in the evidential value of this material (Stevenson, 1987b, p. 104).

Louisa E. Rhine's new technique for case surveys certainly facilitated research on spontaneous cases and, as we shall see, much interesting material emerged through investigations of this type. Admittedly, the new approach did provide an opportunity for critics to declare (in apparent ignorance of Rhine's argument) that parapsychologists would accept as "evidence for the paranormal" anyone's delusion or fantasy if only the individual would state that it was a parapsychological experience; if you have grasped the rationale and method of L.E. Rhine's technique you should have little difficulty in establishing the fallacy of that criticism. At the same time a few parapsychologists, while acknowledging the value of case analyses, do caution that collections of uninvestigated reports possibly could yield data statistically unrepresentative of carefully investigated cases (Dingwall, 1961; White, 1964b; Stevenson, 1987b).

In the remainder of this chapter we will consider the application of case study analyses to a major parapsychological phenomenon, the extrasensory experience, and then examine in more depth the strengths and weaknesses of this approach.

Surveys of ESP Experiences

One way in which spontaneous case material has been utilized entails a survey technique. In a typical survey people are asked if they have had a certain parapsychological experience, and are given other questions on potential psychological correlates of that experience. The objective here is to find the sorts of people who have (or at least who report) the parapsychological experience. Thus the incidence of these experiences can be related to various demographic and other personalistic variables. In the specific context of ESP experiences, one such survey in the form of a postal questionnaire was conducted in 1974 by an American parapsychologist, John Palmer (1979). His data indicated that 51 percent of Charlottesville, Virginia, residents and 55 percent of University of Virginia students had had some form of extrasensory experience.

Some of Palmer's other findings on waking ESP (as distinct from ESP during dreams) may be summarized by way of illustration of the survey approach. About 38 percent of the sample reported having had an extrasensory experience while awake. People who acknowledged such experiences generally tended to recall their dreams, to analyze their dreams, to have lucid dreams, to have had a moving spiritual or transcendental experience, to have consulted a psychic, to have a positive attitude toward parapsychological research, to place some credence in astrology, to believe in reincarnation, to be divorced or separated, and to have a lower level of education. No trends, however, were found in relation to the variables of sex, age, birth order, political convictions, religiosity, religious denomination, occupation, income, practice of meditation, use of "mind expanding" drugs, or vividness of dreams.

Although there are other survey data on extrasensory experiences, the above review of Palmer's findings suffices to indicate that the survey technique is most pertinent to the issue of underlying processes. It can generate ideas about the ways in which extrasensory experiences come about. Those issues will be taken up in the next chapter. If the survey questionnaire includes items about the experience itself it may well be useful also in studying the phenomenology of extrasensory experience. But the latter sort of information has come predominantly from a rather different perspective on the study of case material.

The Phenomenology of ESP Experiences

Another approach to spontaneous cases, that exploited most notably by L.E. Rhine, is to analyze the content of case reports and locate trends in the character of the various categories of parapsychological experience. It is this method that has provided the most direct access to the phenomenology of a parapsychological experience (or, the features of the phenomenon as it is experienced by the individual).

Louisa E. Rhine's data on the phenomenology of extrasensory experiences confirmed some of the categories defined in Chapter 1. In particular she noted the occurrence of precognitive, contemporaneous, and retrocognitive experiences. Because the issue of the temporal displacement of ESP has major theoretical implications, Rhine's data in this regard are given separate coverage in Chapter 5. The most basic of her phenomenological results however, relate to the *form* of the extrasensory experience. Rhine (1953a) observed that broadly speaking, each of the case reports could be categorized as an intuitive impression, a hallucination, a realistic dream, or an unrealistic dream. Each of these forms of spontaneous ESP experience now will be described.

Intuitive impressions. These extrasensory experiences consist of a simple, unreasoned impression or hunch. There is no imagery accompanying the experience, nor any conscious process of linear or rational thought leading to the impression. The individual reports suddenly "just knowing" something that upon subsequent investigation was borne out. Occasionally the informational element is minimal and the experience comprises little else than a strong, unexpected emotion; usually, however, the experient has some appreciation of the identity of the person to whom, or the situation to which, the felt emotion relates.

An example of an intuitive impression is given by the following experience of mine. The day before my family and I were to leave on a holiday I had a nagging impression that something was wrong with one of the wheels of our car. I had no logical grounds for this notion but it was sufficiently intense and compelling that I made a superficial examination of the wheels and also noted carefully the handling of the car when I went out that evening. During the trip on the following day one of the tires blew out. According to the garage attendant who fixed the tire at our destination the blow-out was due to a small stone lodged between the tire and the inner tube. In time the pebble had abraded the inner tube to the point of disintegration. Note that the content of the original impression ("something is wrong with one of the wheels") is limited and unelaborated: there was no associated imagery nor any conscious ideation converging toward the idea. (I cite this personal experience purely for illustrative purposes. In itself it should not convince anyone of the authenticity of ESP.)

Hallucinations. In a hallucinatory ESP experience the "message" is conveyed in the form of a sensory hallucination. For example, at the time of the unexpected death of a loved one in some distant place, many people report seeing an apparition of the individual or hearing his or her voice calling them. An apparent case of hallucinatory ESP concerns a servant who twice heard her master call her. At the time the servant's employer in fact was many miles away and allegedly was dreaming that he twice called his servant to request some hot water (Gurney, Myers & Podmore, 1886, Vol. 2, p. 105).

The information in hallucinatory experiences often is incomplete. In cases where the experient's name is heard being called, she or he may speculate about the safety of the person identified with the hallucinated voice but have no precise knowledge of that person's situation at the time of the experience.

Realistic dreams. In some extrasensory experiences information seemingly is acquired by way of a clear, realistic mental image. By far the most common form of this type is a dream which later is confirmed. It is on this basis that Louisa E. Rhine designated experiences of this sort, "realistic dreams." The term is not, however, entirely appropriate because the category also is intended to accommodate waking imagery (e.g., a "vision") which is not projected on to the environment (as is the case with a hallucinatory experience).

The following example of ESP in a realistic dream was sent to me several years ago by a young Australian man aged 17. "On a Wednesday night (mid–1977) I had an extremely vivid dream that I was watching an operation which I felt was for cancer. I did not know immediately who the person was who was undergoing the operation, but recognition came slowly. Gradually I sensed that the surgery was taking place in America and I associated it consciously with my sister. [The fellow wrote regularly to his elder sister in America but had had no indication that his sister may have been ill.] . . . Upon waking I described the dream to my mother. The next night the same dream was experienced except this time . . . I became far more agitated. . . . A certain urgency was felt. As the dream ended this urgency gave way to peace. Once again I told my mother about it. About one week later a letter arrived [in Australia] from America telling my family that my sister had undergone two operations for cancer [each on the night, or day as it was in the U.S., on which the young man had had his dreams]. The operation was a success."

Note that "realistic" in this context does not necessarily mean completely literal. If the above correspondent's sister had actually had only one operation or if the operation was for something other than cancer the dreams still would be regarded as realistic in the sense that the information they conveyed was not in a disguised form. By their nature realistic cases generally are more detailed in content than those of the two preceding categories, although much of the detail here may well be unconscious elaboration of a single basic item of information.

Unrealistic dreams. These are similar to realistic dream experiences but here the imagery is of a fanciful unreal sort. Although these cases do include a few waking experiences the category is predominated by dreams.

Sometimes the information conveyed by the extrasensory experience is dramatized as a fantasy. By way of illustration L.E. Rhine cited a case

Figure 5. Louisa E. Rhine and her file of case reports (photo: FRNM).

in which an elderly lady dreamt her daughter was pregnant and that she was teasing her daughter about it. Nothing like this interaction between mother and daughter ever took place but it subsequently emerged that the latter indeed was pregnant at the time. In other instances the information may be disguised, as in symbolic form. You may recall the biblical story of the pharaoh who dreamt of seven fat kine (cattle) and seven lean kine, a dream which was interpreted as a precognition of seven years of plenty to be followed by seven years of drought and famine.

As with any taxonomic scheme there are occasional instances of spontaneous extrasensory experience that do not fit conveniently into any single component of Rhine's quadripartite system. A few extrasensory dreams, for example, contain both realistic and unrealistic elements. With continued application of this taxonomy over another two decades of research, Rhine nevertheless was satisfied with its efficacy and saw no substantial reason to revise it. That view generally has been endorsed by other case analysts who utilized schemes similar to Rhine's (e.g., Green, 1960; Irwin, 1987c; Prasad & Stevenson, 1968; Sannwald, 1963; Schouten, 1981).

Before surveying more of L.E. Rhine's phenomenological findings it again should be emphasized that none of Rhine's cases is presented as evidence of the authenticity of ESP. The examples cited above serve only to illustrate a taxonomic scheme; any one of them could be "explained away" as a chance event or otherwise attributed to normal rather than paranormal factors.

Over an extended series of analyses beginning in 1951 Louisa E. Rhine noted several more trends in the phenomenological characteristics of extrasensory experience. The principal findings are summarized below (except that data relating to precognition and retrocognition are deferred for consideration in Chapter 5).

Distribution. The relative incidence of the different forms of ESP experience in Rhine's collection was approximately as follows: intuitive 26 percent, hallucinatory 9, realistic dreams 44, and unrealistic dreams 21 percent (e.g., Rhine, 1962a, p. 93). This pattern generally is confirmed by other surveys: that by Sannwald (1963) in Western Europe put the relative frequencies at 27, 10, 48 and 15 percent respectively. A few studies nevertheless have yielded somewhat different results (Schouten, 1982). It must be said that the incidence of a particular type of case in a collection can be affected by various factors. If in a radio interview the researcher cites as an example a case of realistic dream ESP many listeners who have had this type of experience will write to the researcher with details of their case. If these reports are included in the parapsychologist's case collection, the occurrence of realistic dream ESP then could be exaggerated. The experient's reticence is another pertinent factor. People may be relatively reluctant to report hallucinatory cases, fearing that hallucinations might be taken as indicative of mental disorder. Dreams on the other hand may be acknowledged more readily, even if they seem bizarre, because "after all, they are only fantasy."

Taken simply at face value these data nevertheless generate interesting questions for research into processes underlying the extrasensory experience. That a half or more of the experiences occur in the form of a dream might be taken to suggest these processes operate best when the experient's intellectual defenses are down or when the experient is engrossed in the contents of mentation and largely out of touch with sensory inputs from the environment. The association of ESP experiences with dreams and intuition also prompts the notion that the content of the experience has its origins deep in subconscious levels of the human mind. Each of these themes will be addressed again in the context of process-oriented research (see Chapter 4).

Completeness of Content. Extrasensory experiences typically incorporate information on only some aspects of the environmental event to which they ostensibly relate. L.E. Rhine (1962a,b) examined the four forms of ESP experience for their completeness of content, the latter being defined operationally in the fairly gross terms of whether or not the experience conveyed the general meaning of *what* occurred and to *whom* (Weiner & Haight, 1986, p. 18). This analysis showed realistic dreams to exhibit the highest level (91 percent) of completeness of content, followed in order by unrealistic dreams (72 percent), intuitive impressions (55 percent), and hallucinatory experiences (32 pecent).

The skeptic probably would be inclined to argue that because the content of dreams is so much more complex than that of intuitions and hallucinatory experiences, one would expect purely on the basis of chance that dreams will show the greatest number of points corresponding to reality. On the other hand, if the informational origins of extrasensory experience lie deep below the level of consciousness one might expect dreams also to be relatively efficient vehicles for processing or "working up" the information to the point where it is comparatively available for access to consciousness. In any event the evidently differential completeness of the content of the various forms of ESP experience is a phenomenological feature that warrants appropriate empirical investigation and explanation.

Personal Significance of Content. In those cases in which the extrasensory experience related to another person, commonly it was someone emotionally close to the experient, according to L.E. Rhine (1956). That general trend has been confirmed in analyses of several other case collections from various countries (Green, 1960; Irwin, 1987c; Prasad & Stevenson, 1968; Sannwald, 1963; Schouten, 1981; Stevenson, 1970). This may indicate that an emotional bond between people is conducive to extrasensory "communication." Again it is possible that there is greater opportunity for the content of the experience to be confirmed by a close individual than by a stranger, so that the impression about the friend is relatively likely to be categorized by the experient as being extrasensory instead of being dismissed as baseless fantasy. In any event examination of ESP cases as a whole does suggest that their content has some significance for the experient. The experiences seem to be *purposive*.

This is borne out too by L.E. Rhine's analysis of the events depicted in extrasensory experiences. The vast majority of cases in her collection concerned deaths, personal crises (illnesses, accidents, births, marriages) and other events of general importance to the experient. Similar findings are reported for other case collections of extrasensory experience (Prasad & Stevenson, 1968; Schouten, 1981; Stevenson, 1970). Perhaps experiences concerned with personally significant events are intrinsically easy to recall and hence they readily are reported to the collector of case reports, although the trend in the data is so consistent that it seems unlikely to be a mere report artifact.

While extrasensory experiences generally may relate to personally significant events the various forms of the experience may be differentially associated with particular kinds of events. Schouten (1981) for example, suggests that the death of the referent person is relatively more likely to be depicted in waking imagery than in an imageless intuition.

Conviction. When describing an extrasensory experience people often give particular emphasis to their impression that the experience was highly compelling and meaningful. As we shall see in the following chapter this contrasts markedly with the behavior of subjects in ESP experiments: typically they simply do not know if their impressions of a sensorially concealed target are correct. The sense of conviction in spontaneous extrasensory experience therefore is a matter warranting some study.

L.E. Rhine began her investigation of the issue in 1951 and found a sense of conviction in the experience's content to be lowest in dreams and hallucinatory experiences, a tendency confirmed by Green (1960). Perhaps this is due to the fact that the individual has learned that (normal) dreams and hallucinations usually are based in fantasy and thus not to be accorded much credence. Rhine (1951) on the other hand suggested that conviction is emotional rather than an objective item of information and hence cannot be represented as a mental image. She contrasts the situation for imaginal experiences with that of intuitive ESP in which no imagery and little objective information emerges in consciousness, yet conviction often is high.

Telepathic Experiences. In her study of telepathic experiences L.E. Rhine (1953b) focused on an instructive form of the hallucinatory ESP experience known as "call cases." These are ones in which the individual heard a loved one calling and learned later that the "caller" was in distress some distance away. It was noted that in few of these cases did the caller or *agent* actually call to the experient or indeed even think of the latter person. Rhine speculated that in ESP the notion of an agent sending a message to the experient might be invalid. Rather the experient may be the "active" member of the association, in some way seeking out information on people emotionally close to him or her. Support for this idea emerged in a later study (Rhine, 1956) in which it was found that although experients in telepathic cases did need to know about the agent, in about a sixth of cases there seemed to be no conceivable reason for the agent to communicate to the experient. Rhine's suggestion certainly raises questions about the popular view of extrasensory "perception" as a perceptual-like process, a "sixth sense" in which some unidentified sort of environmental "stimulus" is mediated to a percipient.

Louisa E. Rhine's investigation of the phenomenology of extrasensory experience is a most valuable pioneering effort, but regrettably it has inspired few parapsychologists to continue and to extend her research. As far as its implications for process-oriented research is concerned, arguably the most interesting ideas thrown up by Rhine's analyses of spontaneous case reports are that ESP seems purposive in its orientation and that it may well be instigated by the experient rather than being received passively by him or her.

Other Phenomenological Features. The meager information available on other aspects of ESP phenomenology falls into two main classes, that relating to the situation in which the experience occurred and that to do with the experience's impact upon the individual.

The social context of extrasensory experiences was surveyed in a sample of 124 Australian university students (a report on the focal objective of the survey is provided by Irwin, 1987c). Approximately two-thirds of the group reported being alone at the time of the experience. Given that the substantial majority of the sample had had their most recent extrasensory experience before the age of eighteen and that a sizeable proportion of such experiences arise during sleep, perhaps it is not surprising that most of these respondents claimed to have been without company. Certainly the result should not necessarily be taken as applicable to the general population of extrasensory experients. The social context of an ESP experience might additionally affect its form; in one case collection Schouten (1981) found intuitive impressions to occur more often when the experient was with other people than when alone.

Also surveyed in the Australian study was the experient's level of physical activity at the time. Ninety percent of the sample reported being engaged in minimal activity such as sleeping, sitting, or standing. The activity level was moderate (as in walking or playing a piano) in 7 percent and substantial (as in jogging or playing tennis) in only 3 percent. This tendency for a very low level of physical activity at the onset of the extrasensory experience is found in association also with some other parapsychological phenomena (e.g., Irwin, 1985a, pp. 151–152) and is consistent with the idea that these experiences are facilitated by an unforced engrossment in one's mentation or in a repetitive, highly practiced motor act (Honorton, 1977; Irwin, 1985b).

The latter notion also sits reasonably well with data on the individual's state of mind at the experience's onset. The strong association between extrasensory experience and dreaming already has been noted. In my

Australian student survey very few people felt they were concentrating strongly on the occasion of their experience; most were either engaged in minimally demanding mental activity (28 percent) or not really thinking about anything in particular (50 percent).

Apart from L.E. Rhine's attention to the experient's conviction in their extrasensory experience, the experience's *impact* upon the individual has received surprisingly little attention from researchers. Stevenson (1970, pp. 23–26) sought to operationalize the issue of conviction by examining whether or not the experient took any action after an intuitive telepathic experience. Action reportedly was taken in about half of the cases, most particularly when the "agent" in the experience was identified and when that person's thoughts were said to have been focused on the experient at the time.

The experience's emotional impact is an important but neglected aspect of ESP phenomenology. Sannwald (1963, p. 282) noted that about 85 percent of cases in his collection referred to unpleasant or sad events, but he did not ascertain how experients actually felt about their extrasensory impression of these events. It is feasible for example, that if conviction in the experience is low the experient will be relatively unmoved by its negatively-toned content. Stevenson's (1970, pp. 26–27) analysis of intuitive telepathic impressions examined original case reports for evidence of the emotions felt by the experient. Although many of the reports made no reference to the matter, the dominant emotions educed in the remainder were anxiety (61 percent), depression (36), and joy (3 percent). In the Australian student sample an attempt was made to survey the individual's feelings immediately after their extrasensory experience. Here 18 percent were happy or joyful, 25 percent anxious, and 5 percent depressed. The other 52 percent indicated they had felt "otherwise"; in a written elaboration of this response option many said their reaction was one of surprise/curiosity/intrigue, a few noted they were confused or displeased, and several claimed to have been quite indifferent to the content of their experience. There clearly is scope for further research into the emotional impact of extrasensory experiences.

Another facet of the experience's impact is whether or not the experient tells anyone about it. This undoubtedly is linked to the experient's level of conviction and the nature of the event depicted in the experience, among other things. Respondents in my Australian survey were asked if they had told someone of their experience before they learned by conventional means of the depicted event's actual occurrence. Thirty percent had done so; 53 percent had not because of no inclination to do so, and 17 percent had not told anyone because of the lack of an opportunity.

This completes the review of ESP phenomenology. It may seem surprising that we know comparatively little about an experience acknowledged to have been had by approximately half the population. But despite the substantial efforts of Louisa E. Rhine, phenomenological research on extrasensory experience is still in its formative stage.

The Value of Spontaneous Case Material

Spontaneous cases may be of use to parapsychologists in several ways. First, it must be said that these "real life" experiences are what we are endeavoring to explain. It is all very well to take ESP into the laboratory for controlled investigation and precise statistical evaluation, but once this is done our hope surely is that we will be in a position to explain how and why people have these parapsychological experiences in the course of everyday life. Collections of spontaneous cases at least should serve to remind experimental parapsychologists of the ultimate goal of their research.

A second function of case material is to indicate the different ways in which ESP (if there is such a thing) may be expressed. For example, in real life ESP experiences seem to relate to past, present, and future events, and may take the form of an intuition, a hallucination, or a mental image (e.g., dream). The researcher should be alert to these various vehicles of expression and consider the extent to which specific laboratory findings may be generalized to the various forms.

Perhaps a primary role of spontaneous cases is to suggest hypotheses for experimental investigation. Content analyses of case collections provide a valuable source of inspiration on the nature of extrasensory processes. For example, if spontaneous ESP experiences tend to occur when the percipient is in a mentally relaxed state, the parapsychologist can examine the effect of relaxation on experimental ESP scoring and then, if appropriate, go on to explore precisely what specific aspects of relaxation are involved in this relationship and on what basis. By and large, experimental parapsychologists have shown insufficient cognizance of the indications of case material for process-oriented research. Given that the subject matter of spontaneous cases seems to be something of particular significance to the experient, why have parapsychologists conducted so much ESP testing with geometrical shapes and alphanumeric characters that have little personal meaning for experimental participants?

Finally, as we have seen from L.E. Rhine's work, spontaneous cases can be examined from a phenomenological viewpoint. Quite apart from the matter of the bases of parapsychological phenomena it is legitimate to inquire into the character of the experiences from the percipient's point of view. Whether or not the phenomena are paranormal, people do have these experiences and we as students of behavior should be interested in ascertaining what is distinctive about the content and personal interpretation of these experiences. Only by knowing what happens from the experient's viewpoint will we be able to decide, for example, whether the experience of a person we see in the psychological clinic is parapsychological or psychopathological. If experiences of these two types can be distinguished phenomenologically perhaps we can avoid classifying people as schizophrenic when all they require is some counseling to come to terms with their personal parapsychological event.

In these respects therefore, collections and surveys of spontaneous parapsychological experiences can make a substantial contribution to research. At the same time there are certain limitations in such data of which we must take account.

The Limitations of Spontaneous Case Material

The evidential limitations of spontaneous cases essentially spring from the possible incidence of self-deception, deception and fraud on the part of the people reporting the experience. Some of the limitations will be discussed in relation to the issues of authenticity and the nature of parapsychological experience.

Case Material and Authenticity

Despite the hopes of the founders of the SPR the general feeling among modern parapsychologists is that no spontaneous experience, no matter how carefully investigated, can be considered to provide unequivocal evidence of the authenticity of parapsychological phenomena (West, 1982). Any such experience might have been due to the unknown operation of one or more of the following factors.

(i) **Inaccuracies of recall.** Cognitive psychologists have demonstrated that people's recall of everyday events can be highly inaccurate. Human memory is not a device permitting literal replay of previously experienced incidents. Once a particular interpretation is placed on an event, features of the experience consistent with that interpretation might be recalled but inconsistent features will tend to be forgotten. If, for example, you witness an altercation between Smith and Jones and attribute the blame to Jones you later may tend to recall Jones's provocative actions but not those of Smith. A similar type of distortion may occur in some reports of parapsychological experiences. By way of illustration, I may dream that Uncle John and Aunt Mary have food poisoning and both die. A few weeks later I learn that Aunt Mary has died of cancer. I then may declare that I had a precognitive dream to this effect, forgetting that the dream related also to Uncle John and to food poisoning rather than cancer. As time passes the consistency between the event and my precognition of it will tend to increase.

Having placed an interpretation on an experience, recalling it may prompt embellishments to reinforce that interpretation. If Jones is seen to have provoked the argument with Smith you involuntarily may elaborate on the nature of Jones's provocation. Similarly, in the retelling of my precognitive dream of Aunt Mary's death I may incorporate details about her anger over the doctor's inability to effect a cure for her condition.

(ii) Misperception of ambiguous situations. Perceptual psychologists point out that human perception of the world is not veridical but rather is a construction based on sensory inputs, past experience, and expectations. Particularly in perceptually ambiguous situations, past experience and expectations play a substantial role in determining what we consciously "perceive."

One way in which past experience influences our perception of an incident as paranormal is in regard to causality. In childhood people have learned that events occurring in quick succession are causally linked, that is, one event is seen to cause the other or both events are seen to be caused by a common factor. This conception has been borne out on so many occasions that it often is taken for granted. Even where two events are causally independent their temporal contiguity is a compelling suggestion of a meaningful connection between them. Someone who happens to be pulling the handle of a poker machine in a distinctive way when the jackpot drops is inclined to believe that this technique of pulling is a cause of poker machine payouts. In a parapsychological context, if we are thinking of a long-lost friend at the very moment that person phones us it is natural to assume a causal connection between these events, yet they may well have arisen coincidentally.

Past experience also governs our assessment of the probability of an incident, and incidents with a low probability are intrinsically more likely to be construed as paranormal. Nevertheless our estimates of probability may be very inaccurate. For example, you may think it extraordinary for two people in a small group to have the same birthday, but for a group of 23 people the odds are better than 50/50 that at least two of them share a birthdate. Often our estimates of probability are distorted by the forgetting of things which at the time were inconsequential. Try to recall how many times you have read your horoscope in a magazine and subsequently found the predictions to be fulfilled. Most likely you will recall having looked at horoscopes but cannot really say whether or not they were realized. Yet if you read in tomorrow's horoscope that you were about to make a financial gain and in the afternoon were told that you had won the lottery you probably would be inclined to conclude that horoscopes should be given some credence. Many would proclaim, "The probability of winning the lottery is so small that the horoscope could not have been correct just by chance!" Nevertheless the horoscope predicted not a lottery win but a more probable event, a financial gain; and on closer examination our impression of the probability of a horoscope's fulfillment is based on a very vague memory of the record of past predictions.

Perception also is influenced by expectations and beliefs, particularly in ambiguous situations. Often expectations make perception or cognitive processing more efficient. Having read "They bought some chocolates at the...," we expect to encounter "shop" in the next few words. When "shop" does appear it therefore requires little processing for its recognition and our reading thereby becomes more proficient. On the other hand, expectations can lead to misperceptions. If in the above example a typographical error resulted in "shep" being printed instead of "shop" many readers would not even notice the misprint, that is, their perception would not be veridical. Magicians rely heavily on creating inappropriate perceptual expectations. By various maneuvers they effect the impression that an object is located under a black cloth, and when the cloth is removed to reveal the absense of the object the audience "perceives" the object's dematerialization. In a more parapsychological context the nervous person spending a night in an unfamiliar old house may be prone to perceive naturally occurring noises as the footsteps of a ghost: there is an expectation (even subconscious) that such houses could be haunted.

Beliefs also serve to influence the search for alternative explanations of the perceived event (Jones & Russell, 1980). An individual who is extremely skeptical about the paranormal will look for natural causes of the event and if this should prove unproductive will dismiss the experience as a coincidence or mental aberration and quickly forget it. In contrast a person who is overly gullible about the paranormal will accept any unusual event as such without giving due consideration to other possibilities. A report of a spontaneous experience thus might spring largely from motivated misperception.

(iii) Subconscious perceptions. In the literature of cognitive psychology there are indications that some sensory stimuli may be registered by the individual's processing system without evoking a conscious sensation (e.g., subliminal perception). This subconscious information later may break through into consciousness in the form of a dream or in thought associations. For example, you may be concentrating on some activity when an old friend happens to speak in your vicinity. Shortly afterwards you may start daydreaming about your old friend; at that moment the latter taps you on the shoulder and you cry in amazement, "Why, I was just thinking about you!" It is conceivable that some reports of ESP are based on such subconscious perception. Consider another example. Some very subtle changes in behavior may signify that a friend is very ill but is hiding the fact from you. If these cues are not perceived consciously they may be registered subconsciously and emerge subsequently as the basis of a "precognitive" dream of your friend's death. Some instances of apparent telepathy between close friends might reflect similar factors. One individual will make a comment and the other will remark that such a thought had just passed through his or her mind too. Rather than attributing this to ESP, each person might review their recent mentation to find what prompted that particular thought. It may turn out to be an association to a fleeting image or remark on television which by virtue of the pair's common history evoked the same train of thought.

(iv) **Deception and fraud.** The preceding sources of inaccuracy in spontaneous case reports basically are unintentional: the experient has no deliberate objective of deceiving the case collector. Other respondents however, may well engage in premeditated deception and fraud. Their motives may be diverse. Some may have an infantile sense of mischief, others may get a feeling of superiority from misleading a "know-all academic." People aspiring to be professional psychics also may be seeking a university department's "stamp of approval" to enhance their credibility among members of the public.

There is nothing especially difficult in concocting a tale of a fictional parapsychological experience and passing the fabrication on to a collector of case reports. Perhaps of more interest are some of the techniques used by professional psychics or stage mentalists to demonstrate they have "extrasensory" abilities (for a broader review see Abbott, 1909). Although these sorts of performances can hardly be deemed "spontaneous" some of the underlying techniques might well be used in instances presented to the parapsychologist as reports of spontaneous ESP.

One technique is called billet reading and is useful for performance before a large group. Members of the audience are each invited to write on a card the name of a loved one and a short description of some distinctive characteristic of that person. Each card is sealed in an envelope and passed to the "psychic" who then selects envelopes at random to read by ESP. After attempting to read a card clairvoyantly the envelope is opened, the card read to the audience to establish the accuracy of the ESP attempt, and the person who wrote that card is asked to acknowledge its authenticity. The mentalist proceeds through several cards in this fashion with great success and the audience's donations are gratefully received to support the good work. How is this performance achieved?

The trick in billet reading is fiendishly simple. The reading of the first card is sham. There are (at least) two options here. One is to report that little information can be obtained from the card ("because the writer is a skeptic"), make an ostensibly weak stab at the envelope's contents, open the envelope, pretend to read out something which is quite discrepant from the attempted ESP reading, and finally retain the sympathy of the audience by not asking the "obviously embarrassed" skeptical writer of the card to acknowledge it. Alternatively, a reading may be given and a stooge in the audience deceitfully acknowledges its complete accuracy. Under either of these arrangements for the reading of the first card the contents of this envelope in reality are not divulged to the audience and thus can be used as the message that the psychic pretends to obtain from the second envelope. Ostensibly to provide authentication of the second reading, this envelope is opened and its contents become the message to be reported for the third reading. This procedure can be repeated indefinitely, although the performer would stop after five or six readings to ensure that cynics will not have sufficient time to discern the technique being employed. A feature of billet reading is that authentication of readings is given by several members of the audience known to other people there not to be a stooge of the performer.

Let us now consider a method more applicable to the circumstance where there is only one sitter. This is the classical situation of the fortune-teller or consultant medium. Where the sitter is a regular patron the fortune-teller has tremendous scope for obtaining information about the client and presenting it as inspiration from the spirits. Rather extreme measures include engaging a private detective to gather suitable data or recruiting a housebreaker to search the individual's home for information (and also to steal one or two small items of sentimental value which can be "apported" in a sitting some months later). According to one reformed (or retired) medium there is a network of mediums in America within which dossiers of major (wealthy) clients are circulated (Keene, 1976). A rather less extreme but equally effective tactic is to get the client talking during each session and to report some of this information in a reading at a later date. Since sitters are more interested in what the psychic says to them than in what they say to the psychic they often are convinced that the subsequent reading derived from paranormal sources.

Where the fortune-teller has not met the client before some rather different measures must be employed. One possibility with a female sitter is to invite her to leave her coat and handbag in the waiting room where they are searched by an accomplice for any useful data. More subtle avenues, however, may be utilized; these are known as "cold reading" techniques (Hyman, 1977). The sitter can be sized up on the basis of grooming, clothing, jewelry, mannerisms and speech, and this information can provide a basis for the initial stages of the reading. The impact of these statements can be noted, even in minor changes of facial expression, and the comment quickly may be hedged and if necessary completely reversed.

If data on the individual's background can be extracted a medium familiar with the latest opinion polls and surveys can predict with high probability the client's beliefs on a range of issues. All of this information can be interwoven with statements the client would like to hear: "You have several abilities which you have not been given an opportunity to demonstrate," "You have a tendency to underestimate your achievements," and so forth. Even if the factual material is mistaken the client will remember the reading in glowing terms if it contained a good measure of carefully presented flattery.

Apart from the informational facet of the performance there are points of showmanship involved in a successful reading. The medium will be confident and act as if she or he believed in the performance, at the same time remaining modest and making no excessive claims. The cooperation of the sitter will be sought; then if the reading is a failure it is the sitter's fault. Cooperation is said to be needed particularly because of the "vagaries of language": as it might not be possible for the medium to convey adequately the intended meaning, the sitter is called upon to endeavor to clarify the message by restating it in their own words or in relation to their own life. This of course gives the fortune-teller additional information and clues as to the direction the reading should take. Various dramatic devices such as a crystal ball or palm reading will provide an air of mysticism and also an excuse for stalling: while formulating the next part of the reading the medium can be seen to be following the lines of the client's hand or to be peering through the mists in the crystal ball. Stock phrases will be used to fill out the reading and to provide further time in which to organize thoughts. Statements will be given in an uncertain tone or posed as a question, then modified in accordance with the client's reaction so as to leave the sitter with the impression of having received a positive statement. In short, the skills of a fake medium are very much those of an adept used car salesman.

(v) Chance. Perhaps the major argument against the use of spontaneous case material for the purpose of authenticating parapsychological phenomena is that the role of chance in such cases in unknown. You may intuit the unlikelihood that a given case is due purely to chance or coincidence but the fact remains that almost invariably the investigator is not able to specify the statistical probability of the event's occurrence by chance.

Consider for example my apocryphal tale of precognitively dreaming about Aunt Mary's demise. On the basis of chance alone the likelihood of my having this dream and my aunt dying shortly thereafter would seem remote. But how can you tell? How many people in the world had a similar dream that night and found it not fulfilled? We simply cannot say. The point is that with one's having a number of dreams each night, over a lifetime one surely would get by chance alone a correspondence between some dreams and actual events of the immediately following days. Unless the level of statistical significance of a spontaneous experience can be determined, parapsychologists cannot justifiably be confident that the event was unlikely to have been a coincidence.

The move toward testing the authenticity of parapsychological phenomena in the laboratory reflected the realization that the level of statistical significance must be ascertained and there must be control exercised over such potentially confounding factors as those cited above, namely, inaccuracies of memory, misperception, subliminal cues, and deliberate deception.

Case Material and the Nature of Parapsychological Phenomena

As you will recall, L.E. Rhine argued that collections of spontaneous case material could be used to gather data on the nature of parapsychological phenomena. If such trends are used as hypotheses for experimental investigation there is much merit in her position. On the other hand, where the data are to be used for other purposes one must recognize certain limitations in collections of case material. The limitations here generally relate to sampling, that is, the extent to which the collection can be regarded as representative of spontaneous experiences as a whole.

Investigators are one potential source of bias in this respect, since they decide which reports will be included in a collection and which will not. Such decisions are by their nature subjective. For one to reject some reports as not pertaining to a parapsychological phenomenon may in the eyes of other researchers be construed as imposing upon the data one particular interpretation of what should constitute a parapsychological phenomenon. For one to reject other reports on the grounds that they are too poorly written for use in the analysis might be seen as biasing the sample towards people who are more verbally fluent and perhaps thereby prone to embellishment. To accept all reports would leave the researcher open to the charge that the collection contains identifiable instances of psychotic hallucination, hoaxes, and other nonparapsychological material.

The case collection also may be biased by the manner in which contributions are solicited. If examples of particular parapsychological experiences are given to potential respondents they tend to elicit very similar experiences rather than the full range of forms which the phenomena can take. A researcher who makes an appeal for cases in the media may be sampling a population of uncertain, and thus possibly atypical, characteristics. It is not simply a matter that the listeners to a particular radio program are unrepresentative of the general population but also that the researcher has little idea what sort of people actually listen to the program.

Additionally the composition of case collections may be atypical because of the differing preparedness of people to respond to the researcher's plea for case reports. People who believe in parapsychological phenomena may well be much more inclined to participate in a survey of spontaneous ESP experiences than folk who do not. Individuals sympathetic to the objectives of science and general academic research may be relatively common among the respondents. It is also the case that females tend to be more willing than males to write out an account of their experiences and send it to an investigator. Even if an individual is prepared to take part in the project she or he may tend to report experiences of a certain type, such as the more credible instances or ones less suggestive of maladjustment.

There are procedures for minimizing the effects of these various potential sources of bias but in general it is advisable to seek replication of case study data in other samples and with other research techniques. At the same time it must be said that in spite of the potential for sampling bias, many phenomenological trends do seem remarkably consistent across different case collections.

In this section a number of limitations of spontaneous case material have been highlighted. By means of these arguments it is possible to "explain away" virtually any spontaneous parapsychological experience, and on such grounds many critics maintain that parapsychological research is futile. While acknowledging that case collections cannot be used as conclusive evidence of the authenticity of parapsychological phenomena the position taken here is that this does not warrant the abandonment of research into these experiences.

First, the fact that cases may plausibly have been due to the operation of any number of normal factors does not demonstrate that any given case was indeed due to such factors. The case still could be authentically paranormal. As Dow (1987) notes, psychological research on human attributional and information-processing errors might equally be used to argue that some people could have been mistaken in construing their anomalous experiences *not* to have involved paranormal processes. The only fair way of assessing the authenticity of a parapsychological phenomenon is to employ a research technique suited to that task, a carefully designed experimental procedure.

Second, even if the phenomena prove not to be paranormal, people do report them and hence we as behavioral scientists should endeavor to understand why they are reported. Far from prompting an end to research, the points raised in this section indicate the necessity of further, if different, research.

Key Terms and Concepts

intuitive impressions
hallucinations
realistic dreams
unrealistic dreams
Gurney, Myers & Podmore
Henry Sidgwick
Eleanor Sidgwick
Prince
Louisa E. Rhine

Saltmarsh
Sannwald
Stevenson
Palmer
telepathic agent
completeness of content
conviction
call cases
billet reading

Study Questions

1. Recall one of your own extrasensory experiences. To what extent does it meet the Society for Psychical Research criteria for the acceptability of a case report? What additional evidence would have been demanded of your case by the founders of the SPR, and why would they think this evidence was necessary?

2. Were the SPR criteria needlessly severe? Or were they appropriate for their intended purpose?

3. Distinguish between a case collection and a case survey. Methodologically speaking, might there be some overlap between the two approaches?

4. How did Louisa E. Rhine's technique for analysis of case collections differ from that of earlier studies?

5. Try to locate among your own extrasensory experiences instances of intuitive impressions, hallucinations, realistic dreams, and unrealistic dreams. Do any of your experiences not fit neatly into L.E. Rhine's proposed taxonomy?

6. What were the principal results of L.E. Rhine's analyses of spontaneous cases of ESP?

7. Of what use to parapsychologists are spontaneous case reports?

8. What are the evidential limitations of spontaneous case material?

9. Recall one of your own extrasensory experiences and explore ways in which an independent critic might seek to explain your experience in terms of recognized psychological processes. To what extent do you feel your experience demonstrates the existence of the paranormal process ESP?

10. On what sort of evidence should parapsychologists assess the authenticity of ESP?

4

Experimental Research
on Extrasensory Perception

The Authenticity of ESP

A central issue in ESP research is that of authenticity: Are (some) extrasensory experiences due to the operation of a process presently not acknowledged to exist by conventional scientists? Parapsychologists' interest in this issue often is represented as a pursuit of the paranormal and thus in a sense a crusade against science itself, but in essence the research on the authenticity of ESP has been a pursuit of the normal, a use of the methods of science in an attempt to establish the bases of ESP and to "normalize" them, either by demonstrating their compatibility with accepted scientific principles or by establishing sufficient reason for that framework to be expanded in order to accommodate the occurrence of extrasensory experiences. In addition to its significance for parapsychology's legitimization as an academic discipline, the investigation of ESP's authenticity is a fascinating study in the sociology of science.

The Move to Experimental Inquiry

Following the establishment of the Society for Psychical Research in Great Britain, and particularly in the first quarter of this century, there was a growing realization that the authenticity of ESP could be investigated only through a controlled test in a laboratory situation. That appreciation evolved naturally from researchers' experience in investigating mediums, although it was to be some time before there developed a standard experimental paradigm for ESP research. The first step toward operationalizing the ESP hypothesis entailed an emphasis upon controlled observation whereby the investigator should select some target material, ensure it was sensorially inaccessible to the subject of the study, and then invite the individual to identify the material by psychic means. Some of the SPR's early investigations of mental mediums or "sensitives" comprised controlled tasks of this sort. Thus, Guthrie's study in 1883 required subjects to telepathically identify sensations concurrently being experienced by agents in visual, gustatory, olfactory and tactile modalities (Guthrie & Birchall, 1883; Gurney et al., 1886, Vol. 1, pp. 36–58).

Controlled tests in which the range of extrasensory targets is unknown (and hence conceptually unlimited) to the subject are known as *free-response* experiments. These investigations were to make a major contribution to our understanding of processes underlying extrasensory experience, particularly through the work of Sinclair (1930/1962) and Warcollier (1938/1975). But in the early period of experimentation their value to the issue of ESP's authenticity was limited because the evaluation of their data necessarily was qualitative. In Guthrie's study with drawings for example, the evidence for the occurrence of telepathy relied upon the apparent similarity between the pictures viewed by the agents and the subjects' sketched impressions of those targets. Whatever their value for process-oriented research such studies did not attest to the reality of ESP because it was not (then) possible to be sure that correspondences between targets and responses were anything more than lucky guesses.

The next step in the development of a paradigmatic ESP experiment therefore was marked by an emerging awareness of the need for quantification of the observed correspondence between targets and responses. This entails both the representation of the subject's performance as a numerical score and the assessment of the probability that this performance was due simply to guessing or "chance." A few of the earliest SPR investigations instance a glimmering appreciation of this requirement. Beginning in the year before the SPR's statutory foundation, ESP tests were conducted by Barrett, Gurney and Myers with the five young daughters of an English clergyman, the Reverend Creery; here an agent concentrated on the thought of various types of target including a randomly selected playing card and a two-digit number, and the subject sought to determine each target telepathically (Gurney et al., 1886, Vol. 1, pp. 20–31). In the case of these targets the investigators evaluated the girls' performance on the assumption that the probability of correctly guessing the identity of a playing card on the basis of chance alone was 1 in 52, and that of guessing a two-digit number, 1 in 90. The probability that the observed results are due to random guesses thus was determined to be typically very low (Gurney et al., 1886, Vol. 1, p. 25). (It should be noted in passing that evidence of the girls' cheating was reported a few years later.)

The notions of quantification and probabilistic assessment of ESP data, and the associated need for a sizeable number of "guesses" or trials, were enunciated formally in 1884 by Charles Richet, an eminent physiologist and later Nobel Prize laureate at the University of Paris (Gurney et al.,

1886, Vol. 1, p. 31; Richet, 1923, p. 85). Richet's thesis was indeed a crucial insight in the history of experimental parapsychology, principally for two reasons. First, although critics of ESP research had ample scope to quibble about the claimed extent of target-response correspondence in free-response studies like that by Guthrie, this became a much more difficult proposition when the data were quantified and objectively evaluated in these *restricted-choice* experiments. Second, quantification permitted the detection of very weak or intermittent extrasensory effects, eventually opening the way for research into the authenticity question with so-called *unselected* subjects instead of people with supposedly high and controllable skills in ESP. Typical of his era however, Richet himself still preferred to have data that encouraged conviction qualitatively as well as quantitatively; in tests to identify extrasensorially the suit of 2927 playing cards, Richet recorded 789 correct responses compared to an expected 732, but despite the statistical improbability of achieving this result by chance he could not regard it as conclusive.

Although there were relatively few experimentally-inclined psychical researchers active during the fifty years immediately following the foundation of the SPR, a surprising number of simple card-guessing tests of ESP were undertaken; Pratt, Rhine, Smith, Stuart and Greenwood (1940, Table 29) catalog about 80 such experiments. While many of these had experimental personnel of unknown standing, a small number of trials, an inadequately controlled experimental setting, other methodological flaws, or poorly reported procedures, some of the studies do seem procedurally adequate.

A Harvard University researcher, George Estabrooks (1927/1961), for example, conducted four series of tests with individual unselected students as subjects in one room and himself as the telepathic agent in another room. Each of the 83 participants completed 20 trials with playing cards as targets. The identification of target color and of target suit were substantially better than expected on the basis of chance.

A few skeptics also undertook card-guessing experiments. One of these was the often-cited study by Coover (1917/1975) at Stanford University in 1915. Individual subjects sat in one room while a telepathic agent sat with Coover in an adjacent room. The targets were a shuffled 40-card deck of playing cards. On the roll of a die each trial was performed under one of two conditions. In the "telepathy" condition the telepathic agent looked at the card while the subject sought to identify it. The other type of trial was designed as a control or "nontelepathic" condition; here the telepathic agent did not view the card when the subject attempted to guess its identity. After some 10,000 trials Coover found no substantial difference between scores under the two conditions and he concluded there was no support for the telepathy hypothesis.

Critics of Coover's study later pointed out that although the control condition may have been "nontelepathic" it was hardly a "non–ESP" procedure; on the contrary, it admitted the operation of clairvoyance, a possibility Coover simply could not take seriously. Comparison of the scores to that expected purely on the basis of random guessing showed performance under both conditions to be above chance, significantly so when data for the two conditions were (rather inappropriately) combined. Coover himself was inclined to attribute the scores' elevation over chance to the possibility of involuntary auditory cues passing from the agent's room to the adjoining subject's room (Kennedy, 1939, p. 63).

There certainly were some innovative studies in the period to 1930. Some researchers examined the idea that ESP might operate over long distances; Usher and Burt (1909) obtained above-chance data in a card-guessing test conducted with the two men attempting telepathic contact between London and Bristol (120 miles) and between London and Prague (960 miles). In the Psychological Laboratory of the University of Groningen in the Netherlands, experimenters tried to influence by telepathic means a subject's selection of one of 48 squares on a 6×8 grid in front of him (see Schouten & Kelly, 1978). The subject's success rate was remarkably high, but because target selection and scoring procedure may have been biased the results cannot be regarded as conclusive for the authenticity of ESP.

An experiment well ahead of its time was designed by Troland (1917/1976) at Harvard University. Troland constructed an electrically operated machine that randomly selected one of two targets, presented it to a telepathic agent for a specified duration, recorded both the target and the subject's guess at its identity, and terminated the series when a specified number of trials had been completed. In a test comprising 605 trials, 284 correct responses were recorded, a result of mere borderline statistical significance. The methodological precision permitted by Troland's device nevertheless was noteworthy, yet it received scant subsequent use. Troland also accepted as informative an ESP performance that was significantly *below* that expected by chance; this issue will be taken up later in the context of *psi-missing*.

But despite all this activity, before 1930 research on the authenticity of ESP had a negligible impact upon the scientific community. In part this was due to the fact that only a small proportion of the work was conducted in a university setting and published in sources where it might come to the notice of other scientists. A more fundamental factor was that the research effort was sporadic and uncoordinated. Although some qualified researchers (such as Troland and Coover) did perform ESP tests they typically completed just a single study and then made no further empirical contribution to the field. No coherent, sustained program of research had been instigated by this work and no dominant standardized experimental paradigm had evolved. The scientific researchers' sense of frustration was reflected in increasing disunity within the SPR and the American Society for Psychical Research (ASPR), with major rifts arising between the ardent experimentalists and other, more spiritualistically oriented members (Mauskopf & McVaugh, 1980; Tietze, 1985).

The program of ESP experimentation that was to confront the academic world with the authenticity issue began in 1927 at Duke University, in Durham, North Carolina, when J.B. Rhine (husband of Louisa E. Rhine) developed the classical ESP cards and techniques for their use. This style of research became so fundamental to the discipline that J.B. Rhine generally is regarded as the father of modern experimental parapsychology, although like any intellectual pioneer he had his conceptual predecessors, as we have seen.

Joseph Banks Rhine (1895–1980) studied botany and plant physiology at the University of Chicago, where both he and Louisa obtained their Ph.D. This may seem an odd background for a person who taught psychology and engaged in parapsychological research, but two factors conspired to help Rhine along his chosen path. First, in the 1920s botanists were in the forefront of work in statistical theory and Rhine's knowledge in this area served him well in his later efforts to devise laboratory tests of ESP. Second, Rhine's interest in parapsychological research endeared him to William McDougall, the newly appointed head of the Psychology Department at Duke University. Rhine thus became an instructor in psychology in 1928 and an assistant professor in 1929.

J.B. Rhine's first topic for study was clairvoyance. Although earlier psychical researchers generally felt telepathy had been adequately attested many of them were dubious about the existence of clairvoyance; as was the case with Coover, some even dismissed the notion out of hand, in spite of the formal experiments on clairvoyance by Richet (1888) many years before. Between 1924 and 1928, however, Ina Jephson of the SPR performed a sizeable card-guessing investigation, the results of which she claimed to support the hypothesis of clairvoyance. She then proceeded to argue that because former experimental studies of apparent telepathy also admitted the possibility of clairvoyance of the cards being viewed by the agent, the concept of telepathy was in fact redundant (Jephson, 1928). The occurrence of ESP without the mediation of an agent or "sender" therefore became a salient issue.

Now, Rhine was aware that previous ESP studies had relied on packs of ordinary playing cards as target material, but there were objections to the use of these cards. The probability of correctly guessing the identity of a playing card theoretically was 1 in 52, but it was clear that subjects had preferences for certain cards (e.g., aces) that might make a random-

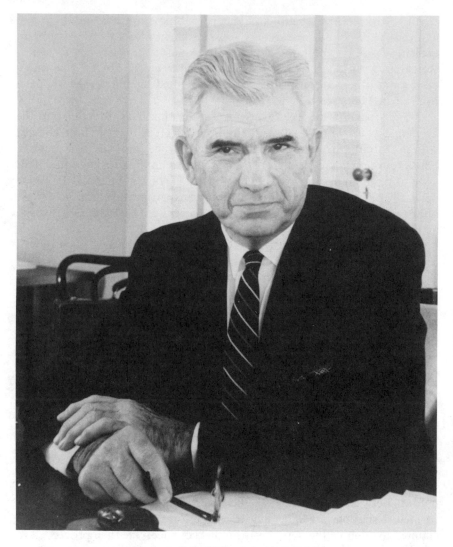

Figure 6. J.B. Rhine (photo: FRNM).

guessing model of performance invalid regardless of the existence or otherwise of clairvoyance.

   Additionally, there was the problem that the identity of playing cards
is determined by two bits of information, the suit (hearts, diamonds, clubs,
spades) and the face value (ace, two, three, etc.). This made for some inconvenience in scoring. If a guess had to be precisely correct to be credited
then a person who, for example, always guessed the suit but rarely the value
would unjustly be rated as a poor performer.

The elasticity of scoring criteria also allowed critics to level the charge of "hypothesis saving": if the parapsychologist failed to find significant results when scoring the responses holistically, the data could be reprocessed for correctness of the suit, and then for correctness of the face value, and then for correctness of the suit color, all in the hope of eventually locating a statistically significant effect.

To avoid these various difficulties Rhine sought some simple stimulus cards to which a statistical random-guessing model would be applicable. He initially used digits and letters as targets for the participant to identify by clairvoyant means, but again subjects exhibited marked preferences for some digits/letters over others. An experimental psychologist at Duke University, Karl Zener, suggested some elementary geometrical symbols and thus the now famous ESP symbols (formerly known as Zener symbols) came into being. There are five different symbols: a square (formerly a rectangle), a circle, a cross (or plus sign), a star, and wavy lines. The standard ESP pack comprises 25 cards, five of each symbol. The essential task of an experimental participant is to guess, perhaps with the assistance of some form of ESP, the identity of each card in a shuffled deck. An unusually high and sustained level of correct responses on the part of an individual was proposed as a demonstration of the authenticity of ESP.

Some basic terminology of card-guessing tests may be collated at this point. The subject's guess is termed a *call*. Correct guesses are *hits,* incorrect calls are *misses.* A set of 25 guesses (for a full pack) is a *run;* often a test session would comprise a number of runs. The symbol on a given trial is known as the *target* for that trial.

Several different experimental techniques were devised by the Rhines. Two are methods for testing clairvoyance. In the "down-through" (DT) technique the subject has to guess the order of symbols in a shuffled downward-facing deck, starting from the top and working down. After the 25 guesses are recorded, each card is turned over and checked against the subject's corresponding call. In an alternative technique the experimenter takes one card at a time from the shuffled pack, places it face down, records the subject's call, and then repeats the process until all 25 cards have been used. The calls and targets finally are checked for correspondence.

Each of these techniques was held by Rhine to be a test of clairvoyance because at the time of the subject's guesses the experimenter was unaware of the order of the cards and thus telepathy was excluded. Another procedure tapped general ESP (GESP), that is, clairvoyance and or telepathy. Here the experimenter (or an agent) takes one card from the pack, looks at it, records the subject's call, and continues in this fashion through the whole deck. Since the subject theoretically may rely on extrasensory information either from the card itself (clairvoyance) or from the mind of the

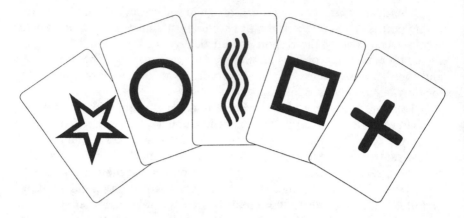

Figure 7. The ESP symbols (© FRNM).

experimenter (telepathy) this technique was proposed as a measure of GESP (rather than of telepathy as had been assumed in many earlier studies).

Rhine then formulated the statistical means of evaluating data yielded by these procedures. As the probability of guessing the identity of an ESP card is 1 in 5 one would expect the subject to produce on average 1/5 of 25, or 5, córrect calls purely by random guessing. That is to say, the *mean chance expectation* (MCE) is 5 per run. By conducting the subject through an extended series of runs the actual performance could be compared to MCE. The statistic used for this comparison is a form of a standard on Z score known as a *critical ratio* (CR).

The formula for the critical ratio varies slightly according to the nature of the ESP deck used. Consider an *open deck* in which there are 25 randomly selected symbols but in which the number of each symbol is not fixed in advance. Thus, although the probability of correctly guessing a target is 1/5 there need not be five of each symbol in a deck of 25 cards. For example, the experimenter by chance might draw a deck consisting of four squares, six circles, three crosses, seven stars, and five wavy lines. For an open deck the critical ratio is given by the following formula (more sophisticated formulae, including ones with a correction for continuity, can be found in Burdick & Kelly, 1977; Edge, Morris, Palmer & Rush, 1986, Ch. 6):

$$CR = \frac{X - Np}{Npq} \quad \text{for an open deck experiment,}$$

where X is the total number of hits in the series,
        N is the number of trials in the series (or 25 times the
           number of runs),

p is the probability of success per trial, here 1/5,
and q is the probability of failure per trial, that is
$$q = 1 - p = 4/5.$$

For example, suppose a participant completed 30 runs with an open ESP deck and had 175 hits. The number of trials would be $N = 30 \times 25 = 750$, and

$$CR = \frac{175 - 750 \times 1/5}{\sqrt{750 \times 1/5 \times 4/5}}$$

$$= \frac{175 - 150}{\sqrt{120}}$$

$$= 2.28.$$

That is, instead of yielding the MCE of 150 the subject exceeded this level of performance with a CR of 2.28. If you look in a table of areas under the normal curve the two-tailed probability of obtaining a Z score of 2.28 or larger is 0.0226. This (hypothetical) subject therefore has exhibited a level of success that statistically is unlikely to have been due simply to chance ($p < .05$).

Most of J.B. Rhine's early tests however, were conducted with *closed decks,* that is, there were exactly five of each symbol in each deck or run. This places constraints on the statistical model of a pure chance guesser: for example, once the *hypothetical* chance guesser has called "circle" five times that symbol will not be called again in the run. To compensate for this factor the above value of the CR has to be divided by 1.02 (in the case of decks of 5 lots of 5 symbols). That is,

$$CR = \frac{X - Np}{1.02\sqrt{Npq}} \qquad \text{for closed deck experiments.}$$

(Again, compare this formula with the more sophisticated ones provided by Burdick & Kelly, 1977; Edge et al., 1986, Ch. 6.) If the subject in the above example had worked with closed decks and yielded the same performance we would have

$$CR = \frac{175 - 750 \times 1/5}{1.02\sqrt{750 \times 1/5 \times 4/5}} = 2.24,$$

a value that again is significantly different from chance at the .05 level.

After devising an experimental paradigm and suitable statistical procedures Rhine set about finding some "sensitive" people who could perform consistently well in his test. His first significant result was obtained in a series of tests conducted in 1931 to 1932. Using a clairvoyance procedure 24 student subjects gave a total 207 hits in 800 trials (as against a MCE of 160), for which the value of p is less than one in a million (Mauskopf & McVaugh, 1980, p. 90).

Rhine also worked toward tightening his experimental procedure, particularly in regard to the elimination of sensory cues. For example, some of the earlier packs of ESP cards had very slight differences in the pattern on the back of each card and it was realized that if subjects could see the backs of the cards they might learn (either deliberately or subconsciously) to distinguish certain cards by the pattern on the obverse face. Similarly, subjects who could see or hear the experimenter could be aware of subtle changes in the experimenter's facial expression or tone of voice when a correct call was made. With a closed deck, knowing that a square (for example) had been drawn from the deck the subject would have a slightly increased chance of correctly guessing cards bearing other symbols.

When J.B. Rhine published his book *Extra-Sensory Perception* in 1934 he described his gradual improvements in technique (although critics were quick to seize upon earlier experiments and criticize them for poor control). Nevertheless, the main function of Rhine's book was to show how the ESP hypothesis could be approached in a rigorously scientific fashion, encouraging other psychologists to undertake similar research. The success of some of his own studies was cited not so much to establish the authenticity of ESP but to indicate that there were individuals who may be able to perform consistently better than chance level and thereby an experimental research program on ESP might well be viable. For example, one of Rhine's outstanding subjects was a Methodist theological student, Hubert Pearce, who averaged about 8 hits per run (compared to a MCE of 5) over 690 runs (17250 trials). Rhine's *Extra-Sensory Perception* also reviewed the history of experimental parapsychological research in an attempt to demonstrate that such work could be divorced from occultism and to support some of the trends he had found in the analyses of his own data.

The book initially was received with cautious interest among the American psychological community. The book then fell under the public eye and not only became a best seller but also elicited much comment in the popular press and instigated a fad for ESP cards. Reaction among psychologists soon was strongly antipathetic; it is uncertain if this was due to the publicity given to the Duke University research, to the exaggerated claims made in the media, or to a resurgence of awareness that ESP was incompatible with accepted principles of behavioral science. In any event, between 1934 and 1940 ESP raged as a major psychological controversy, with Rhine's work subjected to vehement criticism. Much of the comment was purely rhetorical: for example, the Duke research was ridiculed as being rooted in superstition and mysticism and as such it was held to be putting the science of psychology in disrepute. Some of the more rational arguments of the critics may be mentioned briefly, together with Rhine's accommodations of these criticisms in his later research (Pratt et al., 1940).

Invalid statistical analyses. Some psychologists were concerned that the statistical analyses did not rely upon a comparison between an ESP condition and a non–ESP condition. The ESP data were compared to a hypothetical value rather than to data from a control group. Of course the notion of a "non–ESP condition" is meaningless. Rhine's subjects had no idea of how they achieved an excessive number of hits, so it would have been pointless to ask participants not to use ESP on some trials. In any event the distaste for comparing performance to a theoretical model is inappropriate. Even when experimental and control conditions are used in other psychological experiments we are comparing the observed difference between means to a theoretical model of the distribution of differences between means. The statistical techniques employed in the Duke research were further refined and condoned by eminent statisticians of the day, including R.A. Fisher (1929; Mauskopf & McVaugh, 1980, pp. 195–200).

Uncontrolled sensory cues. If the subjects can see the backs of the ESP cards or see or hear the experimenter there may be sensory cues in the test situation which can be used to enhance the level of performance. Subjects' obtaining sensory rather than extrasensory information from the cards themselves was termed *sensory leakage.* Lack of adequate control over such sensory cues was suggested as the basis for Rhine's observation of above-chance card-guessing performances. Nevertheless, Rhine and his colleagues had conducted several successful experiments in which the subject and the experimenter were located in different rooms (and even in different buildings), thereby eliminating potential sensory cues. The above-chance scores obtained by the subject Pearce did not fall as access to sensory cues progressively was reduced.

Recording errors. In GESP tests where the experimenter knows the identity of the target, on some occasions she or he might unwittingly record as the response the target — what it was hoped the subject would say — instead of the subject's actual call. It became standard practice in later research to use two experimenters in ESP tests, each experimenter making an independent record of targets and calls and later comparing the two records to ensure accuracy. This criticism of course was not applicable to Rhine's series of clairvoyance experiments, because here the experimenter did not know the identity of the target at the time the subject's call was recorded.

Inadequate shuffling. If you note the order in which playing cards occur in a deck, then shuffle them and note their new order you will find that some cards have not been separated in the course of shuffling. For example, if the two of hearts was next to the eight of clubs before shuffling, they may well be together in the reshuffled deck. Hand shuffling therefore does not produce a random reordering of the cards. Since many different packs were used in the Duke research it is unlikely that subjects would have been able to make use of this fact to enhance their performance. Be that as it may, there is the additional problem that if the runs of an experiment are not independent in structure they are not random and hence the random guessing model is not an appropriate statistical model against which to compare the observed data. Rhine devised two solutions to this problem. One was to build large ungainly mechanical shufflers. The other was to use tables of random numbers as a basis for ordering the cards in each run. In ESP research today the problems of shuffling are circumvented by generating the targets with the aid of a computer or microcomputer. Computer-controlled tests have the additional advantage of avoiding recording errors. Significant data still are obtained under these conditions.

Optional stopping. If a subject is tested over a long series of runs, purely by chance there occasionally may be some points in the series where the aggregate score exceeds MCE. Continuation of the series beyond this point would see such a fluke outcome pulled back to chance levels if nothing but random guessing was behind the performance of the task. Some critics argued that Rhine simply had elected to stop testing a given subject when one of these points was reached. In fact Rhine recognized this potential flaw very early in his research and it became customary to specify before testing commenced the total number of trials to be completed by the participants.

Suppression of null results. If you run twenty subjects in an experiment, purely on the basis of chance you would expect (on average) one subject to perform *significantly* at the .05 (i.e., 1 in 20) level. Rhine's critics argued that the Duke researchers merely reported their occasional significant data and suppressed the remaining (19 of every 20) cases that were nonsignificant. Rhine and his colleagues did, of course, obtain some null data: many of these results were for people who were classified as not "sensitive" and whose testing then was discontinued.

The charge of suppression of null results nevertheless can be contested on two grounds. First, the data of all experiments and pilot tests conducted in the Duke parapsychological laboratory were recorded and open to inspection. If the records are accurate then the published studies certainly do not represent only the one in twenty experiments to be expected by chance to reach significance. Second, the level of statistical significance of some reported ESP experiments was extremely high. For example, consider one

(by no means exceptional) result obtained with Hubert Pearce for which the
p value was less than one in a million. Put simply, if this was one of those
statistically significant results that crop up occasionally by chance, one
would predict that there were performed about a million similar ex
periments which did not reach this level of significance and were suppressed. Such a proposition cannot be sustained: the staff of the Duke
laboratory would not have had the capacity to conduct anything like that
number of experiments.

As each of the above arguments was rebutted there remained only one
tactic open to the determined critic, namely, to challenge the bona fides of
the researchers.

Fraud. If the data could not have been obtained by normal means they
must be fraudulent. Psychologists sketched all manner of scenarios in
which Rhine, his colleagues, and their subjects variously were depicted as
having engaged in collusion to yield significant data, to fudge (distort) the
data, or to construct entirely fictitious data. Over the ensuing years, as
more and more researchers in laboratories around the world performed
statistically significant ESP experiments, this argument became increasingly
tenuous. As Eysenck (1957, pp. 131–132) asks, Why should dozens of
academics engage in an international conspiracy of such proportions? If
they achieve anything at all it is only to put their careers in jeopardy.

For many years the techniques developed by Rhine effectively controlled the agenda for ESP research. In more recent times parapsychologists
have devised rather more adventurous experimental procedures, in part as
a response to the sheer tedium of long series of card-guessing trials.
Restricted-choice methods still predominate in the contemporary experimental literature but even they have become somewhat more appealing.
For example, in place of the standard ESP symbols Fisk and Mitchell (1953)
used drawings of a clock face with the hour hand pointing to one of the
hour positions from 1 to 12; unfortunately these targets proved unsatisfactory because participants had preferences for certain times and these
response biases contaminated the data (Chauvin, 1985, p. 26).

Modern electronic developments also contributed to the design of
novel restricted-choice targets. In the late 1960s Schmidt (1969, 1970a) constructed devices by which a sequence of ESP targets was determined in part
by the random emission of particles from either a radioactive or an electronic source. These so-called *random event generators* (REGs) can be connected to a panel of target lights as in Tart's (1976) "ten-choice trainer," or
to a display of target events on a video screen. Not only are ESP test
machines of this sort more entertaining for participants than are card-
guessing tests but data can be collected efficiently and processed
automatically without the risk of human error.

The popularity of free-response techniques also has revived in the last

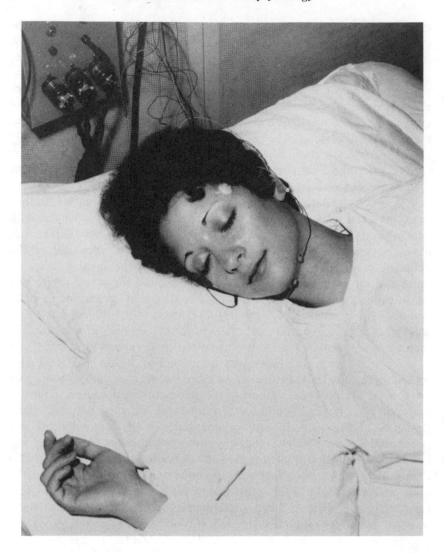

Figure 8. A participant in a Maimonides study of ESP in dreams (photo: Stanley Krippner).

two decades, particularly in the context of research on extrasensory experiences during various altered states of consciousness. At the Maimonides Medical Center in Brooklyn, New York, Ullman, Krippner and Honorton conducted some fascinating studies on ESP during dreams (Child, 1985; Ullman & Krippner, 1970; Ullman & Krippner, with Vaughan, 1973). These investigators report that the content of experimental participants' dreams could relate thematically to sensorially inaccessible prints of famous works of art. The Maimonides team also compiled a set of 1,024 photographic slides representing all combinations of the presence and absence of ten specific dimensions of pictorial content (Honorton, 1975). A target slide and an experimental subject's imagery during an altered state of consciousness then could independently be coded on these ten dimensions and the correspondence between them assessed in a purely quantitative fashion. This and similar target material made a significant contribution to some major series of free-response studies, most notably those concerned with ESP during sensory restriction or ganzfeld conditions, of which more is said later in this chapter.

An experimental procedure that gained considerable public attention was designed by Targ and Puthoff (1978) at the Stanford Research Institute in California. Dubbed *remote viewing*, its experimental subjects are asked to describe a randomly selected outdoor location at which a coexperimenter currently is situated. Judges blind to the identity of the target rate the subjects' imagery protocols for their correspondence to each location in the pool of potential targets. Targ and Puthoff report extrachance correspondence between subjects' imagery and the actual target under the remote viewing procedure and although there has been some dispute as to whether their judges in fact were fully blind to the identity of targets (Marks & Kammann, 1980, Ch. 3), the procedure has been utilized successfully by other researchers (e.g., Dunne, Jahn & Nelson, 1983).

Despite this recent flurry of innovative ESP research, for most contemporary psychologists the atmosphere of the 1934–1940 controversy prevails. For example, the arguments presented in Day's (1969) and Marks' (1986) critiques of ESP research essentially are the same as those dating from the 1930s. Recently some attempt has been made to list the claimed methodological flaws and to examine statistically their possible influence on the reported data. A technique known as *meta-analysis* enables the aggregation of results across all experiments on a given phenomenon (Green & Hall, 1984). By coding each experiment for apparent or potential methodological flaws the bearing of each flaw on the data then might be assessed. For example, the size of the experimental ESP effect found in studies where motivated recording errors theoretically were feasible can be compared to the effect-size for experiments in which such errors could not have occurred. It also is possible under this technique to allow for the existence of unknown and unreported experiments that yielded only chance results. If the extrachance scores in ESP tests were due to the flaws alleged by critics, meta-analysis should bear this out. Meta-analyses of specific classes of ESP experiments have been undertaken (e.g., Child, 1985; Haraldsson, Houtkooper & Hoeltje, 1987; Honorton, 1985; Hyman, 1985; Schechter, 1984).

In the context of methodological criticisms of the ESP research, meta-analyses have yet to prove conclusive, in part because different judges ascribe different flaws to the same experiment. But on the basis of meta-analyses of one set of ESP studies a critic and a parapsychologist have agreed that at least the experimental effect can not reasonably be attributed either to suppression of null results or to invalid statistical procedures (Hyman & Honorton, 1986). It should be added that meta-analysis itself still is regarded as a relatively controversial statistical technique.

In any event the prevailing impression among psychologists today is that so much heat was generated during the original ESP controversy there just has to be something unscientific about parapsychological research into ESP. Although skeptics' rhetoric certainly has served to sustain this attitude, the present position has been compounded by the failure of parapsychologists to devise techniques for controlling this hypothesized ability of ESP. If the very best subjects can sustain an average of only 8 hits per run, and the now typically short studies of groups of unselected subjects yield means of about 5.2 hits (as against MCE of 5), then *regardless* of the level of statistical significance the data are hardly very persuasive that people in some paranormal fashion can direct their awareness to things inaccessible to the recognized senses. Undoubtedly some scientists would require consistent 100 percent accuracy (25 hits per run) before they would sit up and take notice. Although this extreme requirement is unreasonable the onus now is squarely on the parapsychologist to gain sufficient understanding of the nature of ESP as to permit substantial control over the phenomenon, thereby convincing other scientists not merely in statistical terms but at an *emotional* level as well.

But what is the objective status of the available experimental evidence? Does it establish the authenticity of ESP in the eyes of the fair-minded observer? Three approaches to this issue must be explored. The first concerns the existence of a definitive experiment; the second seeks authenticity in the weight of the cumulative record of ESP experimentation; and the third entails the logical evaluation of what an ESP experiment can achieve. These three approaches are addressed in order.

The Existence of the Definitive Experiment

One means of judging if ESP is genuine is to locate an ESP experiment which is definitive as far as the issue of authenticity is concerned. In particular, can we be persuaded of the paranormality of ESP experience by the results of some study which parapsychologists themselves regard as among the most carefully conducted?

The demand for a definitive ESP experiment has been made by several critics (e.g., Price, 1955, 1956), and parapsychologists intermittently have responded by nominating past studies believed to provide the best evidence for authenticity (e.g., Beloff, 1980; Rao, 1984). The study I have chosen to examine for its standing as a definitive demonstration is the so-called Pearce-Pratt series conducted in Rhine's laboratory at Duke University in 1933–1934.

The selection of an experiment for this analysis clearly is a subjective and to some extent arbitrary process, so it is appropriate to indicate the criteria upon which my choice was made. The criteria, essentially those advocated by Beloff (1980), are enumerated below in relation to the Pearce-Pratt experiment.

First, the experimenter had to be a competent person of good standing and well known to the parapsychological community. In the target study the experimenter was J.G. Pratt, at that time Rhine's research assistant. Pratt went on to pursue a long and distinguished career in parapsychological research, publishing more than a hundred papers over a period of forty years, and was widely respected by others in the field (see Pratt, 1987; Stevenson, 1980). He died suddenly in 1979.

Second, the report of the experiment had to be published in a reputable scientific journal that routinely subjects its papers to a searching process of editorial scrutiny and refereeing by qualified peers. The first account of the Pearce-Pratt series appeared in the *Journal of Abnormal and Social Psychology* (Rhine, 1936), and a more detailed report was published in the *Journal of Parapsychology* (Rhine & Pratt, 1954); each of these journals qualifies under the second criterion. The study is mentioned also in various books by Rhine and by Pratt (for example, Pratt et al., 1940).

Third, the overall experimental ESP scores had to be so highly significant that selective reporting, optional stopping, or any minor procedural artifact such as nonrandom shuffling could be discounted. Aggregate data over four subseries in the Pearce-Pratt experiment were significant at the 10^{-22} level. If these results reflected a methodological flaw it evidently was a substantial one.

Fourth, the experiment had to be deemed by eminent parapsychologists as one of the best available. Rhine himself believed the Pearce-Pratt study to be beyond all reasonable criticism; this is evident from his analysis of it in terms of alternative hypotheses to that of ESP (Pratt et al., 1940, pp. 160–163). The noted Indian parapsychologist K.R. Rao (1984) included the report by Rhine and Pratt (1954) in his anthology of "the basic experiments" in the field of parapsychology; he regards the Pearce-Pratt experiment as "one of the highly evidential studies we have in parapsychology" (Rao, 1981, p. 191), a view he holds to be shared by "many parapsychologists" (Rao, 1984, p. 12). In a pamphlet produced for the SPR, Hitching (1980) also cites the Pearce-Pratt data as one of twelve "crucial" findings in the field. The target study therefore is highly regarded by at least some prestigious parapsychologists. It cannot be said I have chosen for scrutiny an experimental report no one regards as evidential.

The procedure of the study at Duke University was as follows. Between August 1933 and March 1934, 37 sessions each comprising two runs were completed in four subseries A, B, C and D; the scheduling of the individual subseries was governed by the availability of the student subject, Hubert Pearce. Immediately before each session Pearce met the experimenter Gaither Pratt in the latter's office situated in the Physics building of the university. The two men synchronized their watches and agreed upon a time at which the test session would commence. Pearce left the Physics building and walked across to the library 100 yards away. In subseries A, C and D Pratt remained in his office; in subseries B Pratt conducted the session from the Medical School some 250 yards from Pearce's position in a library cubicle. Seated at his table Pratt selected one of several packs of ESP cards used in the study, shuffled and finally cut the deck, keeping the cards face down at all times. At the prearranged time Pratt took the top card and placed it face down in front of him. This "clairvoyance" procedure was followed with the other cards in the deck at the rate of one per minute. In the library Pearce meanwhile recorded his call for each target's identity, minute by minute. After 25 cards and calls the participants had a five minute rest and then repeated the whole procedure with a second pack.

The experimenter Pratt then turned over the cards and recorded their order; a signed duplicate of this record of targets was handed to Rhine. Pearce also made a signed copy of his calls for the two runs and gave it to Rhine upon his return to the Physics building. Finally, Pearce and Pratt met to compare their lists and to score the number of hits on each run. As a check on the accuracy of scoring Rhine independently scored Pearce's performance from the duplicate records. It had been agreed beforehand that in the case of any discrepancy between the two sets of results (whether arising from faulty duplication of lists or from an error in scoring) a miss would be recorded. Clearly, the data were to be processed conservatively; in the event, only one such discrepancy arose. The sole variations in procedure were the increase in distance between targets and subject in subseries B and the presence of Rhine in Pratt's office as an observer in subseries D.

The general results of the Pearce-Pratt series may be stated briefly. Compared to an MCE of 5 the mean number of hits in the four subseries were 9.9, 6.7, 7.3 and 9.3 respectively. Each of these means significantly exceeds chance expectation. In the complete series of 74 runs (1850 calls) Pearce achieved 558 hits as against an expected 370; this corresponds to a CR or Z score of 10.71 (for *closed* decks), with $p < 10^{-22}$.

What are the particular strengths of this experiment? Several come to mind. The distance between the two participants ruled out sensory leakage

Figure 9. Hubert Pearce (left) being tested for ESP by Rhine (photo: FRNM).

from the back of the cards. Both the separation and the clairvoyance procedure also eliminated the possibility of unwitting sensory cues from the experimenter. The clairvoyance procedure prevented the experimenter's in-
advertent recording of the subject's call as the identity of the target. The
presence of an observer (Rhine) in subseries D enhanced security. And the
dual independent scoring procedure acted as a check on the processing of
the data. A further testimony to the study's authenticity is that on a subsequent occasion the Pearce-Pratt data were reanalyzed for an effect
unknown at the time of the study's execution and the effect was evidenced
in those data; the performance pattern, formally termed a within-runs
decline effect, will be examined later in this chapter, but its presence in
Pearce's performance does encourage the view that the data were obtained
in a proper manner.

The Pearce-Pratt experiment therefore appears to have been conducted with due regard to the control of artifactual variables and its data
are impressive in the sense that their significance level is very high, so high
in fact that the possibility of minor procedural flaws can safely be discounted. But in the interests of balance, account must be taken of criticisms
of the study. The shuffling of the decks by hand might be one cause for concern, although this factor in itself surely could not be the basis of the results'
high level of statistical significance. A second fault is that the number of
trials was not specified in advance; this was not taken, however, as an

opportunity for optional stopping because the number of sessions completed was governed simply by Pearce's availability. Additionally, in a very pedantic sense the Pearce-Pratt experiment is not replicable, that is, it cannot be undertaken again with Pearce as the subject and Pratt as the experimenter. As noted earlier, Pratt now is dead. So too is Pearce, but replication of the study might not have been possible even in Pearce's lifetime: some time after this experiment Pearce was under some emotional strain and announced he did not expect to do well in further tests, and despite two years of relatively regular performance he then ceased to score reliably above chance (Pratt et al., 1940, pp. 313–314).

The major critique of the Pearce-Pratt series however, is that presented by the British psychologist Hansel (1966, 1980). He argues that the results of this experiment *could* have been fraudulent, and in support of this contention he offers several scenarios.

One scenario entails fraudulent activity solely on the part of the subject Pearce. Hansel suggests that while Pratt sat at his table at the end of the session and recorded the order of the targets, Pearce could have left the library and spied on Pratt, noting the identity of some of the targets. For example, claims Hansel, Pearce may have stood in the corridor outside the experimenter's room and looked through a small window located about 5′10″ above floor-level, or have stood on a chair outside Pratt's door and peeped through a small transom above the door. Hansel even thought it possible for Pearce to have seen the cards on Pratt's table from a transom over the door of a room situated down the corridor from the experimental room. In relation to subseries B, when Pratt was stationed in the Medical School, Hansel reports the existence of a trap door in the ceiling directly above the table at which Pratt sat; Pearce therefore might have spied on the targets from this vantage point. The scenario of Pearce's deceit has been challenged by parapsychologists on many grounds, including its physical possibility, its likelihood in terms of Pearce's character (Pearce was a Methodist divinity student), and the probability of its passing undetected in every one of the 37 sessions.

A second scenario proposed by Hansel is that Pratt and Pearce acted in collusion. Specifically, these two men may have adjusted their records to show an impressive performance before each list was handed to Rhine for checking. Again, this would not account for the independently significant results in subseries D in which Rhine remained in the experimental room with Pratt.

Another possibility, proposes Hansel, is that there was collusion on the part of all three men. That is, Rhine, Pratt and Pearce simply agreed to invent the data. It is difficult however, to accommodate under this scenario the post hoc finding of the within-runs decline effect in the Pearce-Pratt data.

Note that Hansel does not establish evidence that any of these scenarios actually did take place; for him it is sufficient that they *could* have occurred. He admittedly does make much of the claim that Hubert Pearce never gave a written assurance of not having cheated in the experimental work at Duke University. It transpires however, that Hansel simply did not approach Pearce for such an assurance; certainly Stevenson was able to obtain one and he published it (Stevenson, 1967, p. 258) in his review of Hansel's (1966) book. In addition to Hansel's failure to approach Pearce, his slight on Pearce's reputation is compounded by the fact that the claim of Pearce's lack of an assurance of honesty is reiterated in the revised version of the book (Hansel, 1980, p. 123), despite the contrary evidence in Stevenson's review.

Although Hansel's skeptical fervor may occasionally have had the better of him his central argument nevertheless is legitimate. It is possible to make a charge of the opportunity for fraud in *any* scientific experiment. Hansel (1966, p. 241) initially proposed that a computer-controlled ESP study would obviate this charge, but in the meantime many such investigations have been successfully completed and the proposal was withdrawn from the book's revised edition. Because any experimental report, whether in parapsychology or any other science, might conceivably be the product of fraudulent activity it therefore cannot constitute a watertight case for the phenomenon under investigation.

Irrespective of the professional eminence of the investigator and the reported attention to precision in the execution of the study, and regardless too of the standing and the number of scientists who endorse the study's findings, there always is the possibility, no matter how remote we judge it to be, that experimental personnel colluded to manipulate or invent the data. Although Hansel's use of that argument may be politically motivated to the extent that he evidently sees no reason to apply it to any other phenomenon investigated by psychologists, its validity stands inviolate. In short, there is and can be no definitive experiment on the authenticity of ESP.

The Cumulative Record

Given that some fault can be found with any single experiment perhaps the best evidence for ESP's authenticity may be provided by the trend in the cumulative record of ESP research. Some experiments in the literature may well be based on bogus data; indeed there are a few cases of fraudulent experimenters in parapsychology, just as there are some in psychology and in other sciences. Other experiments may have yielded significant results through shoddy experimental procedures, as in failure to eliminate sensory cues. Still other reports of significant data might be attributable to those uncommon occasions on which significance is achieved purely by chance. Be this as it may, if a substantial proportion of experimental reports cite significant data surely it is unreasonable to maintain that *all* of them were due to these sorts of artifacts. That is, surely we may rely upon at least one of the significant studies in the cumulative record being indicative of a genuine effect. If one accepts this argument, the relative frequency of experiments yielding statistically significant results indicates there is something here that warrants explaining.

Again, not all psychologists would endorse the above argument, at least as far as ESP research is concerned. They would maintain that if one cannot point to a *specific* experiment as definitive, then having a multiplicity of experimental reports does not testify to the quality of the data: the sum of any number of zeroes is still zero. This puts the parapsychologist in a "no win" situation: the cumulative research record is not compelling if the definitive study cannot be identified, and anyway the definitive study can not exist.

Where does this leave you, the novice wandering between neighboring camps of psychology and parapsychology? As there are arguments favoring each side you must choose the interpretation that strikes you as logically most satisfactory, or else be forced to accept that the issue of authenticity is unresolved or inherently unresolvable. In my own view it is fair to say that the experimental evidence for ESP meets the criteria generally demanded for other psychological phenomena. To be sure, ESP experiments are not replicable in the sense that anyone could guarantee to obtain a significant ESP score with the first person they happen to meet after 10 o'clock next Tuesday morning. But in my experience of undergraduate laboratory exercises, psychologists generally delude themselves of the level and quality of replicability entailed in many of their accepted phenomena.

In any event I remain unconvinced that authenticity demands replicability of this sort; an intrinsically weak and unstable phenomenon could be resistant to attempts to elicit it experimentally, yet still be "real" (Beloff, 1985). With any conventional (intuitively acceptable) psychological phenomenon no one would dream of demanding an experiment in which fraud was utterly inconceivable. If a large number of independent investigators had obtained significant data on such a phenomenon, the existence of some null results notwithstanding, psychologists unhesitatingly would conclude that the phenomenon was not an artifact of fraud, poor experimental procedure, or the like. Unless there are to be one set of rules for intuitively acceptable data and another set for parapsychological and other "radical" data, I find myself persuaded that the ESP studies are indicative of a genuine phenomenon. That this phenomenon is extrasensory perception remains equivocal, however, as I endeavor to show in the next section.

Logical Scrutiny of the ESP Data

Even if it is conceded that there does exist a definitive experiment or that the cumulative experimental record constitutes an adequate substitute for this requirement, it remains to be shown that the statistically significant data are conclusive on the matter of ESP's authenticity.

In essence ESP tests show nothing else than that some subjects, or groups of subjects, are able to guess the identity of sensorially inaccessible targets at a level beyond that expected by chance. This is consistent with the existence of a paranormal means of acquiring information but it does not prove its existence, for the following reason. Parapsychologists have not demonstrated that there was an actual passage of information from the targets to the percipient's mind. The channel for ESP, if it is appropriate to think in those terms, has not been determined and until it is, other explanations of the extrachance or *anomalous* data are possible. For example, perhaps there is some force in nature that effects a measure of extrachance convergence or isomorphism between two series of comparable objects (such as a series of targets and a series of calls) without any actual flow of information between the series. Perhaps our current notion of how "chance" processes should operate is invalid. The merits of such hypotheses do not warrant examination at this juncture (see Chapter 8), but the possibility of formulating a range of optional hypotheses illustrates that although the data of ESP experiments may testify to a genuine phenomenon, they might also be attributable to factors other than ESP.

Following Alcock (1981, pp. 147–148), the fallacy of regarding the card-guessing data as evidence of ESP's authenticity can be shown also by casting the argument in the form of a syllogism, as follows.

> People who have ESP would score above chance.
> These subjects scored above chance.
> Therefore, these subjects (are people who) have ESP.

This entails a logical error known as "affirming the consequent." Its potential for generating unjustified conclusions from valid premises is illustrated by another syllogism of precisely the same form.

> People who have X-ray vision, a red cape and a big "S" on their chest would score above chance.
> These subjects scored above chance.
> Therefore these subjects (are people who) have X-ray vision, a red cape and a big "S" on their chest.

It might be argued that alternative explanations of the extrachance data are merely hypotheses about the *modus operandi* of ESP and as such they do not bring into question the reality of ESP but on the contrary subsume it. To sustain this view it would be necessary to label the extrachance effect as ESP, an effect to be explained but nonetheless genuine. Now, certainly it is legitimate to name a phenomenon to facilitate discussion of it, but care must be taken not to use a definition as its own justification. If the extrachance effect is *named* ESP it is not acceptable to say that the extrachance effect is *due to* ESP. The question of ESP's authenticity then would become tautological.

In practice, parapsychologists do not define ESP as the extrachance effect but rather as some paranormal process of access to information. The latter is not established by a significant ESP test result in itself, as there may be posed other hypothetical accounts of the anomaly that are not formulated in terms of information access.

In short, to promote ESP from a data-consistent hypothesis to an authentic phenomenon, parapsychologists must also ascertain there are objective processes which mediate ESP in the ESP test situation. This requirement is not peculiar to ESP. Suppose for example, we are visited by an alien scientist who knows little of our earthly perceptual systems. He acquires spontaneous case reports in which earthlings purport to be aware of their immediate environment by an ocular process they call "vision" and he decides to investigate these claims scientifically. His subjects are presented with a series of designs on cards and these are identified to a level exceeding chance (he fails to appreciate the contribution of ambient illumination to completely accurate identification).

Now, on the basis of this significant result our alien friend could not conclude that vision, a means of sensory access to the environment, is authentic. Such a conclusion would require additional evidence that there actually occurs a passage of sensory information from the stimulus cards to the observer (in the form of electromagnetic radiation within a limited range of wavelengths) and that the individual has a device for detecting and processing this information (the eye and the rest of the visual information processing system).

In the absence of such evidence the visiting investigator would be forced into some circular arguments. If he were asked why his data were significant he would talk of the existence of "vision"; asked how he knows "vision" exists he would point to the significance of his data. When the mediating processes of vision are shown to be open to observation, the alien would then have grounds for construing vision as an objectively authentic (as distinct from a phenomenologically or experientially real) phenomenon.

This is not to say that ESP must be shown to rely on some source of radiation as its vehicle and to be registered by a specifiable organ of the body. Perhaps ESP does not work that way. Whatever its underlying processes they nevertheless must be shown to be open to measurement independently of the extrachance performance they enable. In this respect the authenticity of ESP must be resolved in light of some appreciation of the nature of ESP. That is, the significance of proof-oriented research depends upon results from process-oriented research. In addition to determining whether the underlying process is ESP or something more familiar to mainstream psychologists, process-oriented research could yield coherent functional relationships the pattern of which might indicate if the anomalous card-guessing data are likely to reflect ESP or instead some procedural artifact. The focus of experimental research into ESP thus shifts to process-oriented study.

Process-Oriented Research on ESP

The remainder of this chapter is devoted to a review of experimental work designed to reveal the characteristics of processes underlying the hypothetical phenomenon of ESP. As noted in Chapter 1 this so-called process-oriented research does not assume the authenticity of ESP per se. If ESP were shown not to exist the results of process-oriented research would still apply to the nature of the anomaly in card-guessing performances, whatever its identity.

The authenticity issue nevertheless has had an apparent effect upon the conduct of process-oriented research. Recently Akers (1984) undertook a methodological analysis of experiments concerned with correlates of ESP performance in the domains of personality, attitudes, and states of consciousness. In the considerable majority of these he identified at least the opportunity for such methodological flaws as nonrandomness of target sequences, sensory leakage, subject cheating, recording errors, scoring errors, statistical violations (e.g., optional stopping), and experimenter fraud.

Parapsychologists undertaking process-oriented research evidently have tended to assume the authenticity of ESP has been established at a sufficient level of certainty that precision in procedural control no longer is necessary in the investigation of the characteristics of ESP. That assumption of course, is grossly inappropriate. If we cannot be confident that a process-oriented study in fact is tapping ESP or the card-guessing anomaly, then we also cannot be confident that the data of the study reveal anything about the characteristics of that anomaly. Of course, Akers typically could not show that the potential flaws were realized and had an identifiable role in generating the statistically significant results, but his analysis does serve as a caution not to put too much faith in the findings of any single study, but rather to take greater cognizance of process-oriented data that have been replicated by various researchers.

Process-Oriented Research and
the Parapsychological Experimenter Effect

Before reviewing research into the nature of ESP one further methodological issue must be raised. It is known as the *parapsychological experimenter effect* and it raises the problem that if ESP and other parapsychological phenomena are authentic and can operate outside the individual's
conscious control, parapsychologists may have no reliable avenue for
determining the nature of ESP. That is, process-oriented research might
well be futile.

As in other types of psychological research, the performance of subjects in ESP experiments can be influenced by the behavior of the experimenter (e.g., see White, 1977). The experimenter's level of motivation
and handling of the participants can influence the subjects' motivation and
expectations which in turn may have an effect on the level of their scores.
Similarly, if any of the experimenter's actions suggest to the subjects the
precise nature of the experimental hypothesis, they may strive to perform
in a way that otherwise they would not. These sorts of biases in the procedure of human experiments are familiar to psychologists and deliberate
steps can be taken to minimize their operation and influence. Methodological problems arising from the influence of the experimenter on the data
generically are termed *experimenter effects*.

There is however, an additional bias of this type that raises such special
difficulties for parapsychological experimentation that it has come to be
designated specifically as the *parapsychological experimenter effect*. Essentially the parapsychological experimenter effect in psi research is the partial
dependence of the obtained data on the parapsychological abilities of the
experimenter (Kennedy & Taddonio, 1976; White, 1976). As the parapsychological experimenter effect assumes the existence of psi it is not
especially problematic for the issue of the authenticity of ESP, but it does
raise the question of whether it is possible for a researcher to investigate the
nature of ESP.

Suppose, for example, that a researcher wanted to test the hypothesis
that extraverts were better ESP scorers than introverts. It is possible that the
experimenter subconsciously might use his or her own precognitive and extrasensory abilities to locate series of targets which are more susceptible to
good scoring and allocate these to the group of extraverted participants.
There is indeed some empirical evidence that extrasensory abilities may be
utilized nonintentionally (Schechter, 1977). If account is taken of the
possibility of psychokinesis (a paranormal influence on physical systems by
the mind) it is conceivable that the experimenter subconsciously might influence even the production of target sequences for each subject in a direction favoring the hypothesis. Hence an observed relationship between

extraversion and ESP performance might be nothing more than an artifact of the experimenter's subconscious use of psi to generate results in accordance with this relationship.

To what extent does the parapsychological experimenter effect operate? That remains unknown, but some study of the issue is being undertaken. It has been noted for example, that some parapsychologists seem to get a higher rate of significant results than others. Charles Honorton in America and Carl Sargent in England seem to have achieved a high proportion of significant ESP results in their research; they evidently are *psi-conducive experimenters*. The British parapsychologists John Beloff and Susan Blackmore, on the other hand, very rarely obtain a statistically significant finding in ESP tests and appear to be *psi-inhibitory experimenters*. This could be due to the familiar psychological experimenter effects (e.g., upon the subject's motivation), or to the greater psi abilities of the more successful experimenters (the parapsychological experimenter effect), or to other factors such as differences in the professionalism of experimenters and in the conservatism of their hypotheses.

Parker's (1977) study to investigate this required a sample of parapsychologists to complete two personality scales, one of which was actually a disguised ESP test. Independent judges then classified the respondents according to the level of the latter's success in conducting parapsychological experiments. No differences in personality were found between groups but the more successful experimenters did yield higher scores on the covert ESP test. Notwithstanding the possibility that Parker's study itself was influenced by the parapsychological experimenter effect, it is consistent with the notion that the parapsychologist's psi might be a factor in successful research. The number of participants in Parker's study, however, was very small. The correlation he obtained also might reflect another type of experimenter effect; for example, experimenters with high personal psi ability might be more confident that their studies will be successful, and this confidence could be communicated to their experimental participants and influence the performance by nonparapsychological means. Schmeidler and Maher (1981) also report that students rate psi-conducive experimenters' "body language" as communicating greater friendliness and flexibility than does that of psi-inhibitory experimenters. For these and other reasons the parapsychological experimenter effect does require more extensive empirical substantiation.

Parapsychologists' only general defense against the parapsychological experimenter effect is to conduct replications of one another's experiments. As a given result is confirmed by several independent experimenters perhaps it becomes increasingly unlikely to have been an artifact of an isolated researcher's subconscious use of his or her own psi. Disinterested parties could be hired to conduct replications, but we simply do not know the limits of the experimenter effect; even disinterested assistants might learn telepathically of the experimenter's expectations and use their own psi to oblige the experimenter.

A more limited means of dealing with the effect is a strategy known as *retrodiction* (Beloff, 1986). In some circumstances it may be possible to study a given process-oriented relationship by analyzing data from an old ESP experiment originally performed for other purposes. In discussing the Pearce-Pratt study for example, we noted that support for the "within-runs decline effect" was found through a reanalysis of these data some years later. There are several examples of this tactic being applied in ESP research (Beloff, 1986; Kelly, 1982). Retrodiction nevertheless has limited application and in any event its circumvention of the parapsychological experimenter effect assumes that future analysts of the data cannot influence them retrospectively by paranormal means; there are some indications that the latter assumption might not be justified (Schmidt, 1976; Weiner & Zingrone, 1986).

Until the issue of the parapsychological experimenter effect is resolved, most emphasis should be put on findings that have been replicated in several laboratories and which exhibit consistency with data on allied relationships.

With due cognizance of these methodological points, we now may review the literature on the experimental investigation of the nature of ESP. Because of the incidence of potential methodological flaws in process-oriented studies (Akers, 1984), the parapsychological experimenter effect, and the inherent unreliability of ESP scores, consideration must be focused on findings that have been replicated or that at least show consistency with related data. Matters to be examined here are patterns of ESP test performance and the role of variables related to the targets, the test environment, and the people engaged in the test. The surveys by Palmer (1978a, 1982) are recommended as an invaluable resource in this regard.

ESP Performance: Patterns and Improvement

What is the character of performance in an experimental ESP task? Apart from the overall hit rate there have been observed certain consistencies in individuals' patterns of performance and these will be described briefly.

The Bidirectionality of ESP: Psi-Missing

One would expect that if a person had ESP the level of performance on an experimental ESP test should be higher than MCE, that is, significantly better than 5 hits per run in a card-guessing test. Some individuals (and some groups in specific experiments) on the other hand have been found to score significantly *below* chance. This is termed *psi-missing*. It is important to note that this does not indicate a lack of ESP (or of psi in general) since the latter would be associated with nonsignificant scores. Rather, psi-missing might be viewed as an expression of psi in a way that produces a result different from the conscious intent. The participant's guesses are wrong more often than would be expected by chance; that is, the participant shows sensitivity to the targets' identity but tends to make calls at odds with this sensitivity.

As we shall see, psi-missing is thought to be in part a consequence of negative elements in mood and attitude or of aspects of personality; these elements may cause *psi-missers* to focus their ESP inaccurately (Crandall, 1985). While observations of psi-missing are much less common than those of *psi-hitting,* the former are sufficiently numerous to suggest there is an effect here to be explained (Rao, 1965).

Critics would be inclined to argue that the occurrence of so-called psi-missing confirms their view of reported card-guessing data as statistical freaks. These below-chance scores are seen as nothing else than the negative tail of the normal distribution of random guessing scores centered on a mean of 5 hits per run. Two points count against this interpretation. First, under this "normal curve" model the incidence of psi-missing data should be the same as that of psi-hitting results, yet in fact the former is much lower than the latter. Second, the occurrence of psi-missing seems to be correlated with certain psychological variables; this should not be the case if properly controlled ESP tests entail purely random guessing.

Consistent Missing

A variety of psi-missing entails poor scoring on one symbol due to a consistent tendency to call it another particular symbol. For example a subject may tend to guess "square" whenever the target is a circle. The evidence for this so-called *consistent missing* is limited (Cadoret & Pratt, 1950; Kennedy, 1979), although few researchers may have bothered to examine their data for such an effect. It may prove to be one (but not the sole) mechanism by which psi-missing is enacted (Timm, 1969).

Kennedy (1979) suggests consistent missing might be linked to similarities in the appearance of targets or semantic associations between them. Thus in an ESP study using playing cards as targets (Kelly, Kanthamani, Child & Young, 1975), a selected subject, Bill Delmore, tended to show consistent confusions between colors (e.g., calling "heart" for a diamond) and between court cards (e.g., calling "king" for a queen).

The Focusing Effect

Some subjects show a preference for a particular symbol and their significant performance is due largely to their superior scoring on targets featuring this symbol. This is called the *focusing effect* and it is documented principally with one special subject, Pavel Stepanek (Pratt, 1973), although, again, parapsychologists might not have looked for such a tendency in their experimental participants.

Position Effects and Decline Effects

It was noted early in experimental ESP research that performance often declines within defined units or sections of the test (Rhine, 1969; Schmeidler, 1944). Within a run (25 guesses), scoring on the first half frequently is superior to that on the second half. More detailed analyses suggest that performance within a run follows an asymmetrical U-curve, with high scoring just after the start of the run followed by a consistent decline and a slight recovery toward the end of the deck *(terminal salience)*. A decline in hit rate also may be found across runs within a test session, with the best performance in the first quarter of the session. Within-run and within-session declines are termed *episodic* declines. Another type is the *chronological* decline in which a subject's performance gradually falls over time, much to the annoyance of the parapsychologist who waited so long for a consistently good ESP performer. Episodic declines, and possibly chronological declines too, may be due to the effects of boredom and the comparative revival of interest at the beginning and the end of each unit of experimentation.

Although the occurrence of episodic decline effects received a lot of empirical scrutiny in earlier years, the progression from a card-guessing methodology to computerized procedures has been associated with a lessening of attention to these effects (Palmer, 1978a, p. 171).

The Differential Effect

The use of two contrasting conditions in an experiment may result in contrasting levels of performance under the two conditions, usually with psi-hitting in one and psi-missing in the other. This is the *differential effect* (Rao, 1965). Often the differential effect across contrasting conditions appears meaningful (e.g., Carpenter, 1971), but in other instances it seems quite capricious, perhaps signaling the operation of some kind of experimenter effect.

A proposed variety of the differential effect is the *preferential effect.* Here each subject performs in contrasting conditions (often unknowingly, as with two different categories of targets) and shows superior performance under the condition they most prefer. It would be more appropriate however, to say simply that subjects' preferences may be one factor underlying the differential effect.

Displacement

In some experiments it has been found that while a subject's guesses match the intended targets only at chance level, there is a significant tendency for each call to match the target before (or the target after) the intended one. That is, ESP seems to have been displaced either temporally or spatially, an effect known as *displacement.* The effect was discovered serendipitously in 1938 by a prominent American experimental physicist and announced by him anonymously ([Abbot], 1938), but apart from some early work by Carington (see Chapter 5) and by Soal (Soal & Bateman, 1954), until recent years little had been done either to authenticate displacement or to ascertain its bases.

In a series of studies Crandall (e.g., 1985) has found a replicable association between displacement and psi missing. Specifically, subjects who scored below MCE on the intended targets performed above chance on the target immediately before and the target immediately after the intended one, suggesting that psi-missers simply have their ESP inaccurately focused.

Conversely, Tart (1978) reports that subjects who score positively on the nominated target show displaced psi-missing on adjacent targets. Tart suggests the successful ESP performer is able both to focus on the target and to inhibit information from adjacent targets; this focusing process he terms "transtemporal inhibition."

Braud's (1987) review of the empirical literature suggests that displacement effects are linked to negative moods and attitudes, including those induced by unfavorable test situations; impatience, especially when aggravated by the experimental procedure; and distractability, or lack of absorption in the immediate goal or target. Braud suspects too that the ESP subject's curiosity to explore beyond the immediate target may be a significant factor, although this might be interpreted as a motivational element of the distractability/absorption dimension. There is scope for further experimental study of displacement in relation to the concepts of ESP focusing and absorption in experiencing the target.

Response Bias Hypothesis

When people guess at the identity of an ESP target they may be habitually inclined to call some symbols more often than others. Scientists refer to this as an inherent response bias. American parapsychologist Rex Stanford (1967) claims that the most infrequently used responses are more likely to be correct when they are used. Evidence for such a trend is supportive but not yet conclusive (Palmer, 1982, p. 67). Care needs to be taken here to distinguish between response *habits* in Stanford's sense and the observed frequency of calls in an isolated run (Nash, 1978).

Variance Effects

Sometimes a statistical deviation from chance expectation may be manifest not in terms of the average score but in the variance of the data. A variety of variance effects have been reported (for a review see Carpenter, 1977, pp. 243–252), but one of the most instructive is known as *clustering*.

In a recent post hoc analysis of the ESP performance of some consistently high scoring subjects it was noted that the majority did not produce hits at random intervals but rather tended to have hits in groups or clusters (Kelly, 1982). The trend toward stringing hits together instead of having each in isolation from the rest is called clustering. It seems to suggest that at certain stages of the experiment a subject may slip into a psiconducive state of mind and for a short period show strong ESP. Work on the clustering effect is beginning to be undertaken.

Effects in Post Hoc Analyses

In the comments on some of the above effects it was noted that parapsychologists generally do not bother to look for patterns of performance other than is evidenced by the mean and perhaps by the variance. The reason is that the occurrence of many such effects cannot yet be anticipated, and in undertaking all manner of post hoc analyses to test for the presence of these various patterns there is a fair probability of turning up a significant result purely by chance; as you will recall, if data are purely random and twenty different statistical analyses are applied to them, then on average one of these analyses nevertheless will yield a "significant" result at the .05 level of probability. Such a blind search for a significant trend through continued reanalysis of performance obviously would leave the experimenter open to the charge of "data bashing" or "hypothesis saving."

While these various effects in ESP performance may well be valid and warrant investigation they therefore do not have the breadth of empirical documentation that one might have expected.

Improvement and the Role of Feedback

As indicated previously, often a subject's ESP scores are observed to decline. An American psychologist/parapsychologist, Charles Tart (1966, 1977), has argued that chronological declines and poor performance overall are due to inadequate opportunities for learning. If at the end of a run or at the end of a session the participant is told the aggregate level of performance (as was usual in the Duke University studies, for example), this would do little to help the individual learn when she or he was "using ESP." Tart recommends that the subject be informed of the correctness of each call as it is made, thereby providing a chance for the subject to determine (even intuitively) what they were doing differently in those trials on which calls were correct. In other words, the ESP task can become one of learning, with appropriate responses being reinforced through provision of immediate feedback. Tart (1976) and others (e.g., Honorton, 1970; Sandford, 1977) have reported some improvement in ESP scores under trial-by-trial feedback, but the available data are inconsistent and the situation appears rather more complex than a simple learning hypothesis would allow (e.g., Jackson, Franzoi & Schmeidler, 1977). If learning effects do occur they may require much longer training periods than typically studied in experiments to date.

It is still too early to say if ESP performance can be enhanced by application of learning principles but the issue is of such importance as to attract considerable research effort.

Target Variables in ESP Performance

In tests of ESP the target may be mental as in a telepathic procedure, physical as in clairvoyance, or mental and or physical as in GESP. Among the targets used by researchers have been the standard ESP symbols, digits, letters, words, colors, line drawings (of animals, for example), paintings, photographs, three-dimensional objects, and distant environmental settings. There are some indications that simple target material such as colors or geometrical figures (the ESP symbols) may be superior to other sorts, particularly words, but then again such an advantage may depend greatly on the manner in which the test is conducted. To ascertain the aspects of target material pertinent to extrachance performance, some studies have focused on various specific physical and psychological dimensions.

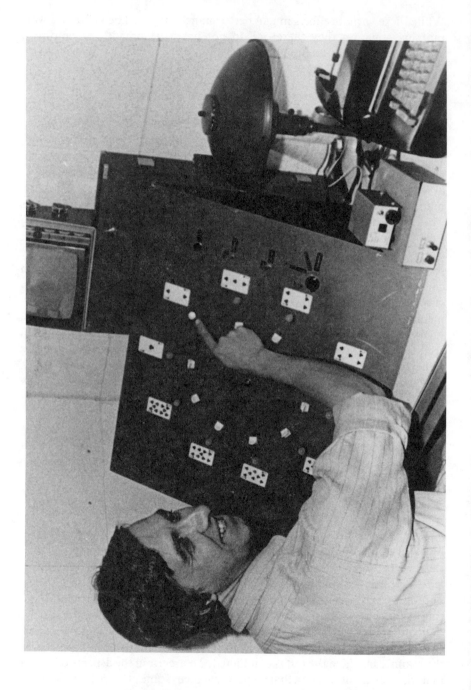

Physical Aspects

The size of the targets does not seem to affect performance in restricted-choice ESP tests, particularly if the participants are not informed that target size is to be manipulated. Of the few significant results associated with the dimension of size nearly all seem attributable to other factors such as novelty and subject preferences for a particular size. The number of times the target symbol appears on a card evidently has no effect on the level of scoring (Rhine, 1937). In one study the standard ESP symbols were distorted (unbeknownst to the participants) but this did not affect the subjects' significant level of psi-hitting (MacFarland & George, 1937). Likewise the distance of the ESP targets from the subject seems to have no clear linear effect upon performance; such effects as do occur are thought to be explicable in terms of the subject's differential perception of the task. (This should not be interpreted as showing conclusively that the extrasensory "signal" is not attenuated by distance; an ESP score is hardly a pure measure of "signal strength.")

Psychological Aspects

Psychological preferences for targets vary across subjects. Generally speaking, higher ESP scoring has been found with targets which subjects favor for emotional reasons. Three studies may be cited by way of illustration. In one study (Dean & Nash, 1967), in which a measure of physiological arousal was used as the index of extrasensory awareness, greater responsiveness was found when the targets were names of friends than when strangers' names were used. An experiment by Carpenter (1971) used the standard ESP cards, some with erotic pictures taped to them and others with neutral pictures. A differential effect was observed in accordance with each subject's "guilt level": although the high school student participants knew nothing of the presence of any pictures on the target cards, the more anxious subjects performed better on the neutral cards while less anxious participants yielded higher scores on the erotic cards.

In another experiment by Johnson and Nordbeck (1972) a single neurotic subject was used. On the basis of personality tests some words were selected which had emotional significance for the subject, half positively and half negatively so. The participant scored above chance on the positively toned words and below chance on the negative, emotionally disturbing words. After the subject was informed of the nature of the target

Opposite: Figure 10. Tart used his ten-choice trainer to study learning effects in ESP (photo: Charles Tart).

material she was highly displeased and a subsequent experiment with her using the same targets was not successful. (Proposals to conduct this type of study today would be given very close scrutiny on ethical grounds.)

The evidence suggests therefore that psychological aspects of the target material rather than purely physical aspects govern the level of ESP performance. It may be recalled that analyses of spontaneous ESP cases reveal that the content of the extrasensory experience tends to have some personal significance for the percipient. These results should not, however, be taken to imply that, if it exists, ESP operates independently of the physical features of the situation. Rather, it may be that the magnitude of any such effects is overshadowed by the role of psychological factors in the flow of extrasensory information from subconscious to conscious levels of mentation.

Multiple-aspect Targets

A multiple-aspect target has several different dimensions; not merely symbol shape but also color, size, numerosity, and so on. A few studies have been conducted with such targets and the general trend seems to be that participants score more highly on the target as a whole than would be expected on the basis of the performance on each of the individual dimensions (e.g., Schmeidler & Lewis, 1968). Although more work needs to be undertaken on this issue, it does raise the possibility that percipients are not getting several isolated pieces of information on a target but are responding to it as a whole. Some parapsychologists have even proposed that ESP entails a holistic style of cognitive processing, one for which the right hemisphere of the brain is more suited. Support for such an idea is meager.

Other Situational Variables in ESP Performance

Facets of the testing situation other than the target material may influence the level of ESP scores. Pertinent variables here include the experimental personnel, the procedure, and the physical setting.

Experimental Personnel

The possible influence of the experimenter on the outcome of the study was noted earlier, specifically in relation to the parapsychological experimenter effect. There is now a substantial literature documenting the operation of experimenter effects in the broader sense (see White, 1977, for a review). For example, Honorton, Ramsey and Cabibbo (1975) tested two groups of subjects, one with an experimenter acting in a friendly and supportive way and the other with an experimenter who affected an abrupt, formal and unfriendly manner. The former group achieved significant psi-hitting and the latter, psi-missing.

There also are suggestions that the people who score or "check" the subject's responses against the targets have differential influences upon the scores obtained. This so-called *checker effect* presumably would be psi-mediated, paralleling the parapsychological experimenter effect (Weiner & Zingrone, 1986), and it raises the possibility that in an ESP test there may be several potential "psi sources."

Apart from the experimenter (that is, the person who designs and supervises the study), the "checker," and the subjects themselves, there may be another major person involved in the experimental procedure. In a telepathic or GESP task an agent or "sender" has to be employed. Sometimes the agent's role is taken by the experimenter (or a coexperimenter) while in other studies, particularly those concerned with the nature of the agent's contribution to the participants performance, other people are recruited to act as agents.

Regrettably little research has been devoted to the contribution of the agent (Carpenter, 1977, pp. 252–257). A fundamental issue here is whether the agent is essential to significant scoring. One means of assessing this is to compare performance under GESP conditions to that on a clairvoyance task. In some studies of this type the participants were aware of the difference in procedure and thus the results may have been an artifact of the effect of this knowledge on the subjects' expectations and motivation. The better studies kept the subjects blind to the fact that some trials were clairvoyant and others permitted GESP. A number of these experiments show evidence of superior scoring in the GESP condition, suggesting that the agent did make some contribution, but this pattern by no means is universal.

Another approach used by two Israeli parapsychologists, the Kreitlers, is to ask the agent to actively "send" the target information on some trials and simply to think about it on other trials. The active trials yielded significantly higher ESP scores (Kreitler & Kreitler, 1973). This result warrants independent confirmation. A third approach makes use of a number of different agents. There are no clear trends for two agents to be better than one or for higher scores when agent and subject are emotionally close rather than strangers. Hence the agent's role, and indeed the authenticity of the concept of telepathy, have yet to be demonstrated conclusively (Palmer, 1978a, pp. 96–102).

Experimental Procedure and Setting

The success of an ESP experiment might be affected by the procedure and the physical conditions under which the subject completes the test.

One factor examined in this regard is the *rate of response*. Where subjects work at their own preferred rate there are some indications that those who work more slowly gain higher scores (e.g., Stuart, 1938). A similar finding is noted in studies where subjects were required to respond at a rate defined by the experimenter. Most experiments on rate of response have relied, however, upon selected or "gifted" subjects and hence their generality is uncertain (Palmer, 1978a, pp. 89–90). In any event the data might be due not to response rate as such but to level of relaxation: people who respond slowly or who are not "rushed" by the experimenter may be relatively relaxed.

A more general variable, *spontaneity* of response, also has been subject to investigation. It is a conventional wisdom among experienced experimental parapsychologists that subjects should be encouraged to let target-related information simply come to mind rather than concentrating intensely on the task or being governed by rational considerations of what would be a judicious choice of response on a given trial. Some experimental evidence indeed does suggest that response spontaneity does facilitate ESP performance (Palmer, 1978a, pp. 90–92).

The physical setting of the experiment can influence the results, at least if the comparative adversity of the conditions is reasonably extreme. For example, having to do the ESP test in the dark can lead to a decline in scores, and even produce psi-missing (Bevan, 1947). In one study different sorts of background music had no effect on performance levels (Eilbert & Schmeidler, 1950), but in another (Quider, 1984), baroque music was more conducive to high scores than was a no-music control condition.

One way in which variations of procedure may function to influence performance is through *motivation*. Some experimental procedures or situations may enhance the participant's level of motivation to perform well. Several attempts to examine this factor directly have relied on the use of tangible incentives. Monetary rewards for good performance do not appear to be efficacious and may even be detrimental (perhaps by inhibiting relaxation) (Casler, 1976). One study (in the 1950s) used electric shock to punish the subject for incorrect calls, and performance did improve (McElroy & Brown, 1950); confirmatory investigations are lacking, however, and today the use of such a procedure would be frowned upon. Intangible incentives have been examined, principally in regard to the experimenter's provision of feedback. As noted earlier in comments upon Tart's research, the value of feedback is still an equivocal issue, so this aspect of motivation also warrants further research. Somewhat surprisingly, other types of intangible incentives such as praise by the experimenter have not been investigated systematically.

A procedural feature that has received much empirical attention is the participant's state of mind during the test. More specifically, researchers have examined the conduciveness to ESP of various states of consciousness. The main states employed in such studies have been hypnosis, sensory (perceptual) deprivation or the *ganzfeld,* meditation, progressive relaxation, hypnagogic states, dreaming, and drug intoxication. Except perhaps for the last of these there is substantial evidence suggesting that each of the above states of consciousness is psi conducive (see Honorton, 1977, for a review).

In recent years the ganzfeld procedure has been given particular attention. Under this procedure structured visual stimulation is excluded by placing half a ping-pong ball over each eye of the subject and directing a bright light at them; structured auditory stimulation is excluded by presenting electronic noise (rather like continual, soft radio static) through headphones; and the subject lies on a mattress or in a reclining chair so as to become habituated also to a uniform level of tactile and proprioceptive stimulation. After the first half hour or so the ESP test is begun, with the subject simply permitting target-related imagery to come to mind. According to Honorton (1978), 23 of 42 experiments conducted in ten different laboratories have yielded significant ESP performance under ganzfeld conditions; this success rate of 55 percent is far beyond that expected by chance. Because the ganzfeld effect loomed as a highly replicable phenomenon in parapsychology it became in the mid-eighties the focus of intense critical debate (Honorton, 1985; Hyman, 1985), the result of which was that it is agreed there is an effect here to be explained, whether or not the underlying process is authentically extrasensory (Hyman & Honorton, 1986). Other commentators (e.g., Parker & Wiklund, 1987) nevertheless remain skeptical of the quality of the experimental evidence for the ganzfeld effect.

The reported success of these various psi-conducive states might stem from several sources. Attitudinal factors may be affected: ESP performance may be enhanced by virtue of the fact that while in one of these states of consciousness the individual is more inclined to believe that ESP is possible; the state of consciousness thus may help to break down or suspend the subject's socially-conditioned intellectual defenses against the notion of ESP. Other pertinent factors relate more to information-processing characteristics. These psi-conducive states generally encourage greater levels of relaxation and withdrawal of attention from the external world. Thus, ESP appears to be facilitated by minimizing concurrent sensory and proprioceptive stimulation, and by promoting absorption in the internal processes of mentation (Honorton, 1977; Irwin, 1985b). Psi-conducive

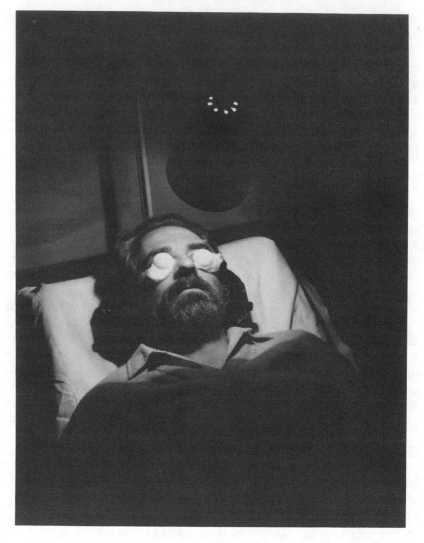

Figure 11. Ganzfeld stimulation (photo: author).

states of consciousness represent a major area of research in contemporary parapsychology.

Subject Variables in ESP Performance

Parapsychologists have given much attention to the identification of successful ESP subjects. Apart from throwing some light on the nature of

ESP such research has the pragmatic justification that if investigators can select a sample of people who are relatively open to extrasensory experiences, then there is a greater chance of achieving statistically significant results in experimental work.

The major personalistic variables that have been investigated are attitudes, mood, and personality, although increasing attention is being given to physiological and cognitive variables.

Attitudes and Beliefs

The best known work on the contribution of attitudes to ESP performance was conducted by Gertrude Schmeidler (1952; Schmeidler & McConnell, 1958). She began by dividing ESP subjects into two groups. One group, designated "sheep," was comprised of people who believed in the possibility of ESP; a second group, of so-called "goats," rejected that possibility. On pooling scores on ESP tests over a number of such groups Schmeidler established a trend for sheep to score above MCE and for goats to score significantly below chance level.

Separating "the sheep from the goats" in terms of ESP belief therefore also tends to differentiate two types of ESP performer. The result for sheep is interesting although perhaps not surprising: it is consistent with other cognitive research that suggests people attend to information they want to and perceive what they believe can be perceived. The result for goats is most fascinating. Not only does it confirm an effect of attitudes on the occurrence of ESP, it also reminds us of the adage that there are none so blind as those who will not see. But the fact that goats' mean ESP score is significantly below chance suggests these people are not merely directing their attention away from extrasensory information nor blocking its cognitive processing; rather they seem to be identifying ESP targets at an extrachance level and then choosing a different target as their response. By making more incorrect responses than expected by chance, goats seemingly use ESP in a self-defeating endeavor to support their belief that ESP does not exist. It is not that goats are intrinsically insensitive to extrasensory information, but that their attitude affects how they deal with such information.

The *sheep-goat effect* is one of the more successfully replicated relationships in experimental ESP research (Palmer, 1977). Later work, however, indicates that "attitude to ESP" is more complex than one at first might think. "Do I believe in ESP?" may subsume many distinct attitudes and beliefs, including "Would I like ESP to exist?" "Do I think I have ESP?" "Do I think I will exhibit ESP in this particular experiment?" "Do I think this ESP experiment will work (for people in general)?" and "Do I think this experimenter can elicit my ESP?" The measurement, scope and correlates of paranormal belief currently represent a very active area of research (e.g., Irwin, 1985d; Thalbourne & Haraldsson, 1980; Zusne & Jones, 1982, Chapter 7).

That beliefs are more fundamental in the sheep-goat effect than are specific dimensions of personality and adjustment remains to be established. One experiment by Lovitts (1981), however, suggests the effect does stem from beliefs. When she disguised an ESP test as a procedure for "disproving ESP," the usual scoring pattern was reversed, that is, sheep tended to perform below chance and goats showed psi-hitting. This indicates that the sheep-goat effect arises from subjects' use of ESP in conformance with their beliefs about it. Replication of Lovitts' most elegant study is called for.

A related attitudinal variable that recently has received attention is *fear of psi*. There are suggestions that some people reject the notion of psi because they find it threatening. In relation to ESP, for example, survey respondents have expressed anxiety that if ESP were to exist, their mind would be flooded by other people's thoughts, they might not utilize ESP in a responsible and sensitive way, and there would be a threat to people's rights to privacy (Irwin, 1985c; Tart & LaBore, 1986). It is feasible that fear of psi may be one element of the sheep-goat effect. It also has been suggested (Braud, 1985; Tart, 1984) that parapsychologists' subconscious fear of psi might be involved in various sorts of experimenter effects in ESP studies. As yet there have been no experiments relating ESP performance directly to subjects' fear of psi. The nearest we have to this is a replicable relationship between ESP scores and the strength of general defense mechanisms as indexed by the *Defense Mechanism Test* (DMT): whereas highly defensive subjects tend to score at or below chance expectation in an ESP test, people with low defensiveness show psi-hitting (Haraldsson, Houtkooper & Hoeltje, 1987; Haraldsson & Johnson, 1979).

Mood

Another psychological dimension that has been linked with performance on laboratory ESP tasks is that of *graphic expansiveness*. If a person is asked to draw on a sheet of paper his or her utilization of the space on the sheet is variable. On some occasions the person will produce large drawings that fill the page, and at these times the individual typically appears to be in an outgoing, cheerful mood; this type of drawing performance is categorized as "expansive." On other occasions that same individual may be depressed, inhibited and unsociable, and in this state the drawings produced generally are small and located in a corner of the page rather than filling the available space; this style is called "compressive." Graphic expansiveness is linked to personality to the degree that a given person may exhibit one style of drawing much more frequently than the other. Nonetheless, the style does vary across time and hence graphic expansiveness is best regarded as an index of mood.

Several studies indicate a relationship between ESP scores and graphic expansiveness. The earliest of these was conducted by Betty Humphrey (1946a,b). In clairvoyance tests expansive subjects obtained higher ESP scores than did compressive subjects. On the other hand, in a series of telepathy or GESP tests in which an agent was concentrating on the ESP targets, the compressive subjects showed the superior ESP performance. Later studies tend to confirm this pattern. Evidently mood does influence ESP scores, but there is an interaction effect between the mood variable and the type of ESP test.

Personality

There has been considerable empirical interest in determining the personality correlates of ESP. The two principal variables investigated in this regard are *neuroticism* and *extraversion*.

Neurotic people display either high levels of anxiety or marked reliance upon defense mechanisms directed against anxiety. On the evidence of a substantial number of studies it seems that ESP performance correlates negatively with neuroticism; that is, neurotic subjects tend to score at chance or below MCE, while stable and well-adjusted people yield above-chance ESP scores (Palmer, 1978a, pp. 130–132). This at least is the dominant trend in studies in which the ESP test is conducted with subjects on an individual basis. When ESP tests are administered to a group of people at one time, the relationship with neuroticism does not always emerge, possibly because in this situation neurotic individuals can lose themselves in the crowd and thereby their anxiety is not evoked to the same degree as in the one-on-one setting of an individual assessment of ESP.

Extraversion is a personality type in which the individual's interests are directed outward to the world and other people rather than inwards to thoughts and feelings (introversion). A number of studies employing this personality measure have found a positive relationship between extraversion and ESP performance; that is, extraverts typically yield higher ESP scores than introverts (Palmer, 1978a, pp. 132–133).

While research on the personality correlates of ESP performance is moderately encouraging by its level of consistency and replicability, there is some question over its generalization to ESP in everyday situations. The general trend in the research is for the best ESP scorers to have superior social adjustment, enabling them more readily to adapt to novel social situations like a psychology experiment. Perhaps, then, ESP can occur if the individual is comfortable or relaxed in a given situation. Should this be so, virtually anybody could experience ESP at some time or another, regardless of their personality. This may account for the fact that if experients of spontaneous ESP are surveyed there is no definitive trend for them to exhibit the distinctive personality profile thrown up by the experimental research (e.g., Haight, 1979); of course, other explanations of this discrepancy are possible.

Physiological Variables

There is meager evidence of relationships between ESP scores and electroencephalographic (EEG) measures. A high amount or density of alpha wave (8 to 13Hz) activity during the ESP test may be a good predictor of performance, at least if the individual also reports having been in an altered state of consciousness at the time (Palmer, 1978a, pp. 123–128). Alpha waves usually are associated with a relaxed, passive state of mind.

Some studies have examined the role of cerebral hemispheric specialization under the hypothesis that ESP is a "right hemisphere" task. There is some experimental data to support this view but one study indicates that "left hemisphere" processes also can be a vehicle for psi (Maher & Schmeidler, 1977). In these investigations the distribution of demands upon processing capacity seems to be critical (Irwin, 1979a, pp. 128–137).

Work on other physiological measures such as galvanic skin response (GSR) and heart rate is too scant to warrant generalizations.

Cognitive Variables

A number of studies have correlated ESP performance with scores on standard intelligence tests. Only a few of these experiments have yielded significant data, but interestingly enough the findings generally indicate a positive relationship between ESP scores and IQ (e.g., Nash & Nash, 1958). This is seemingly at odds with the trend for a disproportionally high incidence of spontaneous ("real life") ESP experiences among people with a poor educational background (Haraldsson, 1985; Palmer, 1979, p. 245). If the relationship between ESP and IQ is valid it suggests the relatively low level of reporting by people with higher education is a function not of intelligence but of some other (e.g., social) factor. At the same time the experimental data are not only weak but typically based on very narrow samples of intelligence (e.g., university students). Further, it is notable that there are some reports of highly significant psi-hitting in groups of mentally retarded children. Possibly therefore the reported IQ-ESP correlations reflect the operation of some intervening factor such as a capacity to settle into the test situation quickly.

Some recent work by an American anthropological parapsychologist, Michael Winkelman (e.g., 1981), suggests that formal education tends to reduce capacity for ESP performance. Testing a group of children in a remote Mexican rural village Winkelman found that with the factor of age controlled, ESP scores correlated negatively with years of schooling. Mathematical education particularly seemed to have an adverse association with ESP. Further research is needed to support and clarify this finding. The underlying effect might spring from the inculcation of a style of linear thinking, exposure to the attitude that "educated" people do not believe in the authenticity of ESP, or several other possibilities.

Allied to the popular perception of intelligence is that of creativity. A few studies have sought to compare ESP scores across groups high and low in creativity, but no clear evidence of a relationship between these variables has emerged. Account may have to be taken of the nature of both the measure of creativity and the ESP task (Palmer, 1978a, p. 139).

The memory skills of the ESP subject have received some measure of attention for theoretical reasons (see Chapter 8). The experimental literature on this topic at first sight shows little consistency but some order may be introduced if account is taken of the type of memory skills entailed. Thus there are indications that ESP scores correlate positively with the ability to retrieve information about past events (long-term memory performance). Additionally there is some suggestive evidence of a negative correlation between ESP and short-term memory, or ability to keep information in mind just for a minute or so; this relationship is evidentially rather more equivocal than that for long-term memory skills (Irwin, 1979b).

In spontaneous cases of ESP, information often is mediated in the form of visual (or other mental) imagery (e.g., White, 1964a). In one of my own surveys (Irwin, 1979c) I found that people who in a variety of "normal" psychological tasks adopted the style of a *visualizer* (as opposed to that of a *verbalizer)* tended more often to have their ESP experiences by way of imagery; verbalizers on the other hand more often had intuitive (imageless) extrasensory impressions, although the latter trend did not reach significance. It is appropriate, therefore, to explore experimentally the relationship between ESP scores and performance on various measures of mental imagery (for a review see George, 1981; Irwin, 1979a, pp. 98–100; Palmer, 1978a, pp. 139–140).

There are reports of a dependence of ESP scores on spatial abilities (e.g., Freeman, 1970), but the results of research using questionnaire measures of mental imagery are rather inconsistent.

The most frequently used questionnaire in this context has been the *Betts Questionnaire upon Mental Imagery* (QMI), about which two points may be made. First, the QMI is a global measure of mental imagery over seven sensory modalities (visual, auditory, tactile, etc.) and thus the reported data may be obscured by the fact that strong *mental* imagery may not necessarily mean strong *visual* imagery. That is, there may well be a relationship between ESP and vividness of visual imagery, but because the global QMI score is not a pure measure of the latter the experimental results have not been consistent. Second, QMI reponses are particularly open to distortion by the respondents. If people suspect that vivid mental imagery is regarded by the investigator as desirable they can inflate their QMI score. If the participants in the experiments were sensitive to the experimenters' expectations, the inconsistency of results may reflect inconsistency of expectations across experimenters. Research with a better measure of vividness of visual imagery is called for.

Another research questionnaire that has been employed is the *Gordon Test of Visual Imagery Control*. Some people can exercise a high degree of control over their visual images, whereas for others images seem to have a will of their own. In one study (Price, 1973) the latter group, the autonomous imagers, evinced more ESP by way of greater variance of scores. The effect, however, was educed in a post hoc analysis and no one appears to have attempted to replicate the study. Other experiments asking participants to use imagery on some trials of an ESP test and not on other trials generally have not found any consistent differential effect (George, 1981, pp. 130–132). Perhaps the conscious effort toward controlled use of imagery in an ESP task is counterproductive, decreasing the spontaneity of performance and thereby negating any advantages to be had from skills in relation to vividness of imagery.

The cognitive style dimension of imagery noted by Irwin (1979c) to be pertinent to spontaneous extrasensory experience has also been investigated tangentially by Mitchell and Drewes (1982). In that experiment subjects with highly verbal interests scored more highly in a verbal ESP task than in a performance ESP task.

Dream recall is another factor of some interest. Several surveys (e.g., Haraldsson, Gudmundsdottir, Ragnarsson, Loftsson & Jonsson, 1977; Palmer, 1979) have obtained a positive relationship between the frequency with which people can recall their dreams and the incidence of spontaneous extrasensory experiences. In laboratory testing two of seven experiments have reported a positive correlation between dream recall and ESP scores (Honorton, 1972; Palmer, 1978a, p. 140; Palmer, 1982, p. 61). The trend is suggestive but not conclusive. Further, the basis of this correlation is far from clear. It may indicate a psychodynamic factor: people who repress their dreams might not be open to ESP. It may reflect imagery processes:

people with certain sorts of skills in mental imagery may recall their dreams more often and achieve high ESP scores. Again, memory might be the connecting link: it has been found that high ESP scorers tend to have good long-term memory and so too may frequent dream recallers.

Another personalistic domain examined in this context is cognitive style, or what could be called preferred modes of perception and information processing. One such style is that of field dependence, the tendency not to differentiate sharply an object from its surrounding environment. The relationship between ESP in general and field dependence is not adequately documented but there does seem to be a trend for field dependent subjects to do relatively well in precognitive ESP tests (Nash & Nash, 1968). It has been suggested that field dependent persons have a less rigid psychological boundary between the present and the future and thus are less inclined to "block out" information about a future situation. Such a notion does warrant further empirical scrutiny.

A dimension that incorporates elements of a cognitive style and other cognitive skills is that of *absorption*. Originally derived as the central cognitive feature of the state of hypnosis, absorption is defined formally as "a 'total' attention, involving a full commitment of available perceptual, motoric, imaginative and ideational resources to a unified representation of the attentional object" (Tellegen & Atkinson, 1974, p. 274). Inherent to a state of absorption, it is supposed, are an imperviousness to normally distracting events and a heightened sense of the reality of the object of attention. As noted earlier in this chapter, situations that are conducive to a state of absorption are recognized as common contexts both for spontaneous extrasensory experience and for high performance in laboratory ESP tests; these situations include hypnosis, sensory deprivation (ganzfeld), meditation, progressive relaxation, and dreaming.

A second factor of the absorption domain, the *capacity* to achieve an absorbed state, also is related to ESP. Stanford and Angelini (1984) report a significant positive correlation between absorption capacity and a measure of ESP under ganzfeld conditions, at least when participants are bombarded with pink (random) noise in the ESP sessions. Palmer and van der Velden (1983) observed no such correlation but they also failed to find evidence of ESP in their experiment; according to Stanford (1987a, p. 58) an inappropriate cognitive set was encouraged in this study.

A third element of the absorption domain is more concerned with motivation or cognitive style, and it is known as the "need for absorption"; a given person may have adequate absorption capacity and be in a conducive situation yet rarely enter an absorbed state simply because of a disinclination to do so. A recurrent desire to engage in absorbed mentation was found by Irwin (1985b) to be strongly related to the occurrence of spontaneous extrasensory experiences. This result warrants replication but is consistent with the reported association between these experiences and the individual's inclination to fantasize a large part of the time (Myers & Austrin, 1985; Wilson & Barber, 1983). There is nevertheless some scope for further experimental research into the role of the absorption domain in ESP performance.

Demographic Variables

While demographic variables have been incorporated almost as a matter of course in the analyses of data from spontaneous case surveys they have been given rather less attention in the laboratory setting.

Sex differences have been subject to some investigation. Women tend to predominate in ESP case collections, but that seems to be a consequence of willingness to participate in surveys rather than of openness to spontaneous experiences as such. In ESP tests there is no clear trend for differential scoring between the sexes (Palmer, 1978a, pp. 144–146), although in some circumstances gender may interact with other variables to influence performance (Rao, Kanthamani & Norwood, 1983). For example, in GESP and telepathy experiments it is possible that the gender of the subject and that of the agent have some bearing on the ability of the pair to form some sort of rapport which in turn might influence scoring.

In a few experiments age has had an effect on ESP scoring, with children tending to perform better than adolescents and adults. On the other hand, many similar studies have been unsuccessful in demonstrating age-dependent differences in scoring (Palmer, 1978a, pp. 146–148). Like gender, age may be a factor which moderates the influence of more fundamental variables. In spontaneous extrasensory experiences, gender is reported to be linked to the *form* of the experience; according to Haraldsson et al. (1977) ESP in a dream was more commonly reported by women in an Icelandic sample, but this pattern seems to vary across nationalities (Haraldsson, 1985).

The demographic variable of educational background has been discussed in the preceding section on cognitive variables.

Little systematic investigation into the pertinence of race and culture has been undertaken. Certainly the incidence of acknowledged spontaneous telepathic and clairvoyant experiences varies from one country to another, being higher in America than in Europe, for example (Haraldsson, 1985, p. 155), but as the available data are from Western nations the full range of cultural differences in this regard is unknown. Members of so-called primitive societies have been given ESP tests and some have performed well (Rose & Rose, 1951), but there are no data with which adequate cross-cultural comparisons may be made. This has not prevented a few parapsychologists from interpreting the occurrence of ostensibly paranormal experiences in primitive cultures as evidence for the view that ESP is a relic of a form of communication characteristic of a distant epoch of our evolution and, indeed, that ESP itself may have been a major mechanism of evolution (Hardy, 1950). Freud (1933, p. 76) too regarded ESP as an atavistic phenomenon.

In the preceding sections some factors that affect experimental ESP performance have been discussed. At this point no attempt will be made to draw these findings together, if indeed that is possible. Their relevance to our conception of psi will be considered after we have looked at other aspects of psi.

Nevertheless, it already should be clear that on some points there is a reasonable degree of consistency and coherence in the process-oriented experimental data. A number of relationships have been replicated by independent researchers in disparate contexts, and some observed relationships are compatible with those on allied matters. To the extent that there are consistencies in the data on the nature of ESP it might be argued that there is further support for the authenticity of ESP (Edge et al., 1986, p. 185). Surely if the results of ESP tests were fortuitous or artifactual there would be rather less consistency across experiments linking ESP performance to psychological variables.

While there is some merit in this view it should not be given undue weight. First, the observed level of consistency may indicate that the extrachance performance in ESP tests is a real phenomenon, but for reasons outlined earlier this does not demonstrate the authenticity of ESP as opposed to alternative explanations of the anomaly. Second, it is feasible that the operation of artifacts in ESP experiments (unintentional sensory cues, subject fraud, etc.) is correlated with various psychological variables and that it is actually these correlations that process-oriented experiments have revealed. For example, ESP scores may be related to extraversion because extraverts are more inclined than introverts to seek means of cheating.

Within these constraints the available data nevertheless might offer some encouragement to researchers who believe that the concept of ESP is viable, and certainly they provide foundations for theory building.

Key Terms and Concepts

Richet	open/closed decks
J.B. Rhine	restricted-choice tests
Duke University	free-response tests
Zener cards/ESP cards	selected/unselected subjects

target
call
run
hits
misses
critical ratio
mean chance expectation (MCE)
Extra-sensory Perception
replication
meta-analysis
the definitive experiment
the cumulative record
experimenter effects
the parapsychological experimenter effect
retrodiction
nonintentional psi
bidirectionality
psi-hitting
psi-missing
consistent missing
focusing effect
position effects
terminal salience
differential effect
preferential effect
displacement
ESP focusing
response bias

variance effects
clustering
multiple-aspect targets
checker effect
psi-conducive states
hypnosis
sensory/perceptual deprivation
ganzfeld
meditation
progressive relaxation
hypnagogic states
dreaming
drug intoxication
the sheep-goat effect
fear of psi
Defense Mechanism Test
graphic expansiveness
neuroticism
extraversion
alpha activity
hemispheric specialization
intelligence/scholastic ability
memory skills
imagery skills
visualizer/verbalizer
cognitive style
field dependence
absorption
demographic factors

Study Questions

1. The work of Charles Richet generally is not as widely acknowledged as it deserves to be. In what respects was it significant?

2. What were J.B. Rhine's principal contributions to parapsychology as a scientific discipline?

3. Why did J.B. Rhine devise the ESP cards?

4. What are the elements of an adequate experimental test of the ESP hypothesis?

5. Discuss the proposition, "ESP is defined ultimately as a statistical anomaly."

6. What criticisms were leveled at the Duke University research into ESP, and how were these taken into account in subsequent research?

7. Subseries D of the Pearce-Pratt study was limited to a mere six runs, but because of Rhine's presence in the experimenter's room as an observer it perhaps had the highest level of security of the four subseries. Pearce's scores in subseries D were 12, 3, 10, 11, 10 and 10. Determine the statistical significance of this set of data using the CR formula for closed decks.

8. On what grounds could ESP be shown to be authentic? Has it been authenticated? If so, how? If not, why not?

9. Do Hansel's scenarios of fraud in the Pearce-Pratt study constitute proper criticism?

10. What is the parapsychological experimenter effect in parapsychology, and why is it of major concern?

11. Akers (1984) notes a range of potential flaws in recent process-oriented ESP experiments. Do such studies really have to be as tightly controlled as proof-oriented experiments?

12. Does the notion of a below-chance score in an ESP test make sense? Do the correlates of psi-missing help in any way to bring credibility to the notion?

13. Some ESP experiments have incorporated erotic pictures in the target material without informing the participants. Consider the ethical aspects of this procedure.

14. The physical characteristics of targets seem to have scant impact upon ESP scores. Can we therefore discount the idea that ESP is mediated by some unknown form of physical (e.g., electromagnetic) radiation?

15. In light of the findings of process-oriented research, how would you best seek to elicit high scores from subjects in a controlled ESP experiment?

16. As an exercise, set up a simple ganzfeld situation in your own home and experience its (nonparapsychological) effects for about an hour.

17. Under what circumstances have you encountered a spontaneous extrasensory experience? Do these circumstances lend support to the experimental research on psi-conducive states?

18. Drawing on your own experience, what sorts of people do you imagine "sheep" to be? What do you think "goats" are like? How might these differences between sheep and goats actually produce differential performance on ESP tests?

19. Construct a psychological profile of people who perform well in ESP tests. Does this accord with your own impression of people who report spontaneous extrasensory experiences?

20. To what extent do you feel the authenticity of ESP is supported by the coherence of the functional relationships identified in process-oriented ESP research?

5
Extrasensory Perception and Time

Many psychologists reject the notion of ESP on the grounds that if ESP existed it would be at odds with known scientific principles. According to Alcock (1981, p. 191), for example, "if psi exists, science as we know it cannot." As far as contemporaneous ESP is concerned such a view is dubious. Although contemporaneous ESP apparently involves information transfer that cannot be attributed to the operation of the known human senses, by no means is it clear that this is contrary to any scientific principle. That environmental information must come through the senses is a tacit assumption, not a proven principle. Thus contemporaneous ESP, if it exists, could be accommodated by *extending* the present philosophical framework of behavioral science; there is no established principle that would have to be revised or discounted. The conflict between contemporaneous ESP and accepted laws of psychology and physics has been grossly exaggerated by critics, for rhetorical purposes, according to Collins and Pinch (1982).

Where ESP seems to relate to events displaced in time the compatibility of ESP and science nevertheless becomes rather strained, and for this reason the issue of ESP and time warrants discussion in its own right. It is to the temporal properties of ESP that we now turn.

Temporal Displacement

In Chapter 4 mention was made of displacement effects. A little more detail on *temporal* displacement is appropriate at this point.

In 1939 an English parapsychologist, Whately Carington (1940, 1945), began a series of free-response ESP studies using simple line drawings as targets. The typical procedure of these investigations was as follows. The object drawn as the ESP target for a given night was chosen at random from a dictionary using one of two methods. Carington would randomly insert the blade of a pocketknife into his copy of Webster's dictionary and open it at that page; or he selected a three-digit number from a table of random numbers and interpreted this as a page number in his dictionary. On that particular page Carington located the first word that corresponded to an item which could be drawn, and either he or his wife then drew the item. This became the target picture for the night. The drawing was pinned to Carington's study bookcase from 7 p.m. to 9:30 a.m. the next morning; usually some security measures were observed. This procedure was followed on ten nights, with a different target drawing for each night. About 250 unselected people participated in the investigation. Each night in their own homes they would make a sketch of what they thought to be the target picture for that night, adding a word that named it.

The number of words counted as hits was determined simply as the frequency of participants who labeled their drawing with the very word Carington had selected from the dictionary. But because some drawable objects (e.g., "cat") are intrinsically more likely to come to a subject's mind than others (e.g., "dolphin") the number of hits on the target night was compared to the incidence of this word on the nights for which it was not the target. That is, Carington operationalized the occurrence of telepathy in terms of a higher incidence of calls of the target word on the night he had selected it than on other nights of the series. A similar procedure was used to rate the presence of hits in the participants' drawings. These were assessed by an independent panel of people who judged each drawing against each target, scoring them 1 point if they unmistakably portrayed the same thing, ½ point if the correspondence was less clear cut, and 0 points if there was no correspondence. The panel was not aware of the date on which each target was used and hence the judges were making blind ratings of the correspondence between subjects' drawings and the targets.

The experiment indicated the presence of ESP (or extrachance guessing). For example, if the target for Night 6 was "pony," the number of people who drew a pony (or horse, etc.) and labeled it "pony" was distinctly higher on Night 6 than that for any other night of the experiment. More interestingly in the present context, the incidence of (say) "pony" drawings on the other nights of the investigation was not uniformly low. Indeed for the nights immediately before and after the night for a given target there were relatively higher frequencies of sketches matching that target than at other stages of the series; these were arranged roughly in a step-like fashion rising to a maximum on the night of the given target and then falling in a similar (but asymmetrical) manner. The effects of an ESP "stimulus" evidently are not confined to the period in which the target is presented but indeed seem to reach into the future and into the past to some degree.

Further experimental work on these bidirectional displacements was undertaken with card-guessing tests. In the 1930s the British parapsychologist S.G. Soal had conducted numerous ESP tests in an effort to replicate the work of Rhine and of Jephson but had been so unsuccessful that he became utterly pessimistic about the viability of an experimental approach to psi. Nevertheless, on the urging first of Robert Thouless and then of Whately Carington (Mauskopf & McVaugh, 1980, p. 237), Soal in 1939 reprocessed his data in a search for displacement effects. Two of his 160 subjects, Gloria Stewart and Basil Shackleton, were indeed found to exhibit such effects. Each showed a significant level of psi-hitting on the target before or on the target after the intended one (Soal & Bateman, 1954). Further tests with these people reportedly confirmed the pattern of performance. That the displacement was temporal in nature was supported by the fact that when Shackleton was required to increase his rate of response, psi-hitting was found not on the target for the following trial but on that for two trials ahead.

A quarter of a century later, Markwick (1978) presented evidence suggesting Soal tampered with the data in at least two sessions with Shackleton. As yet there is no direct evidence that records of Mrs. Stewart's sittings were similarly manipulated, but the confidence that now can be placed in any of Soal's work is necessarily undermined.

Research into the bases of temporal displacement was reviewed in Chapter 4. In the present context the very occurrence of displacement is the crucial point, for the reason that it suggests a temporal dispersion of the extrasensory "signal" into the future and into the past. Additional investigation of this putative phenomenon has tended to focus either on ESP of future events *(precognition)* or on ESP of past events *(retrocognition)*. Each of these facets therefore will be discussed separately.

Precognition

Many inspirations of prophets and soothsayers throughout recorded history have a precognitive tone. The previously cited pharaoh's dream of the seven fat kine and the seven lean kine is of this type. Omens, oracles, and premonitory visions have been accorded great significance in many cultures (Zohar, 1982, Chapter 1). Precognition therefore is not a peculiarly modern belief.

The Phenomenology of Precognitive Experience

As with other extrasensory experiences, spontaneous case collections have been used to ascertain the phenomenological features of precognitive experience. You will recall that the collections by Sidgwick (1888–1889) and Saltmarsh (1934) comprised precognitive cases, and other more general case

Table 1
Form of Precognitive and Contemporaneous
ESP Experiences *(after Rhine, 1962a)*

FORM	TEMPORAL CATEGORY	
	Precognitive	Contemporaneous
Intuitive	19%	35%
Hallucinatory	6%	25%
Realistic dream	60%	19%
Unrealistic dream	15%	21%
TOTAL	100%	100%

collections such as that compiled by L.E. Rhine have been utilized in comparing precognitive with contemporaneous extrasensory experiences.

Although spontaneous precognitive experiences can take any of the forms shown by contemporaneous extrasensory experiences, there is a relatively high incidence of dreams in precognitive case collections (see Table 1). In L.E. Rhine's (1962a) American sample 75 percent of precognitive cases were dreams. The corresponding figure in Sannwald's (1963) Western European collection is 60 percent and in a British study by Orme (1974), 74 percent; similar data are reported by Green (1960), Saltmarsh (1934) and Sidgwick (1888–1889). Most of these are realistic dreams, that is, the precognized event is represented in a fairly literal way. It is quite possible that unrealistic or symbolic dreams are not recognized for what they are and thus their reported incidence is depressed.

Why might dreams predominate in collections of precognitive cases? Rhine suggested that the thought of obtaining information about a future event might be so philosophically distasteful to people that such information is permitted to enter consciousness only when their intellectual defenses are down, as during a dream. Other explanations are, of course, possible. People's alleged "philosophical distaste" for the concept of precognition might affect their willingness to report such experiences of their own; relatively speaking, dreams might then be more readily acknowledged because if need be, they can hastily be qualified as being mere irrational fantasy and thereby not necessarily indicative of any belief on the part of the experient.

Another major characteristic of precognitive experiences noted by L.E. Rhine was that typically the apparent setting of the experience was in the present, not in the future. Thus in the precognitive dream the dreamer perceived the events to be occurring at that time; rarely was there any indication that they related to the future. Again, this might reflect the individual's unease with the idea of seeing into the future, although Rhine suggests that since time is not a concrete thing it cannot readily be represented in the form of imagery and thus generally cannot be conveyed in a dream.

Two British analyses, one by Green (1960) and the other by Orme (1974), have examined the length of time between the precognitive experience and the actual occurrence of the event to which the experience related. In both studies the observed incidence of cases fell as the interval increased. For about half of all cases the precognized event had occurred within two days of the experience, and only about 20 percent of experiences were fulfilled after an interval exceeding one month. A similar trend is reported by Sondow (1988) in her analysis of her own precognitive dreams. These results are consistent with the suggestion of the ESP displacement studies, that the ESP "signal" becomes weaker with time. On the other hand, the data might be due simply to the tendency to forget precognitive experiences that concern events far into the future; admittedly this is a less cogent argument in the case of Sondow's (1988) report, because she recorded her dreams each day and thereby avoided the problem of memory lapses.

Precognitive experiences, like other types of ESP, tend to concern incidents which are emotionally significant to the percipient. In premonitions the content often tends to be tragic (e.g., Saltmarsh, 1934; Sannwald, 1963). The death of a close friend or relative is a common theme, as is the occurrence of natural disasters. The sinking of the *Titanic,* the assassination of President Kennedy, and the 1966 Aberfan disaster have been productive areas of research for collectors of precognitive experiences (Barker, 1967; Stevenson, 1960).

Major conceptual problems are raised by the possibility of intervening in precognitive cases (see Struckmeyer, 1970, for an analysis of these). For example, if someone foresees a particular event and takes effective steps to avoid it the precognized event will not have taken place; how then could the case be regarded as knowledge of a future event?

L.E. Rhine (1955) first examined her case file to see if successful intervention ever was reported. In many cases intervention was not attempted, for a variety of reasons: the information was too unspecific, was not believed, or was not understood for what it was, or the events were beyond the individual's control or too far developed to be prevented. Some experients evidently did try to intervene in the course of events but were not successful. In other cases the precognized event allegedly was successfully avoided or prevented, but many of these Rhine felt to be evidentially dubious; it remained questionable that the precognized event would have occurred had the subject not taken the steps she or he did. In Rhine's assessment there nevertheless were nine instances in which the event not only was avoided or prevented but seemed bound to have occurred had not the percipient intervened.

As a possible example of intervention, American parapsychologist W.E. Cox (1956) cites data showing that on days on which trains are involved in an accident the level of passenger traffic is relatively low. Cox suggests that people subconsciously precognize the occurrence of train accidents and avoid traveling by train on those days. Again it is possible that railway accidents and low passenger traffic both tend to occur when weather conditions are bad.

If both precognition and intervention are authentic phenomena then on the basis of L.E. Rhine's data it would seem that the future is not immutable as some people assume. Rhine also argues from her analysis that information is not sent from the future back to the percipient but rather (as in other sorts of extrasensory experiences) the percipient is the active element in the situation, paranormally reaching into the future.

Few studies appear to have addressed the personality correlates of reporting precognitive experiences. Hearne (1984) reports experients to be more neurotic than the general population. He did not, however, recruit an appropriate control group of nonexperients. Also Hearne's experients obtained high scores on the personality inventory's "lie scale," suggesting the data are of uncertain reliability.

Spontaneous precognitive cases exhibit much the same evidential problems as other types of ESP. Nevertheless, because precognized events relate to the future it is possible to investigate their accuracy in prediction. To this end several "premonition bureaus" have been established, including one in London and another in New York. People who have a premonition are invited to register it with one of the bureaus before the precognized event takes place. Unfortunately for the proponents of the concept of precognition, the percentage of registered premonitions that prove correct is very low (Shadowitz & Walsh, 1976, p. 117).

Experimental Investigation of Precognition

J.B. Rhine began experimental investigation of precognitive ESP in 1933, although his accumulated results were not published until 1938 (Rhine, 1938). In one of these studies Rhine asked the gifted subject Hubert Pearce to endeavor to predict the order in which ESP targets would appear in a deck that was to be shuffled and cut *after* the calls were recorded. In a series of 212 runs an average of 6.3 hits per run was obtained. A second series of 223 runs yielded an average of 7.1 hits per run. Another experiment with a group of subjects produced a mean of only 5.14, but this was associated with a high level of statistical significance for the total of 113,075 trials completed by the subjects. These results are consistent with the idea that experimental subjects can foresee by paranormal means the order of a subsequently generated set of targets.

In J.B. Rhine's early studies it was the experimenter's practice to shuffle the ESP deck without knowledge of the order of the subject's guesses, thereby avoiding the potential criticism of having biased the shuffle. Rhine realized it might be possible for the experimenter unconsciously to use his or her own ESP to get information on the subject's set of calls and to bias the shuffle accordingly. Experiments on the so-called "psychic shuffle" added support to this speculation (Rhine, Smith & Woodruff, 1938). When the Duke laboratory staff constructed mechanical shufflers, Rhine (1941) conducted a further investigation of precognition and again obtained sup-portive data, although on this occasion only at the 0.03 level of significance. With the development of computerized and other instrumented ESP tests, significant data in precognition tasks have continued to be reported in the literature (e.g., Schmidt, 1969).

Some process-oriented experimental research has been directed to the nature of precognitive ESP but the quantity of data is very limited in com-parison to that for ESP in general. One of the few distinctive trends to emerge is for good precognition performers to be field dependent, or in-clined not to draw too strong a boundary between elements of the percep-tual field. There are only a few studies documenting this effect (e.g., Nash & Nash, 1968). Another single investigation suggests that females' precognition scores are on average lower than their clairvoyance scores while for males the trend is in the opposite direction (Zenhausern, Stanford & Esposito, 1977). The basis of such an effect, if authentic, is not known. Such other data as are available generally indicate that precognitive test performance has much the same characteristics as contemporaneous ESP.

A few studies have attempted to investigate the tendency in spon-taneous case collections for reports of precognition of more distant events to be relatively infrequent. Hutchinson (1940) obtained significantly lower precognition scores on runs for which the targets were selected ten days later than for runs for which target selection took place on the day after the test. This is consistent with the idea that the ESP "signal" becomes weaker in time. On the other hand the participants in this study knew which runs were to be checked after one day and which after ten days, so the data merely may have reflected the subjects' expectations. Also the tests for the ten-day condition usually were conducted last and hence the poorer scores in this condition may be nothing more than a within-session decline effect (Palmer, 1978a, p. 81). Another experiment by Hutchinson with these fac-tors controlled was not successful. Three other experiments failed to find any significant negative correlation between precognition scores and the interval between testing and target selection (Palmer, 1978a, p. 81). Although further investigation would be justified it does seem likely that people report few spontaneous precognitions of events set far into the future largely because the experience often is forgotten by the time the event takes place. The attenuating temporal displacement effects reported by Carington may therefore have been more a consequence of the nature of experient's information processing mechanisms (particularly in relation to temporal "focusing" on the target) than an indication of the temporal attenuation of an ESP "signal."

Theoretical Approaches to Precognition

Theories to account for psi phenomena in general will be surveyed in Chapter 8, but precognition warrants brief individual consideration for one fundamental reason: it is not merely that the hypothetical processes underlying precognitive experience are unrecognized in conventional science, but that these processes seem to fly in the face of one of science's central tenets. The apparent paradox in the concept of precognition is that it implies access to information which does not exist. In other words it implies a backward flow of information and this is contrary to the principal of causation, that a cause must precede its effect. Broadly speaking there have been four main approaches to the resolution of this paradox.

Some theorists maintain the paradox springs from the inadequacy of our commonsense view of the world or more precisely, the "naive realism prevalent before the development of modern physics" (Targ & Puthoff, 1978, p. 169). That the latter is inadequate is demonstrated, they argue, by recent developments in quantum physics which suggest, for example, the possibility of a subatomic particle with the property of moving backwards in time. Other parapsychologists reject the notion that the laws of subatomic physics are applicable to aspects of human behavior but nevertheless maintain there is no logical objection to backward causation as would be entailed in the flow of information from the future to the present (e.g., Beloff, 1977a). One of the difficulties with this view concerns the issue of intervention. Suppose that after precognizing a particular event the experient takes steps to prevent that event from happening. If these steps are successful the precognized event does not exist and hence there is nothing from which information can flow back to an earlier time. Under the above approach to precognition, therefore, intervention should not be possible. This in turn has implications for the concept of free will (Murphy, 1967).

A few researchers have sought to accommodate the notion of precognition by proposing more complex theories of time (e.g., Dunne, 1927). Our commonsense impression of time is purely linear: at a given moment we are at one point on a dimension linking the past, the present, and the future. It has been proposed that it is possible to move above this linear channel to another temporal plane where points in the past and in the future may be observed. The means of subjecting this and other more sophisticated theories of time (see Stokes, 1987, pp. 102–107) to empirical testing is by no means obvious.

Another possibility is that precognitive experiences merely entail unconscious inferences from extrasensory perception of factors that exist in the *present* (Morris, 1980, p. 22). For example, a premonition of the death of a loved one may be due to extrasensory awareness of such things as that person's present state of health or the unsafe condition of their car, or some other factor. This idea readily accommodates the occurrence of intervention. On the other hand, to account for the significant results in laboratory studies of precognition it would be necessary under this approach to argue that subjects are able to obtain extrasensorially some information about the experimenter or the test equipment that helps them to guess (at an extrachance level) how the targets will be ordered. What such information might comprise is not clear but proponents of this approach argue that assumptions of this nature are far less contentious than those necessitated by a literal awareness of the future. Experimental work on this view of precognition is beginning to be undertaken (Radin, 1987).

A further option is to reverse the ostensible causal relationship and argue that the precognitive experience in some normal or paranormal way causes the subsequent event. Thus the experience might be communicated extrasensorially to other people who unwittingly act on this information to bring about the incident. Indeed if the possibility of psychokinesis is taken into consideration perhaps the experient actually brings about the precognized event by psychokinetic means. In response to this approach it must be said that while there may be something in the notion of a self-fulfilling prophecy there are some precognized incidents it is hard to envisage as having been instigated by the experient whether by normal or paranormal means. Is it reasonable to suppose that a person who has a premonition about an earthquake or about the commencement of World War III can then actually cause these events?

These are just some of the attempts to resolve the paradox of precognition. Another approach is to deny the existence of precognition and to attribute the reported data to the operation of artifactual factors. For example, extrachance scores in precognition tests might reflect the experimenter effect: experimenters may use their own psi abilities to produce target series that significantly correspond to the earlier calls of their subjects. Certainly of all proposed forms of psi, precognition is the one that parapsychologists themselves feel most uneasy about. In part this lack of conviction stems from the data: among ESP experiments as a whole those on precognition have yielded the results closest to MCE and regardless of the significance level, precognition data thereby are the least convincing of a genuine paranormal means of access to information. Additionally, there is the paradoxical nature of the underlying concept. This is enunciated in an extreme form by McMullen (1978), who asserts the notion of precognition as incoherent because its definition is internally inconsistent: "the self-contradiction is the claim that something which does not exist can be directly known" (p. 19). The resolution of this issue nevertheless will come not through logical analysis but by way of empirical investigation.

Retrocognition

Retrocognition literally means "backward knowing" and is defined as direct paranormal access to events that occurred in the past. In this sense retrocognition conceptually is the obverse face of precognition.

An ostensible instance of retrocognition is the so-called Dieppe Raid case (Hastings, 1969; Lambert & Gay, 1952). In August 1951 two English women were holidaying in Puys, France (two miles east of Dieppe). A little after 4 a.m. one night both women were awakened by the sounds of heavy artillery fire, dive-bombing aircraft, and people's cries. This continued for nearly an hour and occurred twice more during the early hours of the morning. The sounds are said to have been similar to those which would have been audible at Puys during an air and sea raid on Dieppe in 1942.

The frequency of retrocognitive experiences evidently is very low (L.E. Rhine, 1981, p. 53). When Celia Green (1960) analyzed a collection of spontaneous case reports accumulated by the Society for Psychical Research, she found 166 were contemporaneous, 108 precognitive, and only 15 retrocognitive. Similarly, in a tally of extrasensory dreams that had been cited in the publications of the American Society for Psychical Research, only 4 of 372 were retrocognitive (Stevenson, 1963, p. 182).

The rarity of retrocognitive case reports could be due to several factors (Stevenson, 1963, p. 201). First, if the interval between the retrocognized event and the experience is short the percipient may be inclined to report it as a contemporaneous experience. Second, some experiences which might be construed as retrocognitive may be assigned to other taxonomic categories such as apparitions, reincarnation memories, psychometry, and spirit possession. If the retrocognized event occurred within living memory it is possible too that the experience will be construed as a contemporaneous telepathic impression (Sabine, 1950, p. 43). Third, and probably most important, both experients and researchers may discount experiences occurring after the event because of the possibility of obtaining the information by normal means. For example, the individual may have read of the event or seen a television program on it and have forgotten having done so; information about the event later may be revived from memory as a basis for an imaginal experience with a retrocognitive quality. People alert to the possibility of *cryptomnesia* therefore might not be inclined to make (or in the researcher's case, accept) a report on a retrocognitive experience.

Little effort has been made to subject the collections of retrocognitive experiences to content analysis, presumably because the number of such cases in any one collection was too small to justify such analysis. Forman (1978) proposes that retrocognitive experiences begin and end very abruptly, have a dream-like character, focus on some sensory modalities at the exclusion of others, and are specific to a particular place or object. Additionally, the thematic content of these experiences often relates to battles of long ago (Ellwood, 1971; Murphy, 1967, p. 4). The evidence for such generalizations nevertheless is limited.

There have been no attempts to investigate retrocognition experimentally, for the simple reason that no suitable research technique has yet been devised and indeed may well be impossible to devise. The problem in this regard is that if performance in a retrocognition task is to be scored there must be a record of the past event against which to check the subject's call, but if such a record exists it would permit the possibility of contemporaneous ESP. That is, the subject may have paranormal access not to the past event but to the existing record of it. While retrocognition is regarded conceptually by some parapsychologists as a feasible form of ESP it does not appear to be one that is open to experimental investigation.

Contemporaneous ESP, precognition and retrocognition can be described as the *receptive* aspect of psi in that they seemingly entail paranormal reception of information from the environment. Before examining theories of this process we will look at the other side of psi, namely the *expressive* aspect in which the mind ostensibly influences the structure of a physical system in the environment. The general topic of psychokinesis is the subject of the next chapter.

Key Terms and Concepts

temporal displacement
Carington
Soal
precognition
intervention
premonition bureaus

psychic shuffle
retrocognition
Dieppe Raid case
receptive psi
expressive psi

Study Questions

1. Compare the phenomenological characteristics of precognitive experiences to those of contemporaneous extrasensory experiences.

2. What generally is regarded as the fundamental paradox in the notion of precognition? Which of the conceptual attempts to resolve this paradox strikes you as the most satisfactory?

3. Consider the implications of precognition for the existence of free will.

4. What is the basic difficulty in casting the concept of retrocognition in an operational form?

5. Consider the following scenario. Euclid the geometer and mathematician of ancient Greece is known to have derived several theorems in plane geometry but the proofs of these particular theorems have not survived. A medium is selected on the basis that his or her own mathematics skills, as evidenced at school, were poor. On being invited to relate psychically to the golden era of ancient Greece the medium produces a proof of a geometrical theorem by way of automatic writing. Contemporary mathematicians confirm both the validity of the proof and the script's identity as the subject of one of Euclid's lost theorems. Would this constitute a definitive demonstration of retrocognition?

6. Compare and contrast temporal displacement in ESP with the phenomena of precognition and retrocognition.

6
Psychokinesis

To this point our study of parapsychological phenomena has focused on the "receptive" aspects of psi. Thus in ESP the experient acquires some information supposedly by some paranormal means. Chapters 6 and 7 consider the other face of psi, namely its "expressive" character. As well as acquiring information from the environment it may be possible for information to flow from the individual to the environment in a paranormal fashion. One form of such influence already has been referred to, and that is telepathy. In this extrasensory process it is said that information can be conveyed directly from one mind to another. As was noted in Chapter 4 little productive research has been undertaken in regard to the agent's possible contribution to ESP and consequently the authenticity of this expressive form of psi still is equivocal.

Another general type of expressive psi nevertheless has attracted rather more systematic research and it is known as *psychokinesis* (PK). The term "psychokinesis" literally means movement by the mind or psyche. That is, PK may entail observable movements of objects paranormally produced by an effort of will. More generally PK is regarded as any direct mental influence upon the structure of a physical system, whether or not observable movement occurs. In short, PK is a phenomenon of mind over matter. Psychokinesis and ESP are said to be the two fundamental forms of *psi*.

Spontaneous Cases of PK Experience

Many physical phenomena of spiritualist seances implied the existence of PK. Apports, levitation, spirit raps, materialization, and paranormal movement of objects in the seance room might be categorized as psychokinetic feats (Braude, 1986; Randall, 1982). More recently we have seen the spoon-bending fad inspired by Uri Geller, with many youngsters claiming to have produced distortions in cutlery, keys, and other metal objects by paranormal means.

Other people are said to have a similar power to influence the state of a biological system (psychic healing) or that of photographic film (psychic photography); these two specific expressions of PK will be discussed later in Chapter 7.

For the main part, ostensible occurrences of the PK experience in everyday life are rather less spectacular, as is evidenced in the following anecdotal examples.

Maurice Marsh has been a colleague of mine for many years and has a long association with parapsychology; he completed his doctoral dissertation on ESP at Rhodes University in South Africa. One time Marsh was testing a university student for ESP and found she was yielding some promising scores. This trend was appreciated not only by Marsh but by the student herself. One evening the student visited another member of the faculty (a social anthropologist) and described how well she was performing on the ESP tests. This particular staff member was concerned that his student might be wasting her time participating in such work and after some attempts at gentle discouragement became sufficiently exasperated to exclaim, "Look, the only thing that could convince me there is anything to this business [i.e., ESP] is if that picture fell down this very instant!" At the moment he pointed to the picture on the wall it fell to the floor. Examination of the picture revealed that the wire on the back of the frame had neither broken nor come adrift, and the hook upon which the picture had been hanging was intact.

A relatively common example of spontaneous PK experience is the stopping of a watch or clock at the time of death of a relative or friend. Of course, clocks and watches can stop through natural causes, but often in these cases the respondent notes that the timepiece had not wound down, nor was it broken (L.E. Rhine, 1981, p. 196). There also are cases in which at the moment an individual experiences a severe crisis a clock starts to tick after years of inaction (L.E. Rhine, 1963, p. 98).

In a case reported to L.E. Rhine (1961, pp. 223–224) a bulb in a floor lamp exploded. According to the woman who witnessed the event the light bulb "had been cold for hours" and there seemed no reason for its explosion. Intuitively she associated the incident with some sort of family trauma. A few days later she learned that at the time of the PK experience her brother's farmhouse had been destroyed by fire, apparently as the result of an electrical fault.

Another example was reported by the Swiss psychologist Carl Jung (1963, pp. 108–109). His mother heard a loud cracking sound from the sideboard; upon investigation Jung found that the blade of their breadknife had broken into four pieces.

The Phenomenology of PK Experience

Regrettably there are very few sizeable collections of spontaneous PK case reports and even fewer attempts to subject such collections to content analysis. Nevertheless, following along the lines of her work on spontaneous cases of ESP, Louisa E. Rhine has analyzed reports of PK submitted to the parapsychology laboratory at Duke University. The principal trends found in that case collection now will be summarized.

The incidence of spontaneous PK cases is relatively low. At the time Rhine conducted her analysis, she had on file over 10,000 reports presumptive of ESP and only 178 cases of PK experience (L.E. Rhine, 1963, p. 88). These data may underestimate the occurrence of PK. For example, in Palmer's (1979) survey of psychic experiences about 7 percent of the sample acknowledged having seen an object move without any natural mechanisms being evident. But with the incidence of ESP experiences at over 50 percent in Palmer's study, PK does seem to be by far the less common of the two fundamental forms of psi experience.

Again it is possible that this comparative trend is exaggerated by various circumstances. Perhaps people do not countenance the possibility of paranormal factors in physical events as readily as they do in mental events. The concept of ESP is sufficiently familiar that it may be used to "explain" certain mental events, but as PK is a less familiar notion it might not occur to the observer that a particular physical effect could have had a paranormal basis and the unaccountable event may soon be forgotten as "just an accident," something of no great interest. The meaningfulness of the event also may be less obvious in PK experiences. While the content of an ESP experience may have very clear links with an actual event it simply may not strike the individual that for example, the stopping of a clock had some connection with the death of a loved one. Further, in comparison with ESP, it typically is difficult in PK experiences to be sure that an undetected but natural cause was not responsible for the observed event. Finally, for some reason a "mind over matter" effect is much less credible than one of ESP and as a consequence the experient may be comparatively reluctant to acknowledge having had a PK experience.

Nearly all PK cases in Rhine's collection involved two people, one who observed the physical effect and another (usually some distance away) who was undergoing a crisis of some sort. In over a half of L.E. Rhine's (1963) cases the crisis was death. Typically the two people in the case were relatives or close friends so that one individual's crisis normally would have elicited an emotional response from the other person.

This might be taken to imply that the individual undergoing the crisis had used a physical effect as a paranormal means of communicating with the observer. This interpretation is challenged by Rhine. Her reason is that there are a few cases in which only one person was involved. For example, a clock may start ticking when the observer is in a state of crisis. L.E. Rhine (1963, p. 106) cites another case in which a man's watch stopped at the moment he himself died. In such cases there would not seem to be any "message" being sent to an observer. On these grounds Rhine suggests that even when two people feature in a PK case it might be not the distant friend but the observer who is directly responsible for the physical effect. It is hypothesized that the observer extrasensorially perceives the danger faced by the distant friend but rather than admitting this information into consciousness as an intuitive impression or mental image, the subconscious mind of the observer uses a physical object as a means of expressing the information.

Certainly the repression of information from consciousness is indicated in many instances. For example, in one case a woman was sitting in her office when suddenly she began to cry. Her employer repeatedly asked her what was the matter but she could not tell him, nor could she stop crying. After some twenty minutes a huge decorative vase fell off its shelf when no one was near it. Subsequently the woman learned that her father had died on the day of the incident (Rhine, 1963, p. 112). In such cases PK seems to reflect the defense mechanism of *displacement:* extrasensory knowledge for one reason or another cannot be admitted to consciousness and this leads to a state of tension which is released through displacement onto a physical object, a parapsychological version of frustratedly thumping the table with one's fist. (In some cases it is possible that once the tension is released via PK, the extrasensory knowledge may begin to break through into consciousness.)

According to Rhine's analysis it typically is the case that the observer is situated near the object affected and the person in crisis is some distance from it. Some researchers propose that this indicates PK is uninhibited by distance, but their interpretation assumes that the psychokinetic influence stems from the person in crisis rather than from the observer. As noted above such an assumption is questionable. It should be remembered too that there are cases of PK experience in which the presumed referent person was deceased. Forty-six of Rhine's (1963, p. 91) 178 cases were of this sort; usually they were construed by the experient as a sign of the referent person's postmortem survival.

There is some variety in the type of physical effect featured in spontaneous PK experiences. Objects may fall, or they may fracture without falling; mechanical objects may stop functioning or restart after a period of inactivity. Commonly the target object is part of the household decor, an object such as a clock, vase, mirror or framed picture. On the other hand this merely may reflect the frequency with which the respondent is in particular situations or the likelihood of the physical effect's being noticed or acknowledged. For example, few reported cases may be set in a shopping center because, firstly, observers may spend relatively little time shopping and, secondly, if an object falls from a shop shelf its original position is assumed to have been precarious and the involvement of PK simply is not countenanced.

The physical phenomena in spontaneous PK experiences are not likely to be hallucinatory, according to Rhine. She cites a number of cases in which the effects were seen or heard by several people.

Of the above phenomenological trends perhaps the most interesting from the viewpoint of research is that PK might represent a displaced expression of extrasensorially acquired information. Somewhat surprisingly this notion has received little attention in the parapsychological laboratory, although it has been explored to some degree in the context of recurrent spontaneous PK phenomena or poltergeist experiences (as we shall see in Chapter 10).

Although it could be said the consistencies in spontaneous PK case reports do testify to the authenticity of this phenomenon, there are many uncertainties associated with these reports as far as their evidential value is concerned. Several of these were discussed in Chapter 3 in the context of ESP. The factor of chance particularly is problematic here. How often do clocks stop and pictures fall at a time when a close friend or relative is *not* in a state of crisis? Unless we have estimates of such occurrences it cannot confidently be asserted that alleged PK incidents of these forms are beyond the realms of pure chance.

Further, it is even more difficult in PK experiences than in those of ESP to rule out the operation of "normal" causes. It is one thing to be reasonably sure that the content of an ESP experience could not have been acquired by normal means, but rarely can the experient or the researcher demonstrate that a supposed PK effect could not have been due to some normal physical process. Investigation of the authenticity of PK would require properly controlled conditions of observation.

In this light we now turn to a review of experimental PK research.

Experimental Research and the Authenticity of PK

Experimental PK research began at the Duke University parapsychology laboratory in 1934 when a young professional gambler walked into J.B. Rhine's office and claimed that he could influence the fall of dice purely by his will power. The two men then got down on the floor and began throwing dice. Although Rhine was not particularly convinced by the gambler's demonstration it did occur to him that dice throwing was an appropriate task to use in the laboratory investigation of the authenticity of PK (L.E. Rhine, 1970, pp. 2–4).

In J.B. Rhine's initial experiment subjects rolled a pair of dice with the aim of achieving a total in excess of seven on the uppermost faces of the dice. The probability of this event is 5/12, that is in a run of 12 throws of the two dice it would be expected that purely by chance the sum of the faces would exceed seven on 5 of the throws. A group of 25 participants completed 562 runs (each of 12 rolls) and yielded 5.53 hits per run compared to the MCE of 5, a highly significant result.

The first experimental study therefore was encouraging, but Rhine realized that the dice may have been biased and the data hence were inconclusive. To test whether the results reflected a bias in the dice Rhine repeated the study, first with participants asked to throw a score *less* than seven, and then with the target set at seven itself. Above-chance performance was obtained also under these procedures, suggesting that the initial result was not an artifact of poorly balanced dice.

Later studies utilized high quality dice as are used in casinos (where slight biases in dice could cause the casino proprietors to lose heavily). Additionally, the face to be thrown in a given run, the so-called *target,* was selected randomly. Methodological improvements also were made in the throwing process. In the early studies subjects held the dice in their hands and threw them against a wall. With throwing by hand some degree of "fudging" by the subject may be possible. Subsequent experiments relied on other means of releasing the dice: progressively these included tipping the dice off a ruler and down a slide, pulling a cord to release the dice through a shutter and thence down a slide, spinning the dice in a machine-driven, fully enclosed wire-mesh tube, and spinning the dice in a similar perspex device which contained baffles to make the fall of the dice even less open to artifactual manipulation.

L.E. and J.B. Rhine (1943) published a cumulative report on their PK investigations in 1943, by which time the controversy over their ESP work had died down somewhat (L.E. Rhine, 1970, pp. 26–27). The PK task became standardized at 24 throws of a single die; with the probability of throwing the target face on any trial being 1/6, the MCE was 4 hits per run. A number of PK experiments were conducted within this framework, primarily looking at the influence upon performance of various physical factors such as size, weight, and number of dice.

In the 1950s and 1960s interest in laboratory PK research tended to wane, although W.E. Cox in America and Haakon Forwald in Sweden pioneered a novel approach known as the placement method. In placement tests objects were released down a slide and the subject endeavored to influence the objects' movement towards coming to rest in a specified target location at the bottom of the slide. The placement of objects by chance

Figure 12. One of Rhine's dice-rolling machines (photo: FRNM).

factors alone could be calculated and thus it was argued that this type of PK test permitted an estimation of the amount of energy attributable to application of the PK "force."

The 1970s saw a marked resurgence of PK research. Several factors underlying this revival are identified by Stanford (1977, pp. 328–329), but the primary element of the revival was Helmut Schmidt's (1970a) contribution to the development of random event generators (REGs) based on radioactive decay and his use of these devices in PK research.

Figure 13. Schmidt demonstrating one of his REGs (photo: Helmut Schmidt).

The operation of an REG can be described (somewhat simplistically) as follows. In essence an REG comprises electronic circuitry connecting three components: a radioactive source (or in some cases a source of electronic noise, rather like intermittent radio static), a counter, and a visual display. The electronic counter has a clock-like face and its indicator can be stopped in any one of a limited number of positions (e.g., four), just as a hand on a clock may point to one of the hours. The indicator on the counter spins around the face at a very high frequency until it is stopped by a signal produced upon the emission of a particle from the radioactive source. The nature of the visual display (the only part of the apparatus open to the observer) is governed by the stopping point of the counter on each trial. Now, the interval between successive emissions of particles from the radioactive source is conceptually random, that is, theoretically it is not possible to predict accurately the position in which the counter next will stop. Hence if an individual can focus on the visual display over a substantial number of trials and in some way "will" it to change in a specified way to a level beyond chance expectation, a psychokinetic effect is said to be evidenced. The statistical randomness of the REG's output when subjects are *not* attempting to achieve PK effects must periodically be checked.

With REG technology current PK research is methodologically superior to that of the dice-throwing days. The REG can be interfaced with a micro-computer so that the targets and outcomes automatically are recorded and scored without the opportunity for human error. A huge data base also can be obtained in a relatively short period (e.g., Jahn, Nelson & Dunne, 1986). As significant data continue to be obtained under these more sophisticated procedures (Radin, May & Thomson, 1986) it would seem that there is a genuine phenomenon here to be explained. That this phenomenon neces-sarily entails a "mind over matter" effect as implied by the PK hypothesis is another issue. As is the case for ESP research, unless parapsychologists can demonstrate the nature of the channel for PK interaction it cannot be said that a "mind over matter" effect has been authenticated.

Process-Oriented Experimental Research on PK

By means of the techniques described above some experimental research into the nature of PK has been conducted, but the quantity and scope of available data are far more restricted than for ESP. Detailed reviews of the literature are provided by Rush (1977, 1982), Schmeidler (1977, 1982, 1987) and Stanford (1977).

If ESP and PK are to be regarded as expressions of some unitary capac-ity termed "psi" the comparison of PK with ESP becomes crucial and it therefore may be instructive to outline the trends in experimental PK research under the same sequence of headings used in the summary of the ESP literature (see Chapter 4). The following presentation draws in part upon Irwin (1985e).

PK Performance: Patterns and Improvement

Most of the data on patterns of PK performance are derived from the old research paradigm of dice throwing. In many cases it remains to be shown that the same patterns can be demonstrated under the methodo-logically superior REG approach.

The bidirectionality of PK: psi missing. In some experimental inves-tigations of PK (e.g., Steilberg, 1975), subjects have scored below MCE to a significant extent, that is, incorrect outcomes were obtained more often than expected by chance. Psi-missing therefore occurs in PK. Sometimes this arises in the context of a differential effect (e.g., Gibson & J.B. Rhine, 1943). The occurrence of "PK missing" in association with negative elements in mood or personality is not well documented (Stanford, 1977, p. 330 & pp. 345–348).

There seem to be no reports of consistent missing, or a trend towards producing one particular outcome when another is intended.

The focusing effect? In some of the early dice-throwing research at Duke University many subjects performed best on trials in which the target was a six. This may have been due to a preference for sixes acquired in playing children's dice games and thereby it would constitute a focusing effect. Again, a bias in the dice may have contributed to the excess of sixes: with pitted dice the higher numbered faces are lighter and hence these may tend to turn up more frequently than the lower numbered faces.

Position effects. One of the factors prompting the Rhines' publication of their accumulated data in 1943 was the observation of a decline in scoring within each session (L.E. Rhine, 1970, p. 29). This suggested to the Rhines that PK has an affinity with ESP. Like ESP tests, the majority of dice-throwing studies show better performance in the first quarter of the session than in the last quarter; within-run declines also were reported (McConnell, Snowdon & Powell, 1955; Rush, 1977, pp. 34–36). Critics (e.g., Girden, 1962) nevertheless continued to maintain that position effects in these studies were due to chance, bias in the dice, or nonrandom effects in the operation of the dice-rolling apparatus.

Subsequent research with REG methodology has not given much attention to position effects, although some experiments have confirmed the within-session decline (Honorton & May, 1976; Schmeidler, 1987, p. 19).

The differential effect. As with ESP, PK experiments featuring two contrasting conditions may yield contrasting levels of performance, often with hitting in one condition and missing in the other (e.g., Cox, 1971; McMahan, 1947).

Displacement? It is not clear that spatial or temporal displacement of PK can occur within a run of trials. In the dice research the identity of the target usually was changed for each run rather than for each trial; hence it would not have been meaningful to look for a displacement of PK onto the target for the trial after (or before) the intended one, since both trials had the same target. Nevertheless some researchers (Pratt & Woodruff, 1946; Palmer & Kramer, 1984) have noted positive scoring on the target that was just abandoned, an effect which is suggestive of temporal displacement. Braud (1987, p. 215) also asserts the possibility of spatial displacement, with significant scores being found for dice-face outcomes other than the intended one.

Among the more recent REG studies, Schmidt (e.g., 1976) has performed several experiments consistent with the concept of *retro–PK,* that is, the operation of a psychokinetic influence on a past event (or perhaps a future event's influence upon the present). The methodology used by Schmidt can be questioned on the grounds that its data also are interpretable in terms of a precognitive parapsychological experimenter effect.

The experimenter may unwittingly have used his or her own psi to select targets that would yield significant results in relation to subjects' subsequent efforts.

Clustering? There are no indications that PK "hits" tend to cluster together rather than being spaced randomly through the run (Stanford, 1977, p. 354). This is in contrast with Kelly's (1982) suggestions of ESP clustering. You will recall that the latter data are based on post hoc analyses and a direct investigation of ESP clustering has yet to be undertaken. Additionally, a trend toward clustering might be affected by the frequency with which the targets are changed, whether from trial to trial (as in ESP work) or from run to run (as in most of the PK research).

Improvement and the role of feedback. Providing the subject with trial-by-trial feedback does not seem to lead to an improvement in PK performance: scoring continues to decline within the session (Stanford, 1977, pp. 359–360). In the context of PK, Tart's argument for the importance of feedback therefore is not supported. Tart (1983) argues, however, that a prerequisite level of PK ability is necessary for his predicted learning effects to take place.

Target Variables

Among the target systems that have been used in experimental PK research are rolling dice, tossed coins, falling spheres, falling drops of water, spinning roulette wheels, and various sorts of video displays governed by an REG.

Physical aspects of the target objects have been given some experimental scrutiny.

In the older dice-throwing work the size of the dice had no significant or consistent effect upon PK scores (e.g., Humphrey & J.B. Rhine, 1945). Forwald's (1961) methodologically superior study did reveal die size as a factor in level of performance but the nature of the data suggests that size as such was not as fundamental as the extent to which the dice bounded and spun before coming to rest.

The die's density (weight with size held constant) or its component material has not proved to have any linear effect upon scoring. In one study using celluloid dice and lead dice of the same size, the former yielded significant above-chance scoring and the latter scored below chance to an equal degree (Cox, 1971). This differential effect occurred without the participants' knowing that dice of different densities were being used.

The number of dice thrown on each trial does not seem a pertinent variable at least in the physical sense (J.B. Rhine & Humphrey, 1944). At the same time, if only one die is thrown per trial a greater number of trials is required to yield a given quantity of data and as the test progresses the subject working with a single die could become increasingly bored, a situation which might well depress performance. There also are some complex methodological issues in the multiple-dice studies (see Kennedy, 1978, pp. 92–94 for an analysis).

In PK studies with electronically generated targets, a very high rate of target generation may impair performance (Schmidt, 1973), but there is evidence to suggest that this effect springs from the participant's perception of the tasks rather than from any intrinsic limitations of PK (Stanford, 1977, pp. 353–354).

In a study with pictorial stimuli Stanford (1983) obtained higher PK performance when the target slide had low similarity to other pictures that could be selected by the REG. Although "similarity" here was judged partly in terms of contours and thereby might be deemed a physical dimension, it also entailed some semantic interpretation of the pictures. Whether Stanford's data reflect purely physical or psychological target characteristics therefore is unclear. Certainly the variable of physical similarity or discriminability of REG outcomes warrants further investigation.

In REG research there also is some indication that PK scoring is not influenced by the complexity of the device which generates the target (Schmidt, 1974).

One physical characteristic which may influence PK is the *lability* of the target system. This is the ease with which the system can change from one state to another, or the amount of "free variability" in the system. In a series of experiments recently conducted by the American parapsychologist William Braud (1980), labile target systems appeared more open to psychokinetic influence than were systems characterized by high inertia. This is not to say that static targets are impervious to PK (see the section on macro–PK in Chapter 7). Again, it is feasible that Braud's results are due more to psychological than to physical factors: a highly stable system may strike unselected experimental subjects (consciously or subconsciously) as so immutable as to discourage attempts to influence its state.

Looking globally at the research on physical aspects of PK target systems, it would appear that such factors have little effect on PK performance except perhaps by way of their psychological impact on the participant. This accords with similar research into ESP. Further, these data suggest that it might not be appropriate to think of PK as a paranormally produced physical force. It must be acknowledged, however, that the scope of the PK studies in this regard has been limited. Faith may move mountains, but that PK can do so as readily as it appears to influence dice is a matter yet to be resolved conclusively. Braud's research also serves as a caution that there may be important physical dimensions yet to be explored in this context.

While on the subject of the pertinent characteristics of the target it should be mentioned that PK can occur even when the participant is unaware of the nature or even the existence of the target system. For example, in most REG experiments the subjects are asked to try to influence a video display and as far as they are concerned this display is the "target." On the other hand, it might be presumed that the point at which the REG system is open to PK influence is in the emission of particles from the radioactive source, a part of the system that is unknown to the subjects. Indeed the subjects may even be unaware that they are taking part in a PK experiment. In one study the uninformed participants were given either a boring task or a pleasant task according to the outcome of a REG situated in an adjacent room; the number of people gaining access to the pleasant task exceeded chance (Stanford, Zenhausern, Taylor & Dwyer, 1975). It seems then that PK is directed toward a *goal* rather than necessarily to the underlying physical mechanisms of the target event. This aspect of PK is particularly important in the context of constructing a theoretical account of the phenomenon, and it also offers a viable alternative to the view that PK operates like a physical force. The *teleological* (goal-directed) character of PK is discussed by Stanford (1978); see also Chapter 8.

Other Situational Variables

Performance in a PK task may vary with the physical setting of the experiment presumably by way of an effect on the motivation of participants. With psychological factors controlled, most physical variables appear irrelevant. For example, PK does not decline with increased distance between the subject and the target system, provided the subject remains unaware of the actual distance (Dickstein & Davis, 1979). There is one study in which PK scoring was significantly higher in light than in darkness (Gibson & J.B. Rhine, 1943), but in another study the reverse was observed (McMahan, 1947). Perhaps some subjects find darkness unnerving, while for others it is conducive to relaxation.

As with ESP the experimenter's motivation, attitudes and handling of subjects can have some bearing on the outcome of a PK study. Some evidence of this is cited in White's (1977) review.

A little work has been conducted on the states of consciousness most conducive to good PK scores. There are indications that a relaxed frame of mind is more advantageous than intense striving for an effect (Debes & Morris, 1982; Steilberg, 1975). Thus superior performance may be obtained when the PK task is presented as a kind of game. Passive visualization of the target also seems more efficacious than thoughts about imagined processes leading to the goal (Levi, 1979; Morris, Nanko & Phillips, 1982).

These findings are consistent with the idea that PK performance is facilitated by an unforced state of absorption in the goal of the task (Isaacs, 1986), although the occurrence of spontaneous PK experiences does not seem to be related to a need for absorption (Irwin, 1985b).

The number of subjects tested at one time may be regarded as a situational factor. In one early study employing the dice methodology, two subjects trying to achieve the same target face were more effective than when each tried for a different target (Humphrey, 1947). In another experiment the run variance was greater when the pair of subjects aimed for the same target (Feather & L.E. Rhine, 1969). Few of these so-called "help or hinder" studies have been undertaken with the more sophisticated REG methodology. An interesting variation of this approach was used by Schmidt (1985), with two subjects making *successive* attempts to influence prerecorded events by means of retro–PK; only the individual who made the first such attempt was associated with a significant effect. There still are too few data upon which to base a decision about additive PK effects across different people.

Subject Variables

Some studies have examined PK performance in relation to the beliefs of the experimental participants. A few sheep-goat experiments have been conducted but unlike ESP a belief in the possibility of PK evidently has little if any effect upon dice-throwing performance (Dale, 1946; Stanford, 1977, pp. 330–331). As PK is even more sensitive than ESP to the subject's level of mental relaxation, it is possible that the advantage of a stronger positive attitude to PK is offset to some degree by a concomitant increase in level of arousal. Nevertheless in one study with an REG-PK task, Weiner (1982) found a strong positive correlation between performance and belief in the existence of PK; this result was not obtained in her attempted replication of the experiment.

There is scant evidence that the subject's mood during the test affects scoring level although few studies have addressed this issue directly. Van de Castle (1958) reports that the expansive/compressive index of mood may be related to PK performance, although the data are weak and lack independent confirmation. Research on personality correlates of PK has not fared much better. Van de Castle's study indicated also that spontaneous people exhibit higher scores than inhibited subjects. Other studies suggest a negative correlation with anxiety (Broughton & Perlstrom, 1985). Few experiments, however, have sought to relate PK performance to major personality variables.

Some research on cognitive variables has been undertaken. Stanford

(1969) found that people tend to do better in a PK task when they use their preferred mode of cognitive processing; thus habitual visualizers achieve higher PK scores when they visualize the target than when forming free associations to the target. Another investigation by Krieger (1977) revealed a significant relationship between PK and a test of depth of semantic processing; the latter is a factor in establishing information as a secondary (long-term) memory trace, so perhaps PK is linked with long-term memory skills. Although there is some coherence in reported associations between cognitive style and PK performance it must be said that there are attempted replications and other studies that have yielded nonsignificant results.

The experimental literature therefore evidences similarity between PK and ESP in certain respects. But in other respects the parallelism is less clear. To be sure there are reports of people who are adept in both ESP and PK (Stanford, 1977, pp. 346–347), but this might be due to an attitudinal factor or the like rather than to any fundamental commonality between "two forms of psi." The principal difficulty here is that little research has been directed to the psychological dimensions of PK performance. Much of the current work, despite the welcome improvements in precision and control, still is concerned with the existence of PK and the forms it may take. More of this material is reviewed in the following chapter but at the present point it must be regretted that we are left with comparatively little process-oriented data from which to deduce the modus operandi of PK.

Key Terms and Concepts

psychokinesis (PK)
PK as a displaced reaction
dice methodology
target face
PK placement test
random event generator (REG)
PK missing
position effects

retro–PK
target variables
lability
teleological approach
situational variables
subject variables
cognitive variables

Study Questions

1. Define psychokinesis and describe the principal techniques employed in its experimental investigation.
2. Have you had a spontaneous PK experience? If so, did it exhibit any of the phenomenological characteristics reported by Louisa E. Rhine?

3. What trends have been deduced from collections of spontaneous PK case reports? What is the evidential value of such material?

4. To what extent do the patterns in PK test performance parallel those of ESP?

5. Is retro–PK a testable hypothesis?

6. Some people are inclined to think of PK as a mentally-produced physical force. What experimental findings cast doubt on this simple notion?

7. Suppose you throw a die 100 times, on each throw attempting to call the outcome, and the correspondence between the throws and the calls is statistically significant. How could you determine whether this result was due to ESP or instead to PK?

8. What is an REG and how do these devices work? What precautions must be observed in using an REG in parapsychological research?

9. The results of an REG-PK experiment might be construed as being due to precognition. Explain the rationale of this view. Might spontaneous cases of PK similarly be attributable to precognition? Conversely, might spontaneous cases of precognition be attributable to PK?

7

Special Topics
in PK Research

This chapter examines several issues some of which might be said to be on the periphery of PK research but which nevertheless have some affinity with the notion of a "mind over matter" effect. The issues to be discussed are PK and the parapsychological experimenter effect; macro–PK and metal-bending; psychic healing; psychic photography; and the electronic voice phenomenon.

PK and the Parapsychological Experimenter Effect

The authenticity of PK would add a new dimension to the parapsychological experimenter effect. As you will recall, if we assume the authenticity of ESP, investigations of the nature of psi would be faced with the possibility that before testing begins, parapsychologists unwittingly use their own ESP abilities to identify subjects and target sequences favorable to their hypotheses. If additionally it is assumed that the experimenter may have PK abilities, it is conceivable that these too could be used (even subconsciously) to influence the experimental equipment in such a way as to facilitate the production of data consistent with the hypothesis under investigation. Indeed the experimenter's psychokinetic influence might conceivably extend to control over the subjects' responses.

The potential PK component of the parapsychological experimenter effect may be considered in relation to some research into the parapsychological abilities of animals, a field called *anpsi*. A number of laboratory experiments have utilized an REG device to investigate the precognitive or psychokinetic skills of animal subjects (for a review of this work see Nash, 1986, p. 146; Rush, 1982, p. 100). A fairly common procedure here is to apply a moderate electric current to one half of the grid that forms the floor of the test cage. The particular half of the grid to be electrified on each trial is determined randomly by the output of the REG.

The objective of such a procedure is to see if an animal can use psi to avoid shocks to a statistically significant degree: thus, the animal might employ precognition to ascertain which part of the grid is to be electrified next and then move to the other section of the cage, or PK might be used to ensure that the current tends to be applied to the empty side of the cage. This procedure has been used with some success to evidence psi in various species including hamsters, guinea pigs, gerbils, cats, laboratory rats, and brine shrimp. Each of these species appeared able to prevent or avoid the electric shocks to a statistically significant degree.

A rather curious result, however, was obtained in an experiment conducted by Schmidt (1970b). The subjects in this investigation were cockroaches! And they too yielded significant data, but in the opposite direction. That is, the cockroaches received *more* shocks than would be expected by chance. There are many possible interpretations of this contrary result. Perhaps cockroaches are masochistic by nature and actually enjoyed receiving more than their fair share of electric shocks. The sample of cockroaches used by Schmidt may not have been typical of the species: for example, a group numerically dominated by neurotic cockroaches (?) may be inclined to psi-missing. Again, a plausible explanation may be contrived in terms of the parapsychological experimenter effect. Specifically, Schmidt could dislike cockroaches and therefore subconsciously have used his own psychokinetic abilities to influence the REG, ensuring that these creatures were punished for being objectionable.

It is not suggested that the data of Schmidt's cockroach study conclusively evince the parapsychological experimenter effect in operation, but the fact that such an account can be formulated illustrates the problematic character of the "parapsychological experimenter effect" hypothesis. If ESP and PK are authentic the results of *any* process-oriented psi research could be explained away in such terms. Indeed parapsychologists themselves are beginning to resort to this hypothesis in order to "account for" discrepant experimental outcomes. The experimenter effect represents a major conceptual obstacle in contemporary parapsychology.

Macro–PK

In the classical dice-throwing work the effect of PK upon the rolling die was not directly observable. The die could not be seen to move in a noticeably different way when PK was being "applied." The evidence for PK here was statistical, not perceptual. The same can be said of the more modern REG research. The PK influence upon the decay of the radioactive source (assuming that to be the physical locus of the effect) is not directly accessible to observation: we have no device which signals that particle

Figure 14. Cockroaches in Schmidt's experiment (photo: FRNM).

n_i is being emitted by virtue of natural causes while particle n_{i+1} is being helped along by PK. Psychokinetic phenomena which are discernible solely upon statistical analysis are termed *micro-PK*. The magnitude of micro-PK effects (like that of experimental ESP data) typically is small. The deviation from MCE while statistically significant is minor compared with that part of the average performance attributable to chance. Consequently this sort of experimental evidence is scientifically consistent with the notion of PK but is not very convincing at a purely emotional level.

For the latter reason, directly observable PK phenomena would be of considerable interest. Such phenomena collectively are termed *macro-PK*. Thus if it were possible to produce paranormal movement of a stationary object under controlled conditions the testimony of our own senses would be most compelling and the question of the level of statistical significance would virtually be superfluous.

Many of the alleged phenomena of the spiritualistic seance would be categorized as macro-PK. Levitation of objects and people, apportation of objects from distant locations, table tipping, and effects upon weights in a set of scales all involved observable physical effects of an ostensibly paranormal character. Many such incidents, of course, occurred under conditions that cannot be regarded as scientifically controlled. As increasing numbers of physical mediums were detected in fraud, reports of such phenomena became less frequent.

The revival of interest in macro-PK with static objects was sparked by a Russian psychic, Nina Kulagina, in the late 1960s. Films brought out of the Soviet Union showed Kulagina apparently moving various nonmagnetic objects by paranormal means. In 1968 parapsychologists attending an international conference in Moscow saw one such film and through contacts made at that conference several Western researchers arranged brief visits to the U.S.S.R. in subsequent years to conduct their own tests with Kulagina. The Soviet authorities evidently did not want to be seen to be encouraging parapsychological research and adequate laboratory facilities unfortunately were not made available. The investigations of Kulagina's macro-PK feats, therefore, were conducted either in her own apartment or in the researchers' hotel rooms, and to this extent controls might not have been of the highest quality. A number of reputable Western parapsychologists nevertheless have reported observing and filming movement of objects without finding the slightest suggestion of any trickery (Keil, Herbert, Ullman & Pratt, 1976). For example, in one instance Kulagina apparently moved a small glass that was inverted inside another inverted glass.

Because of the vagaries of international politics, parapsychologists have not been able to conduct the kinds of studies necessary to elucidate the nature of Kulagina's performance. Similar phenomena rarely are reported in the West. The ability to psychokinetically displace objects reportedly is possessed by a Frenchman, Jean-Pierre Girard, by Felicia Parise in America, and by Suzanne Padfield in Britain, but access to these subjects has been limited and few incisive investigations with them have been published.

The principal macro-PK phenomenon currently being investigated in the West sprang from the Geller affair. In 1973 the Israeli entertainer Uri Geller appeared on a BBC television program and by apparently paranormal means he bent keys, cutlery and other metal objects, and started allegedly broken watches. The authenticity of Geller's performance is a matter of much debate (as it must be with all folk who derive their living from such performances). Generally Geller has been reluctant to participate in scientific research, preferring the more lucrative television and lecture circuit. He has tended to be uncooperative in projects in which he has agreed to participate and curiously enough the few "scientific" studies

Figure 15. Spoons claimed by an Australian mini–Geller to have been bent paranormally (photo: author).

with Geller by and large have been methodologically weak (Targ & Puthoff, 1974; cf. Marks & Kammann, 1980). There are instances in which Geller has been shown to cheat and, of course, there are many magicians who claim to be able to replicate Geller's feats under the same conditions in which Geller performs (Fuller, 1975; Randi, 1975). Without adequate testing in properly controlled conditions it is impossible to validate Geller's psychic talents.

More important in the present context is the fact that Geller's performances have encouranged other people to try to achieve macro–PK effects. Many children, the so-called *mini–Gellers,* have reported to parapsychologists with claims of spoon-bending abilities. The majority of these people have been unable to demonstrate their alleged talents in the parapsychological laboratory and when given an opportunity to cheat, many (particularly the children) do so (Bender, 1977; Hanlon, 1975; Pamplin & Collins, 1975). Nevertheless there occasionally have been located individuals who are said to bend metal strips by paranormal means under laboratory conditions.

One commonly employed research technique is to enclose a metal strip in a sealed glass tube or other container and to invite the subject to distort the metal psychokinetically (e.g., Wolkowski, 1977). Another method used by the British researcher John Hasted (1981) is to attach piezoelectric sensors or strain gauges to a metal strip and record the deformation of the strip while the subject is under observation; a strain gauge is a filament whose electrical resistance varies as it is stretched or bent. There are reports from several researchers (Dierkens, 1978; Hasted, 1981; J. Isaacs, 1983; Scutt, 1981) that paranormal metal bending is recorded in these sorts of tests. In other attempts to authenticate this macro–PK phenomenon, nitinol wire has been used as the target material. Nitinol has the property of "shape memory": it is machined to a specific shape at a particular temperature and when bent by normal physical means it will revert to its original shape upon reheating to the critical temperature. There are some reports that certain subjects have used PK to destroy the nitinol wire's shape memory (Hasted, 1981, p. 38; Randall & Davis, 1982). Recently however, there has been a report that a permanent kink can be produced in nitinol wire by normal means (Couttie, 1986). The status of this element of PK research therefore remains uncertain.

Some research has been undertaken into the physical characteristics of paranormal metal bending. Metallurgical analysis of some specimens has suggested that macro–PK produces changes in the crystalline structure of the metal in many respects unlike that associated with deformation by normal means. Various effects are cited in this regard, including anomalous hardening, anomalous softening, loop dislocations, a churning-like distortion of the crystals, and chemical transformations (Hasted, 1981). Recordings from strain gauges attached to the metal strip suggest that the macro–PK effect involves a surface of action that moves along the strip and that may rotate about an axis in its own plane to produce twists in the strip (Hasted & Robertson, 1979).

Little investigation of the psychological correlates of paranormal metal bending has been undertaken. Informal observations suggest the importance of mental relaxation and passive attention rather than concentration (Hasted, 1981, p. 160). This characterization of the conducive state of consciousness is consistent with one report of an association between the phenomenon and EEG activity in the alpha band (Dierkens, 1978). Before the psychokinetic event however, some arousal of the sympathetic nervous system appears necessary.

Paranormal metal bending remains a controversial phenomenon in parapsychology. One source of difficulty is that comparatively few people are actively involved in this area of research and thus the standing of the research relies heavily upon the reputation of a small number of individuals; this is not to denigrate that reputation in any way, but simply to make the point that the acceptability of a phenomenon as authentic is in part a function of the number of researchers who have elicited that phenomenon in their laboratory. This issue is all the more cogent in light of the fact that one team of parapsychologists researching the "Geller effect" was deceived at least to some extent by two conjurors masquerading as psychics (Randi, 1983a,b; Truzzi, 1987). Despite the controversy, metal-bending research is important in two respects. First, by entailing an observable event it could offer more emotionally convincing evidence of the authenticity of PK than have most of the micro–PK experiments. Second, research on the temporal course of the metal-bending action may provide some insight into the physical characteristics of PK, an issue upon which other research paradigms have not been particularly enlightening.

Psychic Healing

Some forms of healing might involve an element of PK. Indeed, according to some commentators even conventional healing features psychokinetic factors. For example, in the evaluation of medicinal drugs it is usual to include a "placebo" control condition because patients who believe prescribed treatment will alleviate their illness often show an improvement attributable largely to that belief. Mental processes also are known to affect the body's immune system, a matter that is the subject of a new medical field called psychoneuroimmunology (Braud, 1986). It has been argued that placebo and other psychosomatic effects instance a "mind over matter" process and thereby can be construed as psychokinetic in nature.

On these grounds the distinction between psychic healing and other sorts of healing may be dubious. But for the sake of definition *psychic healing* is taken here to entail a mode of healing in which there is claimed to be a direct transfer of some form of energy from the healer to the patient. At a purely conceptual level psychic healing in that sense can be differentiated from orthodox healing, faith healing (in which the effect evidently stems from the authority vested in the healer), and psychic surgery (in which diseased tissue allegedly is removed without the use of surgical instruments). In discussing psychic healing therefore, the focal question is whether it represents a form of PK. That other sorts of healing could also have a PK component is not central to the inquiry.

Throughout recorded history there have been people who claimed the power of healing by "the laying-on of hands" and other paranormal techniques. Phenomenologically speaking, healers often report they feel such sensations as heat, cold, tingling and prickling in their hands while performing the healing ritual, and the patients describe a similar range of sensations as the healer's hands move around their body (Benor, 1986). Pain is the symptom most frequently reported to be ameliorated. Few healers, however, have had the objective effects of their practices confirmed by scientific investigation. One of Britain's most renowned psychic healers, Harry Edwards, was investigated by a psychiatrist, Dr. Louis Rose (1955). The study by Rose focused on 95 patients who claimed to have had their condition alleviated by Edwards. Independent medical records were available for only 37 of the sample, but these data indicated that the efforts of the psychic healer were of no substantial benefit in 34 cases. Only in three patients was there some sustained improvement that might conceivably be attributed to Edwards' powers; again, the observed improvement in these few cases may have been due to spontaneous recovery or to a placebo effect. In any event there evidently was a marked discrepancy between clients' claims of improvement and the actual medical evidence. Whether the results for Edwards would be comparable to those for other kinds of psychic healers is unknown. One study of a German healer also yielded an essentially null outcome, although there were indications that an improvement in the patient's condition is more likely if the medical disorder is functional rather than organic (Strauch, 1963).

Rose's research nevertheless highlights a problem in the investigation of psychic healing. As long as human patients are employed in the study it becomes difficult to rule out alternative explanations of any observed alleviation of illness. A "placebo" control condition might be incorporated in the design, but it is very difficult to ensure that the "psychological" treatment given to the placebo group is precisely equivalent to the presumed psychological component of the "psychic healing" condition, and further it could always be argued that the person administering the placebo procedure had unrecognized powers of psychic healing. Considerations such as these have encouraged researchers in this area to make use of animal and other nonhuman target material. It is assumed that animals do not form expectations of a treatment's curative potential in the way that human patients may.

Arguably the best research program conducted along these lines is that by Bernard Grad, an expert in experimental morphology at McGill University in Montreal. In the 1960s Grad worked with Hungarian psychic Oskar Estebany, who was said to have the power of healing by the method of laying-on of hands. A review of these studies is provided by Grad (1976). In his first experiment mice were placed on an iodine-deficient diet to produce goiters and then were divided into three groups. The experimental group was treated by Estebany: the healer placed his hands on the outside of the animals' cage for fifteen minutes about ten times per week. A control group of mice was kept in a similar cage but was left completely alone. In a second control condition the mice's cage was warmed by electrothermal tapes intended to produce heat equivalent to that from Estebany's hands. Grad found that the rate of goiter development was significantly slower in

the experimental group than in the control mice. A second experiment excluded Estebany from the vicinity of the cages. In this study the healer
merely held pieces of wool and cotton material that then were put in the
cage with the experimental animals. Untreated material was deposited in
the control mice's cage. Again the goiters on the control mice grew more
quickly than those on the experimental animals, suggesting that the intervention of the healer was beneficial.

Another of Grad's investigations involved the surgical removal of a
small piece of skin from the back of each mouse. The wounds on the
animals treated by Estebany healed more quickly than those of the control
group. A more elaborate replication of this study was conducted with controls on the size of the original wound, temperature and humidity of the
animals' housing, amount of handling, and other factors. Mice in the cages
held by Estebany showed faster healing than those in other groups; additionally, mice in cages held by skeptical medical students showed *less* improvement than other control animals.

Other psychic healing research with animals has not been so sound.
Watkins and Watkins (1971) required a subject to try to make one
anesthetized mouse recover consciousness more quickly than another control mouse; a significant effect was reported in several runs of their experiment. In some of the earlier runs however, the person who timed the
recovery knew which mouse was the target animal. Further, the selection
of the experimental animal was not random. Because there are so many factors that can influence rate of recovery from anesthesia, any future research with this novel design would have to utilize sizeable samples of
animals.

Consistent with the hypothesis of mental healing there is now a growing literature on the occurrence of PK influences upon the state of living
systems. This material is surveyed by Solfvin (1984).

A more process-oriented line of research in this area is of a biochemical nature. Studies by Sister Justa Smith (1968) and by Rein (1978) report
that enzymes kept in a flask show a significantly increased rate of chemical
transformation when held by a healer. Further work of this sort might
reveal the mechanism underlying the phenomenon of psychic healing. It is
feasible, of course, that psychic healing may function in several different
ways. For example, as well as affecting the body's enzyme activity a healer
may be able to exercise a direct influence upon organic tissue. Thus Braud,
Davis and Wood (1979) report PK effects on some biochemical processes in
human blood cells.

There is, therefore, a measure of experimental support for the notion
of a psychokinetic effect upon healing processes, but further investigation is required to broaden and strengthen the field's empirical foundation.

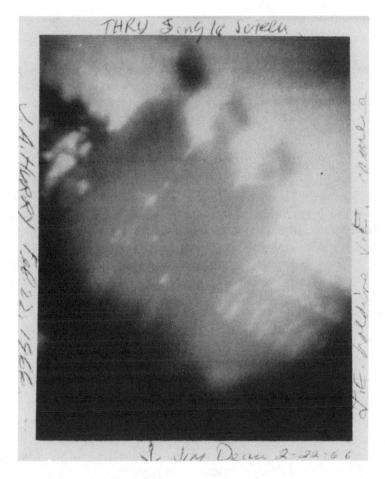

Figure 16. A psychic photograph produced by Ted Serios (photo: Jule Eisenbud).

Psychic Photography

If it is possible to influence paranormally the state of a physical system perhaps photographic film might provide a potential target material for such an effect. The psychokinetic production of an image on unexposed film or photographic plates is termed *psychic photography*.

Psychic photography arose historically from spirit photography. From the earliest days of spiritualism some people claimed that when they took a photograph of an individual, faces of deceased folk (often "identified" as the individual's late relatives) also would be found on the processed plate. Others purported to be able to photograph spirits that were summoned to certain mediums' seances. Several psychical researchers investigated these alleged phenomena, but the evidence for spirit photography was not impressive and in many instances clear proof of fraud was established.

Perhaps photographic effects said to depend upon spirit agencies were bound to encounter an antagonistic reception among serious researchers. But in other work there appeared to be evidence that living persons paranormally could affect unexposed photographic materials. Sometimes the individual's mental image seemed to have been projected on to a photographic plate, a phenomenon dubbed "thoughtography" by the Japanese researcher Tomokichi Fukurai. Psychic photography thereby came to be recognized as a field of parapsychological research that could be distinguished from spirit photography.

In recent years interest in psychic photography has been maintained very largely through the work of the American psychiatrist and parapsychologist Jule Eisenbud with the subject Ted Serios (Eisenbud, 1967, 1977). Under Eisenbud's supervision Serios reportedly was able to produce anomalous effects on unexposed Polaroid film. The typical procedure here was that Eisenbud would point the camera toward Serios and press the shutter release at the moment signaled by Serios. In some sessions Serios was permitted to hold a small tube in front of the camera lens; this so-called "gismo" became the target of criticism by skeptics (Diaconis, 1978), but even without the device, apparently paranormal effects on the film were obtained. These images included completely black or completely white photographs; fuzzy shadows and silhouettes; and pictures of varying clarity, some of which were of specifically identifiable objects. On many occasions Serios was asked to produce a photographic image of a target defined by the experimenter; some of the resulting prints bear an impressive structural resemblance to Serios's mental image of the target. Ian Stevenson and J.G. Pratt also conducted experiments with Serios.

As an area of research psychic photography remains controversial even among parapsychologists. In part this attitude is due to the small number of experimenters and subjects upon which the literature relies. A greater involvement of independent researchers would be needed to put psychic photography on a more sound empirical footing. Additionally, parapsychologists' unease over this area of research reflects the fact that fraudulent production of effects upon film is such a simple matter. Photographic technicians have revealed various methods of achieving results similar to the psychics' but by normal means. This has impaired not only the acceptance of the data by other scientists but also the readiness with which parapsychologists are prepared to conduct experiments on psychic photography: charges of being a "pseudoscientist" are hard enough to bear without becoming involved in an activity which is so open to the suspicion of fraud regardless of the care taken in conducting the research.

The Electronic Voice Phenomenon

Even more controversial than psychic photography is the electronic voice phenomenon (EVP). In the EVP voicelike sounds are found on a magnetic tape when they had not been present on the occasion of the original recording. The sounds generally are faint, isolated, very brief and banal phrases or sentences. If these sounds have a paranormal origin the EVP might be deemed an example of PK.

The EVP apparently was first noted by an American parapsychologist, Raymond Bayless, in the 1950s. Bayless (1976) was working with Los Angeles psychic Attila von Szalay and found "extra voices" on tape recordings of his interviews with von Szalay. In some instances these voices were quite loud and even appeared to be comments upon the recorded conversation. Similar instances were described by a Swedish film producer Friedrich Jurgenson (1967) and by Konstantin Raudive (1971), a Latvian living in Germany. Both Jurgenson and Raudive interpreted the voices as communications from discarnate entities, and Raudive in particular attracted much criticism which continued well after his death in 1974. The EVP has variously been interpreted by critics as misperception of electrical static, the unwitting whispers and spontaneous exclamations of people present during the original recording, and interference from radio broadcasts and short-wave transmissions (Ellis, 1975; Keil, 1980; Smith, 1972).

If PK can affect photographic film it does not seem altogether unreasonable to suppose that magnetic tape might similarly be affected. Perhaps it is on this basis that the majority of parapsychologists have doubts about the authenticity of both the EVP and psychic photography. The relative incredibility of these phenomena may stem also from the probably unjustified assumption that PK, while paranormal in origin, does behave like a mechanical force. While this notion superficially accords with certain macro–PK and dice-throwing phenomena it is more difficult to conceive of a mechanical-like force with such dexterity as to transform individual molecules of unexposed film or those of magnetic tape to produce respectively a finely detailed photographic image and a voicelike acoustic sequence. Perhaps a teleological model of PK is more accommodating not only of the more widely acknowledged PK effects but also of these more controversial forms. In the meantime, many more parapsychologists would have to become interested in the EVP before its authenticity could be said to have been tested adequately.

While some of the alleged forms of PK may be poorly documented it would seem that in many PK experiments there is evidence of a genuine effect. That this effect necessarily entails a "mind over matter" transfer of information is less clear. Discussion of the theoretical aspects of PK and of psi in general is undertaken in the next chapter.

Key Terms and Concepts

PK experimenter effect

anpsi

micro-PK

macro-PK

Nina Kulagina

Uri Geller

mini-Gellers

paranormal metal bending

Hasted

psychic healing

laying-on of hands

faith healing

Grad

enzyme activity

psychic photography

spirit photography

Fukurai

Eisenbud

Ted Serios

electronic voice phenomenon

  (EVP)

Study Questions

1. How would the existence of PK add to the complexity of the parapsychological experimenter effect?

2. What are the major sources of evidence for macro-PK?

3. Compare the research techniques used to study macro-PK with those for micro-PK. In your view, which of these two areas has generated the more convincing evidence for the authenticity of PK?

4. Discuss the methodological problems of research into psychic healing. To what extent did Grad deal successfully with these problems?

5. What evidence suggests that PK might affect photographic film and magnetic tape? Why are many parapsychologists dubious about such effects? If the effects were authentic what light could they throw on the nature of PK?

8
Theories of Psi

This chapter considers the major theories designed to account for the two proposed fundamental forms of psi, ESP and PK. It should be noted at the outset that attention is to be focused upon scientific rather than mystical theories.

Theorization has a crucial role to play in scientific endeavor. Empirical research does not achieve scientific advancement merely through the collection of data and the evaluation of isolated hypotheses. Understanding requires that the derived factual information be ordered, integrated, generalized, and interpreted. Further, to permit continuing progress, the hypotheses being investigated in isolated projects must be interrelated and coordinated, forming a gradual (albeit not always linear) kind of conceptual progression. These various functions are served by the formulation of a powerful scientific theory or more typically, a few competing theories of this type. Without such theories empirical inquiry achieves no more than a massive collection of piecemeal observations, and genuine progress is inhibited by the lack of any overriding conceptual momentum to steer ongoing hypothesis generation into purposeful channels. Ancillary functions of scientific theories are the prediction of new findings and the clarification of assumptions underlying a particular area of research.

The Australian philosopher Michael Scriven (1962, p. 104) has asserted that whereas psychoanalysis is all theory without any hard facts, parapsychology is just a collection of facts without any theory. At least with regard to the latter part of this comment the position is overdrawn, as there has been a good deal of theorizing about the nature of psi. The point of Scriven's assessment of parapsychology, however, is that the field lacks what could be called an agreed theory. Indeed many scientists ignore the efforts of parapsychologists not simply because the facts themselves are controversial but because the facts are not accommodated by any widely endorsed scientific theory (Beloff, 1972; Flew, 1980). Thus the development of a viable theory of psi is essential both to progress within parapsychology and to the acceptance of the field by other scientists.

In essence theories of psi have to address two basic questions: first, how is information mediated between the environment and the individual (in either direction, if ESP and PK are construed as reciprocal processes in this regard); and, second, how does psi come to manifest itself in the individual's consciousness and actions in the ways that it does? Most theories have focused on the first issue, that of mediation, as can be seen from earlier commentaries (Chari, 1977; Rao, 1978; Stokes, 1987). This preoccupation is understandable: if there is no clear conceptual appreciation of the mediational phase then the experiential phase might well be dismissed as fantasy or autosuggestion. This survey of theories of psi therefore is organized in three major sections: theories which address the mediational issue, those that are concerned with the experiential phase, and some that in a sense encompass both. Finally there is a discussion of the view that theories of psi are unnecessary because psi does not exist; here some skeptical interpretations of the available data are presented.

Theories of Psi Mediation

Electromagnetic Theories

According to some accounts psi is mediated by some form of electromagnetic radiation. In ESP this radiation is held to affect electrical activity in the brain directly, that is, without going through any recognized sensory organ. In PK, electrical activity in the brain is "transmitted" as electromagnetic radiation. Under this approach telepathy, for exTample, would be deemed a sort of "mental radio."

Two modern proponents of this view are the Russian I.M. Kogan (1966) and the Canadian Michael Persinger (1975). Each of these theorists proposes that psi is mediated by *extremely low frequency* (ELF) waves whose wavelength is so great that they are not impeded by walls or other objects in the manner that light and sound are. Persinger (1985) argues that the ELF wave hypothesis is supported by correlations between the incidence of spontaneous ESP experiences and low levels of geomagnetic activity, although Hubbard and May (1987) maintain that for statistical reasons current indices of geomagnetic activity are inappropriate to a correlational assessment of the hypothesis.

There are numerous objections to electromagnetic theories. If psi is mediated by electromagnetic radiation, both ESP and PK should obey the inverse square law as do other forms of such radiation; thus if the distance between target and percipient is doubled then the psi "signal" should be attenuated to a quarter of its original strength. That ESP and PK seem independent of distance casts doubt on this suggestion, notwithstanding the fact that performance on ESP/PK tasks is hardly a pure measure of "signal strength." Again, if psi tests were to be conducted in a Faraday cage which is designed to exclude electromagnetic radiation of certain wavelengths, then subjects' scores should be at chance level. In experimental investigations, however, this sort of screening does not appear to eliminate extra-chance ESP or PK effects (Eisenbud, 1977; Tart, 1988; Vasiliev, 1963/1976). The proponents of the ELF wave theory could argue that a Faraday cage would pose no obstacle to ELF waves because the whole cage would resonate at the frequency of these signals; on the other hand it is not clear how the experimental participant could sense and interpret these resonant vibrations.

Apart from the context of Faraday cages it has been calculated that direct cortical detection of ELF waves would require an antenna of considerable proportions, far larger than the human brain. The low information transmission rate of ELF waves and their poor capacity to carry information over a large distance raise further serious doubts about this form of the electromagnetic theory (Stokes, 1987, p. 115). An account of precognition under any of these theories would have to make appeal to the hypothetical existence of so-called "advanced" electromagnetic waves that can travel backward in time, but even this assumption cannot cope with the precognition of an event set even as much as one day into the future (Stokes, 1987, p. 127). It is difficult also to conceive of brain activity as initiating powerful electromagnetic radiation, as is proposed to occur in expressive psi: with current technology the electrical activity of the brain cannot be detected more than a few millimeters from the scalp.

Finally, electromagnetic theories do not explain what variations in the pattern of radiation are the cues to the identity of targets: for example, how does the radiation associated with a square on an ESP card or in a telepathic agent's thoughts differ from that for a circle?

The story of the fate of one ELF wave theory may be added here by way of a footnote. John Taylor (1975), a British physicist and mathematician, investigated the feats of Uri Geller and some mini–Gellers and came to the conclusion that these could best be accounted for in terms of ELF waves. The conservative scientific establishment was most critical of Taylor's involvement in this "murky subject," a factor which may have some bearing on his subsequent behavior. After some further research which suggested the ELF wave hypothesis was inadequate, Taylor concluded (Taylor & Balanovski, 1979) that psi phenomena (presumably including those instances he observed under his "controlled laboratory conditions") do not exist!

Energy Field Theories

Other theorists attribute psi to some other undiscovered or unrecognized form of physical energy (e.g., Wassermann, 1956). This energy is said to radiate from the individual as a *field effect* and mediates extrasensory and psychokinetic phenomena. The quanta of which the energy is comprised are so small that they do not interact with matter, and hence the energy field may pass through solid objects with no difficulty. Interest in these sorts of energy fields (e.g., "bioenergy") is greatest in Europe, particularly in communist countries, and in Japan; research with this orientation often is termed *psychotronics*.

One query to be leveled at this theory is that if the energy passes through matter unimpeded, how is it stopped and detected by the brain in receptive psi? One would have to suppose that the energy is not "stopped" as such but has its effect through an interaction with neurological processes as it passes through the brain, just as a magnetic field can induce a flow of electricity.

A more serious criticism is that despite efforts in psychotronic research there is no generally acknowledged demonstration that an energy with the required characteristics actually exists. In terms of theory building it would be legitimate if the energy field was purely hypothetical, but in such circumstances to fulfill the requirements of a scientific theory the postulated energy form still would have to be specified in such a way as to lead to novel implications that can be subjected to empirical testing. Energy field theories of psi unfortunately have not been markedly successful in this regard.

Elementary Particle Theories

It is possible that certain elementary particles may pass through matter yet also set up a field which interacts with the percipient's brain or with the psychokinetic target object to engender psi phemonena. Theories devised around this theme variously have nominated electrons, protons, neutrinos, tachyons, or hypothetical "psitrons" to serve this function. An advantage of the tachyon theory is that since these particles are defined to travel faster than the speed of light it is possible to accommodate precognition in this framework.

Again it is not clear how in ESP the central nervous system might detect these particles and use them as a basis for a perceptual-like experience. For example, given that we are engulfed by a sea of neutrinos, how would these particles' activity be affected in one way by a square on an ESP card and in another discernible way when the target symbol is a circle? And how would the brain tell the difference? Generally the theories of this type have focused on the physical characteristics of psi mediation and have taken insufficient account of how information initially could be encoded in the particles' activity and how the information could be extracted from this activity at the other end of the psi process.

Observational Theories

According to quantum mechanics a physical system such as an atom has an infinite number of potential states, and observation of the system is associated with its "collapse" into one of its component states. An American theoretical physicist, Evan Harris Walker (1975), believes the observer's consciousness or intention is responsible for the collapse and he interprets PK phenomena as instances of just this sort of effect. Walker explains ESP in a similar if rather contorted way: here the selection of ESP targets collapses in (partial) accordance with the "percipient's" consciousness of them. In neither of these paranormal processes is there held to be any transfer of energy; only information is transferred. As quantum state collapse is independent of space and time, psi phenomena are not related to these variables. Hence an experimental subject can affect the output of an REG irrespective of the complexity of the device. Even macro–PK and effects on rolling dice are possible because there are quantum processes occurring in individual atoms of the target object, according to Walker.

A broadly similar observational theory by Schmidt (1975) is couched in terms of feedback to a "psi source" or observer by which the probability of a given outcome in a quantum state collapse may be altered, depending on the "strength" of the psi source. In Schmidt's model, ESP comprises an influence upon the quantum indeterminancy of neural processes in the brain. The latter notion is developed by Jahn and Dunne (1983), who draw parallels between aspects of mentation and various dimensions of quantum processes.

An advantage of these observational theories is that they are formulated in mathematical terms. Theories of this sort are relatively powerful because they generate precise predictions and thereby are readily accessible to empirical assessment. The level of REG-PK research has risen sharply in the last decade, in part because of the questions raised by the observational theories. Although Schmidt's theoretical predictions accord with most of those yielded by Walker's theory there are some differences and this too has stimulated experimental investigation. For example, both theories maintain the dependence of a psi effect upon feedback of the outcome to the experimental subject or source of that effect (Millar, 1978); some experimental results (e.g., Braud, 1978) query this assumption, although it is difficult to be sure who the psi source really is and what manner of feedback is sufficient. On the other hand, PK performance is predicted to be inversely related to the presentation rate of trials under Walker's theory but not under Schmidt's. Experiments to test between the models on this score have yielded somewhat inconsistent results (Stanford, 1977, pp. 351–354).

One of the less satisfactory aspects of the observational theories is that they imply a quantum process may be affected by many observers at various times. For example, the results of a completed PK experiment conceivably might have been due in large measure to some particularly powerful psi sources who in the future get feedback about the quantum state collapse by reading the published report of the experimental data. The possibility of contributions by any number of unknown observers at any time is termed the *divergence problem*. That such an effect is possible has yet to be resolved empirically, although in one study Schmidt (1985) found evidence that a quantum process can become fixed after the first observation and thenceforth be immune to further PK influence. Recently Schmidt (1984) modified his theory to permit observation to be "complete" at some stage so that the quantum state collapse could not proceed beyond this point. Because additional PK influences by later observers would then not be possible the divergence problem is eliminated by Schmidt's amendment. In ruling out the occurrence of a further PK effect beyond a certain point in time however, the revised model essentially abandons the assumption of PK's space-time independence.

Another criticism of observational theories is raised by Braude (1979). He points out that they involve a closed causal loop. A psi effect supposedly begins with the observation of its outcome and this retroactively affects the quantum state collapse that underlies the outcome that is observed. In other words, in order to bring about an event through psi the occurrence of that event must first be observed. Walker (1984, pp. 282–283) responds to this criticism by arguing that it is misleading to apply everyday temporal logic to a quantum process; rather, under observational theories the observation and the quantum state collapse are aspects of a single event. A more practical limitation of the observational theories is that because the measurement of psi is so unreliable the parameters of the theories' equations are difficult to determine with any precision.

The observational theories have been productive of novel predictions and of research. Their validity nevertheless is yet to be tested effectively. It should also be said that some parapsychologists are uneasy about borrowing from theoretical physics some laws that relate to the subatomic world and applying them to human behavior and to macrophysical events. Whether this translation is best regarded as literal or as an analogy, or indeed is appropriate at all, must be answered by further research. Some of these difficulties would seem to be avoided in an observational theory recently proposed by von Lucadou (1987; von Lucadou & Kornwachs, 1980). While retaining many of the relational properties of the earlier theories, this model is formulated in the more general terms of systems theory rather than starting at the level of quantum events. Von Lucadou agrees that information obtained from a system can interact with the measurement process or "observation," but he does not think it necessary to reduce processes of the mind to features of the quantum theoretical structure of atomic systems. The merits of his approach still are under investigation.

Theories of the Experiential Phase of Psi

Assuming some means of mediating psi information between the (ESP or PK) target and the individual, there remains to be explained the experiential facet of the phenomena. In ESP, where is the information admitted to the central nervous system or information processing system, and how does the system deal with it? In PK, what manner of information processing takes place, and at what point of the system is it transmitted or emitted into the environment? As noted above, parapsychological theorization on these aspects of psi phenomena has been relatively limited.

Theories of the ESP experience will be considered first. The basic issue here is whether or not ESP operates in a sensory-like fashion, despite the absence of an obvious organ for extrasensory "perception." On this basis a distinction may be drawn between two approaches to the experiential phase of ESP, the *pseudosensory models* and the *memory models*.

Extrasensory perception popularly is spoken of as a "sixth sense," and in essence this is the theoretical orientation of the pseudosensory models. That is, although ESP apparently is not mediated by any of the *known* sensory modalities, perhaps there is some as yet undiscovered organ, a "third eye," responsible for the reception of so-called extrasensory information. Under this pseudosensory approach psi inputs would be processed by the mind in essentially the same manner as sensory inputs.

A means of assessing this model of ESP is to conceptualize the mind as an information processing system, to establish the stages of information processing to which sensory inputs are subject, and then to see if the nature of ESP performance conforms to the characteristics of these respective sensory processing stages. A detailed analysis in these terms is presented by Irwin (1979a; see also Irwin, 1978a,b, 1980a). The conclusion reached there is that the available evidence does not encourage the view that extrasensory information receives the same sorts of processing as a sensory input. For example, unlike a sensory stimulus, the sensory discriminability or "quality" of the ESP target (its contrast, size, form, orientation, etc.) has no systematic effect on ESP performance (apart from effects interpretable in terms of psychological reactions rather than discriminability as such). On current evidence, depiction of ESP in a pseudosensory framework does not emerge as a viable approach.

But sensory processing is only one mode of human information processing. Another is the ideational mode, in which the information processed by the system (or mind) is obtained not direct from the external environment but from within the system itself. For example, typically a dream or a reminiscence entails the processing of information that already is in the system, in the individual's (long-term) memory. Perhaps the processing of extrasensory information is akin to processing more in the ideational mode than in the sensory mode.

This possibility is encapsulated by the so-called memory models of ESP. According to the memory models, in ESP a trace (or set of traces) in long-term memory becomes activated and the information in these traces represents the foundation of the content of the extrasensory experience. The activated memorial information is mediated from a preconscious to a conscious level by the very same processes that characterize the normal operation of the information processing system in the ideational mode. Just how the memory traces become activated in ESP is unknown and is the subject of speculation: perhaps the process entails the passage of information from the ESP target directly to the relevant memory trace or, again, memory activation may be a nonmechanistic, teleological process (see the discussion of noncybernetic theories several paragraphs below). At the same time it must be said that this issue pertains to the mediational phase of psi rather than to the experiential phase in itself.

Memory models of ESP have been proposed by Roll (1966) and Irwin (1979a). In Irwin's version it is held that the activated memorial information is *structurally* similar to the ESP target. For example, if the target is a star, then memories relating to a radial structure (e.g., those for a star, a daisy, a bicycle wheel and so on) will tend to become activated. Among the evidence in support of this notion is the work of Sinclair (1930/1962) and Warcollier (1938/1975) in which selected subjects frequently drew remarkably accurate representations of an ESP target but showed little appreciation of its identity or meaning.

On the assumption that the systemic source of extrasensory information is in long-term memory a good deal of ESP data begins to become intelligible. For example, the models readily accommodate the known forms of spontaneous ESP experience (including even those rare cases comprising purely emotional reactions or purely semantic associations), as well as such characteristics of experimental ESP performance as position effects and psi-missing. The central assumption of the memory models is consistent with reported correlations between ESP scores and long-term memory skills. Further, an experiment by Kanthamani and Rao (1974) employing a task with both memory and ESP components suggests more directly that extrasensory processes are not merely *similar* to those underlying performance in memory tasks but *depend* upon memory processes for their expression. In addition to this empirical support the memory models are proving of considerable heuristic value in integrating diverse aspects of the experiential phase of ESP (Edge et al., 1986, Ch. 8).

The experiential phase of PK phenomena has received scant attention, primarily because parapsychologists have so few experimental data on the psychological (especially cognitive) correlates of PK. Theorization along these lines nevertheless is pertinent if only to encourage further empirical investigation. The possibility of incorporating PK in a memory framework is pursued by Irwin (1979a, 1980b). Essentially the proposed account is the converse of the memory model of ESP. Thus in PK it is suggested a long-term memory trace (or set of such traces) is active and by some means (whether mechanistic or teleological) a relationship is formed between the nature of the memory trace and the structure of a physical system in the environment. This approach has yet to prove as successful in its application to PK as it has been with ESP. One reason for this may spring from the theory's tenet that so-called receptive and expressive psi are in fact converse facets of a single process. Despite broad implicit endorsement of this idea by parapsychologists, and explicit attempts to argue ESP and PK are indivisible (Nash, 1983), the evidence for it is meager (Irwin, 1985e). Indeed a few differences are emerging between the performance characteristics of ESP and those of PK. For example, indications of clustering of ESP hits and the personality and attitudinal correlates of ESP performance are not paralleled in PK. These differences if confirmed and elaborated by further research would suggest the unitarian approach to psi has shaky foundations. There certainly is scope for further theoretical development in the domain of PK's information-processing bases.

Other approaches to the experiential phase of psi have not been expounded in adequate detail. There is some exploration within a neurophysiological framework, most notably implicating the temporal lobe as a neuroanatomical locus for psi experiences (e.g., Neppe, 1983; Persinger & Roll, 1986), but this has not yet been refined sufficiently to qualify as a model of the experiential phase.

Noncybernetic Theories

There is one more group of theories which might be said to address both the mediational and the experiential phases of psi. More properly they might be regarded as alternatives to the concepts of ESP and PK. These theories abandon the notion of information flow in psi phenomena and hence they are referred to here as *noncybernetic* models.

The best known theory of this sort is Carl Jung's synchronicity hypothesis. Jung (1955/1985) argued that there exists in nature a tendency for two separate systems to conform to a common structure or to coincide. This tendency, however, is held not to involve a cause-effect relationship. It is not a matter of one system's being physically linked to the other system and mechanistically causing the latter to conform with it in some degree. Synchronicity is not a causal process, it is *acausal*. When elements of the two systems coincide, this "just happens" as a characteristic of the natural world. Hence a series of ESP targets may show extrachance agreement with a subject's set of calls not because of any transfer of information between targets and the person's mind but because of this acausal tendency of synchronicity. The phenomena of PK are explained similarly. In short, psi experiences are instances of synchronicity or meaningful coincidence.

For people socially conditioned to structure their world conceptually in terms of cause and effect, the notion of acausal relationships is difficult to appreciate. Not unexpectedly Jung's hypothesis has met with a measure of criticism. The British philosopher Antony Flew (1953) has argued it is nonsensical to speak of a "meaningful coincidence" because this is tautological: a situation is a coincidence only because the association between the two separate events is meaningful and thus the coincidence is defined, not accounted for, by its meaningfulness.

Also meaningfulness is a subjective matter: what is meaningful to one person is not so to another. It is difficult to credit the existence of a tendency in the physical world such that a certain situation arises simply because one particular person would find meaning in that situation. The alternative to this interpretation of synchronicity is to suppose that there exists some ultrahuman domain of meaningfulness, where meaning in a coincidence of events is defined in objective terms independent of people's culture and personal history. More crucially perhaps for parapsychological research, if ESP and PK are acausal events then there is no point in conducting experiments on the phenomena: manipulating conditions in such a way as to elicit psi necessarily implies a causal process (Beloff, 1972, 1977b). If a "synchronistic" relationship is shown to be more likely to occur in some situations or with certain sorts of people the relationship may be said to be governed by these situational and personalistic variables and thereby cannot be acausal.

In that synchronicity does not imply any flow of information between mind and target in a psi task, it could be argued that it is not an explanation of ESP and PK but an alternative to these concepts. That is, since ESP and PK have been *defined* in terms of information flow they cannot be attributed to synchronicity; rather they would be supplanted by Jung's hypothesis (if the evidence warranted doing so). Another theory that abandons the assumption of information flow is Rex Stanford's (1978) conformance theory. Unlike synchronistic accounts the conformance theory proposes that the link between targets and mind is causal but is not physically mediated as often implied in the information-flow or cybernetic approach. Stanford depicts the causal relationship in terms of the *goal* that the relationship achieves; it could be said that the formation of the relationship is a teleological process. Psi therefore is viewed as organizing loose, chaotic or random processes such that their outcomes accord with the dispositions of someone who (or some organism which) has an interest in those outcomes. A similar model is presented by Ballard (1987).

Noncybernetic models do offer a simple account of psi's evident independence of physical variables such as size, distance, and time. Admittedly scientists are so wedded to explanations in terms of physical or mechanistic causes that the teleological approach is unlikely to appeal to people outside the field of parapsychology (or for that matter to many people within this field). But the viability of a theory must be based on its performance in explanation and prediction, not simply on the conditioned emotions it evokes among conventional scientists. Unlike the synchronicity hypothesis the conformance model is open to empirical testing and thereby is admissible as a scientific theory.

Only time will tell if teleological causation provides a satisfactory account of the characteristics of psi. Stanford's model nevertheless does require supplementation in regard to the experiential phase of psi. All it has to offer here are the ideas that the overall process is goal-oriented and that information does not actually enter or leave the information processing system. The model provides no other explanation of the personalistic and situational correlates of psi performance. In this light the conformance model and a memory model could usefully be treated as complementary; of course memory models do not demand the assumption of teleological processes and would sit happily in conjunction with various models of psi mediation.

Skeptical Theories of Psi Phenomena

To this point the analysis has focused on theories that seek to explain the paranormal mediation of information between an individual and the environment and the means by which this information is utilized as the basis of a parapsychological experience. Skeptics on the other hand maintain there is no need to devise any theory of paranormal processes because the available data can be accommodated satisfactorily by appeal to "normal" or conventionally recognized factors.

Under a skeptical approach all spontaneous psi experiences are attributed to such processes as misperception, misinterpretation, inaccurate recall of events, deception, and coincidence. The feasibility of these accounts of individual experiences was surveyed in Chapter 3 and generally is acknowledged by parapsychologists themselves. The central issue for the skeptic therefore is the explanation of the experimental psi data. As noted in Chapter 4 the common assumption here is that the data are variously an artifact of procedural flaws, a freak outcome of chance, or a product of fraud. In the critics' view this is supported by the reportedly low level of replicability of the data and by the fact that there is no definitive psi experiment, none that is immune to claims of actual or potential methodological deficiencies.

At the same time it is possible to maintain that the data of psi experiments attest to a genuine phenomenon (as opposed to an artifact) but that this underlying phenomenon is a normal process rather than psi. Most skeptics have been so intent on dismissing the data that they have given little thought to the development of a theory to account for any valid effect yielded by psi research. One skeptical theory that did take the data seriously was proposed by Goodfellow (1938, 1940).

Goodfellow's argument, originally applied to the data of an ESP experiment conducted during a series of weekly broadcasts by the Zenith Radio Corporation late in 1937, was that the extrachance correspondence between ESP targets and calls was due purely to nonrandomness in the subjects' selection of calls. When people try to produce any random series (such as in guessing the identities of a random series of ESP symbols) they may in fact show various biases in their responses. Some symbols may be called much more frequently than others; calling the same symbol two or more times in succession may be avoided to the extent that such strings appear more rarely than in a truly random series; and other idiosyncratic sequential interdependencies may arise, such as a tendency to call "circle" immediately after a call of "square." The nonrandomness in the ESP subject's calls is responsible for the deviation of the number of hits from that expected under a random-guessing statistical model, according to Goodfellow.

Can this theory account for the observed correlates of experimental ESP performance? That is, does the tendency to produce a nonrandom series of responses have the same pattern of correlates as ESP scores? Presumably the extent of nonrandomness in a set of calls would be little dependent upon the distance of the targets from the subject, the presence of intervening physical barriers, the size and orientation of the targets, and similar physical variables.

Call randomness may be affected by the subject's mood (Stanford, 1975, p. 156). With regard to attitudinal variables, sheep (believers in ESP) have a poorer understanding of statistical probability than do goats or disbelievers (Blackmore & Trościanko, 1985), so the sheep-goat effect reported in the ESP literature conceivably could reflect nonrandomness of guesses (although the data of Blackmore and Trościanko do not go so far as to confirm this).

Like ESP scores, nonrandomness of response sequences correlates negatively with mathematical education and short-term memory (Tune, 1964) and is subject to experimenter effects (Gault & Goodfellow, 1940).

On the other hand, other correlates of nonrandomness seem to be contrary to those of ESP performance. For example, nonrandomness correlates positively with neuroticism (Wagenaar, 1972) and with age (Tune, 1964).

It would be thought too that the identified psi-conducive states of consciousness would work to facilitate response spontaneity rather than to encourage nonrandomness. Perhaps some account needs to be taken of the *type* of nonrandomness in response series. A given psychological variable might well be related positively to one style of nonrandomness and negatively to another.

The importance of distinguishing types of nonrandomness becomes evident when the issue of psi-missing is countenanced in the context of Goodfellow's approach. Both psi-hitting and psi-missing entail deviations from chance but their contrasting direction signals the insufficiency of an undifferentiated concept of nonrandomness as an explanation of ESP scores. Different styles of nonrandomness have indeed been found in association with psi-hitting and missing; Morris and Cohen (1971) found subjects who rarely called the same symbol twice in succession in ESP tests achieved psi-hitting and those who frequently called doubles showed psi-missing. On these grounds, if a psychological variable reportedly correlates in one direction with ESP scores and in the other direction with response nonrandomness, this might not be contrary to Goodfellow's theory but instead be a mere consequence of the selected index of nonrandomness. That ESP and nonrandomness show so many of the same correlates (when direction is ignored) might be taken, therefore, as encouraging for the spirit of Goodfellow's theory.

A relatively direct test of the theory may be considered. In Goodfellow's opinion the extrachance scores yielded by an ESP experiment stem from the comparison of a nonrandom series (the subject's calls) to a random series (the targets). The effect therefore should be evident regardless of the choice of the random series against which the comparison is made; that is, extrachance scores should be equally likely whether the calls are scored against the actual targets used for that individual or against some other run of ESP symbols not even used as targets in the experiment. But when ESP calls are compared to symbols for which they were not intended the correspondence is found to be at the level of chance (e.g., Greenwood, 1938). (Appeal to the parapsychological experimenter effect to excuse such a finding of course is inappropriate because Goodfellow's theory would not admit any manner of parapsychological influence.) This represents a substantial empirical stumbling-block for the approach advocated by Goodfellow. In the view of some parapsychologists a further cause for unease may be that the theory is applicable only to ESP and not at all to PK; in a PK experiment the subject does not generate the series of targets and thus psychological sources of nonrandomness are not a pertinent issue.

Other skeptical theories of the psi data have not been developed in detail. Spencer-Brown (1953) has argued that scientific understanding of chance processes may be flawed and that the data thought to attest to psi are therefore nothing more than a consequence of inappropriate notions about chance expectation. This argument has yet to be shown to accommodate the observed pattern of correlates of psi performance. Because probability theory has been widely applied in scientific fields other than parapsychology, even skeptics are loath to pursue Spencer-Brown's suggestion.

Contemporary skeptics generally do not believe the psi data attest to any phenomenon, paranormal or otherwise. Thus the anomalous data are dismissed as unworthy of consideration because of the perceived possibility of fraud (e.g., Hansel, 1966, 1980) or because of claimed procedural errors (e.g., Diaconis, 1978; Hyman, 1985). In that these views deny the existence of any nonartifactual effect they are strictly speaking not theories of psi. Further, they are not open to falsification. In the unlikely event there was a psi experiment for which the skeptic was at a loss to identify openings for fraud or procedural shortcomings it would not prove that an effect could occur in the absence of these artifacts: the latter might exist without being immediately obvious.

There remains a demand for other skeptical theories that address the psi data as indicative of a valid but nonparapsychological effect. The debate over the authenticity of psi is best conducted not by skeptics' seeking to "explain away" the data but by the construction of skeptical theories that generate predictions capable of being pitted against those of the parapsychological models. Such theoretical development would have the fruitful effects of sharpening the assumptions underlying the authenticity issue and encouraging critical empirical investigation of them.

These then are the major types of theory designed to explain psi; some additional approaches, including more mystical accounts, are described by Chari (1977), Rao (1978) and Stokes (1987). Probably a fair if sweeping summary assessment of the position is that older accounts are either not viable or relatively inaccessible to empirical scrutiny, while the more recent models have yet to be given sufficiently exhaustive empirical evaluation for their viability to be assessed. Nevertheless the sophistication of recent theories may signal that the time is near when it will be inappropriate to describe parapsychology as "a set of facts in search of a theory."

Key Terms and Concepts

mediational phase
experiential phase

electromagnetic theories
ELF waves

inverse square law
energy field theories
bioenergy
psychotronics
elementary particle theories
observational theories
pseudosensory models

memory models
noncybernetic models
synchronicity
acausal phcnomena
conformance theory
teleological
skeptical theories

Study Questions

1. What are the functions to be served by a theory in parapsychology?

2. Outline the major types of theory designed to explain the way in which psi is mediated. What objections to each type may be raised?

3. What is the fundamental objective of theories of the experiential phase of psi? Given the range of theories of the mediational phase of psi, are experiential models even necessary?

4. Two noncybernetic models of psi have been formulated by Jung and Stanford respectively. Compare these theories and comment on their capacity to explain what is known about psi.

5. What contributions to parapsychology can be made by skeptical theories of psi phenomena?

9

The Survival Hypothesis

The three classical domains of parapsychological research are ESP, PK, and the postmortem survival hypothesis. This chapter is concerned with a general introduction to survival research; subsequent chapters will discuss in more depth some topics in parapsychological research which originally were motivated by interest in the survival hypothesis but which now attract research effort in their own right.

The survival hypothesis concerns the notion that a disembodied consciousness or some such discarnate element of human personality might survive bodily death at least for a time. The survival hypothesis has obvious religious connotations but these are of no concern in scientific parapsychology. Further, it should be noted that survival does not necessarily imply immortality or eternal existence as promoted in many religious systems (Thouless, 1979).

Mediumship and the Survival Hypothesis

You will recall that the early activities of the Society for Psychical Research were concerned fundamentally with the issue of discarnate survival. The SPR's investigation of phenomena of the seance room and the collection of cases of spontaneous psychic experiences were designed largely to accumulate empirical data upon which the survival hypothesis might be assessed. Indeed the development of interest in ESP to some degree grew from survival research: ESP was seen to be a possible mode of interaction with the "spirit world" or as an artifact in mediums' acquisition of information that was presented as if gathered from discarnate personalities. Spiritualistic mediumship thus stands as an historically important component of survival research. Evidentially speaking the most notable seance phenomena bearing on the survival hypothesis have been proxy sittings, "drop-in" communicators, xenoglossy, and cross-correspondences.

Proxy Sittings

As mentioned above, one of the problems with so-called spirit communications as evidence for survival is that the medium could be held to
have obtained the reported information telepathically from one or more of
the sitters at the seance rather than from any discarnate personality. One
methodological device to circumvent the possibility of ESP from sitters entails the use of *proxy sitters*. That is, a sitter asks the medium to contact
the spirits for information known only to some third party who is not present at the seance. There are some notable cases of successful proxy sittings
in which the medium cited specific data not familiar to any of the sitters but
which were verified on subsequent consultation with the absent party (e.g.,
Saltmarsh, 1930–1931; Thomas, 1932–1933).

An objection to proxy sittings as a source of support for the survival
hypothesis is that we simply do not know the limits of ESP. For some parapsychologists it is not inconceivable that the medium could use ESP to
"reach out" to any sources, including the absent person, from which or
from whom the required information may be gleaned. This account of the
evidence from proxy sittings assumes that it is not necessary for the medium
to know either the identity or the location of pertinent sources in order to
achieve extrasensory contact with them; such an interpretation consequently is known as the *super–ESP hypothesis* (Gauld, 1961). In support of
this idea it may be noted that some ostensible spirit communications do appear to have entailed unintentional extrasensory contact with a living
source (e.g., Dallas, 1924).

"Drop-in" Communicators

A "drop-in" communicator is an apparently discarnate personality
who intrudes uninvited upon a seance yet is not known to either the medium
or the sitters. If the drop-in communicator provides information with
which the sitters are unfamiliar and this information subsequently proves
accurate, it can be argued that the survival hypothesis is enhanced because
the medium here could not have relied upon telepathic contact with the sitters as the basis for the communicated material.

An appeal to the super–ESP hypothesis again might be made as an
alternative to the survival interpretation of this phenomenon. That is, the
medium conceivably may have used ESP to acquire data from any source
about any deceased person; in the dissociated state of the mediumistic
trance these data then would form the subconscious informational foundation for a dramatized "spirit" communication. Additionally, while
acknowledging there are some impressive reports of drop-in communi-

cators (Gauld, 1982, Ch. 5), it is difficult if not impossible to demonstrate that the medium could not have had access by normal means to the communicated information at some time prior to the seance; because the experimenter has no *a priori* control over the identity of the drop-in communicator the operation of fraud or cryptomnesia remain potential interpretations of these seance communications. The failure to rule out such optional accounts means that the phenomenon of drop-in communicators cannot constitute conclusive evidence for the survival hypothesis.

Xenoglossy

There are some rare instances in which it appears a discarnate personality communicates to a medium some skill the personality demonstrably possessed while alive but which the medium does not have. One type of such case is termed xenoglossy: here the medium speaks, writes or understands a language known by the deceased communicator and yet, as far as can be ascertained, the medium has never had the opportunity to learn that language. A few cases of mediumistic xenoglossy have been documented in the literature (Gauld, 1982, pp. 101–107; Stevenson, 1974, Ch. 1), although the thoroughness of their investigations generally tends to have been insufficient.

The significance of these cases is that if they are authentic, the super–ESP hypothesis might be held to be hard pressed to accommodate them. Is it really possible for a medium to acquire by the sole means of ESP the vocabulary, pronunciation and grammar of a foreign language? Strictly speaking the answer to this question is that parapsychologists do not know; but if ESP can service such a skill, the informational bounds of ESP must virtually be limitless. For this reason the survival hypothesis looks increasingly viable to some parapsychologists. Once again, however, there is the substantial problem of excluding fraud by the medium as another explanation of xenoglossy in seance communications.

The Cross-Correspondences

Three early leaders of the SPR, Myers, Gurney and Henry Sidgwick, died within a short period of one another, and reports soon began to appear that several mediums were receiving communications from these three deceased personalities. The material thus communicated, particularly in the first decade of this century, became quite voluminous (Saltmarsh, 1938). Of primary interest is that there seem to be certain correspondences between the messages received by different mediums.

Now Myers, Gurney and Sidgwick were classical scholars and the scripts of the seance communications contain many classical references and allusions. Some correspondences between the scripts of independent mediums comprise merely the same obscure word or phrase. But others were much more complex and subtle. For example, two seemingly meaningless messages would be obtained by different mediums and then a third medium would receive some key or clue which enabled the meaningless items to be connected in an allusive yet meaningful way, rather like fitting together pieces of a jigsaw puzzle.

Some psychical researchers (e.g., Piddington, 1908) deemed the cross-correspondences to be evidence that communications received by different mediums in fact came from a common discarnate source and that this source was capable of highly intelligent and creative activity in devising these correspondences. Other parapsychologists (e.g., Podmore, 1910) have suggested one of the mediums, a Mrs. Verrall, had a classical education and could therefore have devised the series of cross-correspondences at a subconscious level, then extrasensorially communicated the pieces of the puzzle to the other mediums; the cross-correspondences continued, however, well after Verrall's death. At the same time a hypothesis of some form of ESP or super–ESP from living sources might conceivably accommodate the cross-correspondence data. Additionally, the material of the cross-correspondences data is very complex and to this extent its evidential value for the survival hypothesis is not readily gauged.

Two Experimental Tests of the Survival Hypothesis

Two tests of survival were proposed subsequently in the context of the performances of mediums. The proposals are Thouless's (1946) "cipher test" and Ian Stevenson's (1968) "combination lock test."

The first of these entails a passage of prose translated into code; the passage can be deciphered only by use of a key word or phrase that is known solely by the person who designs the code. During the lifetime of that person others are invited to use either ESP or cryptographic techniques to discover the key and thereby decipher the passage. If they are unable to do so and an alleged postmortem communication from the spirit of the test designer conveys the correct key to a medium, the notion of survival may be held to be supported. Researchers had a long wait for the opportunity to enact Thouless's own instances of the cipher test; having published his coded passages in 1946 Thouless died in 1984 at the age of 90. The SPR and another group immediately invited people (presumably with the aid of Thouless's discarnate personality) to name the clue that would decode the sequences. To date no effective solution has been forthcoming; moreover,

Berger (1984) has shown that for Thouless's method of encipherment there may be no unique key. Several different keys might decode such a sequence if it is relatively short. A medium's identification of a key decoding one of Thouless's passages therefore would not demonstrate that this was the key intended by Thouless and communicated by him posthumously. Berger nevertheless presents an alternative method of encipherment that appears to possess a unique key, so perhaps a cipher test of survival might still be viable. Berger adds that some account may need to be taken, however, of the types of people who could prove to be effective posthumous communicators.

In Stevenson's test a similar procedure is followed with a combination lock instead of a coded passage; the lock's combination is known only to the person conducting the test and is to be communicated in the form of a code word after that person's death. These techniques have a significant advantage over an older practice in which a message in a sealed envelope was to be identified by a medium after the writer's death (Gay, Salter, Thouless, Firebrace, Phillimore & Sitwell, 1955; Salter, 1958). The latter test becomes useless as soon as the envelope is opened to check mediums' guesses about the contents, whereas if some mediums' initial guesses at the identity of a code key or lock combination are incorrect the test still is operative for any other medium who subsequently should claim to have had a communication from the deceased. A satisfactory result from any of these tests has yet to be obtained.

The Survival Hypothesis and the Super-ESP Hypothesis

The prospects look bleak for a critical test between the survival hypothesis and its major alternative, the super-ESP hypothesis. Available evidence can be accommodated by each hypothesis in turn, even if at times they have to be stretched somewhat in order to do so. Moreover, much of the dissatisfaction with each hypothesis seems motivated more by religious beliefs than by objective evaluation of the hypotheses' adequacy. It seems both hypotheses are a little too unspecific for a critical test between them or perhaps even for a crucial test of either one in its own right.

The survival hypothesis has failed to define exactly what it is that is held to survive death and what the fundamental characteristics of this entity would have to be (Grosso, 1979). At the same time the super-ESP hypothesis seeks to explain one unknown (e.g., seance communications) in terms of another unknown, namely ESP. Explanations in terms of a process that has few identifiable constraints (as ESP and in particular super-ESP have) are extremely awkward to refute empirically. According to Alvarado and Martínez-Taboas (1983) the super-ESP hypothesis simply is untestable, because "it postulates an omniscient and omnipotent capacity that cannot be falsified by the scientific method" (p. 58). Even if the survival hypothesis is vague, at least specific forms of it could be open to empirical evaluation (Schmeidler, 1980; Thouless, 1979). On the other hand it is possible this hypothesis itself has an implicit extrasensory component, that is, spirit communications may be mediated extrasensorially and thereby exhibit certain characteristics of ESP. In any event no empirical test has yielded persuasive data in support of either of the rival positions.

There nevertheless are several phenomena that in the view of some researchers strongly testify either to the authenticity or to the feasibility of postmortem survival. Such phenomena include poltergeists, near-death experiences, out-of-body experiences, apparitions and reincarnation experiences. But these phenomena deserve discussion in a broader context than the survival hypothesis. In subsequent chapters each of these phenomena is considered in turn; some reference to the survival issue is made but coverage is not restricted to this aspect.

Key Terms and Concepts

survival hypothesis
super–ESP hypothesis
proxy sittings
"drop-in" communicators

xenoglossy
cross-correspondences
Thouless's cipher test
Stevenson's combination lock test

Study Questions

1. Why has survival research given so much emphasis to evidence from mediumship? Review and evaluate this evidence.

2. "Human personality and dispositions are encoded wholly in the central nervous system." Explore this proposition in relation to the survival hypothesis, and decide if survival research is compatible with mainstream behavioral science.

3. Examine the status of the survival hypothesis and the super–ESP hypothesis as scientific theories, considering such issues as conceptual parsimony and accessibility for empirical evaluation. Are the two hypotheses necessarily mutually exclusive?

4. What data are required before it will be possible to evaluate adequately the super–ESP hypothesis?

5. Critically discuss the potential of cipher tests and combination lock tests for providing a crucial test between the survival hypothesis and the super–ESP hypothesis.

10
Poltergeist Experiences

The German word "poltergeist" does not translate precisely into English but roughly speaking it means a noisy, boisterous, troubling spirit or ghost. The term thus reflects the popular folk belief that poltergeist disturbances were the responsibility of the spirit of a deceased person. In this regard the link between poltergeists and the survival hypothesis has a long history. At the same time there was some realization that poltergeist activity may be associated with a particular living person and according to some accounts (e.g., Roll, 1977, p. 382) the word "geist" now is used to designate either a discarnate spirit or the "spirit" of a living individual.

Poltergeist outbreaks have been reported for centuries; indeed there are accounts dating back to the first century. Each year two or three new cases appear in the press. While poltergeists therefore are not common there are sufficient cases for parapsychologists to investigate. By way of illustration a summary of the so-called Sauchie poltergeist is provided below. (Poltergeist cases usually are identified by the name of the town in which the outbreak occurred, although occasionally they are named after the family which was subjected to the disturbances.) The Sauchie case often is cited in recent literature because it was one of the first modern cases to attract the serious interest of the parapsychological community. The following outline of the case draws upon the detailed report by Owen (1964, Ch. 5).

The outbreak began in November 1960 in the town of Sauchie in Scotland and was documented by A.R.G. Owen, a parapsychologist who at that time was an academic at Trinity College, Cambridge University. Owen did not witness any of the phenomena himself but based his report on interviews with the many witnesses to the disturbances. The Sauchie poltergeist phenomena centered on an 11-year-old girl, Virginia Campbell. Virginia had been raised on a small farm in Ireland where she had led a lonely life, her chief companions being the daughter of the neighbors and a pet dog. In 1960 Virginia's father decided to sell the farm and during the process of winding up the business Virginia was sent to stay with her elder married brother in Sauchie, leaving behind her friend, her dog, and most of her possessions. She appears to have been very upset with this state of affairs.

The first curious incident occurred on the evening of Tuesday, November 22, when a sound like a bouncing ball was heard in Virginia's bedroom, on the stairs, and in the living-room; no cause for this noise was apparent. The following evening Virginia was sitting in the living-room near but not in contact with a heavy sideboard. Her brother and his wife saw the sideboard move outwards about 5 inches (12 cm.) and then return to its original position. Later that evening while Virginia was lying awake in bed loud knocks were heard in her room. A local minister, the Reverend Lund, was summoned and he concluded that the raps came from the bedhead; he moved Virginia down the bed so that no part of her body was touching the bedhead but found the noises continued. Lund then saw a large and full linen chest, which was standing 18 inches (45 cm.) from the bed, rock sideways and move jerkily along parallel to the bed and back again. The chest weighed about 50 pounds (23 kg.). At the suggestion that Virginia's 9-year-old niece sleep with her, there was a burst of violent knocking.

On Thursday evening, November 24, the Reverend Lund again visited and heard more raps and saw the linen chest rocking. He also saw Virginia's pillow rotate horizontally beneath her head about 60 degrees. Dr. Nisbet, a physician accompanying Lund, also heard the knockings and saw a curious rippling movement pass across the pillow on which Virginia's head lay.

At school on Friday, November 25, Virginia's teacher saw her trying to hold down her desk lid which several times raised itself to an angle of 45 to 50 degrees. The teacher could see Virginia's hands flat on the lid of the desk and her legs under the desk. Virginia's teacher also saw an empty desk behind Virginia slowly rise about an inch (2 cm.) above the floor and settle down again. That evening Dr. Nisbet again witnessed knocks, movement of the linen chest, rotation of the pillow, and ripples passing across the bedclothes.

On Monday, November 28, a blackboard pointer on the teacher's table began to vibrate and move across the table until it fell off. The table was felt to be vibrating and it swung around counterclockwise. Virginia started to cry and said that she was not responsible. That afternoon Virginia was taken to stay with a relative in a nearby town and there Dr. Nisbet again heard knockings, this time very loud ones.

Virginia returned to Sauchie and on Thursday, December 1, Dr. Nisbet and a colleague succeeded in recording the noises on tape. After this date the phenomena diminished considerably. Minor occurrences persisted for about three months but these are not as well attested as earlier incidents. One of the more reliably documented incidents in this period occurred on

Monday, January 23, 1961. Virginia placed a bowl of bulbs on her teacher's table and the bowl moved across the tabletop. Both Virginia and her niece also claimed to have been pinched occasionally by unknown means.

The Phenomenology of Poltergeist Experiences

Various sorts of ostensibly paranormal events are associated with the poltergeist experience. In reviewing these frequent reference will be made to two major surveys. One involved the tabulation of 116 poltergeist cases by Bill Roll (1977, 1978a); the other is the monumental compilation of 500 cases by two British parapsychologists, Alan Gauld and Tony Cornell (1979).

Movement of objects. One of the most common features of poltergeist activity is the movement of objects. The Sauchie case reportedly involved movement of several articles such as the sideboard, the linen chest, the pillow, the teacher's table, a child's desk, the blackboard pointer, and the bowl of bulbs. In Roll's (1977, p. 387) sample about 90 percent of the cases mention recurrent movement of objects; Gauld and Cornell (1979, p. 226) found 64 percent of cases to feature movement of small objects and 36 percent, movement of large objects such as furniture.

Sometimes the displaced objects are damaged. In the Miami poltergeist of 1966–1967 (Roll, 1976, Ch. 9) the major incidents were set in the warehouse of a novelty and souvenir firm and many fragile articles were broken.

In some cases the objects move not along the floor but through the air, and when the trajectories of these have been observed they tend to be odd. For example, objects may seem to float or fall slowly, as if being carried: the latter impression was noted in 19 percent of Gauld and Cornell's (1979, p. 226) sample. Roll (1977, p. 389) also reports that in 41 percent of cases entailing object movement the trajectories were unusual, being variously described as floating, wavering, zigzagging, hovering, fluttering, and moving in a sinuous fashion. Even movements across the floor or table may be odd: in the Sauchie case the linen chest was said to move in a jerky and rocking manner.

Apportation also may occur, that is, objects may be transported by apparently paranormal means from a remote location. About 20 percent of cases include this effect (Gauld & Cornell, 1979, p. 226).

The "poltergeist" may be selective in regard to the objects moved. Thus some outbreaks are designated *stone-throwing poltergeists* because they predominantly comprise bombardment by rocks and pebbles. These disturbances have occurred in the same basic form in many cultures over the centuries. For example, in A.D. 530 Deacon Helpidius, the physician to Theodoric, king of an area now part of Germany, was the target of mysterious showers of stones (Thurston, 1953, pp. 187–188). Sometimes the stones in these outbreaks feel hot to the touch. Occasionally the stones have been collected, marked and thrown away, only to reappear in the house plagued by the disturbance (Gauld & Cornell, 1979, p. 228; Roll, 1977, p. 391). In many cases people are hit by the falling stones but it is rare for someone to be hurt: indeed a few witnesses report that stones seemed to "float" down and strike them with less force than expected of a falling object (Roll, 1977, p. 389).

Noises. Another typical manifestation of the poltergeist experience is the outbreak of unaccountable noises, particularly of a percussive type. About half of Gauld and Cornell's (1979, p. 226) sample included mention of rapping, pounding, knocking, and scratching sounds. A similar level of incidence was found in Roll's (1977, p. 387) sample. The poltergeist, therefore, is one of those "things that go bump in the night." There are suggestions that the occurrence of sounds may tend to precede the outbreak of movement of objects (as in the Sauchie case) but data to this effect as yet are weak (Roll, 1977, pp. 387–388).

In several modern cases, of which the Sauchie case is one, the poltergeist noises were recorded on tape. There have been some attempts to compare these noises to ones produced in imitation by the investigator. According to one report the poltergeist noises showed a distinctive sound spectrum: the vibrations were damped (died away) more quickly than were the imitative sounds (Whitton, 1975, 1976).

Fires. Incendiary phenomena were mentioned in 11 percent of Gauld and Cornell's (1979, p. 227) cases. Sometimes these represent the major phenomenon of the disturbances: such cases are termed *fire poltergeists* and entail the sudden outbreak of numerous small fires in the household.

In some instances the objects that burst into flame would otherwise be incombustible or would merely smoulder if ignited by normal means. A recent case in Michigan (Solfvin, personal communication, 1979; Solfvin & Roll, 1976) involved the incineration of a wet towel and a roll of toilet paper burned to the core. Forensic analysis of the latter revealed no evidence of chemical impregnation. If ever you have tried to ignite a tightly rolled newspaper you will appreciate the oddity of this event.

Generally these outbreaks are investigated by officials from the fire or police departments. Some of these investigators admit the inexplicability of the phenomena, at least in private; others attribute them to childish pranks and leave the scene before anyone thinks to ask how normally incombustible objects were set alight.

Water inundations. Some poltergeist disturbances exhibit an obsession with water. Water may begin to seep or spurt from a wall in the house and investigation fails to uncover any natural explanation of this. Other cases focus on the toilet: Brian Nisbet in England once told me of his investigations of three poltergeist cases in which the cistern would flush unaccountably and water would be thrown up on the toilet walls.

Comparatively speaking these effects are not common. Gauld and Cornell (1979, p. 227) found such phenomena in only 5 percent of their collection, and Roll (1977, p. 387) cites only two cases.

Bites, scratches, and pinches. Fifteen percent of Gauld and Cornell's (1979, p. 227) collection included various forms of personal assault of an unaccountable nature. People would report being scratched or bitten, the marks on the body being inconsistent with self-infliction. Pinches are relatively more frequent: these occurred in the terminal stages of the Sauchie case, for example.

Demonic persecution. A few cases are of an even more vicious character, with sustained persecution of a particular individual or family. Often these persecutions have a religious element: they may center on a clergyman and feature desecration of religious artifacts. In the public's mind demonic poltergeists would be most clearly instanced by the case of the "Amityville horror"; there is evidence however, that this case was greatly dramatized (if not completely fabricated) by the author of the book about it and the family concerned (Harris, 1986, pp. 9–17; Morris, 1981).

Other Features of the Poltergeist Experience

Most poltergeist disturbances exhibit recurrent events which tend to diminish rapidly. Usually the outbreaks last between two weeks and two months, although there are cases in the literature said to have persisted for a year or more. In Roll's (1977, p. 388) sample the median duration was two months, but some extraordinarily persistent cases (including one of six years) pulled the mean duration up to five months.

In broad terms there are two types of poltergeists, ones which appear to be associated with a particular place and others which evidently center upon a particular person (Bender, 1982, pp. 124–125). According to some researchers different explanations may be applicable to these two classes of poltergeist outbreaks. In practice, however, it is difficult to be sure that the place-centered phenomena are not linked in some way with an unidentified person. Additionally a few cases might be said to exhibit the characteristics of both categories: the disturbances may seem to center on a particular individual yet continue at least for a short time after that individual has left the district. (The latter phenomenon sometimes is referred to as a *linger effect*.)

Poltergeist activity associated with a particular place is the basis of many instances of the so-called haunted house. Here recurrent poltergeist phenomena persist despite changes of the house's tenants (Osis & McCormick, 1982a; Pierce, 1973). Again, apart from the problem of ensuring that a person outside the house (e.g., a neighbor) is not the center of the activity, it is possible that a process of "psychological infection" occurs whereby person-centered phenomena among one group of tenants inspire similar activity in the house's next occupants. Also new tenants may endeavor to gain commercial advantage from the house's haunted reputation and use fraudulent means to sustain the disturbances. Nevertheless, some parapsychologists believe that place-centered poltergeists do exist. Such cases at least appear to be much rarer yet more durable than the person-centered type (Bender, 1982, pp. 124–125) and they might well have slightly different phenomenological features (Gauld & Cornell, 1979, Ch. 18; Stevenson, 1972).

The major part of poltergeist research has been directed to cases in which the outbreak seems to center upon and generally require the presence of a particular individual, the so-called poltergeist *focus* or *agent*. Roll (1977, p. 386) reports that 79 percent of his cases had an alleged focus, and in 42 percent of cases the disturbances "followed" this individual beyond the home. Gauld and Cornell (1979, p. 226) put the incidence of cases with agents at 40 percent. It is possible that many of their older cases were not documented in sufficient detail to permit a judgment of the existence of a focal person. Even if many of the cases do involve a key figure, any decision that this person was the poltergeist agent is moot and the judged incidence of person-centered cases thus will depend markedly on the conservatism of the case analysts. In any event now that the concept of a focus is more familiar, the considerable majority of contemporary cases investigated by parapsychologists appear to feature a focal person. The Sauchie poltergeist is one such instance.

Another example of a case with a focal individual is the Bremen poltergeist (Bender, 1971, pp. 91–93). In mid–1965 unexplained movements of merchandise occurred in the chinaware department of a Bremen store. Investigations by police and other authorities failed to establish any normal explanation for the events but they evidently were connected in some obscure way with a 15-year-old apprentice employee in the department. The lad was dismissed and the disturbances in the store immediately came to an end. The young man subsequently obtained a job as an apprentice in a Freiburg electrical shop. In March 1966 he was asked to drill holes in a concrete wall and to install wall hooks. The task was done properly but a little later it was found that the hooks came loose in the presence of the young apprentice. He was accused of being to blame. In a test of this a freshly attached hook was observed to come loose within two minutes while the apprentice stood about a yard (meter) from the wall. It is reported that the boy had been "brought up under difficult circumstances" and was living with foster parents at the time of the outbreak.

If a substantial number of poltergeist cases center upon a focal person it is pertinent to inquire into the characteristics of such people. Three biographical factors that have been examined are sex, age and domestic situation.

In both collections of poltergeist cases there is a predominance of female agents. In Roll's (1977, p. 386) sample 61 percent of focal individuals were female; the figure in Gauld and Cornell's (1979, p. 226) collection is 73 percent. Roll suggests that this trend is due to the rarity of male agents in the oldest (1612 to 1899) cases; in the present century the sexes are represented equally. The earlier predominance of females may have been due to the different nature of social pressures across the sexes; again there may have been a reporting bias, with cases either attributed to a "witch" or depicted as place-centered rather than person-centered. In any event the recent data suggest that sex is not a major determinant of poltergeist agency.

In Roll's (1977, pp. 386–387) sample the age of agents ranged from 8 to 78, although the median was 13 years. The tendency for adolescent foci is confirmed in Gauld and Cornell's (1979, p. 226) collection, where over 70 percent of agents were under 20.

An interesting trend is found in regard to the agent's domestic situation. On the assumption that 18 is the age at which a young person might leave home for normal reasons, Roll (1977, p. 402) selected from his sample those cases in which the agent was aged 18 or less. Of this group 62 percent were living away from home when the disturbances commenced. In many poltergeist cases, therefore, a young focal individual was not living with his or her natural parents at the time of the outbreak; this was the situation for both the Sauchie and the Bremen poltergeists, for example. Roll (1977, p. 403) also notes that of those cases in which an agent was identified, 41 percent of disturbances occurred when there were changes or other problems in the home or the family which may have affected the agent. Fifteen percent of focal individuals in Gauld and Cornell's (1979, p. 226) sample were known to be suffering from a mental or emotional problem prior to the outbreak, and in many other cases such a problem was discovered during the period of the poltergeist activities.

The picture of the poltergeist agent that emerges is that of a young adolescent, often near the age of pubescence, with cause for personal turmoil and rebellion. This suggests that poltergeist disturbances in some way are associated with emotional conflict in the focal person. The frequency of adolescent cases may indicate further that the agent typically is not in a position to express the conflict openly. Implications of these trends will be discussed shortly in the context of theories of the poltergeist.

There are some consistencies also in the poltergeist phenomena themselves, despite their superficially erratic quality. For example, there may be an obsessive element in the disturbance with activity concentrated on particular objects, particular types of objects, or particular areas such as a certain room or shelf (Roll, 1977, p. 390). In person-centered cases there are suggestions that the number of incidents decreases with distance from the agent; in other words, most activity may tend to occur in the vicinity of the focal person (Roll, 1977, p. 388). Quantitative documentation of this effect however, is limited.

In cases with moving objects Roll (1968, 1976) has attempted to identify patterns in the movements in the hope of ascertaining the character of a possible "force field" centered on the poltergeist agent. While movements in individual cases do not seem to be entirely random there is limited consistency in patterns across the cases so far analyzed. Nevertheless with so few sets of such data currently available for comparison further research along these lines would be justified.

Theories of the Poltergeist Experience

There are four main theoretical approaches to the poltergeist. The first two emphasize normal causes, the others appeal to either supernatural or paranormal factors.

Fraud. One theory of poltergeist activities is that they simply are childish pranks. Proponents of this view (e.g., Podmore, 1896) point out that it explains why so many cases center around a child and why it reportedly is rare for people to witness the initial stages of movement of a displaced object (Zusne & Jones, 1982, p. 414).

There is a measure of support for this approach. Gauld and Cornell (1979, p. 226) report that in 8 percent of their cases fraud was detected. Roll (1977, p. 392) puts the figure at 16 percent and notes that the identification of fraud is more common in modern cases, presumably because contemporary parapsychologists are more skilled investigators than the people who documented disturbances in earlier times. In the fraudulent cases, trickery usually is of a simple, though sometimes skillfully executed, sort. Thus objects would be thrown at judiciously chosen moments and objects overturned or levitated by use of fine horsehair or cotton thread attached to them (Christopher, 1971, pp. 142–163; Owen, 1964, pp. 26–64). Very rarely a mechanical device has been employed to produce various odd effects.

The generality of the "naughty child" account is open to question. The incidence of fraudulent cases is rather too low to be taken as evidence in support of the theory, although admittedly it is possible that many other cases identified as fraudulent have not been written up by investigators. Again there are some reported poltergeist feats that do not seem possible to achieve by normal means. How did the 11-year-old Virginia Campbell manage to move a heavy sideboard and a large linen chest in the Sauchie case? How do normally incombustible objects burst into flames in certain instances of fire poltergeist? Indeed, far from the literature's suggesting an underestimation of the incidence of fraud, there are grounds for arguing that many supposedly fraudulent cases in fact are not so. For example, the timing of the identified fraudulent activities bears examination. In many such cases the trickery occurred well after the original outbreak had subsided and thus could be construed as a rather puerile attempt by some of the principals of the case to prolong the attention brought to them by the initial genuine phenomena. Further, in a number of allegedly fraudulent cases a confession was extracted from a youngster under the inducement that the interrogation then would terminate and no further action would be taken. In person-centered cases it hardly is surprising that the focal individual feels some responsibility for the phenomena and hence may confess as much.

It should be noted also that it is not correct that the initial stages of an object's movement are rarely witnessed in poltergeist disturbances. There is a substantial number of cases in which a complete movement or trajectory was observed (e.g., the Sauchie poltergeist). While the occurrence of trickery in some cases is not denied the fraud theory, therefore, is inadequate as a general explanation of the poltergeist.

Misinterpretations. Poltergeist phenomena have been deemed to represent misinterpretations of natural events by nervous or overimaginative folk. For example, the sources of indistinct noises are difficult to locate and hence these might be attributed to paranormal factors. Natural sounds like the activities of rodents behind the woodwork and waterhammers could be perceived as poltergeist scratching and rapping noises. Minor seismic activity, underground water flows, and shifting house foundations might not be detected yet produce movement of objects that are interpreted as the effects of a poltergeist (Lambert, 1959). Some instances of (apparent) poltergeist experience have indeed been diagnosed as comprising misinterpretations of natural events (Blackmore, 1986, pp. 195–207).

While "nervous and overimaginative" people might well behave in the above fashion it is unlikely that everyone who witnesses poltergeist phenomena could be categorized thus. At the very least it would seem that the misinterpretation theory would have to be supplemented with such factors as substantial misreporting. Additionally, some of the trends of poltergeist case collections do not sit happily with this approach. In person-centered cases why should the phenomena seem dependent upon the presence of a particular person? And why should these focal individuals tend to be under the age of 20? Also, the trajectories of displaced objects in poltergeist cases are quite unlike those associated with natural shocks to house foundations (Gauld & Cornell, 1979, pp. 334–337). The persistence of poltergeist phenomena does not accord with such natural events as seismic activity. As a broad account of the poltergeist experience this approach leaves much to be desired, although it does fare better if taken in conjunction with the theory of fraudulent activity.

If it proves to be the case that (some) poltergeist phenomena cannot be explained satisfactorily in terms of normal factors there remain two principal theoretical options. The point at issue between these options is encapsulated by the question, "Are poltergeists living or are they dead?" (Stevenson, 1972).

Spirits. In traditional folklore the poltergeist is depicted as the spirit of a deceased person. This account is consistent with many apparently paranormal features of poltergeist phenomena. Thus some poltergeists give the impression of an underlying intelligence. Poltergeists' noises have been used as a basis for meaningful communication (in 16 percent of Gauld and Cornell's sample); objects may move as if they are being carried (19 percent of Gauld and Cornell's sample); and some disturbances, particularly the demonic poltergeist cases, seem to be directed at specific individuals. These indications of an underlying intelligence are consistent with the spirit theory, although they might also be said to support the fraud theory. Other suggestions of the involvement of spirits are that apparitions are reported in some poltergeist cases (29 percent of Gauld and Cornell's sample, 23 percent of Roll's sample) and that exorcism may be successful in attenuating the disturbance (60 percent of Gauld and Cornell's cases in which exorcism was attempted).

The spirit theory has its maximum appeal with place-centered cases. On the other hand these cases are not as well attested as person-centered poltergeists and particularly in recent instances the place-centered outbreak is in a distinct minority. As far as the person-centered disturbances are concerned it is not clear under this theory why the poltergeist focus should have certain psychological characteristics — why only certain sorts of people should attract a poltergeist "spirit." Indeed, why should the "spirit" be attracted only to some people in conflict and not to all of them? Most if not all of the various points of evidence favoring the spirit hypothesis can be accommodated by another theory (see below) that does not rest on an assumption of discarnate entities and to this extent poltergeist experiences in the view of most parapsychologists do not constitute compelling support for the survival hypothesis.

Subconscious PK. A theory of the poltergeist that has gained wide support from parapsychologists in recent years proposes that poltergeist effects are due to the subconscious use of PK as a release from considerable psychological tension. The feasibility of this hypothesis is enhanced by those experimental studies which suggest that a person may be able to employ PK without conscious awareness of either the task to be performed or the situation to which it pertains (e.g., Stanford et al., 1975). Proponents of this approach thus refer to poltergeist activity as *recurrent spontaneous psychokinesis* or RSPK. To the extent that both "poltergeist" and "RSPK" are theory-based terms, neither is really satisfactory as purely descriptive nomenclature for a class of phenomena, but each has become entrenched through widespread usage.

One of the earliest expressions of the subconscious PK theory was provided by a psychoanalytical parapsychologist, Nandor Fodor (1948; Carrington & Fodor, 1951). One of his female patients was the evident focus of poltergeist activity. In therapy with this patient Fodor uncovered (in true psychoanalytic tradition) a deep-seated psychosexual conflict entailing an imagined sexual assault upon the patient by her father. Fodor interpreted the poltergeist events as part of a "poltergeist psychosis," a vehicle for expressing subconscious psychosexual conflict by paranormal displacement of repressed hostility. In many cases the poltergeist activity is blind in its fury and hence primarily represents a means of "letting off steam." Other disturbances appear to reflect an underlying intelligence. Here in effect the agent additionally is denying (to self and perhaps to others too) that she or he is responsible for the events, for the acts seem to be executed by a separate (discarnate) personality.

Many aspects of the poltergeist experience are consistent with this interpretation. The theory implies a high level of tension among poltergeist agents and this is confirmed both by survey data and some case study material which includes detailed psychological assessment of the presumed agent (e.g., Palmer, 1974; Roll, 1968). The identification of the source of the trouble as bottled-up aggression may explain the frequency with which children and adolescents are identified as agents, since in comparison with adults children have fewer skills and opportunities for giving socially acceptable expression to their conflicts. The postulated subconscious basis of the phenomena is compatible with their reported susceptibility to posthypnotic influence (Bender, 1982, p. 131) and with the evident inability of the focal person to bring under conscious control the disturbances that center upon him or her. The childishness of much of the activity accords with the idea that the acts spring from frustration: often our behavior becomes childish when we are intolerably frustrated. Indeed, often it merely needs to be mentioned to the presumed agent that such outbreaks can be a subconscious displacement of tension and the disturbances will dissipate.

Although the psychosexual element is not an essential component of the theory it might account for the common association of the poltergeist experience with pubescence, toilets, beds, and any number of objects possible to construe as genital symbols (linen chests, blackboard pointers, etc.); again, the potential for such interpretation of facets of the poltergeist is so unlimited that it is difficult to imagine where to seek any contrary evidence with which to refute the psychoanalytic element of the theory.

Nevertheless, apart perhaps from the psychoanalytical versions, the subconscious PK theory appears compatible with available phenomenological data on the poltergeist experience. The incidence of apparitions in poltergeist cases may be a source of some inconvenience, but as apparitions constitute a phenomenon in their own right the point need not be pursued at this juncture. A further advantage of the RSPK theory is that it is more open to empirical testing than is the spirit hypothesis. This is not to say that the RSPK approach should be accepted uncritically. Let us look more closely at its two main assumptions, first that poltergeist experiences reflect conflict, and second that they employ a psychokinetic mechanism.

Are poltergeist agents really in the grip of psychological conflict? Survey data to this effect are inconclusive because control subjects have not been surveyed; one might well find similar levels of conflict reported by people (especially adolescents) who are not poltergeist agents. There have been some detailed psychological assessments of focal individuals but often these were methodologically poor: assessments were undertaken by the case researcher or someone who knew the subject was a poltergeist agent and thus had an expectation of finding evidence of conflict. Martínez-Taboas (1984) argues also that these investigators almost exclusively used unreliable projective tests of personality. Those psychological assessments that were performed satisfactorily are too few in number and too neglectful of comparative data from nonagents to be regarded as conclusive support for the theory's "conflict" postulate.

The assumption of a PK mechanism can be tested by investigating the PK abilities of poltergeist foci. Roll (1977, pp. 391–392) reports only three of six such studies to have yielded significant PK performance, and the German parapsychologist Hans Bender (1974, p. 130) notes that in his experience PK cannot be elicited from agents in the laboratory. The direct evidence for the PK postulate therefore is not strong, although it could be argued that conscious PK tests in the laboratory are a poor analogue of subconscious and deeply motivated poltergeist PK. Additionally the attribution of poltergeist events to PK is rather like explaining one unknown in terms of another unknown. Parapsychologists know so little about the limitations of PK that they simply are unable to say whether or not it is plausible to accommodate the variety of poltergeist activities under the concept of PK. For example, no laboratory studies have examined the possibility that PK might produce incendiary phenomena and hence it is precipitate to suppose that PK could explain instances of fire poltergeist activity.

The theory's emphasis upon an individual as the poltergeist agent also might be too simplistic. If one person can use PK activity as a release from psychological conflict then so could several people. Rogo (1982) drew attention to the need to take account of family dynamics in one poltergeist case. More generally, investigation of the psychodynamics of interpersonal relationships in a given case might well serve to identify multiple poltergeist agents each making significant and interdependent contributions to the RSPK phenomena.

It would appear then that the popularity of the RSPK theory does go somewhat beyond the available evidence. Support for this approach probably stems in some measure from modern parapsychologists' unease with any proposal demanding the assumption of spirit entities. Thus the rejection of the spirit theory, while undoubtedly justified on some objective grounds, also is intimately bound up with current fashions in parapsychological theorization. Conceptually the poltergeist is subject to the zeitgeist.

It should be mentioned that Bill Roll has proposed a neurological version of the RSPK approach (Montago & Roll, 1983; Roll, 1977, pp. 405–410; 1978b). He proposes that RSPK activity is due to eruptions within the central nervous system (CNS), rather like epileptic disturbances. Hence the neurotic conflict said to be characteristic of poltergeist agents is not the direct cause of the poltergeist outbreak but just an incidental consequence of the more fundamental factor of CNS disturbances.

In support of this theory Roll has identified a few poltergeist agents whose EEG was symptomatic of epilepsy (e.g., Solfvin & Roll, 1976). He claims further that 4 percent of his collected cases feature behavioral signs of epileptic disorders and argues that this significantly exceeds the 1 percent incidence of such signs in the general population. On the other hand, even a rate of 4 percent cannot be deemed substantial evidence of the potency of this factor in poltergeist cases. Further, among children and adolescents (who form the majority of poltergeist foci) the frequency of EEG abnormalities considerably exceeds 1 percent and thus Roll's figure might not be particularly deviant (Martínez-Taboas, 1984; Martínez-Taboas & Alvarado, 1981). Some of the "behavioral signs" taken by Roll as indicative of CNS disturbances also are diagnostically dubious (Martínez-Taboas, 1984). Although Roll's interpretation of the RSPK theory is both interesting and more open to empirical scrutiny than the purely psychopathological version, its evidential base is not strong.

The general RSPK approach nevertheless does warrant further research effort. In drawing attention to the possible role of psychological conflict in poltergeist cases this theory also merits consideration in the clinical context. Psychologists alert to the theory might be more constructive in their handling of people who come to clinics for guidance in dealing with the poltergeist experience. Counseling in light of an appreciation of the RSPK model at least would be preferable to telling clients that since spooks do not exist, poltergeist disturbances are all in the imagination.

In the final analysis there may be an element of truth in each of the theories of the poltergeist experience. At least some cases do entail fraudulent activity or misinterpretation of natural events. If other cases have paranormal origins it is possible that some are due to an RSPK agent and others to a discarnate entity; this approach is promoted most notably by Stevenson (1972) and Gauld and Cornell (1979, Ch. 18). Although poltergeist cases cannot justifiably be claimed to provide strong evidential support for the survival hypothesis the fact remains that we are not yet in a position to discount any of the major theoretical approaches to the poltergeist experience.

Key Terms and Concepts

poltergeist
poltergeist focus/agent
poltergeist psychosis

recurrent spontaneous psychokinesis (RSPK)
Roll's neurological model

Study Questions

1. What are the principal forms of poltergeist activity? Is there any independent evidence that these forms can be brought about by psycho-kinetic means?

2. What are the principal characteristics and correlates of poltergeist experiences?

3. Outline the major theories of the poltergeist, listing the evidential points for and against each theory.

4. To what extent has poltergeist research lent support to the survival hypothesis?

11
Near-Death Experiences

Many persons suddenly faced with death have experienced a distinctive state of consciousness in which their existence seemed to be bound neither to a physical body nor to earthly environs. Such a state is termed a *near-death experience* (NDE) and may be defined simply as a transcendental experience precipitated by a confrontation with death. Reports of NDEs come from people who survive the threat to their life. These experients may have been in potentially fatal situations but escaped uninjured, or they may have been seriously ill or hurt and recovered unexpectedly; a few may have been pronounced clinically dead but eventually responded to resuscitative measures. According to one estimate (Ring, 1980, p. 32) as many as half of all people suffering a serious accident or grave illness have an NDE, although some other surveys suggest its incidence to be much lower, even as little as 7 percent (Locke & Shontz, 1983).

The following example of an NDE was obtained by one of my former students, Norm McMaster, from a man who had cardiac bypass surgery at the age of 55. The experient reports that as he regained consciousness after the operation he was in a great deal of pain. The description of his NDE is extracted from a recorded interview.

> All of a sudden I was standing at the foot of the bed looking at my own body. I knew it was me in bed because there were certain features I could recognize easily. I felt no pain at all. I was a bit puzzled. I wasn't anxious or worried, I just didn't understand what I was doing at the foot of the bed. Then I was travelling. I was at the entrance of a tunnel. There was a light at the end of the tunnel just like sunlight. I had a feeling of comfort and all the pain was gone, and I had a desire to go towards the light. I seemed to float along in a [horizontal] position. When I reached the other end I was in a strange place. Everything was beautiful, yet it was more of a feeling rather than seeing. I could see other people. They ignored me completely and the next thing I heard a voice saying, "You must go back ... it is not your time." Afterwards I seemed to think it was my father [speaking] but this may have been imagination. Then I was in my bed. There was no sensation of moving back. It was just as though

184

I woke up and all the pain was back and [hospital staff] were working on me.

Interest in NDEs increased greatly in the 1970s. The work of Elisabeth Kübler-Ross drew the attention of researchers and of the general public to the study of death, and in 1975 physician Raymond Moody published a book based on more than a decade of investigation into NDEs during which time he collected about 150 case reports. Moody's (1975) book, *Life After Life,* became an international best seller; its sequel (Moody, 1977) explores the implications of the NDE for the survival hypothesis and in it Moody declares that his case collection convinces him of the existence of life after death. Several other books on NDEs now are available, of which the most scientific are those by Ring (1980, 1984), Sabom (1982), Lundahl (1982), Grey (1985) and Greyson and Flynn (1984). Study of the experience has flourished to the extent that it supports its own specialist journal, the *Journal of Near-Death Studies* (formerly *Anabiosis).*

Study of the NDE necessarily entails retrospective case reports; strict experimental induction of the experience would require us to engineer a perceived threat to a subject's life, a procedure that clearly is unacceptable on ethical grounds. A Canadian researcher, Joel Whitton, claims to have used a hypnotic technique for inducing experiences with much the same elements as are found in NDEs (Whitton & Fisher, 1986, Ch. 4). This technique could conceivably be represented as an experimental method for NDE induction. Such an interpretation, however, has yet to be given serious independent empirical scrutiny. Additionally, Whitton's technique essentially comprises hypnotic regression and thus presumably it would be marked by the inherent methodological ambiguities of that procedure (see Chapter 14). In any event current data on the NDE come from case collections and surveys.

Phenomenological Characteristics of Near-Death Experiences

On the basis of his case collection Moody (1975) identified a common set of elements in NDEs. Broadly speaking these elements are confirmed in the more scientific studies by Ring (1980), Sabom (1982) and Grey (1985). A given NDE might not feature all elements and they need not occur in a fixed order, despite Ring's depiction of them as "stages." The phenomenological elements reported by Moody are:

(a) an overwhelming feeling of peace and well-being, including freedom from pain;

(b) the impression of being located outside one's physical body;

(c) floating or drifting through darkness, sometimes described as a tunnel;

(d) becoming aware of a golden light;

(e) encountering and perhaps communicating with a "presence" described by Moody as a "being of light";

(f) having a rapid succession of visual images of one's past; and

(g) experiencing another world of much beauty, perhaps meeting there spirits of deceased relatives and acquaintances with whom one also might communicate.

The characteristics of each of these features will be reviewed in turn.

The Affective Component

Generally this may be described as a sense of emotional detachment, with an absence of feelings of fear and pain that otherwise the individual might be experiencing. The state of peace and well-being sometimes is depicted as one of happiness or joyfulness. There may be moments of sadness, loneliness and anxiety during the NDE but these tend to be transient, the overall experience later being described as enjoyable.

The affective component seems to be much the same whether the experient is conscious or behaviorally unconscious (Noyes & Slymen, 1979). In other words the reported freedom from pain and fear evidently is not a mere consequence of loss of consciousness.

In Ring's (1980, p. 39) survey the feeling of peace was found to be the most common feature of NDEs, being acknowledged by about 60 percent of experients. The participants in the study by the cardiologist Michael Sabom had their NDEs during a heart attack or in heart surgery, and Sabom (1982, p. 206) claims that all experienced calm and peace in the NDE.

The Out-of-Body Impression

Many experients report the impression of being outside the physical body during the NDE. Estimates of the incidence of this element are rather variable: Ring (1980, p. 45) puts it at 37 percent, a smaller scale study by Greyson and Stevenson (1980, p. 1194) found the incidence to be 75 percent, and in Sabom's (1982, pp. 204–205) sample of NDEs all but one respondent (99 percent) had a sense of bodily separation. Certainly people do describe their NDE as if it had taken place outside their physical body.

The majority of experients have no actual sensations of leaving the physical body, realizing their apparently exteriorized state only when they see their own physical body from the outside. A substantial number of respondents nevertheless do report noises and other sensations accompanying the process of their separation from the body. Many experients also believe that while in the out-of-body state their exteriorized self had a body-like form. These elements will be explored further in Chapter 12 in the context of out-of-body experiences.

It is common for the NDE to consist of an out-of-body impression of nothing more than the experient's immediate environment. The individual can recall apparently looking down upon the physical body and watching the activities of other people trying to lend assistance. Sometimes it is claimed that certain of these out-of-body observations could not have been gathered in any normal fashion (because the individual was unconscious at the time, for example). It is rare however, for the accuracy of these claims to be checked by NDE investigators. Further, the fact that a person is behaviorally unconscious does not preclude the possibility that some sensory (e.g., auditory) inputs are processed. There is, therefore, scant evidence that the out-of-body impression of the environment has a paranormal base and is neither pure fantasy nor imagery built upon expectations and partial sensory information. Even if it can be demonstrated that sensorially inaccessible information was incorporated in some NDEs, it remains to be shown that this was due to some literal separation of consciousness from the body and not to ESP (assuming this distinction to be legitimate).

The Passage Through Darkness

Sometimes the NDE is not limited to earthly environs and may progress to, or consist entirely of, an experience of some allegedly supernaturalistic realm. Often the transition to this realm is characterized as a passage through darkness. This element is found in about a quarter of NDEs (Ring, 1980, p. 53; Sabom, 1982, p. 206). Moody (1975, pp. 30–34) claims that his experients often perceived the darkness as a tunnel, but he does not quantify this trend. In the surveys by Ring (1980) and Sabom (1982) it is more common for the darkness to be described as a completely dark and empty space without shape or size; only a small minority of respondents referred to it as a tunnel, funnel, pipe, or the like.

According to Greyson and Stevenson (1980) the tunnel effect is most often cited by executives and professionals as opposed to service workers and laborers. Perhaps there is a class or educational factor operating here but the pertinence of such a factor is unclear and the association thus warrants independent confirmation. No such occupational association was evident in Sabom's (1982, p. 207) analysis.

Seeing a Light

The transition from darkness to the nonphysical realm sometimes is signaled by the appearance of a brilliant light, often described as golden. The light may be so brilliant as to be blinding but at the same time it generally has a magnetic and reassuring quality. In some cases the light may be experienced without the passage through darkness. This element was mentioned by about 30 percent of experients in both Ring's (1980, p. 56) and Sabom's (1982, p. 206) surveys.

Encountering a "Presence"

Having entered the transcendental environment, the experient may encounter some kind of cosmic being or religious figure; about 40 percent of Ring's (1980, p. 67) cases include this feature. Often the being, or "presence," is not perceived directly but is detected and identified by an intuitive process. Communication between the experient and the being generally concerns the question of whether the experient is to die or to return to the physical body. Many experients had the impression that it was up to themselves to make the choice but sometimes the "presence" commands their return.

Interestingly enough three studies (Greyson & Stevenson, 1980, p. 1195; Ring, 1980, p. 134; Sabom, 1982, p. 207) have revealed no relationship between encounters of a "presence" during an NDE and the experient's prior religious beliefs. On the other hand it is feasible that even the most avowed atheist becomes an instant "believer" when confronted with imminent death, if only for the duration of the threat to life.

Panoramic Life Review

A popular folk belief is that on confrontation with death people will see their lives flash before their eyes, and a number of near-death experients do report this. The frequency of the life review generally is put at about 25 percent of NDEs (Ring, 1980, p. 67; Greyson & Stevenson, 1980, p. 1195; Noyes & Kletti, 1977, p. 181), although Sabom's (1982, p. 206) cardiac cases evidenced an atypically low figure of 3 percent.

The panoramic life review consists of unusually vivid, almost instantaneous visual images of either the person's whole life or selected highlights of it. In some instances the images may appear in an orderly sequence, from

Opposite: **Figure 17. The passage through darkness.**

the present to childhood for example, but often the images seem to appear "all at once." The life review occurs without the conscious effort or control of the experient.

The following example of a panoramic life review is taken from my file of NDE case reports. At the age of 19 the experient had his chest crushed while working between carriages on a railroad.

> I couldn't breathe while I was stuck in there. The locomotive driver did not realize what was happening. I was unconscious. There was something like a film went through my mind. It went that fast! You get every picture and think you have died. It appears to run for a long time although it is only a few seconds. It was the years of my life—what I had done, wrong or good. I think it was from the beginning of my life—what I have done, where I have been. When I think back I can still see the "film" running; I don't see any pictures anymore but I still have it in my mind.

Sometimes the panoramic life review may incorporate fantasies about the future: experients may visualize their death, the reactions of relatives and friends on receiving news of the death, and incidents at the funeral (Ring, 1982).

The Transcendental Realm

People who undergo an NDE may have a perceptual-like experience of a supernaturalistic environment. This occurred in approximately 20 percent of Ring's (1980, p. 60) cases and 54 percent of Sabom's (1982, p. 206) cases.

The transcendental realm typically is described as one of preternatural beauty, a pastoral scene with lush green grass, trees, and beautiful flowers. The vividness of the colors is commonly remarked upon. The identification of the setting as nonphysical seems largely to be an intuitive process, although the overwhelming beauty, color, and the soft diffuse lighting may be cues distinguishing the environment from an earthly scene. Occasionally, lovely music may be heard. It is notable that the nonphysical realm experienced in NDEs is unlike the biblical stereotype of heaven, although Sabom (1982, p. 209) cites three or four cases in which "St. Peter's Gate" and "streets of gold" are mentioned. Nevertheless in a survey of students I found the pastoral image of heaven to be much more popular than the biblical stereotype (Irwin, 1987b); that is, the transcendental realm of the NDE does correspond to a popular stereotypical notion of the nature of the afterlife.

Some experients report meeting deceased relatives and friends in the transcendental realm. These beings usually reassure the individual or advise a return to earthly existence.

Contact with a paradisial environment was not correlated with prior religious beliefs in either Ring's (1980, p. 134) or Sabom's (1982, p. 207) sample. Encounters with this realm have been found more commonly among female experients than male experients (Greyson & Stevenson, 1980, p. 1194); possibly this represents nothing more than a response bias, with women being more prepared to admit such an encounter when interviewed by the researcher.

It is appropriate here to mention too the occurrence of NDEs to a transcendental realm that experients identify as "hell." These cases are extremely rare and their existence is only beginning to be acknowledged (Grey, 1985, Ch. 5; Rawlings, 1978, Ch. 7). In my NDE case collection I have only one example that approaches this "hellish" experience; it was collected by one of my students, Barbara Bramwell. The NDE is that of a woman in her late forties and arose in the context of a car accident. She describes her presence in a pastoral transcendental realm and her entry into a building that looked rather like a church yet was sensed not to be one.

> I started walking down [the aisle] and there were many pews on each side and each pew was filled with people wearing black robes with hoods. I couldn't see their faces but if I turned my eyes I could see the inside of the hoods were lined with red. There was no sound at all, and I kept walking and walking and then came to three steps which I went up then walked a little further. I then saw what looked like an altar on which were six silver goblets and a big silver jug. I stood there wondering where I was and what I was doing there, when a door opened to the right of the altar and out came the Devil. He came over to the altar, looked me straight in the eye and told me to pick up a goblet. I picked up a goblet and he picked up the big silver jug and started pouring. I saw that what he was pouring from the jug was fire and I screamed, dropped the goblet and ran. I didn't know where I was running to and then I saw a big fence, a stone fence, and the gates opened and I passed through. Then I came to another fence made out of iron bars and that just opened and again I passed through. All the time I was getting warmer and warmer and brighter and brighter.

At this point she awoke to find herself in the hospital.

The phenomenological return to the physical body most commonly is instantaneous. The person simply notices that the NDE is over and consciousness is "in" the body. In transcendental cases the termination of the experience ostensibly may be instigated by a command from a discarnate entity. In "earthbound" experiences it may be occasioned by bodily stimulation (e.g., that associated with particular resuscitative measures). Rarely individuals will experience a jolting sensation upon "return." The end of most NDEs however, is both abrupt and a blank.

The Impact of the Experience

An NDE often has an enduring effect upon the individual's attitudes and values, particularly if death was thought to be imminent and if the NDE included a panoramic life review (Greyson & Stevenson, 1980). These effects seem to be due to the NDE as such and not simply to the close brush with death, because the attitudinal changes are not as marked for people who faced death without undergoing an NDE (Berman, 1974).

Reported changes include a renewed sense of the purpose of life; an increased appreciation of life with a determination to live life to the fullest; a more tolerant, compassionate attitude to other people; increased religiosity in a universal rather than sectarian sense; and conviction in life after death, with substantially reduced fear of death (Flynn, 1986; Grey, 1985; Greyson, 1983; Greyson & Stevenson, 1980; Noyes, 1980; Ring, 1980, 1984; Sabom, 1982). The impact upon the experient therefore, is notable for its breadth and depth. If only for this reason the NDE would be worthy of serious investigation.

Correlates of the Near-Death Experience

Several surveys of the NDE have included items about the respondent's background with the intention of determining some correlates of the experience.

Demographic factors such as age, socioeconomic level, race (at least within the United States), and marital status have not been found to differ between people who had and those who did not have an NDE when faced with life-threatening circumstances. The incidence of the various elements of the NDE also did not vary with the above factors except that of occupation: in Sabom's (1982, p. 207) study, professional people reported fewer encounters with discarnate beings, and in the analysis by Greyson and Stevenson (1980, p. 1194) professionals were more likely to report the impression of passing through a dark tunnel. These isolated associations however, were not found in other investigations.

The NDE might nevertheless be affected by the experient's cultural background. In a comparison of NDEs in India with those in America Pasricha and Stevenson (1986) found that Indian experients did not have a panoramic life review nor an out-of-body impression of their physical bodies, and that they were taken directly by "messengers" to a transcendental realm where a discarnate being consulted some records, decided a mistake had been made and ordered their return to terrestrial life. Although the sample of Pasricha and Stevenson was relatively small these findings do suggest the elements of the NDE might not be universal. Indeed Rodabough

(1985, p. 107) argues more generally that claims for the uniformity of NDEs are overstated.

Sex may have some bearing on the experience. Sabom (1982, p. 207) found female experients to report encounters with discarnate beings more often than did males. According to Ring (1980, p. 107) and Twemlow and Gabbard (1984, p. 227) sex may influence the circumstances in which the NDE occurs: women were relatively more likely to have their experience during illness whereas men tended to have their NDE more often in an accident or a suicide attempt. This trend probably reflects a sex difference in life style rather than any inherent difference in susceptibility to the experience.

Religious affiliation and religiosity at the time of the life-threatening incident have no effect upon the likelihood of an NDE nor on the frequency of the various elements of the experience, including the supernaturalistic elements (Ring, 1980; Sabom, 1982). High religiosity seems to be more a consequence than a cause of the experience.

Some experients had heard or read about NDEs prior to their own experience: such was the case in 19 percent of Ring's (1980, p. 136) experients. It might be argued therefore, that this knowledge inspired the occurrence of an NDE when the life-threatening situation arose. Greyson and Stevenson (1980, p. 1195), however, found no relationship between prior knowledge and the incidence of the NDE. More curiously both Ring and Sabom found a *lower* incidence of prior knowledge among experients than among people who had faced death without incurring an NDE. Sabom (1982, p. 57) suggests that this was due to the greater opportunity for nonexperients to have heard of Moody's book before their brush with death: in the surveys by Ring and Sabom nonexperients on average had had their encounter with death more recently than had the experients. Another possibility is that some experients are rather reticent on any items which imply their experience to have been imaginal. In any event experients' seemingly low level of prior knowledge about the NDE makes it unlikely that the claimed degree of uniformity across NDEs is principally an artifact of such knowledge (Alcock, 1978, p. 28), although other sources of social conditioning could still provide the basis for elements of the experience.

Few studies have sought to examine the psychological profile of experients, and even these tend to rely on very small samples. Locke and Shontz (1983) studied a group of students who had had a life-threatening encounter and compared those who experienced an NDE to those who had not. No differences were found between the subgroups in intelligence, extraversion, neuroticism and trait anxiety. Twemlow and Gabbard (1984) similarly report no indications of psychopathology among experients as indexed by measures of psychoticism, hysterical tendencies, danger seeking and general adaptation, although the experients did show a high absorption capacity on Tellegen and Atkinson's (1974) scale. Using larger samples of near-death experients and nonexperients, Council, Greyson and Huff (1986) fond experients to rate highly in absorption and in fantasy-proneness. Further research of this sort may indicate why some people have an NDE in a life-threatening situation while others do not.

Twemlow and Gabbard (1984) also claim that the nature of the NDE may be influenced by the circumstances of its occurrence. For example, they report that awareness of the golden light was slightly more common when the experient was anesthetized and encounters with discarnate beings were more typical of NDEs that arose when the individual's heart stopped beating. This study unfortunately has two flaws. The technique used for the statistical analysis was inappropriate and did not incorporate a correction for multiple analyses. The sample also comprised people who had had an out-of-body experience in a near-death situation; by excluding cases of NDE that did not incorporate the out-of-body element the generality of the data is uncertain. Further research is warranted on the pertinence of the circumstances of the NDE's occurrence.

Theories of the Near-Death Experience

The NDE would offer strong support for the survival hypothesis if it could be shown to be what it superficially seems to be, namely a literal separation of the "soul" from the body and its passage to some realm of postmortem existence. The latter notion is, of course, not a description of the NDE but a theory of its basis. As with so many aspects of the survival issue parapsychologists have yet to devise an adequate test of this theory of the NDE, not really through want of effort but because of the theory's inability to generate unequivocal predictions that a materialistically oriented science can subject to empirical scrutiny. For example, the inclusion of sensorially inaccessible observations in NDEs might be held to discount an imaginal interpretation of the experience in favor of the separationist hypothesis; but such results could equally well be attributed to the operation of ESP in conjunction with a fantasy of separation. In the absence of a conclusive empirical test the evaluation of the "literal separation" theory has become a matter of disproving other potential theories. Let us therefore examine some other options.

For convenience of exposition, accounts of the NDE that fall within the scope of conventional science may be dichotomized as either predominantly neurophysiological or predominantly psychological in their orientation.

Neuropsychological Theories

Temporal lobe paroxysm. The tempero-parietal region of the cerebral cortex plays some role in visual imagery and in body image. Thus temporal lobe epilepsy and electrical stimulation of the temporal lobe are characterized by disturbance of these functions. On this basis some commentators (Carr, 1982; Persinger, 1983) have argued that the NDE is an instance of temporal lobe paroxysm, or seizure-like neural discharges in the temporal lobe or more generally in the limbic system.

Despite some similarities between the NDE and temporal lobe disorders there are several points telling against this approach (Sabom, 1982, pp. 173-174). Perception of the immediate environment typically is distorted in a temporal lobe seizure but seems strikingly realistic in the NDE. A seizure is accompanied by feelings of fear, loneliness, and sadness, whereas the NDE almost invariably is peaceful and calm. Seizures feature auditory imagery more frequently than visual imagery, and sensations of smell and taste are common; the NDE does not conform to this pattern of modalities. In a seizure and in electrical stimulation of the temporal lobe a memory may be revived but invariably it is of no great significance; it is quite unlike the succession of autobiographical highlights that occurs in the panoramic life review associated with the NDE. Finally, seizures and electrocortical stimulation do not evoke images of communicating with deceased relatives in a paradisial setting.

Cerebral anoxia. A shortage of oxygen (or, equivalently, hypercarbia, an increase in carbon dioxide) in brain metabolism can elicit hallucinatory experiences and thus has been suggested as a physiological basis of the NDE (Rodin, 1980, pp. 261-262; Schnaper, 1980). Indeed some subjects with experimentally elevated carbon dioxide levels have experienced an impression of being located outside the body (Sabom, 1982, pp. 176-178). On the other hand people in this state also tend to have bizarre imagery and thoughts that are quite uncharacteristic of the NDE. Also, NDEs do occur in circumstances where cerebral anoxia is extremely unlikely. Perhaps cerebral anoxia is one of many possible physiological cues to a threat to life but at the same time is not the fundamental cause of the experience.

Endorphin release. It might be suggested that the NDE springs from a sudden release of certain neurotransmitters in the brain known as endorphins; these are chemicals that are associated with analgesic effects and a sense of psychological well-being. The properties of endorphins still are not well established but there is little to indicate that any endorphin can evoke the specific perceptual-like experiences characteristic of the NDE. Additionally Sabom (1982, pp. 171-172) has argued that the known analgesic effects of endorphins last much longer than the seconds to minutes typical of the NDE's duration.

Drugs. Some NDEs do occur under the influence of certain medicinal drugs, particularly anesthetics. Perhaps the NDE could be explained as an effect of such drugs. On the other hand, the features of NDEs are rather too specific to be dismissed as drug-induced hallucinations. The latter are notable for their variability across people and they are more bizarre than the NDE. The drug-hallucination theory also is of limited generality since a large number of NDEs, probably the majority, do not occur in the context of drug intoxication.

Massive cortical disinhibition. An American psychologist, Ronald Siegel (1980), proposed that NDEs are due to massive cortical disinhibition. Thus in certain circumstances (including life-threatening events) control is lost over the random activity of the central nervous system and consciousness reflects the system's efforts to make sense of this endogenous activity. One effect of this, holds Siegel, is to destroy the identification of self with the physical body. Another is for endogenous activity in the optic tract to be interpreted as a perceptual-like experience; specifically, information about the intrinsic structures of the optic tract becomes a basis for the experience of a dark tunnel-shaped structure. In support of his theory Siegel points to elements of experiences induced by drugs that are similar to those of the NDE.

Again there is the problem under this theory of why the particular constellation of elements found in the NDE typically occur only as some isolated components of drug experiences. Further, if Siegel's account of the tunnel effect is correct there should be many other so-called "form constant" experiences in the NDE as there are in drug hallucinations, yet these are notable by their absence from NDEs. Thus while Siegel's approach has some novel features it lacks the coherence necessary to accommodate the range of components of NDEs.

Psychological Theories

Depersonalization. Many clinicians, most notably Russell Noyes (1979), are inclined to categorize the NDE as an instance of depersonalization. Depersonalization entails a psychological detachment from one's body; in the case of the NDE the depersonalization would be deemed a defensive psychological reaction to the perceived threat of death.

On the other hand depersonalization by definition involves not merely a sense of psychological detachment from the body but also much confusion over the identity and reality of one's self. The depersonalized individual feels she or he is not a person. This most certainly is not a characteristic of the NDE: experients typically report that during the NDE their sense of self was strong, clear, and even more real than in normal waking consciousness. The depersonalization theory also assumes that the individual first perceives a threat to life and then has an NDE as a psychological defense. Sabom (1982, pp. 162–163) argues that there are cases in which it would appear that the experient had no appreciation of the life-threatening circumstance until after the onset of the NDE or in some instances after the NDE itself.

Motivated fantasy. A milder form of the above theory retains the element of "defensive fantasy" but dispenses with the concept of depersonalization. This approach is associated particularly with the psychoanalytical school and more generally with a psychiatric orientation. The actual motivational basis of the fantasy is variously posited as narcissism (Rank, 1971) or the denial of death (Ehrenwald, 1974; Greyson, 1981; Sagan, 1979).

This is a simple theory, and perhaps too much so. Thus the motivational component of the theory is almost tautological. In essence it seems to be proposing that experients have an impression of surviving death because they desire to survive death. Under this theory one also would expect a strong correlation between the occurrence of NDEs and religiosity at the time of the experience, yet as noted above there is no such correlation. Other consistencies in NDEs do not sit well with the "fantasy" view. Why should so many experients fantasize about passing through a tunnel or darkness, and why should experients' visions of "paradise" be so similar but at the same time so unlike the biblical stereotype? In general, theorists of this school give such scant attention to the details of the NDE that one is tempted to suggest that the motivated fantasy theory is itself motivated fantasy. Perhaps the latter assessment is too harsh but the fact remains that if the NDE is to be depicted as an imaginal event it is necessary to account for the imaginal origins of each element of the experience. The next psychological theory attempts to do just this.

Archetypes. One way of accounting for the commonality of NDE elements is to assume that these images (the tunnel, the light, the "presence," the paradisial landscape) are "wired" into the brain. That is, people of all cultures and of all eras are born with an inclination to generate certain mental images or *archetypes* that form the mythological elements of our common humanity. These archetypes are held to explain the existence of parallel themes in the folklore of disparate cultures, for example. Originally postulated by Jung (1954/1971) the concept of archetypes has been applied to the NDE by an American parapsychologist, Michael Grosso (1981). The near-death archetypal image is envisaged by Grosso as the human race's consensual paradigm of "the best possible way to die."

On the other hand Jung drew upon a diversity of sources to substantiate his proposed archetypal images, but the evidence for the images of the tunnel, the golden light, and so forth seems to be confined to the experience in question. In other words independent evidence for the existence of the alleged "near-death archetypes" is lacking. How this theory might be put to a more general empirical test also is unclear. In these circumstances it does not seem very constructive to attribute the uniformity of NDEs to the uniformity of people's archetypal images: appeal is being made to one unknown in order to explain another.

It is fair to say that no current neurophysiological or psychological theory of the NDE is satisfactory. It is on these grounds that Sabom (1982) is inclined to the view that the NDE must be a literal experience, one entailing the "soul's" excursion to the environs of paradise. Furthermore, none of the rival theories precludes a separationist interpretation, and it is difficult to see how they conclusively could do so: a separation of consciousness from the body could well have the sorts of neurophysiological and psychological correlates upon which the more orthodox theorists focus their attention. Be that as it may, data on NDEs still are too meager to warrant the abandonment of orthodox approaches to the experience. Research into the origins of the individual elements of the experience particularly is required, as it is in this respect that current theories tend to founder. It certainly is premature to assert that the inadequacy of individual orthodox theories enhances the pertinence of the NDE to the survival hypothesis.

Appeal to various conventional psychological factors either singly or in combination may yet provide an adequate account of the experience. In particular, little has been made of Twemlow and Gabbard's (1984) and Council, Greyson and Huff's (1986) finding of high capacity for absorbed mentation among experients. This variable has been given considerably closer attention in relation to an allied phenomenon, the out-of-body experience (Irwin, 1985a); the latter is the subject of the next chapter.

Key Terms and Concepts

near-death experience (NDE)
Raymond Moody
Kenneth Ring
Michael Sabom
religiosity

prior knowledge
separationist theory
neurophysiological theories
psychological theories

Study Questions

1. Describe the principal phenomenological elements of the NDE.
2. Discuss research on the correlates of the NDE, indicating the potential pertinence of each dimension to our understanding of the experience.

3. List the respects in which the NDE has an impact upon the experient and consider why the experience might have these particular effects.

4. Compare and contrast the major theories of the NDE. In what respects do these theories fail?

5. Discuss the use of the NDE as evidential support for the survival hypothesis.

6. Of what help could a near-death experient be to a terminally-ill patient? To what extent should our assessment of this issue depend on the perceived adequacy of the separationist account of the NDE?

12
Out-of-Body Experiences

As noted in the previous chapter, in some NDEs the experient has the impression that consciousness is outside the physical body. This impression, termed an *out-of-body experience,* or OBE, is not confined to near-death circumstances: it may arise in a variety of other situations as is illustrated by the following account from my case collection (Irwin, 1985a, p. 1).

> This event occurred some years ago when I was in my twenties. I was in bed and about to fall asleep when I had the distinct impression that "I" was at ceiling level looking down on my body in the bed. I was very startled and frightened; immediately I felt that, I was consciously back in the bed again.

The out-of-body experience may be defined as one in which the center of awareness appears to the experient to occupy temporarily a position which is spatially remote from his or her body. As with the NDE, the OBE is defined as an experience, not as a literal event. That the OBE entails a literal separation of consciousness from the body is a theoretical interpretation of the experience rather than a definition of it.

The OBE clearly overlaps the phenomenon of the NDE and many experiences could appropriately be designated by either term. The two phenomena are not, however, equivalent: there are OBEs that occur in circumstances not life-threatening and there are NDEs that do not incorporate the impression of the self being exterior to the body. It may strike you as curious that research on the NDE has to a large degree proceeded independently of that on the OBE, but there are two main factors contributing to this situation. First, NDE research evolved primarily in a medical setting and even now a large proportion of NDE researchers are medical professionals; the OBE on the other hand has been more a focus of attention among parapsychologists *per se.* At least in the early phase of work on the NDE, researchers in fact took care to avoid any reference to the OBE literature for fear of being regarded by colleagues as "occultists." Second, the distinctive theoretical orientation to each phenomenon has been facilitated by different styles of definition: whereas the NDE is defined *contextually* or in relation to its circumstances of occurrence, the OBE is defined *phenomenologically* or in relation to its impression upon experients themselves.

Defining the OBE in experiential or phenomenological terms raises some difficulties. For example, if a psychotic patient reported an OBE, should this experience be categorized as a real OBE or as a psychopathological delusion? Under the above definition it would be admitted as an instance of an OBE because, at the time, the experient had the impression of being outside the body. With further research we may be in a position to discriminate the OBEs of psychotics from those of otherwise normal people, but at this stage a distinction between a "real" OBE and a hallucinatory one would be presumptuous. The same applies to OBEs that can be shown to include nonveridical information.

You may recall the story of Hélène Smith's out-of-body excursions to the planet Mars (Chapter 2). That Smith's account of the Martian landscape is at odds with data from space probes does not negate the fact that during the experience Smith believed her "spirit" to be outside her body, and her account thereby qualifies as an OBE report. Veridical and nonveridical OBEs may prove to have different correlates, but this dimension cannot properly be used as a criterion for accepting or rejecting OBE reports: veridical experiences might have the same bases as nonveridical ones.

In other cases people report seeing an apparition of a living individual and assert that the latter was having an OBE. Again, unless the individual concerned had an impression of being out of the body at the time, such a case would not qualify as an OBE under the adopted definition.

Data on OBEs rely heavily on retrospective reports. Thus considerable use is made of OBE case collections, surveys of experients (OBErs) and nonexperients (nonOBErs), and self-observations by so-called OBE adepts who reportedly can induce the experience virtually at will. Irwin (1985a, Ch. 2) reviews the advantages and the limitations of these sources of data; in this regard it is important to note that some of the information on OBEs is available only from the above sources.

Efforts nevertheless have been directed to the development of experimental methods of OBE induction, the objective being to facilitate laboratory investigation of the experience. At the beginning of this century French researchers pioneered hypnotic suggestion as an OBE induction procedure, but that method now is rarely used because of its strong demand characteristics; that is, because the subject merely may produce verbal responses in compliance with the hypnotist's suggestions the hypnotic performance might not be comparable experientially to a spontaneous OBE.

More recently John Palmer (1978c) has sought to induce experimental OBEs by simulating conditions under which spontaneous experiences occur.

His most successful techniques to date involve three fundamental elements. The first is bodily relaxation, usually promoted through a recorded exercise in progressive muscle relaxation. The second involves manipulation of the subject's sensory environment by way of either severe sensory restriction and homogeneity or sensory bombardment; this procedure seems to direct the individual's attention away from exteroceptive processing and to encourage high absorption in mentation. Finally there is an element of expectancy or "mental set" whereby the participant is encouraged to want an OBE and to believe one can occur (Palmer & Lieberman, 1975).

In my own use of Palmer's techniques I have found the induced experiences to be rather weak in comparison to spontaneous OBEs, often marked by little more than a vague dissociative feeling. Demand characteristics may be substantial here too. Experimental procedures in OBE research therefore, are very much in their infancy.

Phenomenological Characteristics of the Out-of-Body Experience

The following review of OBE phenomenology is based upon my earlier collation (Irwin, 1985a, Ch. 3) of data from surveys, case collections, and adepts' self-observation.

Sensations at Onset and Termination

Between 20 and 40 percent of survey respondents report having specific sensations at the onset of the OBE (Irwin, 1985a, pp. 81–82; Poynton, 1975, p. 116). Four main types of experience are cited. There may be percussive noises: the OBEr may hear a buzz, roar, click or crack on "leaving" the body. Vibrations in the physical body may be experienced; these vary from shivering to violent shaking, and from a single jolt to a series of vibrations. Catalepsy sometimes is reported; this state is described as a lack of bodily sensation or a lack of bodily control, with complete rigidity. The start of the experience also may be signaled by a momentary blackout or short period of "mental darkness," after which the experient has the impression of being exteriorized. Some of these onset phenomena are instanced in the following case (Irwin, 1985a, p. 81).

> My first experience was when I was 13 years old. I do not recall anything out of the ordinary at the time nor remember anything that might have led up to it. As I was sleeping I had a strange falling sensation. In my ears and head I had a noise, it went boom boom boom etc. very loudly and quickly. I guess it would be likened to a noise a plane makes but it

throbbed more or vibrated. I tried to wake but I felt frozen. I felt my
whole body just pinned there.

Onset sensations have been found to correlate with the impression of
control during the experience (Irwin, 1985a, p. 84), in that people who experience these phenomena tend to report they had greater control over the
way in which the OBE subsequently unfolded.

It must be emphasized, however, that onset sensations are found
among a minority of cases. In most OBEs the experient suddenly has the impression of being in an exteriorized state, as in the following experience (Irwin, 1985a, p. 81).

I was sitting in the bath when I became aware that I was in the ceiling
corner of the room looking down at myself in the bath. I watched myself
quietly for a while, aware of the light and looking down. Then suddenly
I felt frightened and the scene was rapidly lost—I was back once again
at ground level, in the bath.

This case also terminated instantaneously, as do the majority of OBEs.
Nevertheless up to 40 percent of survey respondents claim to have had definite sensations upon "returning" to the body. These phenomena are much
the same as for the onset of the experience: a momentary blackout, noises,
vibrations in the physical body, and a sense of immobility or catalepsy. If
return to the body is rapid it may be described as a sudden jolt.

The OBE may be terminated by an emotional reaction: in two of the
cases presented above fear produced an immediate end to the experience.
Other cases cite annoyance, mirth, and "consuming love" as having cut
short the OBE. The sight of the physical body from the outside may terminate the experience, in many instances apparently because of the emotional response (fear, contempt, revulsion) this sight evokes, but also
perhaps because attention is diverted back to the body. Another factor
commonly bringing an end to the OBE is the physical body's being touched
by someone. Also the experient may return to the body by a conscious effort
to do so. The OBE therefore may end when attention is drawn to bodily processes or when direction of attention away from such processes begins to
lapse.

Content of the Experience

In the typical OBE, experients find themselves instantaneously exteriorized in the immediate vicinity of the physical body, looking down on
the environment and perceiving it in an apparently realistic fashion. "Astral
flights" to far-off lands and to other planets tend to be the province of the
adept, although it is feasible that survey respondents may simply be less
willing to reveal such experiences.

Most OBErs report having seen their own body from the remote location. This is a feature of 50 to 80 percent of survey cases (Gabbard & Twemlow, 1984, p. 19; Irwin, 1985a, p. 88). The appearance of the physical body during an OBE is of interest in the following regard. There is a psychotic condition known as *autoscopy* in which the individual has an hallucination of coming face to face with their own double. A few psychiatrists want to equate the OBE with autoscopy, despite marked phenomenological differences: for example, in autoscopy the individual realizes the vision is hallucinatory and regards consciousness still to be "in" the physical body. Nevertheless one curious aspect of autoscopy is that the hallucinated double usually is a mirror image of the body, that is, it appears laterally reversed (with hair parted on the opposite side, wedding ring on the wrong hand, etc). Perhaps our mental image of ourselves tends to be laterally reversed because the most common full-length, three-dimensional experience of ourselves is in a mirror. If the OBE is an hallucinated image a perceptual-like experience of the physical body from the outside therefore might be expected to be laterally reversed. I have not been successful in obtaining definitive data on this point, although if OBErs do note the appearance of their physical body from the exteriorized perspective their comments usually are not of the form, "that's just how I look in the mirror," but rather, "so that's how I look to other people."

The out-of-body perception of the environment is described as visually realistic in over 80 percent of cases (Green, 1968a, p. 71). Occasionally some odd effects occur, including wide-angle vision, seeing through objects, and seeing in the dark, but these are uncommon. On the other hand some OBE accounts do imply a lack of realism in certain respects. For example, an experient may report seeing the physical body as if from a height of 30 feet (9 meters) or more, yet this would have entailed seeing through the roof and the ceiling of the house.

Other less common features are associated particularly with OBEs in life-threatening circumstances (Gabbard, Twemlow & Jones, 1981). Passage through a dark tunnel is reported by up to a quarter of survey respondents (Gabbard & Twemlow, 1984, p. 19; Irwin, 1985a, pp. 93–94); this seems to mark a transitional process, for example, between the body and the exteriorized state or between a naturalistic and a transcendental setting. Experiences of a bright light, discarnate entities, and music also are mentioned in a small minority of OBEs.

Sensory Modalities

Over 90 percent of OBEs are visual (Green, 1968a, pp. 67–68), often exclusively so. The involvement of other sensory modalities tends to parallel that of normal perceptual experience, or alternatively it could be said to be consistent with imagery generated so as to provide a maximally convincing representation of the normal environment.

Very occasionally an *asensory* OBE is reported, in which the experient feels exteriorized but has no perceptual-like impression of any environment. In over 300 OBE cases obtained in a British survey, Celia Green (1968a, p. 69) found only "a few" asensory experiences. In my own collection of over a hundred OBE case reports there is only one in which there was an absence of any perceptual-like awareness of the environment.

Vividness

The vividness or clarity of the perceptual-like experience is striking, according to survey respondents. Again there may be some variation in this respect as vividness usually is low in experimentally induced OBEs.

Control

Some OBErs report having been able to control the content of their experience in some way. In one of my surveys (Irwin, 1985a, p. 100), 46 percent of experients made this claim. There is a general consensus among survey respondents and adepts that such control is purely cognitive: it is a matter of directing attention to a desired state of affairs rather than of exerting "physical" effort. Most often control is exercised in relation to the place the exteriorized self wishes to be; according to some accounts the experience may be directed to a person whose location was unknown at the time. Some OBErs mention that the nature and the very existence of objects can be manipulated in the out-of-body state. Females tend to report more control over OBE content than do males (Irwin, 1985a, p. 101).

Aspects other than content are subject to control. These include the termination of the experience and the activities of the out-of-body or *parasomatic* form. Again it should be noted that many OBEs are so brief and so disconcerting that the idea of control is not even entertained.

Naturalism

About 80 percent of OBEs are purely naturalistic. Possibly this figure partly reflects a response bias: an OBE with a transcendental setting is more easily dismissed by the experient as fantasy and thus not reported.

There is some suggestion that naturalistic cases tend to relate to the world as conceived rather than as perceived. Thus people with sensory deficits often report these not to exist in an OBE (Green, 1968a, pp. 32–33; Irwin, 1987d).

As mentioned earlier, transcendental experiences tend to occur more often under life-threatening circumstances (Gabbard et al., 1981).

Veridicality

Experients typically present their naturalistic OBEs as being completely veridical. The accuracy of out-of-body perception often is assumed, however, rather than proven: if the experience matched the individual's memory of the real-life setting then it is held to have been veridical.

One means of investigating the veridicality of OBEs is to see if a person in an out-of-body state can obtain sensorially inaccessible information. In a survey by Palmer (1979) about 15 percent of OBErs claimed to have acquired information in this fashion. During induced OBEs in experimental tests (e.g., Palmer & Lieberman, 1975) subjects have been able to identify remote targets to a statistically significant degree. This might be attributable to the use of ESP, although in a study conducted by one of my students (Smith & Irwin, 1981) a correlation was found between veridicality and independently judged "OBEness"; that is, the more the induced experience was like a spontaneous OBE the more accurate was the subject's description of a remote target. There is, therefore, some indication that OBEs can be veridical to a degree that mere fantasy could not. Further research on this point is warranted.

In some OBEs nonveridical elements nevertheless do occur. One case (Crookall, 1972, pp. 89–90) included mention of nonexistent bars on the bedroom window; these bars seemed to have some symbolic significance for the experient in preventing him from "leaving" his room.

The Astral Body and the Astral Cord

Some OBErs report their exteriorized self to have had a definite form. In occult literature this is termed the "astral body"; in parapsychological work it is known also as the *parasomatic* form. Estimates of the incidence of parasomatic forms vary widely, from 15 to 84 percent of experiences (Irwin, 1985a, p. 114), but the trend is for the slight majority of OBEs to be parasomatic. Further, even in allegedly *asomatic* experiences, the OBEr may imply that the formless exteriorized self had spatial dimensions. For example, the exteriorized self may be said to have had to "squeeze" through a small space or to have been "standing."

The parasomatic form most commonly is a replica of the physical body. A few older experients have depicted their astral bodies as the image of themselves when they were at their physical peak. Occasionally the parasomatic form is localized as a point or a small sphere, while in other cases its dimensions are more vague, being described as a cloud, a mist, or a band of light.

In about 20 percent of survey cases (Irwin, 1985a, p. 125) the parasomatic form is linked to the physical body by a cord-like structure. This so-called *astral cord* is more common in those case collections in which respondents of a spiritualist persuasion are frequent; here the structure tends to be known as "the silver cord." It is much less common in contemporary cases and is very rare in laboratory induced experiences.

The cord reportedly may join the physical body at either the forehead or in the region of the solar plexus; its connection to the astral body often is on the back. Where experients do report having had an astral cord it usually is on the basis of having seen it, but sometimes it is evidenced merely as a sensation of being tugged toward the physical body. Many experients have the impression that if the cord were broken death would be inevitable.

Psychological Processes During the Experience

Experients tend to characterize their psychological state in an OBE as one of relaxed alertness, mental clarity, and effortless concentration. In cognitive terms the OBE is marked by a resistance to distraction and total involvement, the state known as absorption. This recalls the earlier suggestion that the experience may be terminated by a loss or disruption of concentration.

Emotionally the experient seems to be calm, peaceful, and even emotionally detached during the experience, even in otherwise arousing circumstances. It seems that any emotion with strong bodily concomitants tends to terminate the experience.

Circumstances of Occurrence

Other research on the OBE is more explicitly process-oriented, seeking to illuminate factors underlying the experience. Two major foci for this work have been the OBE's circumstances of occurrence and the sorts of people who are prone to the experience.

Under what circumstances does the OBE take place? For convenience of discussion the experient's mental state and physical state will be considered separately; it is not assumed however, that these aspects are independent.

Pre-Experience Mental State

In about 60 percent of survey cases the pre-OBE mental state is described as quiescent or calm, rather like the OBE itself. On the other hand the experience also can arise in emotionally arousing circumstances such as confrontation with death; this is found in 25 to 40 percent of cases (Irwin, 1985a, pp. 144–145).

It would seem then that the OBE may occur under a wide range of mental states, but in fact we can be more specific than this. Irwin (1985a, p. 146) asked a group of OBErs to rate their pre-OBE mental state on a ten point scale. Fifteen rated their emotional arousal as having been low (1, 2, or 3); nine rated it as high (8, 9, or 10); and only two respondents chose intermediate ratings. This trend towards extremes of arousal is statistically significant. On these grounds it may be proposed that the OBE occurs when the level of cortical arousal is extreme (either high or low), perhaps unusually extreme for the experient.

Pre-Experience Physical State

Many OBEs occur when sensory input is minimal or under conditions approximating sensory deprivation. Lying on the bed or meditating are common contexts for the experience. At the other extreme the experience also may be precipitated by sensory bombardment or overload, as in the trance states associated with the rhythms of native drums and the dances of the whirling dervishes; in one case in my collection the experient was listening to very loud rock music. Again it is probable that these physical states have their effect by way of cortical arousal.

At the same time the factor of physical inactivity warrants closer scrutiny. Over 90 percent of OBEs (Green, 1968a, p. 50) occur when the individual is physically inactive (lying down, sitting, etc.). This suggests that a lack of somatic (kinesthetic and proprioceptive) stimulation is an important condition for the OBE. In other words the person must be out of touch with bodily processes. This also accords with the indication that attention to bodily processes brings the experience to an end. Of the 5 to 10 percent of cases in which the experient was physically active at the time of the OBE the considerable majority of activities were automatic (e.g., walking) or so highly practiced as to be automatic for the individual concerned (e.g., a professional musician playing an instrument, a minister reading a sermon).

In cognitive terms these automatic activities require a negligible amount of attention. One may say the individual can perform them while remaining out of touch with bodily processes.

Induction Processes

Many commentators on mystical experiences have published detailed programs for the deliberate self-induction of the OBE (Rogo, 1983). Although most of these have not been put to rigorous scientific investigation they are worthy of consideration as a source of *hypotheses* about the factors critical to the occurrence of the experience.

At first glance there are as many proposed OBE induction techniques as there are commentators, but once the esoteric rigmarole is stripped away some consistencies can be identified (Irwin, 1985a, pp. 155–170). Physical and mental relaxation are given particular emphasis, reinforcing some of the suggestions made above. The use of mental imagery is a common feature; whether this is important for its own sake or as a focus for one's attention is not clear. Certainly attention or absorption is seen as a fundamental factor: many programs include directions for focusing attention upon a particular thought or object, and some even promote some preparatory training in total absorption. The other characteristic general to all techniques, either implicitly or explicitly, is that of expectation: the individual who follows any proposed induction program is to expect an OBE to happen.

The Experient

Further insight into the nature of the OBE may be gained by determining the sorts of people who have these experiences.

Incidence

There have been few surveys of OBEs among the general population, but estimates of their incidence here range from 8 to 15 percent (Blackmore, 1984a; Palmer, 1979).

The most frequent target population has been that of university students. In my own studies (Irwin, 1985a, p. 174) I have found 20 to 48 percent of Australian undergraduate psychology students to have had the experience. These figures are comparable to data from other countries. The higher incidence of reported OBEs among university students may reflect various factors such as better memory, higher capacity for self-observation, recency of experience, more willingness to acknowledge "odd" experiences, greater sympathy with academics' surveys, and more frequent experimentation with psychotropic drugs.

Surveys also indicate that the majority of experients have had more than one OBE (e.g., Palmer, 1979). While the experience may not be an everyday one for the individual it nevertheless seems to be a remarkably familiar one on a population basis.

Age

The OBE evidently can occur at any time of life, although current data are not adequate to indicate if the experience is more common at a given phase of life. Few reported cases occurred when the experient was less than five years old (Irwin, 1985a, p. 179; Woofﬁtt & Blackmore, 1985), but there are difﬁculties of recall for this period (how many experiences can you recall from your preschool years?) and direct questioning of very young children is fraught with such methodological problems as response bias and lack of comprehension.

Sex

In case collections there are more accounts from female experients than from males. Judging from survey data, however, sex does not seem to be a major factor in the incidence of the experience (Irwin, 1985a, p. 181), although it may be linked with the circumstances under which the OBE arises: for example, OBEs under marijuana intoxication are more likely for males presumably because males on average are heavier users of marijuana (Tart, 1971, p. 105).

Other Demographic Variables

The OBE evidently is independent of level of education, marital status, social class and income. Religiosity does not influence either the occurrence of the OBE or the incidence of any specific aspects of OBE content (Irwin, 1985a, pp. 186–189).

There are few data upon which to assess the possible role of race and culture in the OBE. There are differences across cultures in *belief* in the possibility of an OBE, the sorts of people who are thought capable of having an OBE, and the circumstances under which an OBE is held to occur (Sheils,

1978). Some qualitative evidence does suggest that culture may affect OBE content. For example, when shamans of certain primitive tribes have a "magical flight," their parasomatic bodies often are said to take the form of the tribe's totemic animal.

Prior Knowledge

Certainly the OBE can occur without the experient's prior knowledge of the phenomenon. About 50 to 60 percent of survey cases occurred without such knowledge. Further, prior knowledge does not seem to influence the incidence of the various elements of the experience, including sensations at onset and at termination, the possession of an astral body, and the impression of having control over the experience (Irwin, 1985a, pp. 192–196).

Personality

Several studies have investigated the personality of the OBEr. Gabbard and Twemlow (1984, p. 32) found experients to be comparatively low in "danger seeking," but the control group for their investigation makes this result ambiguous. I did not find this tendency among student experients (Irwin, 1980c).

Gackenbach (1978/1979) reports that people who have a high number of OBEs are more unrestrained, imaginative, radical, and "bohemian." This profile of the OBEr as "unconventional" may be misleading. People whose personalities are comparatively unrestrained may have more OBEs not because they are inherently more susceptible to the experience but because they are more likely to delve into occultism and thus to experiment with OBE induction techniques.

Using the *Jackson Personality Inventory,* Myers, Austrin, Grisso and Nickeson (1983) found OBErs had a greater breadth of interest and taste for complexity than did nonexperients. The population they investigated, however, comprised students of a Jesuit college. It is feasible their data say more about nonOBEing Jesuit college students than they do about the personality of the OBEr. Comparison of the data to college student norms supports this view.

Irwin (1985a, p. 201) did not identify any differences between experients and nonexperients on either the extraversion or the neuroticism scales of the *Eysenck Personality Inventory*. Tobacyk and Mitchell (1987) also report no association between the OBE and measures of avoidance defense styles, narcissism and social desirability.

Cognitive Skills

Imagery skills of OBErs warrant some scrutiny. It might be expected that if the OBE is an imaginal experience it would require some dexterity of imagery skills to conjure up a vivid image of how one's physical body and the immediate environment would appear if observed from a point near the ceiling.

Several parapsychologists have examined the ability to generate vivid visual images and to control or manipulate such images. No differences between experients and nonexperients have been established (see Irwin, 1985a, pp. 260–277, for a review). One aspect of visual imagery ability, however, has been found to be pertinent. Cook and Irwin (1983) ascertained that OBErs are comparatively adept in judging how an object would appear from various perspectives.

Although general visual imagery skills do not seem to be pertinent I have found that kinesthetic and somaesthetic imagery is correlated with experients' impression of control over their OBEs (Irwin, 1985a, pp. 272–273). This suggests that in order for the exteriorized self to appear to be doing one thing while the physical body is doing another, some skill in somatic imagery is necessary.

Phenomenological analyses of OBEs, as well as the OBE's association with lucid dreams (Green, 1968a,b; Irwin, 1988a), meditation (Palmer, 1979), and hypnotic susceptibility (Palmer & Lieberman, 1976), raise the possible significance of attentional factors in the OBE. One aspect of this is that during the OBE the individual is out of touch with bodily processes. It therefore may be asked if this is specific to the experience or is a habitual tendency of experients. This issue has not been researched thoroughly but in a questionnaire study I did not find experients to have a permanently low level of "body consciousness" (Irwin, 1985a, pp. 279–280).

The other attentional aspect of the OBE is that of absorption. The nature of the experience suggests that OBErs may have a capacity for resisting distraction. That this is not specific to the period of the OBE is suggested by experients' greater inclination toward lucid dreams and meditation and their superior susceptibility to hypnosis. Irwin (1980c, 1981b, 1985a) has established a substantial advantage of experients over nonexperients in capacity for having absorbing experiences. This result has been confirmed by Myers et al. (1983) in the United States. Further, people who have high absorption scores are more open to an experimental OBE induction technique (Irwin, 1981b). Thus the variable of absorption seems to play a major role in the OBE. There are indications too that experients with high absorption capacity are more likely to report a parasomatic form and sensations at termination of their spontaneous OBEs (Irwin, 1985a, pp. 287–288).

Fantasy proneness, a factor strongly related to absorption capacity, reportedly is higher among OBErs than nonOBErs (Myers et al., 1983; Wilson & Barber, 1983). Stanford (1987b) reports further that various types of fantasy during childhood may correlate differentially with the circumstances in which the individual's OBE arises.

Needs

The content of many OBEs suggests that the experience may serve some social need, such as the need to be with a particular person. On the other hand there are so many other cases in which social motives are lacking that it is likely such motives affect the content rather than the actual occurrence of the OBE.

One psychoanalytic view of the OBE (e.g., Rank, 1971) is that the experience reflects narcissism; experients have a need, it is said, to step outside their physical bodies and admire them as everyone else can. In one of my surveys however, experients did not exhibit a greater obsession with their bodies than did nonexperients (Irwin, 1985a, pp. 296–297). Tobacyk and Mitchell (1987) also observed no difference between OBErs and nonOBErs on the *Narcissistic Personality Inventory*. Thus the need for a narcissistic fantasy does not seem a likely factor in the OBE.

In a more broadly based investigation of the manifest needs of OBErs, Irwin (1981a) found these people to have a higher need for intraception: this entails a concern with and attention to one's mental processes. This finding accords with the earlier result that experients have a high capacity for absorption. To explore this link further the items of the absorption questionnaire were reworded to address the respondent's *need* for absorbing experiences rather than the mere capacity for such experiences. Again OBErs were shown in two studies (Irwin, 1985a, p. 303; Irwin, 1985b) to have a substantially higher need for absorption.

Neurophysiological Correlates

A few studies have recorded neurophysiological data while a subject had an OBE in the laboratory (for a review see Irwin, 1985a, pp. 207–210). For obvious reasons most of these investigations employed adepts as subjects. In general terms the only correlates of the out-of-body state are for the adept to exhibit the neurophysiological signs of being deeply relaxed and of attending to something. These findings have yet to be replicated with unselected subjects.

The Impact of the Experience

An OBE can affect some of the experient's attitudes. The fear of death is reduced in many OBErs (Irwin, 1988b; Osis, 1979). Those OBEs occurring under life-threatening circumstances particularly are associated with a tendency to view death as leading to an afterlife of reward and justification (Irwin, 1988b). The experience will likely be interpreted in spiritual terms if the individual previously was religious or if the OBE occurred in near-death circumstances (Gabbard et al., 1981); however, the OBE generally does not inspire religious conversion in atheists (Irwin, 1985a, pp. 215–216; Palmer, 1979, p. 245). Many experients become interested in psychic phenomena and do some reading in this field (Gabbard & Twemlow, 1984, p. 22; Osis, 1979). Most feel the experience to have been beneficial, providing a better understanding of oneself and increasing awareness of altered states of consciousness and of the possibility of "other realities" (Gabbard & Twemlow, 1984, p. 23; Irwin, 1988b; Osis, 1979). The majority of experients therefore, would be happy to have another OBE.

Theories of the Out-of-Body Experience

How are OBEs and their correlates to be explained? Broadly speaking theories of the OBE fall into two categories. First there are the *ecsomatic theories;* they propose that in an OBE a nonphysical element of existence literally separates from the body and subsequently returns to it. Opposed to this approach are the *imaginal theories* that see the OBE as imaginal or hallucinatory (in a nonpejorative sense), a product of purely psychological or physiological factors. Instances of each type of theory will be described and critically reviewed.

Ecsomatic Theories

According to Crookall (1970) we each possess a "superphysical soul body" that in an OBE separates from the physical body and passes through the objectively real worlds of earth, paradise, and hades. Many aspects of Crookall's theory can be criticized but one of the major difficulties for this type of theory springs from the assumption that the soul body exteriorizes into the physical world. If this is the case why do some OBErs report distortions in reality (e.g., bars on the bedroom window), and how are some experients able to manipulate the nature and existence of objects in the out-of-body environment by an effort of will?

Other ecsomatic theorists such as Yram (c. 1926/1974) maintain that the out-of-body world is constructed from memory and imagination but is every bit as "real" as the physical world. The out-of-body environment is a world of *thought forms* that can be manipulated by mental processes. But while the out-of-body world is imaginary the OBE is not: the experient's entry into and existence within this world are held to be as real as one's existence in the physical world. You may be uneasy with this interpretation of what is real and what is imaginary. The notion of a world created from memory and imagination nevertheless does accommodate the fact that the OBE may relate to the physical world as the experient conceives it yet also feature some fantasized distortions of the real world.

A source of inconvenience for this approach is that in some OBEs it would seem that experients can acquire information about sensorially inaccessible events of which they previously were ignorant. If the out-of-body world is a product of memory and imagination how is this possible? Some theorists in this camp simply deny that such experiences occur. Others such as Yram resort to introducing another conceptual realm, a "clairvoyant dimension," that during an OBE is accessible in much the same way that the thought world is entered. The latter notion seems little else than an assumption of what is to be explained.

Whiteman (1961) and some other ecsomatic theorists propose that there exists an astral world that has varying degrees of correspondence with the physical world. An OBE consists of the soul's movement into this "astral" world. These theorists would appear to be hedging their bets. If an OBE is veridical, that is because the astral and physical worlds corresponded. If the experience is distorted then the two worlds were not quite in correspondence after all. Unless there is an independent measure of the level of correspondence this notion remains *ad hoc* and contrived.

In general terms the ecsomatic approach is intuitively plausible (especially to people who have had an OBE) and at least at first blush it is conceptually parsimonious. The impression of being outside the body, the perceptual-like awareness of the environment in an out-of-body perspective, and the apparent possession of a parasomatic form linked to the body by a cord, all are explained by one basic and simple notion, that the OBE is literally as it seems to be. But the parsimony of the ecsomatic theory is deceptive. As far as making a minimum of conceptual assumptions is concerned, it is just as simple to assert that all out-of-body phenomena are hallucinatory.

On closer inspection the ecsomatic approach is seen not to constitute a very good scientific theory. It tends to provide *post hoc* explanations rather than testable implications. For example, under this theory what sorts of people are susceptible to OBEs? No specific indications are forthcoming; but if it is mentioned that lucid dreamers are more open to the experience this is "explained" by declaring such people to have inherently "loose" astral entities. Similarly the circumstances of the OBE's occurrence are not explained by the theory but merely cited to be the circumstances under which an OBE might be evoked.

This is not to say that there have been no attempts to test the theory. Some researchers have placed various physical detectors in a target location to see if the subject's exteriorized self can be detected there (for reviews see Alvarado, 1982; Irwin, 1985a, pp. 61–66). Most such studies have yielded null results, although in a couple of experiments (e.g., Osis & McCormick, 1980) some unusual recordings from the detectors have been reported. The ecsomatic theory is so pliable however, that it could accommodate any outcome of a detector study. Null data may be explained on the basis that the exteriorized self is nonphysical and hence would not interact with a physical detector. Positive signals from the instruments may be said to be due to certain "semiphysical" properties of the exteriorized self. On the other hand, critics could attribute such signals to subconscious psychokinetic effects rather than to the presence of any exteriorized entity.

Karlis Osis (1974, 1975; Osis & Perskari, 1975), of the American Society for Psychical Research, has conducted another sort of test of the ecsomatic approach. His experimental task requires a subject to exteriorize to a sensorially inaccessible location and to "look" at a target placed there. Now extrachance success in such a task potentially could be due either to an OBE or to ESP, so Osis sought to arrange the experimental task in such a way as to provide a test between these rival interpretations. In an attempt to show that exteriorization was possible Osis devised the following method to rule out target identification by ESP.

The target image was generated inside a box and was visible only through a small viewing window on one side of the box. The target had three independent dimensions: shape, background color, and location in one of four segments of the viewing window. Each of these various dimensions was enacted by a different optical mechanism. Thus, argued Osis, the composite image was not in one single place within the box and could not be "scanned" by ESP; it could be apprehended only through the viewing window, either by normal sight or by "exteriorized sight." Using this device Osis claimed that a few subjects gave responses that suggested they could get either the composite image or nothing at all, a finding he construes as supportive of the ecsomatic hypothesis.

That the result could not have been due to clairvoyance, however, is moot. Osis assumes that clairvoyance relates only to physical objects; that is, in this context he holds that clairvoyance may be applied to the individual physical components within the box but not to the physical (visual) stimuli emitted through the viewing window. Since parapsychologists do not know the limits of ESP, Osis's view of the way in which ESP operates is presumptuous and on these grounds his test of the ecsomatic hypothesis must be deemed inconclusive.

If Osis's work achieves anything at all it is to show how very difficult the ecsomatic theory is to subject to scientific evaluation. Proponents of the approach would respond that this highlights the extent to which a materialistically oriented science is ill-suited to the study of nonphysical phenomena. The problems of ecsomatic theories, however, are more deep-seated than this response would allow. It is not simply a matter of the adequacy of scientific method but whether the ecsomatic hypothesis can predict new relationships and accommodate known relationships without resorting to *ad hoc* assumptions. That ecsomatic theorists in principle can construct a model with these features has yet to be demonstrated.

Imaginal Theories

Probably the majority of psychologists and psychiatrists regard the OBE as hallucinatory. This may very well prove to be the case but in itself it hardly constitutes a sufficient explanation of the experience. The latter demands some consideration of the origins and bases of the out-of-body hallucination, and it is to theories with this level of specificity that we now turn. As with the NDE, imaginal theories of the OBE may be categorized as either predominantly physiological or predominantly psychological.

Physiological theories. An American parapsychologist, Barbara Honegger (1979), attributes the OBE to a mechanism of biological homeostasis. Homeostasis involves a regulatory response to a sudden shift in physiological state in order to preserve biological integrity. According to Honegger, in certain circumstances such as sensory deprivation, sensory overload, and trauma, the human organism loses its biological sense of self and the impression of the existence of self independent of the physical body is created to restore integrity. If the possession of a body is an indispensable part of the individual's sense of self a parasomatic form also will be incorporated in the out-of-body imagery.

Other physiological theories of the OBE are essentially the same as those listed in Chapter 11 for the NDE. The "temporal lobe paroxysm" hypothesis has some adherents (Eastman, 1962; Persinger, 1983).

The criticisms of the physiological models of the NDE apply equally to the equivalent depictions of the OBE and need not be reiterated. Account also needs to be taken of the fact that OBEs do not occur only under life-threatening circumstances. For example, Siegel's (1980) theory of "massive cortical disinhibition" is based on the assumption of high cortical arousal and as noted previously there appear to be some OBEs that arise under conditions of very low cortical arousal.

Psychological theories. An old theory of the OBE is that it represents a schizophrenic hallucination (Rawcliffe, 1959). Some objections to this view were mentioned in the context of the NDE. Personality test scores of OBErs and nonOBErs offer little support for this approach, and it is hard to imagine a quarter to a third of undergraduate psychology students being subject to schizophrenic hallucinations.

The depersonalization model of the NDE has been extrapolated to the OBE by Whitlock (1978). Again it must be said OBErs do not appear strangers to themselves as do depersonalized individuals. Tests of experients' body image also reveal nothing unusual (Irwin, 1985a, pp. 246-247).

Previously mentioned was Rank's (1971) psychoanalytical theory of the OBE centered on the concept of narcissism. That experients are not preoccupied with their physical appearance (Irwin, 1985a, pp. 296-297) and do not score highly on a measure of narcissistic tendencies (Tobacyk & Mitchell, 1987) leaves this theory without an empirical base.

A psychiatrist, Jan Ehrenwald (1974), has described the OBE as an imaginal confirmation of the quest for immortality, a delusory attempt to assure ourselves that we possess a soul that exists independently of the physical body. Two main lines of evidence speak against Ehrenwald's theory. First, neither the occurrence of the OBE nor the incidence of transcendental elements in it are correlated with religiosity (Irwin, 1985a, pp. 186-189). Second, concern with the existence of an afterlife was not found to affect susceptibility to an experimental OBE induction procedure (Smith & Irwin, 1981).

In some older texts (e.g., Tyrrell, 1942/1963) the OBE is termed traveling clairvoyance, or *ESP projection*. Thus it is possible that the perceptual-like content of OBEs is based on ESP, and to provide oneself with a sense of orientation to the remote location, a fantasy of mentally traveling to that point is integrated with the extrasensory information. This theory accounts for both veridical and distorted OBEs, although like many other theories it has difficulty in accounting for some phenomenological elements such as onset sensations and the tunnel effect. According to Blackmore (1982, p. 237) the ESP theory also might not be open to being disproved: this would require a test in which an OBE must be elicited when the possibility of ESP is ruled out, and parapsychologists do not know how to engineer the latter conditions. On the other hand it is possible in principle to establish if the properties of the OBE differ from those of ESP and hence the ESP theory could be testable in these terms.

One of the more detailed psychological accounts of the OBE has been formulated by John Palmer (1978b). In some respects Palmer's theory is similar to a homeostatic approach. Palmer proposes that in certain situations a lack of proprioceptive feedback threatens the individual's sense of self and the OBE then occurs as an imaginal attempt to reestablish this sense of self and to ensure that the ego has not been destroyed. The perceptual-like aspect of the OBE actually is hypnagogic imagery, according to Palmer; any extrasensory content of the experience in a sense is incidental, reflecting hypnagogic imagery's conduciveness to ESP. The postulated involvement of hypnagogic imagery, however, is open to question. Such imagery tends to be bizarre, disconnected, rapidly changing, not subject to volitional control, most common in childhood, and not about oneself (Schacter, 1976); these features are not typical of the OBE. Nevertheless Palmer's notion of being sensorially out of touch with the body does accord with suggestions made earlier in this review of the OBE.

More recently Susan Blackmore (1984b) has offered a cognitive theory of the OBE. She proposes that at any given time the cognitive system is generating many different models of reality and one is chosen on the basis of its compatibility with current sensory input. In certain circumstances such as stress, sensory information processing is not efficacious and the cognitive system then is more inclined to select a model of reality compiled from information in memory and imagination. Some of these memorial representations of the environment incorporate a bird's-eye view. The OBE entails the experient's acceptance of one of these models as "reality." Blackmore's theory is consistent with the finding by Cook and Irwin (1983) that OBErs are better than nonOBErs in imagining a given scene from a different viewpoint. Blackmore also predicts higher imagery skills among people who deliberately induce OBEs than among spontaneous experients; imagery performance data have yet to confirm this. Research by Irwin (1986) suggests that Blackmore's theory might have to take cognizance of the distinction between parasomatic and asomatic OBEs; the disposition to construct bird's-eye models of reality could vary across this dimension.

The principal shortcoming in these imaginal theories of the OBE is that they have tended to focus almost exclusively on explaining why the experient feels that the self literally is exteriorized. The diverse phenomenological elements of the OBE all too often have been neglected. An attempt to formulate a more comprehensive theory of the OBE was undertaken by Irwin (1985a, Ch. 8). His *synesthetic model* is complex, in part a consequence of its comprehensiveness.

The origins of the OBE are hypothesized by Irwin to lie in a confluence of absorption factors. Circumstances associated with extreme (either high or low) levels of cortical arousal evoke a state of high absorption, particularly in the case of a person with a requisite level of absorption capacity and need for absorbing experiences. Alternatively, high absorption may be induced deliberately by the experient. If this state of absorbed mentation is paralleled by a lack of attention to somatic (somaesthetic and kinesthetic) stimuli, an OBE may occur. In instances where the development of absorption is gradual, the imminent cognitive loss of all somatic contact may be signaled by certain innate biological warning signals, the so-called OBE onset sensations.

The continued orientation of attention away from both exteroceptive and somatic stimuli effectively suspends support for the socially conditioned assumption that the perceiving self is "in" the physical body, fostering the impression that consciousness no longer is tied spatially to the body. This abstract, nonverbal idea of a disembodied consciousness is coded by the cognitive processing system into a passive, generalized somaesthetic image of a static floating self. Consciousness of that image corresponds to the so-called asensory OBE.

The somaesthetic image also may be transformed by a synesthetic process into a visual image, given a basic level of visuospatial skills in the experient. Strong absorption in this image is a basis for the OBE's perceptual realism. The somaesthetic image also may be transformed into a more dynamic, kinesthetic form and the experient will have the impression of being able to move in the imaginal out-of-body environment. The somatic imagery entailed in this transformation is held to underlie the phenomenon of the parasomatic form. A drawing of attention back to the physical body's state also may be expressed synesthetically by way of the image of the astral cord.

The perceived content of the out-of-body environment is governed by short-term needs. A life-threatening situation, for example, may prompt imagery about a paradisial environment; the nature of the latter is held to be a product of social conditioning, although the precise sources of these "heavenly" stereotypes have yet to be identified fully (see Irwin, 1987b). Because absorption is psi-conducive it is possible that the out-of-body imagery could incorporate extrasensory information and thereby feature a degree of veridicality not expected of mere fantasy; evidence of extrasensory elements in spontaneous OBEs is not yet convincing, however. Eventual dissipation of absorption or diversion of attention to somatic or exteroceptive processes brings the individual's OBE to an end.

It can fairly be said that parapsychologists' recent empirical and theoretical investigations of the OBE have substantially enhanced scientific understanding of the experience. Although ecsomatic theories have not been conclusively discounted, the OBE currently does not look a promising source of support for the survival hypothesis. Even if the experience were shown to involve a literal separation of a nonphysical element of existence from the physical body there is no certainty that this element could survive the biological death of the body. Notwithstanding that fact, the OBE remains a rewarding topic of scientific study.

Key Terms and Concepts

out-of-body experience (OBE; in earlier works, frequently OOBE)

out-of-body experients (OBErs)

asensory

asomatic

parasomatic

sensations at termination

autoscopy

astral cord

cortical arousal

somatic imagery

somaesthetic

kinesthetic

capacity for absorbing experiences

ecsomatic theories

Crookall

Osis

imaginal theories

homeostasis

narcissism

ESP projection

Palmer

Blackmore

Irwin

synesthetic model

Study Questions

1. Describe a typical OBE and list the principal features of the phenomenon.

2. What are the major methods for researching the OBE? Consider the advantages and disadvantages of each approach.

3. Some OBEs include elements that do not correspond to physical reality. For example, one experient noted that in her OBE the color and pattern of the bedroom wallpaper had changed. Do these cases demonstrate that the OBE is pure fantasy?

4. Many experients describe their OBEs as completely realistic. If the OBE is not a process of literal exteriorization of perceptual functions how can this impression be explained?

5. On the basis of the phenomenology of the OBE what factors emerge as of potential significance in the explanation of the experience?

6. Under what circumstances do OBEs occur? What do these circumstances suggest about the nature of the experience?

7. There has been some investigation into the sorts of people who have OBEs. Has this research indicated anything about the underlying processes of the experience?

8. Outline the major theories of the OBE and discuss their viability.

9. Sit in a comfortable chair in a quiet location, close your eyes and perform the following exercise. Imagine that you can transfer your point of observation to a corner of the ceiling and that you can look down into the room and see yourself seated in the chair.

How difficult was this exercise? What does it suggest about the cognitive skills necessary for an OBE if the imaginal hypothesis is valid? Assuming that you did not feel "out of the body" during the exercise, how then can the OBE be claimed to be an imaginal experience of this sort?

13
Apparitional Experiences

Tales of ghosts, wraiths, and other apparitions have been recorded in virtually all cultures (Rosenblatt, Walsh & Jackson, 1976). In the context of parapsychology these phenomena are so clearly germane to the survival hypothesis that they were accorded special significance from the earliest years of the Society for Psychical Research.

It is difficult to define the term "apparition" without introducing some theoretical assumption about the nature of the phenomena encompassed by that term. In essence an apparition is encountered in a perceptual-like experience and relates to a person or animal that is not physically present, with physical means of communication being ruled out. Note that apparitions are not defined in terms of a "spirit form"; such an approach would incorporate a particular theoretical interpretation of an apparitional experience and thus is best avoided in formulating a definition. On the other hand many parapsychologists, while not committing themselves to the authenticity of apparitions, maintain that these phenomena must be defined as being objective or at least semiobjective. We know that people have apparitional experiences but it is held to be pointless to speak of "apparitions" unless we mean this term to refer to the hypothesis of an objective entity. Having defined the term thus, it is up to parapsychologists to ascertain if these hypothesized objective entities actually exist.

A comparable argument may be raised against any definition of the apparition as hallucination. To the extent that the person represented by the apparition, the so-called *referent person,* is not present in the experient's immediate environment it could be said the apparition is hallucinatory. But this too entails an implicit interpretation of the phenomenon because at least in the view of some researchers the apparition itself could have some manner of objective existence independent of the referent person and thereby be "perceptible" through normal sensory channels. The definition adopted above rightly does not preclude nor presume any theoretical possibility.

The conceptualization of an apparition either as objective or as hallucinatory has been a dominant issue in the past century of parapsychologists' research into these phenomena but as Osis (1986a) points out, this focus has proved hopelessly inconclusive and might even have blinkered investigators to pursue hypotheses along inappropriately narrow paths. In recent years there has been a growing appreciation that we need to study not the apparition per se but rather the *apparitional experience;* that is, it might be best to adopt a phenomenological approach in this field of study. In this context the apparition's seemingly objective features and its seemingly hallucinatory features all are documented simply as aspects of the experience's phenomenology. Thus these featural categories are not deemed *a priori* to be mutually contradictory, nor need they divert research from the determination of other phenomenological dimensions of the apparitional experience. The foregoing definition can readily be reformulated to suit this shift in orientation; thus, the *apparitional experience* is perceptual-like and relates to a person or an animal that is not physically present, with physical means of communication being ruled out.

While an apparitional experience may prove to be hallucinatory it nevertheless should in principle be distinguishable from mirages and perceptual illusions (in which physical means of communication can be ascertained), and rather more problematically, from hallucinations associated with drug states and mental illness (Anderson & Anderson, 1982). Admittedly it may be difficult in practice to decide whether a given report describes an(other) hallucination or is a prima facie case of an apparitional experience, but there are criteria which may help in some instances.

An apparitional experience may convey veridical information of which the experient previously was unaware; this generally is lacking in psychotic and drug-induced hallucinations of another person. An apparitional experience can be related clearly to an identifiable person (or animal); hallucinatory figures typically are anonymous or known to be nonexistent. Finally, an apparition may be experienced by more than one person, whereas a psychotic or drug-related hallucination cannot be shared.

By way of illustration the following collective case of an apparition was researched by the Society for Psychical Research (Gurney et al., 1886, Vol. 2, pp. 617–618). Two brothers sharing a cabin in an old naval ship suddenly were awakened to see the figure of their father standing between their bunks. As one of the brothers sat up the form vanished. The father had died about the time of the incident. (It must be acknowledged that in some collective cases the various accounts of the same experience do show discrepancies; of course, eye-witnesses' reports of objective events also can differ in substantial respects.)

Phenomenological Characteristics of Apparitional Experiences

Data on the phenomenology of apparitional experience necessarily come from collections of spontaneous cases and anecdotes. A good number of cases presented to societies for psychical research have been investigated carefully by society members for their evidential reliability, although the usual problems with spontaneous case material apply (Gauld, 1977, p. 604).

Two additional sources of bias spring from the popularity of ghost stories in fiction. First, some supposedly real-life cases initially may have been devised as a good story but then presented as authentic in the hope of enhancing their commercial potential. Second, fictional ghost stories (and folklore too) promote a particular stereotype of an apparitional experience and it is feasible that witnesses' accounts of their experience unwittingly are distorted to conform to these popular expectations. Parapsychologists therefore must be a little wary of accepting consistencies in spontaneous case accounts as indications of the nature of apparitions: in part these consistencies may reveal only the fictional conception of apparitions. One way of minimizing this problem is to give greater credence to consistencies that are not a feature of the popular stereotype, but if taken to an extreme there is a danger here of throwing out the metaphorical baby with the bathwater: some aspects of the fictional stereotype may well be drawn from authentic experiences.

Ignoring fictional anthologies (especially those labelled "true life ghost stories") there are a few case collections testifying to the phenomenology of apparitional experiences. One of the earliest sizeable collections was the SPR's "Census of Hallucinations" (Sidgwick et al., 1894); this was concerned with apparitions of people occurring about the time of their death. Tyrrell's (1942/1963) book *Apparitions* was based on a smaller number of cases intensively investigated by the SPR and is a classic in its field. A difficulty with these corroborated cases, however, is that the SPR researchers insisted there be evidence that the experience was more than a mere hallucination. A simple report of an apparitional figure was insufficient; the figure had to communicate information of which the experient could be shown to have been unaware, or the experience had to coincide temporally with an unexpected significant event involving the referent person. These cases' representativeness of all apparitional experiences, therefore, is uncertain. One of the few recent studies is Celia Green and Charles McCreery's (1975) *Apparitions;* this surveys uninvestigated experiences. Apart from these there have been a few surveys of parapsychological experiences that have included items on apparitional experiences (e.g., Haraldsson et al., 1977; Palmer, 1979). The major phenomenological findings of these investigations now will be summarized.

The experience of an apparition is not as uncommon as one might think. In Palmer's (1979) survey of Charlottesville, Virginia, residents and students, 17 percent had had an impression of an apparition, and of these about three quarters acknowledged more than one such experience. Twenty percent of a sample of Australian university students reported apparitional experiences (Irwin, 1985b, p. 6). A poll of Icelandic adults by Haraldsson et al. (1977) put the incidence even higher: 31 percent had witnessed an apparition of a deceased person and 11 percent reported an apparition of a living person. In Canada, Persinger (1974, p. 69) found 32 percent of survey respondents to acknowledge an apparition of a person or an animal. A substantial sector of the population therefore has had at least one of these experiences.

The duration of the apparitional experience is rather variable. In Green and McCreery's (1975, p. 143) survey about half of the respondents considered their experience to have lasted less than one minute, although 20 percent estimated its duration to exceed five minutes.

Apparitional experiences tend to be restricted to one or two sensory modalities. Green and McCreery (1975) report that of their cases 61 percent were in one modality only, with a further 25 percent limited to two senses. Most apparitional experiences are visual, 84 percent according to Green and McCreery. About a third of cases nevertheless have an auditory component, with 14 percent being a wholly auditory experience. On the other hand the dominance of visual apparitional experiences is not found in every survey (cf. Palmer, 1979, p. 228). The reported modality of the apparitional imagery may be in a sensory system that is impaired in the given experient; for example, one "totally deaf" man described hearing the rustle of an apparitional figure's dress (Green & McCreery, 1975, p. 169).

A small number of cases are asensory, comprising the intuitive impression of a "presence" nearby. These instances of a sense of presence represented only 8 percent of Green and McCreery's (1975, p. 118) cases, although there was a rather higher incidence in Haraldsson's (1985, p. 152) Icelandic sample and in a sample of Australian university students I surveyed on behalf of Andrew MacKenzie. One of my students reported the experience of strolling along a deserted beach and feeling there was someone walking beside her; although she did not see nor hear anything to indicate there was something there, the sense of presence was very strong and she felt very comfortable with it.

In some cases apparitions are said to have been witnessed by several people at the same time; Green and McCreery (1975, p. 41) report up to eight people simultaneously experiencing an apparition. Collective cases comprise about 12 percent of all reports (Palmer, 1979, p. 228). By the same token not all members of a group necessarily will perceive the apparitional figure. In cases with more than one person present approximately one-third of the apparitions seem to have been collectively experienced (Sidgwick et al., 1894; Tyrrell, 1942/1963).

Most apparitional figures are experienced to be within 10 feet (3 meters) of the subject (Green & McCreery, 1975, p. 123). In the majority of cases however, the figure is not recognized by the experient (Green & McCreery, 1975, p. 178). About 70 percent of recognized apparitions are of people whom the experient knew to be dead (Green & McCreery, 1975, p. 188; Haraldsson, 1985). This may vary with the age of the individual or, more precisely, with the number of deceased persons the individual knew. Thus in Palmer's (1979, p. 228) survey about 60 percent of apparitions witnessed by the older sample of townspeople were of the dead, but for the student sample only 30 percent were of this type.

The distinction between apparitions of the living and apparitions of the dead can be refined into a more detailed taxonomy. Tyrrell (1942/1963, p. 35ff) proposed four classes of apparitional experiences: experimental cases, crisis cases, postmortem cases, and ghosts or haunting cases. Each of these is described below.

(i) **Experimental apparitional experiences.** In these cases living people deliberately have endeavored, allegedly with success, to make an apparition of themselves appear before a chosen percipient.

Some of the most famous cases are attributed to S.H. Beard (Gurney et al., 1886, Vol. 1, pp. 93–94). For example, in December 1882 Beard decided to project an apparition of himself to his fiancée, Miss L.S. Verity. At 9:30 p.m. he determined to appear in Verity's house. He achieved the impression that he was actually in his fiancée's home but he fell asleep and had no further recollection of the experiment. Before going to bed he renewed his determination to appear in Verity's bedroom at midnight, while he was asleep. On the following day Beard visited the Verity family. His fiancée's married sister was visiting her family and without prompting she declared that during the previous night she had seen Beard on two occasions. At approximately 9:30 p.m. she had observed Beard in a passage walking from one room to another and at midnight she had seen him enter the bedroom, walk to her bedside, and take her long hair into his hand. She told her sister of the experience before Beard's (corporeal) visit. Both women corroborated this account.

These experimental cases are rare. They seem to occur when the agent is asleep or in a trance-like state. They are similar in some respects to OBEs and at least one researcher (Hart, 1956) regarded experimental apparitions and OBEs as the same phenomenon. On the other hand it is not usual for the "projector" to have the conscious impression of being outside the body in an experimental apparition case; conversely, when an individual has an OBE it is very uncommon for that person's apparition (or parasomatic form) to be witnessed at the location to which the person consciously has projected.

The behavior of apparitional figures in experimental cases frequently gives the impression of awareness. Thus in the above case of Beard the apparition is said to have moved to the witness's bedside and taken her hair into his hand.

(ii) Crisis apparitional experiences. In crisis cases a recognized apparition is experienced at a time when the person represented by the apparition is undergoing some sort of crisis. By convention an apparitional experience qualifies as a crisis case only if the apparitional figure is experienced no more than twelve hours before or after the crisis. Often the crisis is death; an apparitional experience shortly before or after the referent person's death commonly is known as a wraith. According to Gauld (1977, p. 602) crisis cases are the most frequently reported type of apparitional experience under the SPR criteria for selection. When evidence of veridicality is not required for purposes of corroboration, however, crisis cases are in the minority (Green & McCreery, 1975, p. 179).

The following case of a wraith was investigated by the SPR (Tyrrell, 1942/1963, p. 39). The experient's brother was a pilot and unbeknownst to the woman concerned, had been shot down in France. That same day the experient had a strong feeling that she must turn around; on doing so she was amazed to see her "brother." Assuming that he had been reposted she turned back to put her baby in a safe place, then went to greet her brother only to find that he was not there. Thinking he was playing a joke she called him and searched the house for him. It was only when no trace of her brother could be found that she felt very frightened, suspecting that he was dead. The loss of her brother in combat on the day of the experience was confirmed two weeks later.

Two points about this case should be appreciated. First, the wraith was mistaken for a real person; and second, at the time of the experience the experient was not thinking of her brother.

In the SPR's investigations an attempt was made to show that wraiths did not appear at the time of the referent person's death purely by coincidence (Gurney et al., 1886, Vol. 2, Ch. 3). On the other hand West's (1948) more recent though less extensive survey for the SPR failed to establish that the timing of crisis apparitions was anything else than a chance process.

(iii) Postmortem apparitional experiences. These cases involve an apparition of a person who has been dead for at least twelve hours. About two-thirds of recognized apparitions are of the dead (Green & McCreery, 1975, p. 188). One of the most frequently cited instances of this type is the so-called "Chaffin will" case ("Case...," 1927).

In 1905 James Chaffin, a farmer in North Carolina, made a will leaving his estate to his third son, Marshall, with his wife and other three sons unprovided for. In 1919 he made a new will under which the property was to be divided equally among the four sons, with the provision that they look after their mother. The second will was not witnessed but was valid under North Carolina law, being in Chaffin's own handwriting. The new will was placed in an old family Bible and a note identifying the will's location was sewn inside his overcoat pocket. In 1921 Chaffin died as a result of a fall. As the family did not know of the existence of the new will, the third son Marshall obtained probate of the original will.

In June 1925 the second son, James, experienced an apparition of his father during a vivid dream. The figure was described as wearing the father's overcoat. The apparitional figure pulled back the coat and announced, "You will find my will in my overcoat pocket." It then disappeared. James made enquiries about the whereabouts of his father's overcoat and learned that it had been given to his elder brother, John. In July, James visited his brother and looked inside the overcoat pocket where he found not the will itself but the message revealing the will's location. James returned to his mother's house and after some searching an old Bible was found and the second will located. In December this will was admitted to probate; ten witnesses were prepared to swear that it was in the testator's handwriting.

The Chaffin will case illustrates a common feature of postmortem cases, namely that the apparition seemingly tries to convey specific information that is unknown to the experient. Note also in this case the apparition had both a visual and an auditory component. As with other types of apparition the figure is lifelike and appears suddenly and unexpectedly. A disconcerting feature of the Chaffin will case is that it occurred during a dream. As Gauld (1977, p. 605) comments, on this basis one wonders if almost any extrasensory dream could be regarded also as a veridical apparitional experience. Be that as it may, the case otherwise is representative of postmortem apparitional experiences.

(iv) Experiences of Ghosts. So-called ghosts are recurrent or haunting apparitions, that is, the same figure is witnessed in the same locality on a number of occasions, often by a number of different experients. The ghosts in these experiences reportedly show less awareness of experients and their surroundings than do other apparitional figures. Additionally, ghosts seem more somnambulistic in their movements. Some ghosts reportedly perform the same actions in the same location on each occasion they are experienced. Recurrent apparitional experiences that are less stereotyped in this regard tend to have a deceased friend or relative as the referent person (Green & McCreery, 1975, p. 65). Recurrent apparitions of animals, particularly cats, also are not uncommon (Green & McCreery, 1975, p. 63).

Tyrrell's taxonomy of apparitions has general acceptance although some parapsychologists (e.g., Gauld, 1982, p. 226) prefer to broaden his "experimental" category to include apparitions of the living that are not crisis cases but which also need not necessarily involve the volitional element implied by experimental cases. Other writers (e.g., Bayless, 1973) point out that there are occasional reports of other sorts of apparitional experiences, including apparitions of animals and luminous manifestations such as disks of light or figures in a circle of light.

On the basis of his case collection Tyrrell determined a number of consistencies in the phenomenological characteristics of apparitional figures. Apparitions appear real and solid. Their appearance changes as the experient moves around it. They occlude objects they move in front of and are occluded by objects they move behind. They may cast a shadow and the experient may perceive their reflection in a mirror. In those respects, therefore, apparitional figures are not the transparent misty forms popularized in fiction. Most apparitions evidence awareness of their surroundings (although this is less characteristic of ghosts). For example, if the observer moves around the room the apparitional figure's head reportedly may turn to follow these movements. Also these figures usually are experienced to leave a room by the door rather than to wander through a wall (like the fictional stereotype). Noises made by apparitions tend to be appropriate, like the rustle of clothes or the shuffle of feet rather than clanking chains and soulful moans. Some apparitional images are claimed to have spoken, although this is not common; any spoken communication usually is limited to a few words. If the individual is close to the apparition a sensation of coldness may be felt. Most attempts to touch an apparitional figure are unsuccessful but people who did so generally report their hand to have gone through the apparition. The figure may seem to pick up an object or to open a door when physically these have not moved at all. Apparitions usually leave no physical traces such as footprints, nor can they be photographed or tape-recorded, according to Tyrrell.

Green and McCreery's (1975) analysis of apparitional cases yielded several further characteristics. The apparitional figure's background may remain the same or it may be modified as part of the experience. There usually is no discontinuity of experience at the onset and at the termination of apparitional experiences as there sometimes is in, for example, the OBE. It is more common for the apparition to enter as a complete figure rather than building up or solidifying before the witness's eyes. At the end of the apparitional experience the figure usually vanishes instantly, but in other cases it may fade gradually either as a whole or part by part, or it may be reported to have left as if by its own accord (e.g., by walking out of the room).

Correlates of the Apparitional Experience

Although the apparitional figure almost inevitably is said to have appeared unexpectedly (Green & McCreery, 1975, p. 135) there are some consistencies in the circumstances of occurrence. Typically, an experience arises in familiar everyday surroundings, most often in the experient's home or in its immediate vicinity. Only 12 percent of Green and McCreery's (1975, p. 123) cases occurred in a place that the subject had never visited before. In 83 percent of their reports the experient was indoors (see also Persinger, 1974, pp. 157–158).

Psychological conditions of occurrence also have been surveyed. Over 90 percent of the respondents in Green and McCreery's (1975, p. 123) study claimed to have been in normal health at the time of the apparitional experience; generally the phenomenon would seem therefore, not to be hallucination associated with illness. Most apparitions nevertheless occur when the experient is in a physically inactive state. Concurrent activities reported by Green and McCreery (1975, p. 124) were lying down (38 percent), sitting (23), standing still (19), walking (18) and others (2 percent). Because we spend about a third of our lives lying down (asleep) these data should not be taken to imply that one should adopt a supine position to facilitate an apparitional experience, but the trend toward minimal or "automatic" physical activity is notable. This feature was observed also in a small-scale Australian survey by one of my postgraduate students, Jeanene Campbell (1987), and, as Thouless (cited by MacKenzie, 1982, p. 28) observed, it suggests that apparitional experiences occur either in circumstances conducive to absorbed mentation or for people with an enduring need for absorption.

The latter point raises the general issue of the types of people who have the apparitional experience. Data on the psychological profile of experients are both meager and fragmentary. Traditional tests of personality do not seem to have been administered to matched groups of apparitional experients and nonexperients. Using the *Eysenck Personality Questionnaire,* however, McCreery (1986) has noted that experients' scores on psychoticism, neuroticism and extraversion are comparable to normative data for the general population. The remaining available psychometric data lie in the domain of cognitive functions. In relation to the above suggestion that experients may have a relatively marked *need* for absorbed mentation, such has been found to be the case by Irwin (1985b, p. 6), although experients and nonexperients evidently do not differ in their *capacity* for absorption (Campbell, 1987). The related factor of fantasy-proneness is a strong discriminator: as a group, apparitional experients are highly inclined to fantasize (Cameron & Roll, 1983; Campbell, 1987; Myers & Austrin, 1985; Osis, 1986b; Wilson & Barber, 1983).

It remains to be shown whether these results imply the apparitional experience to be a pure fantasy or to be an experience that tends to arise when the individual is absorbed in fantasy-like mentation. Under the former interpretation an association between apparitional experiences and skills in mental imagery might be predicted. That is, for the experient to interpret a fantasy as a perceptual experience the person might be expected to be capable of extremely vivid imagery. Such seems to be the case for some (other) hallucinations (Mahoney, 1976/1977; Mintz & Alpert, 1972) but in the context of the apparitional experience adequate tests of this elementary hypothesis have yet to be undertaken.

Martin (1915) found three apparitional experients had strong visual imagery and were able to project it onto the environment (so-called eidetic imagery), although she speculated that this capacity is necessary but not sufficient for an apparitional experience. The minuteness of the sample in Martin's study, however, makes generalization inappropriate. In an investigation of 11 experients in a collective apparitional case Osis and McCormick (1982b) found what appears to be a normal distribution of scores on Betts' *Questionnaire Upon Mental Imagery* (QMI), but in the absence of corresponding data for nonexperients no reliable conclusion can be drawn about the relative vividness of experients' mental imagery. One other apparitional experient tested subsequently by Osis (1986b) checked the highest level of imagery vividness on all items of the QMI scale; again, little can be made of the performance of a single subject.

Using Marks' *Vividness of Visual Imagery Questionnaire* (VVIQ) Campbell (1987) compared the scores of 14 experients with those of 28 sex- and age-matched nonexperients and found the experients to exhibit significantly *lower* vividness of visual imagery. Campbell's finding is not anticipated by any interpretation of the apparitional experience and it is possible her experients deliberately depressed their performance on the VVIQ because of its tacit imputation that their apparitional experience was imaginal. Although further research certainly is warranted, there are scant indications here that mental imagery skills make a significant, positive contribution to the apparitional experience.

One recent case study nevertheless raises some interesting possibilities in regard to psychological processes underlying the apparitional experience. The study was conducted by an American psychiatrist living in London, Morton Schatzman (1980). A young married woman called Ruth (a pseudonym) consulted Schatzman when she was seriously troubled by apparitions of her father (the latter was alive and in another country at the time). The apparition had her father's looks, voice and smell. When "he" sat on her bed Ruth allegedly felt and saw the bed sag. The apparition also occluded her view of objects behind it, cast shadows, and was reflected in a mirror. The figure seemed to appear at times not of Ruth's choosing. The case had marked sexual connotations: the apparition would terrify Ruth with recollections of the time her father had tried to rape her as a child, and subsequently it appeared in her husband's place in bed.

Now, many collectors of case reports would not accept Ruth's story as an instance of an apparition. Some features of the case are uncharacteristic of apparitions: for example, when the apparition appeared in Ruth's bed it was by way of a perceived change in her husband's appearance to that of her father. Some of Ruth's behavior and the sexual tone of the experiences might be construed as symptomatic of psychotic disturbance; indeed Ruth was referred to Schatzman by her physican as a possible schizophrenic, although Schatzman himself dealt with her depression and anxiety as a response to the apparitional experiences rather than as signs of psychosis. Additionally some developments during therapy (to be described shortly) suggest that the experiences were hallucinatory. With past researchers' preoccupation with the objectivity of apparitions, Ruth's experiences would be dismissed by many parapsychologists as psychotic hallucinations and not admitted for consideration in relation to apparitions. As far as assessment of the objectivity issue is concerned perhaps this position is a reasonable one. But for the parapsychologist wishing to pursue research on the nature of the apparitional experience Schatzman's treatment of Ruth's case could prove most instructive.

Most psychiatrists in Schatzman's position would work to put an end to Ruth's experiences, but this was not the immediate objective of Schatzman. Rather than encouraging Ruth to dispel the apparition whenever it appeared, he suggested to Ruth that she could and should make the apparition appear at her own wish. Initially she was too frightened to attempt this but with further psychotherapy to relieve the anxiety evoked by the experiences, Ruth achieved some voluntary control over both the occurrences of the experiences and the behavior of the apparitional figure. Later she was able to produce apparitions of other people including her husband, her children, a friend, Schatzman, and even herself (the apparition of herself was *not* her mirror image). By letting her father's apparition "speak" through her, Ruth was able to express his feelings and point of view, thereby lessening her own hatred for her father and her (unjustified) feelings of guilt over her own role in the childhood assault.

One of Schatzman's tests raises some interesting questions about the processes of apparitional experiences. When a person stares at a screen displaying a changing checkerboard pattern the occipital cortex (the visual area of the cerebral cortex) will produce an EEG record (called the evoked response) that changes with the checkerboard stimulus. When Ruth was presented with this stimulus her visual evoked response was normal. Schatzman then asked Ruth to make an apparition appear in front of the screen. The evoked response disappeared, as if something had actually blocked the stimuli, yet the response of the retina and the pupillary reaction to the flashing checkerboard pattern were normal. Evidently low level visual processes are not involved in Ruth's sort of hallucination, but higher level visual processes (say, from the lateral geniculate nucleus) apparently are much the same as in the perception of a real object.

It would be well worth attempting to replicate this result with "normal" subjects in recurrent apparitional cases. Such a study might throw some light on the curious mix of apparently objective and subjective elements of the apparitional experience. In this context it may be noted that later tests of Ruth (Harris & Gregory, 1981) did not reveal evidence of unusual powers of eidetic imagery. If the apparitional experience is hallucinatory the realism of the apparitional figure therefore might be due not so much to the quality of the imaginal processes responsible for its production but rather to the locus of the imaginal input within the visual information processing system.

Schatzman's idea of controlling apparitional experiences opens up many possibilities for research. For example, it might permit exploration of the underlying personality dynamics of the apparitional experience. Through the experient(s), the investigator may administer various psychological tests to the apparitional personality and compare the results of such tests with the manifest needs of the experients and if possible with the psychological profile of the referent person.

The therapeutic technique employed by Schatzman also has implications for current clinical practice. People who attend a psychological clinic for guidance in coming to terms with their apparitional experience are likely to be classified and treated as psychotics or to be told that the experience was a mere perceptual illusion. Schatzman alerts us to other possibilities, but most importantly he shows how clients can be helped to work through the experience to reach their own understanding of it.

Recent studies like that by Schatzman serve to remind us that the objectivity of an apparitional figure is not the only issue of interest or even the most important one. If apparitions should prove to be pure hallucinations the origins and underlying processes of the apparitional experience still would deserve the attention of behavioral scientists.

Theories of Apparitional Experiences

The central issue addressed by the major theories of apparitional experiences is whether apparitional figures are objective or subjective phenomena. As the foregoing review indicates, there would seem to be evidence for both views. Apparitions may be deemed objective because sometimes they are perceived by more than one person, and they have been reported to occlude objects, cast shadows, be reflected in a mirror, and change perspective with the experient's movement. On the other hand apparitions seem to be subjective (hallucinatory) phenomena in that some people present might not perceive them, some apparitions are reported to have moved through solid objects, experients may put their hand through the figure, objects may be perceived to have moved when in fact they did not, and apparitions leave no physical traces in circumstances where such traces should be found. An adequate theory of apparitional experiences should be able to accommodate these ostensibly contradictory characteristics.

The traditional theory of apparitions is the spirit hypothesis, that is, an apparition is an aspect of the individual's existence that survives bodily death. Hart (1956, 1967) and Crookall (1970) each developed a theory of apparitions along these lines. In essence the approach is equivalent to the ecsomatic models of the OBE and the NDE, with the additional assumption that the ecsomatic element has a continued postmortem existence. Some people are comfortable with such a notion as it relates to apparitions of the dead but are dubious about its applicability to apparitions of living persons. Thus if the spirit leaves the physical body, they argue, the person would die.

There are further, more serious difficulties with this model. To account for both objective and subjective characteristics of apparitions, recourse is made to rather vague concepts such as "semiphysical" and "ultraphysical" states of existence. A spirit can have physical qualities that are the basis of its reportedly objective phenomena, yet still be ethereal and pass through solid objects, for example. This would seem little else than an *ad hoc* assumption of what is to be explained. A slightly more subtle approach is to argue that the spirit is nonphysical and projects into space, but is perceived only by extrasensory means. This accounts for several features of the experience, although that an extrasensorially perceived nonphysical spirit should be seen to cast shadows is not explained.

A major problem for the spirit hypothesis is the fact that apparitional figures usually are described as being appropriately attired, sometimes with such accessories as a walking stick and a flower in a lapel. Now, our religious heritage leaves us at least potentially tolerant of the notion of the body's "soul," but the implication that our clothes and favored accessories also possess a "soul" seems to some people to be stretching the bounds of credibility. Ecsomatic theorists' attempts to explain apparitional attire in terms of an "etheric double" of the referent person's own clothes (e.g., Crookall, 1966) are conceptually as flimsy as the ghostly garments themselves. The spirit hypothesis of apparitional experiences now is promoted by a minority of modern parapsychologists (e.g., Osis, 1986a; Stevenson, 1982).

Let us turn now to some alternative theories. One early theory was that proposed by Edmund Gurney, a founding member of the SPR. Gurney (Gurney et al., 1886) held that apparitions were hallucinatory and were mediated by telepathy. Thus the experient acquires certain information from the referent individual by extrasensory means and then admits this information to consciousness as hallucination in the form of that individual's apparition. To accommodate collective cases Gurney had to propose the idea of "contagious telepathy." One person would acquire the extrasensory information and telepathically communicate the nature of the hallucinatory figure to other people present, inducing them to witness the same experience. Again it would seem to be asking a lot of ESP to ensure that different people's images of the apparition exhibit a mutually consistent set of perspectives, as is claimed to have occurred in some collective cases. Also Gurney posed his theory only in relation to apparitions of the living and crisis cases.

An extension of Gurney's theory to postmortem apparitions could require the additional assumptions of the survival hypothesis and of the possibility of telepathic communication by deceased personalities, although some form of super–ESP model might be devised as an alternative. The "telepathic hallucination" theory nevertheless readily accommodates apparitional experiences in which the experient acquires information and those in which the apparitional figure appears appropriately clothed.

Gurney's colleague Frank Podmore (1909) generally reiterated Gurney's theory of veridical apparitions of the living but went further in dismissing out of hand any notion of ghosts as telepathic hallucinations. Experiences of ghosts were a product of an apprehensive subject's imaginative misinterpretation of natural sounds, Podmore (1909, p. 123) asserted.

F.W.H. Myers, another founder of the SPR, devised a theory in many ways similar to that of Gurney. Myers (Gurney et al., 1886, Vol. 2, pp. 277–316; Myers, 1903, Ch. 6 & 7) agreed that apparitions (of the living or of the dead) could be hallucinatory projections of telepathically acquired information, but he proposed further that the referent person sometimes could cause changes in the "metetherial world" which permit the objective perception of his or her image by people in the vicinity of this change. This would account, for example, for the consistency of different experients' perspectives in certain collective cases. Myers is not very lucid in his specification of this metetherial world but evidently it entails some nonphysical dimension of existence that intertwines with physical space. How one would seek independent evidence of the existence of the metetherial world is unknown. But at least Myers appreciated the problem posed by collective cases and sought to address it in a manner he thought to be justified by the evidence accumulated in the SPR investigations. He also implied that apparitional experiences might not all feature exactly the same underlying process. Gauld (1982, Ch. 16) believes Myers' theory to be less problematic than other current approaches.

Tyrrell (1942/1963), like Gurney and Myers, held apparitions to be engendered telepathically. In Tyrrell's view the referent person and the experients effect an hallucination by a mingling of their subconscious minds, a cooperative production of an apparitional drama. Since all participants contribute to the mental staging of the hallucination the apparition has consistent perspectives for the different experients. People who are unable to perceive the apparition are held not to have taken part in the subconscious dramatic production.

The identification of apparitional experiences with hallucinatory ESP experiences was pursued further by Louisa E. Rhine (1957). Consistent with her views on the agent's role in other extrasensory experiences Rhine construed the apparitional experient (rather than the referent person) to be the instigator of the experience, reaching out extrasensorially to the referent person and expressing the subconsciously acquired information through the medium of an hallucination of that person. Unlike earlier theorists, therefore, Rhine saw no need to propose the referent person to be an active contributor to the experience.

Green and McCreery (1975) also accept the apparitional experience as hallucinatory, in some cases inspired by extrasensory information about the referent person. In the view of these researchers both the apparitional figure and the environment in which it seemingly appears are hallucinatory in the majority of cases (see also Green & Leslie, 1987), although there may be some experiences in which the figure is hallucinated upon the real environment of the experient.

The skeptical approach to apparitional experiences is that the apparition is a pure hallucination, that the image has no objective status and its occurrence is not grounded in ESP nor in any other parapsychological process; it is totally a product of the imagination and reflects the experient's suggestibility, expectations, needs, social conditioning and unconscious childhood memories (Rawcliffe, 1959, pp. 372–377; Shapiro, Sherman & Osowsky, 1980). The realism of the experience commonly is ascribed to the properties of hypnagogic imagery (Alcock, 1981, p. 83; Neher, 1980, p. 200; Reed, 1972, p. 39).

The skeptical theory is supported by claims of variations in the apparitional experience across historical periods and across cultures in accordance with the social functions served by belief in apparitions (Emmons, 1982, Ch. 8; Finucane, 1984; Thomas, 1971, Ch. 19). On the other hand Gauld (1984) argues that the evidence for such claims is unsatisfactory because cases of apparitional experience prior to the seventeenth century are very poorly documented and they cannot be regarded in any way as a random sample of such experiences in their respective historical period. Collective apparitional cases presumably are treated as mass hallucinations under the skeptical theory, although there is some doubt that such an account could accommodate the features of these cases if they have been reported accurately.

Little conceptual development has occurred in this area in the last 20 or 30 years. In the 1970s there were some suggestions that Kirlian photography, so-called photographs of the "aura" (Neher, 1980, p. 189), might provide an empirical foundation for spirit/ecsomatic models of apparitional experiences and OBEs, but these were soon discounted. As far as the survival hypothesis is concerned, it is assessed by Gauld (1977, pp. 601–607) to have gleaned little substantive empirical support from apparitional experiences, although this conclusion is disputed by Stevenson (1982). It would seem nonetheless that the spirit theory has not proved a productive approach, yet most proponents of the telepathic theories seem compelled to imply some form of discarnate existence in their attempts to account for postmortem apparitional cases. Additionally, a satisfactory account of collective cases and their characteristics has yet to be formulated. It is to be hoped that the recent phenomenological orientation of research into apparitional experiences will generate a new style of theory that is more fruitful and more comprehensive than past approaches have been.

Key Terms and Concepts

apparition
apparitional experience
hallucination
collective case
"Census of Hallucinations"
Tyrrell
Green & McCreery
incidence
sensory modalities
experimental cases
crisis apparitions

wraiths
postmortem apparitions
ghosts
"objective" characteristics
"subjective" characteristics
Schatzman
spirit hypothesis
ghostly garments
telepathic theories
contagious telepathy
skeptical theory

Study Questions

1. Critically examine the notion that apparitional experiences signify a psychotic disorder.

2. Outline Tyrrell's taxonomy of apparitional experiences and consider the adequacy of the spirit theory in accounting for each type of experience.

3. List the principal phenomenological consistencies in apparitional

case reports. Examine each of these from the perspective of (a) the spirit theory, (b) a telepathic theory, and (c) a skeptical "pure hallucination" approach.

4. Several researchers have given telepathy some emphasis in their accounts of apparitional experiences. What is their purpose in doing this? If one rejects the survival hypothesis is the postulation of a telepathic process viable in all instances of apparitional experience?

5. Of what relevance to apparitional experiences is Schatzman's study of "Ruth"?

14
Reincarnation Experiences

Reincarnation is the notion that a nonphysical element of human existence not only survives death but subsequently is reborn in another body. In the present context we are concerned specifically with the hypothesis of reincarnation in human form and not with that of metempsychosis or transmigration of souls between different species of animal life.

The concept of reincarnation is widely accepted in many cultures, particularly in the Middle East and in Asia, and it is a significant element in several major religious systems (Head & Cranston, 1977). In the West however, the concept generally is regarded with much skepticism, although there are indications that Western interest by no means is negligible (Sigelman, 1977); for example, in the early 1980s nearly a quarter of American adults surveyed by the Gallup organization acknowledged a belief in reincarnation (Gallup & Proctor, 1982, p. 137) and in Britain the incidence of this belief is reported to have increased from 18 to 28 percent during the 1970s (Wilson, 1982, p. 21).

The so-called Pollock case illustrates a claimed instance of reincarnation. This case, documented by Wilson (1982, Ch. 1; 1984), relies heavily on the testimony of an Englishman named John Pollock. At the age of 19 Pollock converted to Roman Catholicism but posed a problem for parish priests by professing a belief in reincarnation; such a belief is heretical in the view of the Catholic church. Despite the priests' efforts to dissuade him, Pollock persisted in his reincarnationist stance and at night would pray that God would provide some proof of reincarnation to resolve the dispute. A few years later Pollock married. His wife, Florence, did not share his belief in reincarnation.

Two daughters, Joanna and Jacqueline, were born to the Pollocks and the family moved home to Hexham. In May 1957 the girls, aged 11 and 6, were hit by a car and killed while walking to an early morning children's mass. Almost immediately John Pollock decided the deaths of his daughters were part of God's response to his prayers for proof of reincarnation and that the girls would be reborn to him. Florence found this attitude most distasteful and for a time their marriage was in serious jeopardy. When

Florence fell pregnant early in 1958 John declared she would have twin daughters because God was returning Joanna and Jacqueline to their parents. Indeed, twin daughters Jennifer and Gillian were born in October. A faint thin line on the second-born ("younger") Jennifer's forehead and a birthmark on her left hip were said to be identical to marks on Jacqueline, the younger of the dead sisters.

When the twins were four months old the Pollocks moved to another town. Three years later the family revisited Hexham and according to John Pollock the twins immediately behaved as if they knew the town. They were said to have recognized the school and the playground previously frequented by their dead sisters and to have identified their former home, all without any prompting from their parents. Similar incidents allegedly followed. For example, some toys of Joanna and Jacqueline were unpacked and Jennifer is said to have correctly named two dolls and to have assigned a toy of the eldest sister Jacqueline to her first-born twin sister Gillian. Pollock also reports coming upon the twins in the backyard screaming hysterically, "The car! The car! It's coming at us!" Such incidents ceased not long after the twins' fifth birthday. Today Jennifer and Gillian claim to have no memories "belonging" to their late sisters. According to John Pollock he did not discuss with the twins their purported reincarnated status until they were 13.

Although this case is convincing to Pollock himself and to others who subscribe to a belief in reincarnation, its evidential bases are not strong. Most of the features of the case rely wholly on the testimony of John Pollock (his wife having died in 1979) and he cannot be regarded as an unbiased observer and reporter of the alleged events. Corroborated facts in the case are scant and not convincing of reincarnation. There is no doubt that Joanna and Jacqueline were killed and that the twins were born subsequently. Further, Jennifer does have a birthmark on her left hip, although there now is no sign of the mark on her forehead. But these data are hardly conclusive. Normal genetic principles can account for the similarity of the birthmarks on Jacqueline and Jennifer; birthmarks are known to run in families. The twins' recognition behavior may have been exaggerated by Pollock because of the fervor of his beliefs and the attention his claims received in the British media. Wilson (1984, p. 51) also raises the possibility that the twins overheard their father discussing his beliefs with his wife and then behaved according to their father's expectations.

A further difficulty with the Pollock case is that it does not strictly entail an experient's giving a firsthand report of what appear to be personal memories of a previous existence. While the Pollock case included claims of alleged reincarnation "behavior" it did not exhibit a *reincarnation experience,* one in which the experient spontaneously recalls details of a personal life seemingly led some time before his or her present one.

Researchers interested in the reincarnation hypothesis have devoted much of their energy to the pursuit of cases which incorporate such an experience. Note, however, that in conformity with the definitions of other parapsychological experiences, there is no assumption that the reincarnation experience necessarily entails recall of a previous existence of the experient; the experience merely *seems* to do so, and it is a task of the researcher to ascertain the bases of these experiences.

The Phenomenology of Reincarnation Experiences

The contemporary parapsychologist who has been most thorough and persistent in the study of reincarnation experiences is Ian Stevenson of the University of Virginia's Division of Parapsychology. Stevenson has visited many countries, recording and investigating numerous cases; his detailed observations have been published in a series of books (e.g., Stevenson, 1966, 1975, 1977c, 1987a). Stevenson has worked almost exclusively with reincarnation experiences in childhood, believing it too difficult to ensure the authenticity of adult cases. Usually he locates cases with the aid of fellow parapsychologists and the media. The experient and witnesses (typically the experient's parents and other family members) are interviewed, usually with the assistance of an interpreter. Where possible, the data in the reincarnation experiences are checked for their veridicality. In some instances, for example, the family of the deceased personality is identified and reported details of the ostensible former life then are checked; a meeting between the experient and the "former" family occasionally can be arranged and the experient's recognition of people and the surroundings is observed. It may be noted that Stevenson trained as a psychiatrist and has written a book on interviewing techniques; one therefore would not expect him to accept human testimony at face value.

Unfortunately the majority of cases documented by Stevenson were no longer "active" at the time of their investigation. That is, the subject of the case had ceased to have recollections of the supposed previous existence and thus the evidence consists mainly of retrospective accounts by other people (e.g., parents) of the experient's statements about that existence. Stevenson nevertheless has been able to interview some experients while they still could access their "past life" memories. One such case is that of Gnanatilleka (Stevenson, 1966, pp. 118-134), a girl born in the village of Hedunawewa, central Sri Lanka, in February 1956.

When Gnanatilleka was one year old she mentioned another mother and father, and at the age of 2 she began to make explicit references to a previous life as a boy. She claimed to have parents, two brothers and many sisters living in another town. At first Gnanatilleka did not identify the town but after hearing some visitors speak of Talawakele she named this as the location of her (or "his") previous existence. Talawakele is a town about 16 miles (26 kilometers) from Hedunawewa; the climate and vegetation of these two settlements differ considerably and travel between them is difficult and infrequently attempted. Gnanatilleka said she wanted to visit her "other" parents and recalled details of her alleged past life including the names of members of her former family, the father's occupation, descriptions of the parents, the location of the family home, and a story she had been taught at school during that previous life.

On the basis of these details a particular family in Talawakele was identified as that of the "previous personality" (as Stevenson terms the subject of an alleged former existence). The previous personality was a lad named Tillekeratne who had died at the age of 12 in November 1954. The cause of Tillekeratne's death remains obscure. He may have had some visceral disease; certainly he is known to have been admitted to a hospital following a fall and to have died within a fortnight. Prior to his death he is said to have developed effeminate tendencies. During Stevenson's interview of Gnanatilleka she reported that when she had been a boy she had wanted to be a girl, and now she was happier as a girl. Members of each family denied having any knowledge of the other prior to Gnanatilleka's statements about her previous existence.

In 1960 Gnanatilleka and her family visited Talawakele where she correctly identified several buildings in the town; when she directed her family to the place of her former residence, however, the home was found to be no longer standing. Gnanatilleka later recognized some teachers from Tillekeratne's school. Early in 1961 Gnanatilleka again went to Talawakele where various relatives and acquaintances of Tillekeratne were brought before her and she was asked if she knew each person. In the presence of an independent observer seven members of the previous personality's family and two other people were identified accurately in terms of their relationship with Tillekeratne. A person unknown to Tillekeratne was not recognized by Gnanatilleka. Two people in a crowd outside the house also were recognized spontaneously. Gnanatilleka's behavior towards the people she recognized was said to have been consistent with Tillekeratne's relationship with them.

During his visit to both Hedunawewa and Talawakele later in 1961 Stevenson was able to confirm the above data of the case by interviewing Gnanatilleka herself, members of the two households concerned, and other witnesses. During the following year, shortly before Gnanatilleka's seventh birthday, Stevenson had word that the young girl's spontaneous recollections of a previous existence had ceased and that she now remembered little about that life.

As Stevenson acknowledges, the Gnanatilleka case is atypical in some

Figure 18. Gnanatilleka and her mother in 1966 (photo: Ian Stevenson).

general respects. The majority of reincarnation experiences do not feature such a wealth of information of the sort that is verifiable. Even in many highly detailed experiences the previous personality cannot be identified conclusively with a known person; Stevenson calls these "unsolved cases" and those of the Gnanatilleka type, "solved." And as noted previously, it is not often that a parapsychologist can locate an "active" case in which an experient still has access to memories of a past life; in most cases the evidence must be compiled from people who witnessed the experient's reminiscences about the previous existence. The Gnanatilleka case nevertheless does serve to illustrate the reincarnation experience, one in which an experient has the spontaneous impression of having lived before and seemingly can recall variously detailed information about that previous existence.

Through the laborious investigations by Stevenson and his assistants an appreciation of the reincarnation experience's phenomenology has emerged.

The incidence of reincarnation experiences is not known precisely. A survey by Barker and Pasricha (1979) in Fatehabad, a district of north India, found the incidence in that population to be about two per thousand, but the generality of this estimate is doubtful. Broadly speaking, cases are more frequent in countries in which the belief in reincarnation is strong (Stevenson, 1977a, p. 646).

A reincarnation experience commonly arises during the waking state in a young child, beginning at the age of 2 to 4 years with the child telling its parents or siblings of a life it led in another time and place. The name of the previous personality often is given, featuring in about one-third of American cases and three-quarters of Indian cases (Stevenson, 1983a, p. 745). The previous personality sometimes is related to the experient (Cook, Pasricha, Samararatne, Win Maung & Stevenson, 1983), almost invariably is ordinary and undistinguished, and his or her living conditions can be either more or less affluent than those of the experient (Stevenson, 1983a, p. 745); Wilson's (1982, p. 50) reanalysis of some of Stevenson's data suggests, however, that a high proportion of cases in India and Sri Lanka relate to a past life of greater wealth or higher caste than that of the experient.

The geographical distance between the settings of the "past" and present lives rarely exceeds 100 miles (160 kilometers) (Wilson, 1982, p. 48); the previous personality and the experient, therefore, in most instances are of the same nationality, speak the same language, and have the same religious background. The previous personality frequently has the same sex as the experient; cross-sex "rebirth" is virtually unknown in Turkish cases but may be as high as 15 percent among American experiences (Stevenson, 1983a, p. 745) and 20 percent in cases from Burma and Thailand (Stevenson, 1977a, p. 655).

Of the various life events of the previous personality recounted by the experient the mode of death often is cited and in a majority of documented cases the mode of death was violent, most particularly in unsolved cases (Cook et al., 1983; Pasricha & Stevenson, 1987; Stevenson, 1983a). The interval between the previous personality's death and the experient's birth seems quite variable, ranging from a few weeks to many years (Wilson, 1982, p. 47) and at least in Indian cases averaging about 14 months (Pasricha & Stevenson, 1987, p. 244).

The child's spontaneous memories of the past life gradually cease, typically between the ages of 5 and 8 (Pasricha & Stevenson, 1987, p. 244; Stevenson, 1983a, p. 745), and soon these apparent recollections have been completely forgotten. Other features of the experience nevertheless may tend to persist somewhat longer. For example, in cross-sex reincarnation experiences the child may show cross-dressing when young and continue to exhibit various signs of cross-gender identification as it grows. A traumatic incident in the former life, particularly in relation to the instrument and the mode of death, may be the ostensible basis of a phobia in the present life (Stevenson, 1977b, pp. 311–312). Likewise, a birthmark might be construed as the remnant of a wound in a previous existence (Stevenson, 1977b, pp. 318–320).

Few correlates of the reincarnation experience have been established. As noted previously, these experiences are reported most frequently among cultures that embrace the concept of reincarnation. This fact might be taken to indicate that belief in reincarnation is a fundamental stimulus for the experience. At the same time many cases are known to have occurred among children whose family did not subscribe to such a belief or even was unfamiliar with it (Stevenson, 1983a, p. 744). It is feasible that cultural endorsement of the reincarnation hypothesis influences readiness to report a reincarnation experience rather than the experience's occurrence as such.

Cultural differences nevertheless do correlate with some phenomenological features of reincarnation experiences, whether because of the impact of belief systems or for other reasons. For example, the frequency of cross-sex experiences varies substantially across cultures. So too does the incidence of reincarnation experiences featuring a violent death, forming a minority among Sri Lankan cases and a sizeable majority in Lebanese Druse cases (Stevenson, 1977a, p. 655) and in American cases (Stevenson, 1983a, p. 745). Cases of "rebirth" of a close relative also have different frequencies across cultures (Stevenson, 1983a, pp. 744–745). Generally these trends are consistent with beliefs about reincarnation in the culture concerned. Stevenson (1977a, p. 634) believes the relationship here to be a circular one, with the incidence of cases serving to sustain the beliefs and the strength of the beliefs encouraging the development and the communication of the experiences.

Solved and unsolved cases differ somewhat in their phenomenology, according to an analysis of Stevenson's data by Cook et al. (1983). Experiences for which the previous personality has not been positively linked to a known person feature a comparatively high incidence of violent death. The experients of these unsolved cases identify the previous personality by name more frequently and stop talking about the previous life earlier than do subjects of solved cases. Cook et al. are unable to provide an unequivocal explanation of these data but they do speculate that some unsolved cases may incorporate elements of fantasy.

In compiling an outline of the phenomenology of reincarnation experiences Stevenson frequently has emphasized that his case reports do not "prove" reincarnation. At best they provide data consistent with the reincarnation hypothesis and for this reason Stevenson continues to refer to them noncommittally as "cases suggestive of reincarnation" or "cases of the reincarnation type." But skeptics have been eager to attack Stevenson's research, presumably because it dares to address a concept that is a scientific heresy. Although he has explored orthodox accounts of reincarnation experiences Stevenson has been accused of being too ready to reject them on insubstantial grounds (Wilson, 1982, p. 50).

Because most of Stevenson's cases rely on retrospective information from witnesses they may have the evidential shortcomings to which such reports usually are vulnerable, but some critics have queried the reliability of Stevenson's observations on the additional ground that so many of them were gathered in communities having a fervent religious commitment to the doctrine of reincarnation. For example, Wilson (1982, p. 50) suggests that Stevenson's frequent reliance on interpreters and assistant investigators, many of whom believe in reincarnation, permits an opportunity for distorting the evidence before it reaches Stevenson. Rogo (1985, p. 85) further asserts that Stevenson has "polished up" some of the weaker cases before their publication. Certainly it must be regretted that such a large part of the data on reincarnation experiences has been accumulated by just one researcher and his associates.

Theories of the Reincarnation Experience

In discussing each of his major cases of reincarnation experience Stevenson addresses a range of possible theoretical explanations and assesses their adequacy in accounting for the case under analysis. In addition to the reincarnation hypothesis he considers the hypotheses of fraud, paramnesia, cryptomnesia, ESP with personation, inherited memory, and possession. The nature of each of these theoretical options now will be outlined.

Stevenson (1977a, p. 650) acknowledges that *fraudulent* cases of reincarnation experience have occurred; indeed he has exposed some of them himself (Stevenson, Pasricha & Samararatne, 1988). In several societies a powerful motive for fraud is the status accorded to the family of a person believed to be a reincarnated being. Any case that depends wholly on the unsupported statements of the alleged experient's parents, as does the Pollock case for example, should therefore be given little evidential weight. With these concessions Stevenson nevertheless feels that reincarnation experiences of young children generally are not likely to be fraudulent because it would be too difficult to coach the child to assume and sustain the unnatural role of being another person. The theatrical skills and the amount of factual information to be learned are thought to be beyond the ability of a young child and any performance thus contrived is expected to be transparent.

Would Gnanatilleka, the experient of Stevenson's Sri Lankan case cited earlier in this chapter, be able and willing at the age of 4 or 5 to simulate her knowledge of and feelings for her "former" family, simply to fulfill some supposedly mischievous scheme devised by her parents? Well, some critics would believe so (Zusne & Jones, 1982, pp. 165–166). Wilson (1982, pp. 50–51) discusses possible motives for fraud in several of Stevenson's cases and concludes that Stevenson has been naive and precipitate in dismissing this theory. One skeptical version of the fraud hypothesis is that in some cases dishonest parents have heard their child talking about its fantasies (e.g., the imaginary playmate) and have fostered and molded the child's subsequent imaginary experiences to give them a reincarnationist flavor (Chari, 1978, pp. 319–320). The skeptical view of features such as cross-gender identification, phobias and birthmarks is that these are seen more properly as a cause than as a consequence of the reincarnation experience; that is, these features are taken by the child or by its parents as one source of inspiration for a reincarnation fantasy.

Another theory of cases of the reincarnation type is that witnesses mistakenly believe the experient is the source of information that actually was obtained elsewhere. For example, in the considerable majority of Stevenson's cases the two families concerned had met before the parapsychologist's investigation and had discussed the life of the previous personality. Some of the details of this discussion could be recalled incorrectly by family members as having been reported by the experient. This process is termed *paramnesia* (Stevenson, 1977a, pp. 650–651). The possible role of paramnesia in reincarnation experiences was suggested long ago by Burnham (1889, p. 432) and still is regarded (Zusne & Jones, 1982, p. 165) as a major flaw in the value of these cases to the reincarnation hypothesis. Stevenson admits that paramnesia may be an element in a few cases but deems it an inadequate explanation of highly detailed experiences reported by careful observers and an inapplicable account of the (regrettably few) cases that have been investigated before any meeting between the two families.

Under the hypothesis of *cryptomnesia* it is supposed that the experient has acquired the facts of the previous life by normal means but has forgotten the source of this information and erroneously has ascribed the existence to their own experience. The process of cryptomnesia is well attested in other contexts (Stevenson, 1983b) but according to Stevenson (1977a, p. 651) as yet no spontaneous reincarnation experience has been demonstrated to have been due to cryptomnesia. He believes further that this hypothesis cannot accommodate the many cases in which an experient gave details of a former life before any contact was likely with relatives and acquaintances of the previous personality. Zusne and Jones (1982, p. 154) believe the historical accuracy of "past life" memories is due to cryptomnesia, but in documenting the evidence for this conclusion these authors make no distinction between spontaneous reincarnation experiences and hypnotic regression (the latter is discussed in the next section of this chapter).

Another theory of the reincarnation experience appeals to a parapsychological mechanism, or more specifically, to a combination of *ESP and personation*. Here the child is held to develop a pathological secondary personality that under the influence of the cultural setting is cast into a reincarnationist form. The delusion is buttressed by the use of ESP to obtain information about the deceased person from surviving relations and acquaintances. A form of this hypothesis is explored by Chari (1962). In many instances the hypothesis implies a super–ESP capacity because the experient would have had to recruit information from sources the existence of which was not known by normal means.

Stevenson (1977a, p. 653) argues it is unreasonable to account for the behavioral aspects of reincarnation experiences in terms of ESP. Additionally Chari (1978, p. 316) and Gauld (1982, p. 184) claim that the majority of reincarnation experients do not show signs of any special ESP abilities. Gauld adds that reincarnation experiences do not merely entail diverse pieces of information but these data are integrated and organized in a style appropriate to the previous personality. It should be said that a super–ESP hypothesis, because of its implied omniscience, is untestable by empirical methods, but by the same token our current inability to rule out conclusively the role of ESP in reincarnation experiences effectively renders the reincarnation hypothesis untestable too (Chari, 1978, p. 314).

In a substantial number of Stevenson's cases the experient is related to the previous personality (see Cook et al., 1983, p. 119). Perhaps it is feasible, therefore, to account for reincarnation experiences in terms of *inherited memory*. On the other hand there appears to be no acceptable independent evidence that personal memories can be genetically encoded (Gauld, 1982,

p. 182). In any event the experient and the previous personality are unrelated in about two-thirds of cases, including the Gnanatilleka case for example.

The final option to the reincarnation hypothesis countenanced by Stevenson is that of *possession*. That is, reincarnation experiences might be due to the experient's being possessed by the spirit of a deceased person. Possession does seem a more apt account of one of Stevenson's (1966, pp. 33–50) cases in which the previous personality did not die until more than three years *after* the birth of the experient. The possession hypothesis does not appeal to skeptics, of course, because both it and the notion of reincarnation subsume the survival hypothesis.

Stevenson also argues against the possession hypothesis on several grounds. First, the experient can recall only a limited amount about the life of the previous personality, whereas a possessing personality would be thought able to provide virtually unlimited data about itself (Stevenson, 1966, p. 346). Second, according to Stevenson (1966, p. 349) the possession hypothesis does not explain the appearance of a birthmark on the experient that is related thematically to the reincarnation experience. Third, there seems no reason for discarnate personalities to be relatively uniform in the period of their possession, "arriving" when the experient is 2 to 4 years and "departing" at 5 to 8 years (Stevenson, 1977a, p. 654). Fourth, although the experient may stop recalling the previous existence the claimed effects on behavior (e.g., by way of a phobia) may persist for some time; under the proposed account why should the possessing personality "vacate" in this piecemeal fashion? Chari (1978, p. 316) maintains additionally that the possession hypothesis does not sit well with the experient's use of the present tense with respect to the current life and the past tense with respect to the previous life.

Stevenson is well aware that arguments against alternative interpretations of the data are in themselves not sufficient to substantially increase the strength of the reincarnation hypothesis. He believes nevertheless that the reincarnation hypothesis is worthy of further serious consideration.

The reincarnation hypothesis itself is not homogeneous. It has a number of varieties, these differing essentially in regard to precisely what it is that is posited to survive death. For example, some versions are couched in terms of the surviving spirit of the deceased person while others focus on the previous personality's "psychic elements" (memories and traits) (Rogo, 1985, Ch. 11). It remains to be seen if these metaphysical distinctions can generate a critical empirical test between them.

As yet it has not been possible to design an effective test between the general reincarnation hypothesis and its conceptual rivals. Further research into the reincarnation experience's phenomenology eventually may enable such a test, but what would really be desirable here is a technique for experimentally evoking reincarnation experiences that permits their investigation under more controlled conditions.

Hypnotic Regression: An Experimental Induction Technique?

It has long been known that suggestions may be made to subjects under hypnosis to return or *regress* to an earlier stage of their life. Participants often respond to these suggestions by behaving as if they were reexperiencing their life at that earlier stage. A logical extension of this technique of hypnotic age regression was to suggest the subject could return to a time before they were born and there encounter a life they had led previously. French spiritualists began to experiment with this procedure in the nineteenth century, and a systematic study of hypnotic regression to past lives was reported by Colonel Albert de Rochas in 1911. Subjects gave variously detailed accounts of a past life, their dramatic performance indicating their experience to be most vivid and personally convincing. During the 1950s the much publicized case of an American woman, Virginia Tighe, who regressed to an existence as Bridey Murphy in nineteenth-century Belfast (Bernstein, 1956), confirmed in the popular mind the view of hypnotic regression as an experimental method for liberating our past lives. This belief has been fostered by a plethora of popular paperbacks citing numerous examples of regressed experiences of claimed past lives.

From the perspective of the professional parapsychologist, however, hypnotic regression has not proved satisfactory as an experimental technique, for the simple reason of its unreliability. Not that a regressed experience is exceptionally difficult to induce in people preselected for their hypnotic susceptibility (Baker, 1982). But the considerable majority of experiences thus induced are clearly fantasies, marked by historical inaccuracies, malapropisms, anachronisms, and loose narrative (Venn, 1986). The hypnotic state is well documented as a context for imaginative roleplaying and for confabulation, a fact that evidently applies also to the majority of performances under the procedure of hypnotic regression (Baker, 1982; Perry, Laurence, Nadon and Labelle, 1986).

The poor efficacy of hypnotic regression as an experimental technique, however, does not necessarily mean that the data it has yielded are of no evidential value to the reincarnation hypothesis. Despite the technique's reputation for generating imaginary past lives there reportedly are occasional cases that appear to show substantial historical and other veridicality, yet the hypnotic subjects declare they have had no opportunity to acquire the information in question by normal means. These cases deserve further scrutiny.

In one type of such case an experient to some degree is conversant in the previous personality's language but has not learned that language during the present lifetime. This phenomenon is known as *xenoglossy*. Sometimes the subject not only makes statements in the "unlearned language" but also can engage in intelligible interactive conversation in that language; this form is termed *responsive xenoglossy*.

Instances of xenoglossy are extremely rare both in the spontaneous reincarnation experience and in the hypnotic state. Of the handful of documented cases one is the so-called Gretchen case (Stevenson, 1984). Here an American woman, Dolores Jay, was hypnotized by her husband and without any suggestions to regress she presented a trance personality named Gretchen who spoke in German. A few biographical details of the previous personality were established during subsequent hypnotic sessions but most of these data were variously unspecific, unverifiable, or simply incorrect. The Gretchen personality nevertheless was able to speak German responsively. Admittedly the utterances typically were short, simple, repetitive and ungrammatical, but nonetheless they were in reasonably well-pronounced German. In the waking state Dolores Jay declared she had never learned this language and Stevenson's quite extensive investigations seem to confirm that Dolores had no opportunity to learn German either at school or from people living in her childhood home town. It is impossible of course, to be absolutely confident on such an issue. This, together with the fact of their exceptional rarity, makes cases of responsive xenoglossy more an extraordinary enigma than definitive evidence of reincarnation. Their major fascination lies in the fact that it is difficult to conceive ESP, or even super–ESP, to be the basis of this unlearned knowledge of a foreign language's vocabulary, pronunciation and grammar.

Other cases of hypnotic regression reportedly have incorporated historically veridical information. One notable series was obtained by a British hypnotherapist, the late Arnall Bloxham, whose work came to public notice through a BBC television documentary and an associated bestselling book (Iverson, 1976). Bloxham claimed to have tape-recorded hypnotic regressions of over 400 people, although only a few were sufficiently specific to warrant detailed investigation. Two of Bloxham's hypnotic subjects were considered particularly suitable for inclusion in the television documentary. An Englishman, Graham Huxtable, regressed as a gunner's mate aboard a British frigate some 200 years ago. During the regression Huxtable named the ship and its officers and in naval slang he vividly described the conditions and events aboard ship, ending in a dramatic enactment of the sailor's severe wounding in a naval battle.

But Bloxham's most prolific subject was a Welsh woman pseudonymously called Jane Evans who regressed to six quite distinct lives, three of which were depicted in impressive detail. Historically speaking the earliest life was as a woman named Livonia in Roman Britain in A.D. 286. Livonia's husband was tutor to the youngest son of Constantius, the governor of Britain, and Livonia described the life of a Roman household and gave an account of an unsuccessful coup intended to overthrow Constantius. Another life was as Rebecca, the wife of a Jewish moneylender in the English city of York in the year 1189. In this regression Rebecca recounted anti-Jewish disturbances and at the climax she seemingly relived a mob's massacre of her children and then of herself as they sheltered in the crypt of a York church. A third reported existence was as Alison, the housekeeper of Jacques Coeur, who was a merchant prince in medieval France in the middle of the fifteenth century. Alison described Coeur's financial dealings with the king and his mistress, the beautiful Agnes Sorel.

Viewers of the televised documentary on Jane Evans' regressions were struck by two features. First, Evans portrayed each of the roles so convincingly that she seemed to be reliving actual experiences. Second, professional historians examined the content of her regressions and although noting occasional curious fallacies they judged the accounts to be historically accurate to a substantial degree. Now, Evans swore she had never researched any of these historical events. Nevertheless there remains the possibility of cryptomnesia; that is, Evans may have acquired the relevant historical information at some stage but now cannot recall doing so.

Is cryptomnesia a viable explanation of veridical hypnotic regressions? Although, as a scientific hypothesis, cryptomnesia suffers the defect of not being open to disproof, there certainly are some confirmatory instances. One of the most frequently cited is the Blanche Poynings case (Dickinson, 1911). Under hypnosis the subject, a young woman identified only as "Miss C.," regressed as Blanche Poynings, a close friend of Maud the Countess of Salisbury in England under the reign of Richard II. The trance personality gave a wealth of information about the life and times of the Countess and the Earl of Salisbury. Dickinson, an SPR investigator, checked the information and found it to be substantially correct. Miss C. on the other hand was unable to imagine how she could have acquired these historically accurate details, as she had never studied the reign of Richard II. To all appearances therefore, this was a classic case of hypnotic regression to a previous life.

Subsequently, however, Dickinson participated in a seance with Miss C. as the medium and contact was made with the "Blanche" personality. Dickinson asked how the information obtained from Blanche during the regression could be verified. After some probing the spirit communicator suggested he read a novel entitled *Countess Maud* and written by Emily Holt. In the normal waking state Miss C. could recall a novel by this name and said she had read it, although she was unable to recall the story.

Dickinson examined the novel and found it to contain virtually all of the factual material obtained during the regression. In the novel, however, Blanche Poynings herself was a minor character. Miss C.'s regression evidently was an instance of cryptomnesia, with "forgotten" memories of a historical novel being used unconsciously to construct a narrative from the perspective of one of the novel's minor characters.

Cryptomnesia has been shown to play a role in other "past lives" generated under hypnotic regression. For example, when hypnotized for a second time but without the suggestions for regression, some subjects have been able to identify the source of the information contained in their reported past life, despite being unable to recall the source in the normal waking state (e.g., Zolik, 1958). Indeed, the investigation of past life regressions by a Finnish psychiatrist, Reima Kampman (e.g., Kampman & Hirvenoja, 1978), suggests that the factual material upon which some regressions are based may be embedded so deeply in unconscious memories that the individual might not have the faintest recollection of it during the waking state.

Given that cryptomnesia *can* be the basis of a past life regression, is there any evidence that the cases collected by Bloxham may be interpreted in this way? This question has been pursued by a researcher in Britain, Melvin Harris (1986, pp. 145–163; Wilson, 1982, pp. 233–243). No specific source has been identified for Graham Huxtable's regression as a gunner's mate. Harris located dozens of novels that contain accounts of shipboard life in the era of the regression, but the historically unattested names of the frigate and its officers have not been traced to any specific book.

Harris's investigations of Jane Evans' regressions have proved more fruitful. Her regression as Livonia in Roman Britain evidently is based on the novel *The Living Wood* by Louis de Wohl. Not only does this book contain the historically accurate information that was incorporated in the regression, but both the book and the regression feature at least two fictitious details that de Wohl had invented for dramatic purposes. T.B. Costain's novel *The Moneyman* is nominated as the source of the regression as Alison, the housekeeper of Jacques Coeur. Factual details of Coeur's dealings with the king are common to the novel and the regression. Further, the Alison personality appears to have been unaware that her master was married and had five children, and Costain's book deliberately omitted any reference to Coeur's family life in order to simplify the story. A probable source for another of Jane Evans' six regressions also has been located by Harris. It would seem that cryptomnesia, if not deceit, is at the root of the Evans cases. Evans herself reportedly has declined to be interviewed about the correspondences between her regressions and the novels nominated by Harris (Wilson, 1982, p. 243).

There may remain, of course, some instances of veridical past life regression that to all appearances do not involve a cryptomnesic mechanism. But such cases, and the Evans regressions too, presumably could be accommodated by a super–ESP hypothesis. Hypnotic *progression* to a "future life" might be a potential research technique in this context. If a veridical account of a future life could be obtained, it would be explicable in terms of (precognitive) super–ESP but surely not in terms of either cryptomnesia or rekindled memories of another existence. The technique of hypnotic progression unfortunately would be inefficient on two grounds. There would be a substantial delay between the experiment and the evaluation of the data concerning a life in a future time. Additionally, there is nothing to encourage an expectation that the yield of veridical "future life" narratives under this procedure would be high, if they occurred at all; thus attempts at hypnotic progression within the subject's present lifetime to date have generated mere fantasies (Rubenstein & Newman, 1954).

On balance it must be said that hypnotic regression has not proved especially useful to the reincarnation hypothesis either as an experimental induction procedure or as a source of supportive data. In light also of the difficulty of ruling out alternative accounts of spontaneous reincarnation experiences the notion of reincarnation has not proved a fruitful domain for research on the survival hypothesis. In one respect this is surprising: perhaps more than any other phenomenon that has been linked to the survival hypothesis, reincarnation raises the issue of precisely what it is that is alleged to survive bodily death. But while survival has yet to prove an authentic phenomenon, reincarnation experiences remain a thought-provoking topic for phenomenological research.

Key Terms and Concepts

reincarnation
reincarnation experience
Stevenson
solved/unsolved cases
phobias
birthmarks
fraud
paramnesia

cryptomnesia
ESP/super–ESP with personation
inherited memory
possession
hypnotic regression
responsive xenoglossy
Bloxham

Study Questions

1. List the features of a typical case of spontaneous reincarnation experience. Which of these features are present in the Gnanatilleka case?

2. How are cases of the reincarnation experience investigated?

3. What potential explanations of reincarnation experiences should be considered by investigators? Is there support for any of these explanations? What are the arguments against them?

4. According to the philosopher of science Karl Popper, a fundamental requirement of a scientific hypothesis is that it be open to disproof. In the context of explanations of reincarnation experiences and past life regressions, why is the hypothesis of cryptomnesia unable to meet the criterion of falsifiability?

5. Do reincarnation experiences vary across different cultures? In light of this, can reincarnation be deemed an objective event?

6. In what respects has the technique of hypnotic regression failed to contribute to an assessment of the reincarnation hypothesis?

7. What features would you require of a case of hypnotic regression before you would accept it as a persuasive example of reincarnation?

15
Matters of Relevance

Parapsychology has been held to be relevant in substantial respects to a wide range of academic disciplines (Angoff & Shapin, 1974; Schmeidler, 1976). This chapter, however, focuses specifically on clinical practice in a parapsychological context and on some suggested practical applications of the findings of parapsychological research. A book could be devoted to each of these topics in their own right, so this chapter aspires to do little more than raise a few major issues.

Parapsychology and Clinical Practice

The parapsychologist, and occasionally the psychologist in the clinic, may be called upon to counsel people about their parapsychological experiences. It is appropriate, therefore, to consider briefly the implications of parapsychology for the clinical context.

One less obvious implication here is the operation of psi in the therapeutic relationship. Thus the client may report telepathic dreams about the therapist, or use psychokinesis in a displaced expression of frustration with the therapeutic relationship, and so on. Some of the most famous examples of psi experiences in the course of therapy were recorded by Freud and Jung. In one case a young woman was describing to Jung (1955/1985, p. 31) a dream in which she was given a golden scarab. At this moment Jung was distracted by the sound of a flying insect knocking against the window. He opened the window, caught the insect and found to his surprise that it strongly resembled a golden scarab. The patient was equally surprised when Jung presented the beetle to her as her "golden scarab." The salutary effect of this experience was to break down the patient's intellectual resistance to therapy. Many other examples of parapsychological experiences during therapy have been documented (e.g., Devereux, 1953; Eisenbud, 1987; Mintz, 1983; Schwarz, 1980).

The psychoanalyst Jan Ehrenwald (1978) gives various explanations of these experiences. For example, they may be indicative of the client's formation of a "symbiotic" relationship with the therapist, something akin to that between mother and child. In other words the parapsychological experience may be due to the development of transference, the patient's strong emotional attachment to the therapist and to this extent it is a cue to the depth of the evolving therapeutic relationship (Servadio, 1956). Again, psi may be employed in the therapeutic relationship to aid the client's efforts to conform to the therapist's interpretation of his or her problem (sometimes called doctrinal compliance). Irrespective of the validity of these particular depictions of in-therapy psi, the fundamental point to be made is that psi experiences may arise in the therapeutic situation; the therapist, therefore, should be alert to this possibility and give thought to the likely function of the experience in the therapeutic relationship (Calvesi, 1983; Ehrenwald, 1978; Schwarz, 1980).

A circumstance more familiar to parapsychologists is that of giving advice to people who report a parapsychological experience or series of such experiences. These cases may reflect various needs and motives, some of which may be considered only by the experient. It is as well to mention at the outset, however, that the suggestions made below are not intended in any sense as counseling "recipes." Because each person is unique the counseling given in a particular case must be individually tailored. The following points therefore, are offered merely as issues to be considered in the clinical context.

The Hoaxers

If your interest in parapsychology is known to the public you are bound to encounter people who approach you with tales of preternatural experiences purely out of a sense of mischief. Often such individuals can be identified readily by the exaggerated character of their account, although evidence cited in some previous chapters warns that even genuine parapsychological experients rate high in fantasy proneness. In any event the very existence of hoaxers serves as a caution that it may be advisable to be noncommital and nonevaluative in commenting on reported experiences especially in the early phases of a consultation. A Rogerian reflective-listening technique, therefore, can be advantageous: the experient is encouraged to do the talking with gentle prods such as, "And how do you feel about that?" "You seem rather bewildered by your experience," or "Would you like to tell me more about that?" Of course, even the hoaxer might benefit from some form of counseling. That the clinician as the intended victim of the hoax would be sufficiently self-controlled to offer counseling is another matter, but it might be borne in mind that the hoax could be a ruse for engaging the counselor's attention, sympathy and support in relation to quite a different problem.

The Seekers of Reassurance

People who genuinely believe they have had a spontaneous parapsychological experience may approach the parapsychologist or clinician for little else than reassurance, placing the therapist in the role of scientific exorcist (Siegel, 1986; Morris, 1976). This need may manifest itself in various degrees. Some people simply may want to talk to someone about their experience rather than seeking counseling as such. Many parapsychological experiences are so uncanny that experients fear friends would only laugh if the incident was confided to them. The opportunity simply to verbalize the experience to a nonevaluative listener permits experients to reassure themselves that the experience really happened and to make the incident seem more coherent in their own mind.

Other people want confirmation that the experience in fact was paranormal and not delusory. Of course, no definitive judgment can be made on the paranormality of spontaneous parapsychological experiences. If the account seems plausible, reference may be made to other similar experiences to indicate that at least they are common (and therefore normal?), but perhaps it is more fruitful to suggest that the question of authenticity is less important than that of the function served by the experience. The parapsychologist might help the individual to work through the experience to establish its personal significance: regardless of the paranormality of the experience, what does the experient take to be its meaning and its place in their life? This is not to suggest that all ostensibly paranormal experiences are crucially meaningful in a psychodynamic sense; the idea of their functional significance certainly should not be pushed dogmatically by the parapsychologist. But the individual's very interest in the status of the experience is often a cue that it is associated with an issue of some psychological significance, and the experient can at least be invited to explore that possibility.

This nonevaluative approach is appropriate also for people who want assurance that parapsychological experiences do not make them abnormal or alien in some sense. Labeling the experience at least may help to normalize it and to reduce the inquirer's level of anxiety and is certainly more constructive than labeling the individual, whether as psychic or as psychotic. It may be useful also to ask about the occurrence of other parapsychological experiences: this may help both experient and clinician to put the focal experience into a broader context.

As Weiner (personal communication, June 17, 1988) has noted, the parapsychologist can substantially enhance rapport with a client by feeling comfortable in discussing parapsychological experiences and by demonstrating a readiness not to dismiss the possibility of psi out of hand. Even if the client then is told their particular experience does not appear parapsychological, the advice can be appreciated as more than a statement of mere prejudice and thereby may encourage the individual to face the implications of alternative explanations.

Clients Needful of Therapy

If psi does exist there is little reason for presuming it could not operate in a psychopathological context. Indeed, if we were extrasensorially aware of other people's thoughts about us we probably would be quite paranoid. The roles of psi in at least some psychoses such as schizophrenia have been prompted by Alberti (1974), Ehrenwald (1978), Ullman (1973) and others, and perhaps are at their clearest in (person-centered) poltergeist outbreaks. Therapy in these cases may be more effective if cognizance is taken of the parapsychological elements rather than dismissing their possible paranormality out of hand (Munson, 1985; Rogo, 1974; Snoyman, 1985), although certainly there is scant experimental evidence that psychotic experients do have heightened psi abilities (Greyson, 1977; Rogo, 1975).

People who report parapsychological experiences may well have problems in personality and adjustment of a less extreme type. For example, perhaps OBEs are being used to escape from certain unpleasant aspects of reality that the individual is not prepared to confront. The clinician should be alert to possible psychopathological factors underlying parapsychological experiences. By way of illustration, Harary (1982) reports a group therapy case in which a high level of frustration and anxiety was uncovered among workmates who frequently experienced an apparition in their department during the night shift. Again this highlights the importance of exploring the functions played by the parapsychological experience rather than merely labeling the client as psychic or psychotic. It also prompts the point that parapsychologists ethically are obliged to put the needs of an experient ahead of their research interests in the experience.

Even if the therapist believes in the existence of psi, the possibility of psychopathology associated with "pseudo-psi" must be countenanced (Greyson, 1977; McHarg, 1982). For example, some schizophrenics claim that someone is in paranormal control of their mind or that they have extraordinary telepathic powers by which they hear voices talking about them. These cases usually are identifiable by the presence of defective reality testing (Greyson, 1977; Hastings, 1983). Patients with temporal lobe epilepsy sometimes experience bizarre images which they might interpret in parapsychological terms. The incidence of psychopathology among parapsychological experients is not known, but Weiner (1980, p. 46) comments that at least half of the experients who called her laboratory for help had a history of some psychological disturbance. While these parapsychological experiences might not be paranormal, neither are they to be grouped with hoaxes. The individuals concerned are very much in need of professional assistance and it would be insensitive of any parapsychologist to have a policy that if a reported experience is not likely to be genuinely paranormal the inquirer should be shown the door as quickly as possible.

Additionally there arise therapeutic cases which may be regarded as *reactive* in the sense that the individual's anxiety and maladaptive behavior spring from the experience rather than vice versa. Many people are quite disturbed by their parapsychological experience (Hastings, 1983; Siegel, 1986; Morris, 1976) and need counseling in order to come to terms with the incident. One of the most common instances of this type is the precognitive experience: the experient had a premonitory dream of a tragic incident and when the latter actually occurred, felt very guilty for not doing more to prevent the tragedy. Often this sense of responsibility is misguided in that nothing the individual could have done would have prevented or avoided the precognized event. Be this as it may, a useful issue to pursue in therapy is the possibility of functions other than intervention that the precognitive experience could be construed to serve. Thus a premonition might be said to have had the purpose of helping the experient to cope with the tragedy when eventually it did occur, or of putting him or her in a better position to help other affected people to cope.

The NDE is another parapsychological experience that may have disturbing effects on the experient quite apart from the actual threat to life. Although most NDErs are reassured by their experience, some are distressed by the command to leave the paradisial realm and to return to their earthly existence, and others are frustrated by the experience's ineffability which prevents its depth from being shared with someone else. Because of the major philosophical and spiritual changes accompanying an NDE, Furn (1987) observes that the NDEr also may feel like a new member of a cultural minority and may need professional guidance to adapt emotionally and interpersonally to the "culture shock" of their newly embraced worldview. In other types of cases, experients may be upset by a friend's reactions upon hearing about the parapsychological experience and some counseling may be required to assist the client adjust to the secondary effects of the experience upon interpersonal relationships. A more serious variety of reactive case may arise when a person has very frequent parapsychological experiences. According to Neppe (1984) such an individual may come to rely upon these experiences as a means of relating to their physical and social environment, with the result that they tend to lose contact with reality to the point of becoming acutely psychotic.

There is a further therapeutic application of parapsychology that warrants acknowledgment and it relates not to people who have had a parapsychological experience but to people who might benefit by having one. For example, you will recall the very profound psychological effects of OBEs and NDEs, particularly with regard to the experient's attitudes to life and death. Whether or not these effects are deemed by others to be delusory they might well be utilized for therapeutic purposes. Thus if parapsychologists develop a powerful and reliable technique for the induction of OBEs (or certain types of OBEs) it could prove of substantial value in counseling programs for terminally ill patients.

A counseling approach to parapsychological experiences clearly raises many considerations of which just a few have been touched on here. As Hastings (1983) observes, there is a great need for both research and training in parapsychological counseling. There are recent indications that interest in this field is growing.

Other Applications of Parapsychology

Parapsychological research may have application in many areas other than the psychological clinic. The *Applied Psi Newsletter* somewhat ambitiously listed potential practical application in the following areas (Mishlove & Kautz, 1982, p. 1):

agriculture and pest control
animal training and interspecies
   communication
contests and gambling
creativity
education and training
entertainment
environmental improvement
executive decision making
finding lost objects
future forecasting
geological exploration

historical investigation
investigative journalism
medicine and dentistry
military intelligence
personnel management
police work
psychotherapy and counseling
safety inspection
scientific discovery
social control
weather prediction and control

To these, other commentators would add dowsing, archeological excavation, and prediction of natural disasters.

A substantial proportion of potential applications concern the phenomenon of precognition. To assess the efficacy of such applications, an evaluative program must be designed before the precognized events occur and preferably before the predictions themselves are made. Thus psychics claim to have foreseen events such as the assassination of President John F. Kennedy, but it is very difficult to assess these performances in retrospect: one must ask how many other predictions were not fulfilled, for instance. Even if predictions in an evaluative program are known in advance, they must be sufficiently precise for success and failure to be defined beforehand and there must be some way of estimating the *a priori* likelihood of the precognized events.

Suppose that a sensitive declares, "There will be serious bushfires in the Sydney area next summer." For this prediction to be included in the program, agreement must be reached on the following questions. How serious is "serious"? When does "summer" start and end? What is the extent of "the Sydney area"? Additionally, official records must be consulted to determine the *a priori* probability of this prediction being realized. Thus if Sydney has serious bushfires almost every summer, this prediction would not be worth including in the evaluative program.

Somewhat surprisingly only a few studies taking the above sorts of precautions have been performed. The subjects of the prediction in these projects have included the time and location of Skylab's return to earth; the time of the release of American hostages in Iran; the time, location, and magnitude of earthquakes; and the solution of particular crimes. In contrast with the ostensibly spectacular records of psychics' past achievements, the outcomes of these planned and carefully documented investigations have been null in the considerable majority of instances (e.g., Hunter & Derr, 1978; McClenon, 1982a; Reiser, Ludwig, Saxe & Wagner, 1979). Critics would be quick to point out that this confirms their view that psi does not exist, but such a conclusion does not take adequate account of the laboratory research on ESP and PK. Perhaps the conscious control of psi for its use in a specific situation is even more difficult than the data of simplistic laboratory tasks would suggest. Like much of the laboratory research the studies of applied precognition largely seem to lack the elements of personal significance and spontaneity that tend to characterize parapsychological experiences in everyday life.

Another possible application of psi is in gambling. There are numerous reports of people dreaming which horse would win a major race or having a strong intuitive impression of which outcome to bet on in roulette or dice games. In these circumstances, however, one cannot disentangle the possible operation of psi from that of chance, knowledge, good judgment, and so on (Nash, 1986, p. 67). Research on the application of parapsychology to gambling is meager. A study by Brier and Tyminski (1970) did indicate some extrachance success in certain "games of chance," but the experimental set-up here was highly artificial: participants were not competing but rather cooperating by betting on the option that a majority of the group agreed upon.

If psi could be used in real-life gambling it is unlikely to be effective: many players (even unknowingly) may be trying to use psi to their individual advantage with the net effect that nobody's psi is noticeably productive. It must be remembered too that in laboratory psi tasks, the deviation from chance is very small. In gambling a deviation of this magnitude would not be sufficient to compensate for the odds in favor of the casino and in any event would be so small as hardly to bring instant wealth. There is also the daunting prospect that one might prove to be a psi-misser in these situations! Finally, it may be noted that the states of consciousness typically associated with gambling are not those thought to be conducive to psi. In short, the prospects for applying parapsychology to gambling do not look promising.

To this point we have been considering applied parapsychology in terms of the intentional use of psi to practical ends. The results of parapsychological research also might be said to have been applied in the development of certain programs for "training psi ability." Little research effort has been devoted to the experimental evaluation of these multifaceted programs. To be sure, there are some programs that superficially appear to entail legitimate extrapolations from the data of parapsychological experiments (Mishlove, 1983), but it is doubtful that the programs' customers are fully aware of the degree of replicability of the original experiments or of the fact that the criterion for a successful psi experiment is not perfectly accurate performance but rather performance beyond chance expectation at the .05 level. To this it must be added that many psi development programs appear more commercially than scientifically inspired. Again, it is feasible that the programs have diverse social, educational, and therapeutic benefits of which the preceding comments fail to take due account.

As will already be evident, parapsychologists have devoted relatively little thought to potential applications of their field. Their reluctance may have been prompted in part by claims that some national governments are interested in the prospect of utilizing parapsychological research findings for military purposes. In the United States, for example, there is evidence of the CIA's involvement in parapsychology for at least 15 years since 1961 (Clemens, 1982), and Soviet attention to military applications has been documented by Ebon (1983). It is said that the world superpowers have been investigating the use of ESP and the OBE in espionage and of PK for sabotage (e.g., of radar equipment or missile guidance systems). Some reports of government involvement in these applications may be instances of disinformation, the objective being to incite rival nations to waste some of their defense budget in monitoring parapsychological research. Many parapsychologists nevertheless are disturbed by the idea of their field being subverted towards military ends. On the other hand the inability to control the phenomena and the minuteness of effect typical of psi experiments give little reason to believe that military applications, or many of the other mooted practical applications, could be successful in the near future. Some commentators (e.g., Jahn, 1984, p. 134) nevertheless believe that a greater emphasis upon practical applications could improve parapsychology's reception among other scientists. The status of parapsychology in the wider scientific community is addressed in the final chapter.

Key Terms and Concepts

psi in therapy	psychopathology in psi
transference	reactive cases
doctrinal compliance	practical applications
hoaxers	psi training programs
psi in psychopathology	military applications
psuedo-psi	

Study Questions

1. As a practicing psychologist how would you be inclined to counsel the person in each of the following cases? If possible, try this as a role-playing exercise with you and a fellow student alternately taking the role of therapist and that of client.

(a) A man is uncertain of his sanity after having experienced an apparition of a sister who is living in a distant city.

(b) While meditating a woman had a spontaneous impression of being outside her body and she is curious about her experience.

(c) A man had a precognitive dream of a major accident to a much-loved aunt and now that the accident actually has occurred he feels guilty that he did not warn his aunt beforehand.

(d) A young man living in a homosexual relationship claims that their house is haunted, loud raps being heard in the walls during the night.

(e) A woman had a vision of a friend's accidental death and fears the vision in some way caused the death.

(f) A man reports that malfunctions of electrical goods in his home are due to a malicious neighbor's use of PK.

(g) With the objective of securing a publishing contract a woman wants you to attest to her ability to communicate mediumistically with the spirit of John Lennon.

(h) A man reports that he had the impression of smelling his late mother's perfume, upon which he was possessed by her spirit and caused to suffer a fit of convulsions.

(i) A woman who has been a client of yours for some weeks describes a dream in which you were going to marry her but instead you sent your brother to the ceremony; in reality you were thinking you might refer this client to a medical colleague for supplementary treatment.

An Introduction to Parapsychology

(j) Following an NDE a hospital patient admits to feeling resentful about being "sent back" to a life of physical pain and even thought fleetingly of suicide as a means of returning to "that beautiful place beyond death."

(k) Under hypnosis during a "quit smoking" program a young man spontaneously "becomes" a Jewish prisoner in a Nazi concentration camp during World War II and he vividly enacts the terrible ordeal of being tortured. After returning him to normal waking consciousness you relate the experience to him and he asks if it arose from a previous life.

2. How might psi be applied in real-life settings? What are the current prospects of such application?

3. In what manner can a psi-development program be evaluated? Is it sufficient that such a program be based entirely on the results of experimentation by parapsychologists?

16
An Evaluation of Parapsychology as a Scientific Enterprise

In this the final chapter of the text it is appropriate to examine parapsychology from the perspective of the sociology of science. As previous chapters have indicated there has been encouraging progress in the experimental investigation of some parapsychological phenomena and the resulting data seem to show substantial coherence despite numerous lacunae. Although an adequate experimental paradigm is lacking for research into many other parapsychological experiences, even here an impressive body of phenomenological data has been accumulated. In short, future prospects for parapsychological research appear exciting if not guaranteed.

But how is parapsychology currently regarded in the broader context of scientific enterprise? Two general issues arising from this question are considered here. The first of these concerns the efforts of parapsychologists to establish their discipline as a legitimate science; the second issue is the nature of the scientific establishment's responses to these efforts.

Efforts to Establish Parapsychology as a Science

Historically speaking there has been a clear progression in parapsychology from the collection of anecdotal material to the experimental investigation of laboratory analogues of psi phenomena. Thus a major element in parapsychologists' efforts to put their discipline on a scientific footing is the recourse to scientific method. Arguably, J.B. Rhine's major contribution to parapsychology was to appreciate the importance of using the investigative mode of the established sciences in order to enquire into the authenticity and nature of ostensibly paranormal events. Certainly people before Rhine had conducted some elementary experiments on ESP, but in the societies for psychical research where much of the work at that time was being undertaken, the development of laboratory analogues of psi phenomena was seen as a minor and indeed somewhat peripheral activity. Rhine's pursuit of a sustained and cohesive experimental program of ESP and PK research, with its attention to the identification and control of artifactual variables and its probabilistic evaluation of data, therefore constituted a significant step toward the goal of gaining scientific status for parapsychology. This initiative has been maintained by contemporary parapsychologists through reliance upon the increasingly sophisticated methods of modern conventional science.

Along with scientific procedures the technological hardware of modern science has been incorporated into psi research. Computers and REGs not only permit tighter experimental methods but also to some degree bring the feature of technical precision that is a hallmark of contemporary science. For example, extrasensory targets can be selected under known parameters of randomness and displayed at the moment chosen by the experimenter or by the participant for an exactly defined interval; the participant's response can be recorded and compared to the target without human bias; and all manner of information on response latency and neurophysiological activity can be plotted across the supposed period of psi processing.

But there is much more to the practice of a scientific discipline than methods and hardware. Science is essentially a social activity. It is undertaken by groups of people who impose upon themselves certain codes of conduct or rules for interacting among themselves and for promoting their interests. Thus the contemporary world of professional science is highly institutionalized.

One consequence of this state of affairs is that it does matter where research is carried out. To be truly scientific, experimental research must be performed in a specialized setting called a "laboratory." If the work has (potential or actual) commercial application it may be conducted in a privately owned facility, but in any event a field of research that has any scientific merit must be represented in the laboratories of recognized universities. In the view of the scientific establishment an area of activity that lacks such representation at the university level cannot be regarded as a "proper" science. In this context it can be said that another important facet of Rhine's contribution was that he undertook his program of research in a university department. The significance of university representation has continued to be recognized with a substantial number of academics pursuing parapsychological research particularly on campuses in the United States and in Europe.

Another characteristic of institutionalized science is that of professionalism. Any genuine science is conducted largely by professionals who specialize in their area of expertise. While amateurs did make acknowledged contributions to conventional science in the last century, this soon changed and today a predominance of amateurs in a field of interest usually would be construed by orthodox scientists as indicative of the field's status as a craft rather than a science. In its early days psychical research was performed, often on a part-time basis, by amateurs, people who in large part saw such work as a recreational pursuit. Part of the effort to achieve scientific status for modern parapsychology has been directed to the growth of professionalism, the full-time employment of suitably trained personnel in parapsychological research (at least to the extent that available funding and resources permit).

Allied to this feature is the formation of professional societies. In recognized areas of scientific research, formal societies are established with the general objectives of promoting the field and facilitating productive interaction among people involved in research. Such societies tend to set high academic qualifications for membership and to accord recognition to major contributors to the discipline by way of higher levels of membership (fellowships) or the conferring of special awards each year. A society of this type has been established for parapsychologists: it is called the Parapsychological Association (PA) and was founded in 1957.

In recent years the number of PA members has varied between 120 and 150 people, with another 160 or so listed as associate members; this membership admittedly is very small in comparison with that of most scientific societies. The Parapsychological Association's qualifications for full membership are that the person (a) hold a doctorate or have a professional affiliation with a recognized academic institution or research organization; (b) have prepared a paper on some aspect of parapsychology that in the opinion of the Association's Council is of high professional caliber and which has been published in a scientific journal or which merits such publication; and (c) be nominated by two members of the Association and elected by a majority vote of the governing Council. (The lower grade of membership, the associate, may be granted to a person with a bachelor's degree and with no publications.) Interaction among researchers is encouraged through various publications and an annual convention. Fellowships and awards are not offered by the PA.

In recent times one of the recognized functions of a scientific society has been to devise guidelines concerning the ethics of experimentation in its field. This has been of particular importance in the context of experiments with human or animal participants. The American Psychological Association, for example, has documented in some detail the ethical considerations that apply to psychological research. Similarly, the Parapsychological Association in 1977 established its own Committee on Professional Standards and Ethics with the objective of developing guidelines on these matters for its members. Advice is given on the protection of the rights of participants in parapsychological research with specific reference to the issues of informed consent to participate in a study, confidentiality, deception about the study's purpose, post-test discussion about the study ("debriefing"), professional treatment of human participants, and humane handling of animal subjects.

Other topics addressed by the ethics committee are the misuse of research funds; openness in the conduct and reporting of research; acknowledgment of contributors to the study in the text of the research report and in assigning authorship; possible conflicts of interest in acting as a referee on a manuscript submitted for publication; ethics in criticism of other researchers' work; fraud by experimenters or participants; dissemination of information through the public news media; and the maintenance of parapsychology's professional image. Parapsychologists generally have shown themselves to be alert to ethical issues (Gregory, 1982; Stanford, 1988; Thomson, 1986).

In addition to a discipline's having its own society it is usual for this society to be affiliated with more general scientific associations to give it a voice in the formulation and promotion of science policy in general. In the United States this general body is the prestigious American Association for the Advancement of Science (AAAS). The Parapsychological Association was admitted to the AAAS in 1969. The annual AAAS convention provides parapsychologists with a forum for presenting their research to scientists from other fields and for advancing parapsychology in the context of the AAAS's lobbying on national science policy.

Another characteristic of a scientific discipline is the publication of specialist journals devoted to the subject matter of the field. These journals permit not only the communication of theoretical and empirical research to interested persons but also the enhancement of the status of the area as a legitimate domain for scientific endeavor. Papers submitted to these journals for publication must fulfill certain requirements in their presentation of methodology and data and are subjected to scrutiny by a panel of qualified referees for evaluation as a substantial scientific contribution worthy of publication. In psychology the earliest journals were very broad in scope, containing papers on the whole range of conventional psychological inquiry; today there are numerous highly specialized journals each of which addresses a particular area of psychological research (e.g., imagery, hypnosis, memory, verbal learning, personality, and so on).

Parapsychological research for much of its history had as its only outlet the journals of a few societies for psychical research. In 1937 Rhine established the *Journal of Parapsychology;* today this and the societies' journals constitute the major channels for the dissemination of research in the field. Recently some other major journals have been established, including the *European Journal of Parapsychology* (from 1975) and *Psi Research* (1982). Additionally there are a few more specialized publications: for example, *Theta* (since 1963) provides a forum for research pertinent to the survival hypothesis, and the *Journal of Near-Death Studies* (formerly *Anabiosis* and published since 1981) features papers on the NDE and related phenomena. Each of these journals observes the rigid code for acceptance of papers that characterizes orthodox scientific journals.

Representation of a discipline in a university setting also is important for training aspiring professionals. The perseverance of academic parapsychologists has seen the establishment of parapsychology courses in many universities and colleges in the United States, Great Britain, Europe, Australia, India and other countries.

One other feature of a genuine science should be mentioned, distasteful though it is. Occasionally professional scientists break the rules of the game and have to be expelled from the field. Such an incident arose in parapsychology with the Levy affair in 1974 (McConnell, 1987, Ch. 11; Rhine, 1974, 1975). Dr. W.J. Levy had worked in Rhine's laboratory for a few years and was interested primarily in psi research with animals (anpsi). In 1974 some students observed Levy tinkering with the automatic recording apparatus being used in one of the laboratory's anpsi experiments. Secret recordings of the data were arranged and, on comparison with Levy's reported results, discrepancies were found. When confronted by Rhine, Levy acknowledged his fraudulent activity and was dismissed. Parapsychologists known to be planning to use any of Levy's published work in their papers immediately were advised not to do so. Rhine (1974) published a statement in the *Journal of Parapsychology* giving the details of the affair and advising that *all* of Levy's publications should now be regarded as unacceptable (although Levy claimed he resorted to fraudulent manipulation only when his recent experiments yielded nonsignificant data). In the Levy case parapsychology was shown to be capable of keeping its house in order and not to be inclined to cover up indiscretions for appearances' sake.

Responses of Critics

How have members of the scientific establishment responded to the efforts of parapsychologists to put their field on a scientific footing? Several anonymous surveys (Evans, 1973; McClenon, 1982b, 1984; Wagner & Monnet, 1979; Warner, 1952; Warner & Clark, 1938) consistently have indicated that while many scientists do not accept unequivocally the existence of psi phenomena they do acknowledge that parapsychological hypotheses should be permitted evaluation in a conventionally scientific manner. The views of the "silent majority" are not always reflected in the voices of the scientific establishment, however, and in science it is the elite groups that wield the greatest political power (Broad & Wade, 1982, Ch. 5).

Some scientists reject parapsychology as a science simply because they cannot accept its empirical findings. On occasion this is tantamount to naked prejudice. For example, the prominent psychologist Donald Hebb wrote in 1951, "why do we not accept ESP as a psychological fact? Rhine has offered us enough evidence to have convinced us on almost any other issue.... I cannot see what other basis my colleagues have for rejecting it.... My own rejection of [Rhine's] views is—in the literal sense—prejudice" (Hebb, 1951, p. 45). And in 1958 the vice president of the AAAS recalled the remarks of the physicist Helmholtz: "I cannot believe it. Neither the testimony of all the Fellows of the Royal Society, nor even the evidence of my own senses would lead me to believe in the transmission of thought from one person to another independently of the recognised channels of sensation. It is clearly impossible" (Birge, 1958, cited by Collins & Pinch, 1979, p. 244). This *a priori* assumption that the experimental findings of parapsychologists just can't be true and hence must be unscientific, persists among the scientific elite and among psychologists in particular, scientists in most other fields being rather more receptive (Alcock, 1975; McClenon, 1982b, 1984; Wagner & Monnet, 1979).

Other commentators reject psi research on grounds derived from the philosophy of science. For example, one such principle is known as Occam's (or Ockham's) Razor and proposes that if two hypotheses account equally well for a given set of data the simplest or most parsimonious should be accepted. Thus, without any regard to the quality of the available data ESP may be ignored under the principle of Occam's Razor because any orthodox alternative hypothesis (fraud, sensory leakage, poor experimental design, etc.) would have the advantage of not positing any new mode of information transfer. If taken to an extreme, application of this principle would preclude almost any further scientific discovery.

A few scientists have sought to dismiss the experimental literature of parapsychology as utterly fraudulent (e.g., Price, 1955). Their motivation in doing so seems to be little else than the *a priori* conviction that parapsychological phenomena are impossible. There nevertheless has been some evidential support for the argument of fraud. The Levy affair in 1974 is perhaps the most notable instance. Additionally, in 1978 a British researcher, Betty Markwick (1978), reported that in comparing S.G. Soal's set of ESP targets with the table of random numbers purported to be the basis of target selection in his experiments with the subject Shackleton, some serious discrepancies were evident, on nearly all occasions with the effect of enhancing Shackleton's ESP score.

Occasionally a parapsychologist may have such an extraordinarily high rate of successful experiments that even the individual's own colleagues may be suspicious of his or her professional integrity. Particularly in the United States a possible motive for experimenter fraud is very evident: American academic parapsychologists commonly are appointed on two- or three-year contracts with their reappointment to these scarce positions governed to some degree by their research productivity.

That some parapsychologists have sometimes cheated is undeniable. What is equivocal is the notion that all parapsychological research is fraudulent, or indeed that there is any justification in Neher's (1980, p. 142) assertion of an unusually high incidence of fraud in this field. Fraud occurs in all branches of science (Broad & Wade, 1982; Kohn, 1987; St. James-Roberts, 1976).

That parapsychology has relatively more frequent cases of experimenter fraud than does psychology is an impression based in part on different modal reactions to such fraud between the two disciplines. When parapsychologists identify an instance of fraud it is given extensive publicity, such is their determination to maintain the integrity of the discipline; indeed the only reason Hansel (1966) was able to cite some attested instances of fraud in ESP experiments was that parapsychologists themselves had published detailed reports of these instances.

On the other hand there is a much stronger tendency among psychologists to turn a blind eye to fraud in their field, the recent posthumous exposure of Burt's deception notwithstanding (Hearnshaw, 1979); their assumption seems to be that the experiment probably would have turned out in the reported manner anyway, so readers are not really being misled (Broad & Wade, 1982, p. 80). In parapsychology there is much effort directed too to the replication of experimental findings and this can assist in the identification of fraudulent practice. Much less interest in experimental replication is shown by psychologists: if the data are theoretically or intuitively plausible academic psychologists today rarely bother with simple replications, if only for the reason that psychology journals generally will not publish a report of such a study. Without routine experimental replications there is no safeguard against experimenter fraud; most exposures of fraud in the orthodox sciences consequently have come through personal disclosure (Broad & Wade, 1982, p. 73). In short, the argument of frequent fraud in parapsychology seems more politically than evidentially founded.

Some recent attacks on parapsychologists have focused not so much on their integrity as on their professional competence. Hansel's (1966, 1980) scenarios of possible fraud in selected experiments typically portray the experimenter as inept in attempting to establish experimental control. This is not to say that parapsychological experiments have been criticized unjustly; methodological weaknesses can be named as readily for these studies (see Akers, 1984) as for the experiments in many areas of orthodox psychology, for example. But skeptics such as Diaconis (1978), Gardner (1981) and Randi (1975, 1982) maintain that parapsychologists' experimental control is so poor that participants are able to use conjuring tricks to achieve above-chance performance.

A majority of parapsychologists now appreciate the point that in designing some of their experiments the professional advice of a magician could be helpful, and indeed many parapsychologists have sought consultations of this sort (Hansen, 1985). Nevertheless the skeptics' generalized slur upon parapsychologists' professional competence still rankles. The issue became acute with Randi's (1983a,b) so-called Project Alpha in which Randi, a professional stage magician, arranged for two young conjurers to present themselves as psychics at a parapsychological laboratory. According to Randi the parapsychologists were deceived effectively by the young men during a series of supposedly controlled experiments. The parapsychologists themselves declared that the conjurers had not been successful in tightly controlled experiments; it was acknowledged, however, that in some exploratory studies fraudulent performances had been taken by the research team as "encouraging" results and had been reported as such in unrefereed conference research briefs.

Much of the subsequent debate over Randi's hoax has concerned the ethics of the procedure (Truzzi, 1987), although it must be remembered that Randi is a showman and thereby is not bound by the professional ethics of scientists. Project Alpha has been constructive in reminding parapsychologists that they need to be especially wary in working with people who volunteer themselves as "psychics." On the other hand the hoax certainly did not show parapsychologists as a group to be incompetent in research. From the perspective of the sociology of science Project Alpha is noteworthy in instancing one form of skeptics' attempts to "debunk" parapsychological research.

Some critics (e.g., Hyman, 1980) have argued for the need to respond to parapsychology in a sober and proper manner, but nonetheless a common tactic of skeptics is the use of ridicule. Parapsychological phenomena are derided as nonsensical and primitive folk beliefs and parapsychological research is belittled as occultism in pseudoscientific garb. This approach especially is characteristic of the Committee for the Scientific Investigation of Claims of the Paranormal (CSICOP). A group of scientists and other people, CSICOP was originally founded to examine objectively the evidence for paranormal phenomena, but it has maintained an inflexible stance against research into the paranormal (Hansen, 1987), some of its affiliates even resorting to deception in experimental reports (Pinch & Collins, 1984). Many of its more evenhanded members consequently have resigned.

Articles published in the *Humanist* and in CSICOP's own periodical, the *Skeptical Inquirer* (see Frazier, 1981, 1986), amalgamate parapsychological research with astrology, vampires, UFOs, pyramid power, numerology, the Bermuda triangle, witchcraft, the Tarot, the Abominable Snowman and the like, encouraging an impression of parapsychology's guilt by association. Parapsychology has been depicted by some skeptics as a spiritualist or occultist movement seeking to maintain popular support by adopting a facade of scientific methodology; for example, the discipline is said to be a "pseudoscience" (Alcock, 1981), its researchers "closet occultists" (Romm, 1977) and its concepts "a reversion to a pre-scientific religio-mystical tradition" (Moss & Butler, 1978, p. 1077). Although parapsychologists deplore these rhetorical devices the fact of the matter is that this is how scientific controversy is waged. As Feyerabend (1975) maintains, it is not so much the logic of the case that determines the outcome of a scientific controversy but rather the rhetorical skills of the advocates for each side.

Other more specific criticisms of parapsychology have been noted in earlier chapters. Some scientists reject the ESP data because while the results may be statistically significant the deviation from chance is so small that it is not convincing of an extrasensory access to information. Others believe that parapsychology cannot be accorded the status of a science as long as it lacks a widely endorsed theory of its phenomena (Flew, 1980). Still other commentators maintain that parapsychology is not a science because its experiments are not guaranteed to be replicable upon demand.

Possibly these aspects of parapsychology could be interpreted as characteristic of a young science, one that has yet to achieve the desired level of control over its phenomena. But again, perhaps psi phenomena are inherently weak or little open to conscious production (Beloff, 1985). Certainly in recent years there are indications that theories of psi are becoming more viable and the experimental findings may be becoming more replicable.

It is not impertinent to note that the above criticisms might equally be applicable to other areas of scientific research. In psychology, for example, many experimental results comprise small but statistically significant effects, and often the replicability of these effects is either poor or untested. This is not to say that effect size and repeatability are unimportant, but merely that critics' emphasis upon them in the parapsychology debate is fundamentally for rhetorical purposes (McClenon, 1984, pp. 89–91). One cannot help but feel that the antagonism of many psychologists toward parapsychological research is in some measure a projection of anxieties over their own discipline.

The motivations of parapsychology's critics have been the object of considerable speculation (e.g., LeShan, 1966; McConnell, 1977; Wren-Lewis, 1974). Critics undoubtedly believe in the rationality of their case against parapsychology, yet this in itself seems inadequate to account for the belligerence and vehemence of their attacks. Although some parapsychologists regard the implications of psi phenomena to be so far-reaching as to augur a major revolution in materialistic science, there is little indication that critics see the fabric of science to be under serious threat, and thus this would not appear to be a significant motive.

Tart (1982) proposes that the critics' behavior is fueled by a very strong unconscious emotion, a "fear of psi." Many people are concerned that if psi really were to exist, social interaction would be disrupted, their personal privacy invaded, and their independence open to unfair manipulation by others. For these people it is too awful that psi should exist, so its existence simply must not be conceded. In support of Tart's hypothesis that critics are motivated by a fear of psi, Irwin (1985c) reports a significant relationship between a measure of the fear of psi and the respondent's attitude to the appropriateness of parapsychological research. There is considerable scope for further research into the psychodynamics of attitudes to parapsychological research.

Criticism is intrinsic to academic science, of course. It plays an important role in the refinement of theories and empirical techniques and thereby serves to stimulate further, more incisive, research. Indeed, some skeptical analyses of parapsychological research have proven very constructive (e.g., Hyman, 1985; Hyman & Honorton, 1986). On the other hand the scientific establishment's reactions to parapsychology tend to go further in using criticisms as grounds for maintaining parapsychology's marginal status and denying it the privileges of a scientific discipline.

One instance of this is the inhibition of parapsychologists' access to orthodox journals. Publications such as *Science* and *Nature* have been shown to be extremely unwilling to publish articles favoring parapsychological concepts (Collins & Pinch, 1979, pp. 257–258; McClenon, 1984, pp. 114–118; Rockwell, 1979). One fascinating documentation of this is provided by Honorton et al. (1975). Honorton submitted to *Science* a report of a study on experimenter effects in ESP. After it had been revised in the light of earlier comments, the manuscript was scrutinized by four referees, three of whom favored its publication. The dissenting referee clearly was not familiar with parapsychological research, being unable for example to countenance the observation of a mean ESP score that was significantly *below* chance. The editors of *Science* decided not to publish the paper.

Those articles that are accepted for publication in *Science* or in *Nature* frequently are diluted by negative comments made in an accompanying editorial or in a commentary by scientists outside the field (Collins & Pinch, 1979, pp. 258–259); often such commentaries do not appear to have been subjected to the usual editorial processes. Psychology journals also appear to publish a higher proportion of unsuccessful psi experiments than do parapsychological journals (Billig, 1972), while in psychology texts the tendency is either to ignore parapsychological research altogether (Child, 1985) or to describe only weak and outdated studies (Rogo, 1980).

Restrictions also are placed on funds for parapsychological research. Committees that assess research proposals and allocate public funds to them typically have been found to be unsympathetic to parapsychology. Even where a university finances much of its own research activity, parapsychological research might not be granted a reasonable level of financial support. Some funds may be available from private sources but limits frequently are imposed on the sorts of investigations that may be conducted under the auspices of these sources; for example, the terms of a grant may constrain the researcher to look into some aspect of the survival hypothesis.

In the university setting there are many other obstacles placed in the way of those who wish to pursue parapsychological research. Such interests may substantially harm one's chances of promotion. Further, there are few openings for academic parapsychologists. Of those Australian academics currently active in parapsychological research or teaching, *none* was appointed originally in this field. There may also be opposition to the teaching of parapsychology in universities and colleges, despite nominal endorsement of the principle of academic freedom in these institutions (Hansen, 1987). McCormick (1987) reports a case of the cancellation of parapsychology courses at the University of Hawaii after pressure from a skeptical group affiliated with CSICOP. The lack of adequate formal acknowledgment of the field on college campuses severely hinders progress in parapsychology and inhibits recruitment of new people to the discipline.

In view of the reactions of certain influential members of the scientific community it might be asked why anyone would persist in their efforts toward parapsychology's acceptance as a legitimate area for scientific inquiry. Some reasons for doing so are idealistic: parapsychologists genuinely may see their work as scientific and want it acknowledged as such. Other reasons ultimately are more selfish: effective recognition of parapsychology should bring more research funds, greater opportunities for and security of employment, and the chance to specialize in parapsychology instead of pursuing it as an ancillary interest. Additionally the promotion of parapsychology as a science has political functions: it constitutes a response to critics and serves to engender in parapsychologists working in academically isolated positions some sense of professional support and unity.

The majority of parapsychologists unfortunately have put themselves at a strategic disadvantage by continuing to present their field as the investigation of the paranormal rather than as the study of parapsychological experiences or experiences that appear to imply the operation of paranormal processes (Blackmore, 1987). Definition in terms of paranormal phenomena inhibits any rapprochement between parapsychologists and their critics because it currently leaves open the question of whether the discipline has any phenomena to investigate: that paranormal phenomena exist is at best uncertain.

The parapsychologist's adherence to scientific procedures in itself is insufficient; for a field of inquiry to be deemed a science there must additionally be identifiable phenomena for investigation by these procedures. The phenomenological context avoids this difficulty. There can be no dispute that people have parapsychological experiences, and the scientific investigation of these experiences by definition then constitutes a science.

This is not to assert that parapsychology should be totally immersed in the world of human consciousness; under a phenomenological definition of the discipline, the performance of psi experiments still is appropriate because some types of subjective parapsychological events might well prove to have an objective foundation, a basis rooted in the physical world. Until parapsychologists can appreciate that parapsychological experiences can be studied whether or not they are paranormal, parapsychological research will maintain its marginal status in the domain of orthodox science and as Moore (1977) argues, parapsychology will run the risk that its cultural significance will progressively fade almost to the point of oblivion, just as happened to nineteenth-century spiritualism.

In the final analysis, what fairly can be said of parapsychology? As far as spontaneous cases are concerned it seems likely that there are numerous instances of self-deception, delusion, and even fraud. Some of the empirical literature likewise might be attributable to shoddy experimental procedures and to fraudulent manipulation of data. Be this as it may, there is sound phenomenological evidence of parapsychological experiences and possibly even experimental evidence of anomalous events too, and behavioral scientists ethically are obliged to encourage the investigation of these phenomena rather than dismissing them out of hand. If all of the phenomena do prove to be explicable within conventional principles of mainstream psychology surely that is something worth knowing, especially in relation to counseling practice; and if just one of the phenomena should be found to demand a revision or an expansion of contemporary psychological principles, how enriched behavioral science would be.

Key Terms and Concepts

scientific method   technological hardware
laboratory analogues   professionalism

scientific societies
Parapsychological Association
(PA)
American Association for the
Advancement of Science
(AAAS)
specialist journals
*Journal of the Society for
Psychical Research*
*Journal of the American Society
for Psychical Research*
Journal of Parapsychology
*European Journal of
Parapsychology*
Psi Research

Theta
Journal of Near-Death Studies
university representation
disclosure of fraud
the Levy affair
fraud by Soal
incidence of fraud
Project Alpha
effect size
replicability
critics' motives
access to journals
research funding
parapsychology teaching

Study Questions

1. Why must science generally be conducted in a laboratory? Discuss this issue in relation to the position of contemporary parapsychology.

2. In what ways has the practice of parapsychology developed toward being scientific?

3. Should parapsychology be permitted representation on university campuses? Why, or why not?

4. In what ways has the scientific establishment sought to frustrate the acknowledgment of parapsychology as a science?

5. "The Levy affair demonstrates that experimenter fraud does occur in parapsychology. This field, therefore, cannot be accorded scientific status." Discuss.

6. Consider (a) the significance for parapsychology and (b) the ethics of Randi's Project Alpha.

7. Imagine scientists invented a drug that made people aware of the thoughts of every person in their immediate surroundings. What feelings do you have about this situation? Can you appreciate that some people would be very anxious about it?

References

[Abbot, C.G.] (1938). A scientist tests his own ESP ability. *Journal of Parapsychology, 2*, 65–70.

Abbott, D.P. (1909). *Behind the scenes with mediums* (3rd ed.). Chicago: Open Court.

Akers, C. (1984). Methodological criticisms of parapsychology. In S. Krippner (Ed.), *Advances in parapsychological research, Vol. 4* (pp. 112–164). Jefferson, NC: McFarland.

Alberti, G. (1974). Psychopathology and parapsychology: Some possible contacts. In A. Angoff & B. Shapin (Eds.), *Parapsychology and the sciences* (pp. 225–233). New York: Parapsychology Foundation.

Alcock, J.E. (1975). *Some correlates of extraordinary belief.* Paper presented at the 36th Annual Meeting of the Canadian Psychological Association, Quebec.

Alcock, J.E. (1978). Psychology and near-death experiences. *Skeptical Inquirer, 3*(2), 25–41.

Alcock, J.E. (1981). *Parapsychology: Science or magic? A psychological perspective.* Oxford: Pergamon.

Alvarado, C.S. (1982). Recent OBE detection studies: A review. *Theta, 10*(2), 35–37.

Alvarado, C.S., & Martínez-Taboas, A. (1983). The super-psi hypothesis: A review. *Theta, 11*, 57–62.

Anderson, R.I. (1987). Spiritualism before the Fox sisters. *Parapsychology Review, 18*(1), 9–13.

Anderson, R., & Anderson, W. (1982). Veridical and psychopathic hallucinations: A comparison of types. *Parapsychology Review, 13*(3), 17–23.

Angoff, A., & Shapin, B. (Eds.) (1974). *Parapsychology and the sciences.* New York: Parapsychology Foundation.

Baker, R.A. (1982). The effect of suggestion on past-lives regression. *American Journal of Clinical Hypnosis, 25*, 71–76.

Ballard, J.A. (1987, August). *Rychlakean theory and parapsychology.* Paper presented at the 30th Annual Convention of the Parapsychological Association, Edinburgh, Scotland.

Barker, D.R., & Pasricha, S.K. (1979). Reincarnation cases in Fatehabad: A systematic survey in North India. *Journal of Asian and African Studies, 14*, 231–240.

Barker, J.C. (1967). Premonitions of the Aberfan disaster. *Journal of the Society for Psychical Research, 44*, 169–181.

Bayless, R. (1973). *Apparitions and survival of death.* New Hyde Park, NY: University Books.

Bayless, R. (1976). *Voices from beyond.* Secaucus, NJ: University Books.

Beloff, J. (1972). The place of theory in parapsychology. In R. Van Over (Ed.), *Psychology and extrasensory perception* (pp. 379–395). New York: New American Library.

Beloff, J. (1977a). Backward causation. *Parapsychology Review, 8*(1), 1–5.

Beloff, J. (1977b). Psi phenomena: Causal versus acausal interpretation. *Journal of the Society for Psychical Research, 49,* 573–582.

Beloff, J. (1980). Seven evidential experiments. *Zetetic Scholar, 6,* 91–94.

Beloff, J. (1985). *Research strategies for dealing with unstable phenomena.* In B. Shapin & L. Coly (Eds.), *The repeatability problem in parapsychology* (pp. 1–21). New York: Parapsychology Foundation.

Beloff, J. (1986). Retrodiction. *Parapsychology Review, 17*(1), 1–5.

Benassi, V.A., Singer, B., & Reynolds, C.B. (1980). Occult belief: Seeing is believing. *Journal for the Scientific Study of Religion, 19,* 337–349.

Bender, H. (1971). New developments in poltergeist research. In W.G. Roll, R.L. Morris, & J.D. Morris (Eds.), *Proceedings of the Parapsychological Association No. 6, 1969* (pp. 81–102). Durham, NC: Parapsychological Association.

Bender, H. (1974). Modern poltergeist research. In J. Beloff (Ed.), *New directions in parapsychology* (pp. 122–143). London: Elek.

Bender, H. (1977). Further investigations of spontaneous and experimental PK by the Freiburg Institute. In J.D. Morris, W.G. Roll, & R.L. Morris (Eds.), *Research in parapsychology 1976* (pp. 202–203). Metuchen, NJ: Scarecrow Press.

Bender, H. (1982). Poltergeists. In I. Grattan-Guinness (Ed.), *Psychical research: A guide to its history, principles and practices* (pp. 123–133). Wellingborough, England: Aquarian Press.

Benor, D.J. (1986). Research in psychic healing. In B. Shapin & L. Coly (Eds.), *Current trends in psi research* (pp. 96–119). New York: Parapsychology Foundation.

Berger, A.S. (1984). Experiments with false keys. *Journal of the American Society for Psychical Research, 78,* 41–54.

Berman, A.L. (1974). Belief in afterlife, religion, religiosity and life-threatening experiences. *Omega, 5,* 127–135.

Bernstein, M. (1956). *The search for Bridey Murphy.* Garden City, NY: Doubleday.

Besterman, T. (1932). The psychology of testimony in relation to paraphysical phenomena: Report of an experiment. *Proceedings of the Society for Psychical Research, 40,* 363–387.

Bevan, J.M. (1947). ESP tests in light and darkness. *Journal of Parapsychology, 11,* 76–89.

Billig, M. (1972). Positive and negative experimental psi results in psychology and parapsychology journals. *Journal of the Society for Psychical Research, 46,* 136–142.

Blackmore, S.J. (1982). *Beyond the body: An investigation of out-of-the-body experiences.* London: Heinemann.

Blackmore, S.J. (1984a). A postal survey of OBEs and other experiences. *Journal of the Society for Psychical Research, 52,* 225–244.

Blackmore, S.J. (1984b). A psychological theory of the out-of-body experience. *Journal of Parapsychology, 48,* 201–218.

Blackmore, S. (1986). *The adventures of a parapsychologist.* Buffalo, NY: Prometheus Books.

Blackmore, S. (1987, August). *The aspirations of psychical research.* Paper presented at the 30th Annual Convention of the Parapsychological Association, Edinburgh, Scotland.

Blackmore, S., & Trościanko, T. (1985). Belief in the paranormal: Probability judgments, illusory control, and the "chance baseline shift." *British Journal of Psychology,* **76,** 459–468.

Braud, W.G. (1978). Recent investigations of microdynamic psychokinesis, with special emphasis on the roles of feedback, effort, and awareness. *European Journal of Parapsychology,* **2,** 137–162.

Braud, W.G. (1980). Lability and inertia in conformance behavior. *Journal of the American Society for Psychical Research,* **74,** 297–318.

Braud, W. (1985). The two faces of psi: Psi revealed and psi obscured. In B. Shapin & L. Coly (Eds.), *The repeatability problem in parapsychology* (pp. 150–175). New York: Parapsychology Foundation.

Braud, W. (1986). Psi and PNI: Exploring the interface between parapsychology and psychoneurology. *Parapsychology Review,* **17**(4), 1–5.

Braud, W. (1987). Dealing with displacement. *Journal of the American Society for Psychical Research,* **81,** 209–231.

Braud, W., Davis, G., & Wood, R. (1979). Experiments with Matthew Manning. *Journal of the Society for Psychical Research,* **50,** 199–223.

Braude, S.E. (1979). The observational theories in parapsychology: A critique. *Journal of the American Society for Psychical Research,* **73,** 349–366.

Braude, S.E. (1986). *The limits of influence: Psychokinesis and the philosophy of science.* New York: Routledge & Kegan Paul.

Brier, R.M., & Tyminski, W.V. (1970). Psi application: Part I. A preliminary attempt. *Journal of Parapsychology,* **34,** 1–25.

Broad, C.D. (1962). *Lectures on psychical research.* London: Routledge & Kegan Paul.

Broad, W., & Wade, N. (1982). *Betrayers of the truth.* New York: Simon & Schuster.

Broughton, R.S., & Perlstrom, J.R. (1985). A competitive computer game in PK research: Some preliminary findings. In R.A. White & J. Solfvin (Eds.), *Research in parapsychology 1984* (pp. 74–77). Metuchen, NJ: Scarecrow Press.

Burdick, D.S., & Kelly, E.F. (1977). Statistical methods in parapsychological research. In B.B. Wolman (Ed.), *Handbook of parapsychology* (pp. 81–130). New York: Van Nostrand Reinhold.

Burnham, W.H. (1889). Memory, historically and experimentally considered. III. Paramnesia. *American Journal of Psychology,* **2,** 431–464.

Cadoret, R., & Pratt, J.G. (1950). The consistent missing effect in ESP. *Journal of Parapsychology,* **14,** 244–256.

Calvesi, A. (1983). The analytic relationship and its therapeutic factors from a parapsychological viewpoint. *Psychoanalytic Review,* **70,** 387–402.

Cameron, T., & Roll, W.G. (1983). An investigation of apparitional experiences. *Theta,* **11,** 74–78.

Campbell, J. (1987). *Cognition and the apparitional experience: An exploratory study.* Unpublished master's thesis, University of New England, Armidale, Australia.

Carington, W.W. (1940). Experiments on the paranormal cognition of drawings. *Journal of Parapsychology,* **4,** 1–129.

Carington, W.W. (1945). *Telepathy: An outline of its facts, theory and implications.* London: Methuen.

Carpenter, J.C. (1971). The differential effect and hidden target differences consisting of erotic and neutral stimuli. *Journal of the American Society for Psychical Research,* **65,** 204–214.

Carpenter, J.C. (1977). Intrasubject and subject-agent effects in ESP experiments. In B.B. Wolman (Ed.), *Handbook of parapsychology* (pp. 202–272). New York: Van Nostrand Reinhold.

Carr, D. (1982). Pathophysiology of stress-induced limbic lobe dysfunction: A hypothesis for NDEs. *Anabiosis, 2,* 75–89.

Carrington, H., & Fodor, N. (1951). *The study of the poltergeist down the centuries.* New York: Dutton.

Case of the will of James L. Chaffin. (1927). *Proceedings of the Society for Psychical Research, 36,* 517–524.

Casler, L. (1976). Hypnotic maximization of ESP motivation. *Journal of Parapsychology, 40,* 187–193.

Chari, C.T.K. (1962). Paramnesia and reincarnation. *Proceedings of the Society for Psychical Research, 53,* 264–286.

Chari, C.T.K. (1977). Some generalized theories and models of psi: A critical evaluation. In B.B. Wolman (Ed.), *Handbook of parapsychology* (pp. 803–822). New York: Van Nostrand Reinhold.

Chari, C.T.K. (1978). Reincarnation research: Method and interpretation. In M. Ebon (Ed.), *The Signet handbook of parapsychology* (pp. 313–324). New York: New American Library.

Chauvin, R. (1985). *Parapsychology: When the irrational rejoins science,* tr. K.M. Banham. Jefferson, NC: McFarland.

Child, I.L. (1985). Psychology and anomalous observations: The question of ESP in dreams. *American Psychologist, 40,* 1219–1230.

Christopher, M. (1971). *Seers, psychics and ESP.* London: Cassell.

Clemens, D.B. (1982). Parapsychology and the CIA. In W.G. Roll, R.L. Morris, & R.A. White (Eds.), *Research in parapsychology 1981* (pp. 192–193). Metuchen, NJ: Scarecrow Press.

Collins, H.M., & Pinch, T.J. (1979). The construction of the paranormal: Nothing unscientific is happening. In R. Wallis (Ed.), On the margins of science: The social construction of rejected knowledge. *Sociological Review Monograph,* No. 27, 237–270.

Collins, H.M., & Pinch, T.J. (1982). *Frames of meaning: The social construction of extraordinary science.* London: Routledge & Kegan Paul.

Cook, A.M., & Irwin, H.J. (1983). Visuospatial skills and the out-of-body experience. *Journal of Parapsychology, 47,* 23–35.

Cook, E.W., Pasricha, S., Samararatne, G., Win Maung, U., & Stevenson, I. (1983). A review and analysis of "unsolved" cases of the reincarnation type: II. Comparison of features of solved and unsolved cases. *Journal of the American Society for Psychical Research, 77,* 115–135.

Coover, J.E. (1975). *Experiments in psychical research at Leland Stanford Junior University.* New York: Arno Press. (Original work published 1917.)

Council, J.R., Greyson, B., & Huff, K.D. (1986, August). *Fantasy-proneness, hypnotizability, and reports of paranormal experiences.* Paper presented at the meeting of the American Psychological Association.

Couttie, R.D. (1986). Correspondence. *Journal of the Society for Psychical Research, 53,* 336–337.

Cox, W.E. (1956). Precognition: An analysis. II. Subliminal precognition. *Journal of the American Society for Psychical Research, 50,* 99–109.

Cox, W.E. (1971). A comparison of different densities of dice in a PK task. *Journal of Parapsychology, 35,* 108–119.

Crandall, J.E. (1985). Effects of favorable and unfavorable conditions on the psi-missing displacement effect. *Journal of the American Society for Psychical Research,* **79,** 27-38.

Crookall, R. (1966). *The next world—and the next. Ghostly garments.* London: Theosophical Publishing House.

Crookall, R. (1970). *Out-of-the-body experiences: A fourth analysis.* New York: University Books.

Crookall, R. (1972). *Case-book of astral projection, 545-746.* Secaucus, NJ: University Books.

Dale, L.A. (1946). The psychokinetic effect: The first ASPR experiment. *Journal of the American Society for Psychical Research,* **40,** 123-151.

Dallas, H.A. (1924). Communications from the still incarnate at a distance from the body. *Occult Review,* **40,** 26-32.

Davey, S.J., & Hodgson, R. (1887). The possibilities of mal-observation and lapse of memory from a practical point of view. *Proceedings of the Society for Psychical Research,* **4,** 381-495.

Day, R.H. (1969). Extrasensory perception and related phenomena. *Australian Rationalist,* **1**(3), 22-26.

Dean, E.D., & Nash, C.B. (1967). Coincident plethysmograph results under controlled conditions. *Journal of the Society for Psychical Research,* **44,** 1-14.

Debes, J., & Morris, R. (1982). Comparison of striving and nonstriving instructional sets in a PK study. *Journal of Parapsychology,* **46,** 297-312.

de Rochas, A. (1911). *Les vies successives.* Paris: Charcornac.

Devereux, G. (Ed.) (1953). *Psychoanalysis and the occult.* New York: International Universities Press.

Diaconis, P. (1978). Statistical problems in ESP research. *Science,* **201,** 131-136.

Dickinson, G.L. (1911). A case of emergence of a latent memory under hypnosis. *Proceedings of the Society for Psychical Research,* **25,** 455-467.

Dickstein, M.L., & Davis, J.W. (1979). A blind PK test over two distances. *Journal of Parapsychology,* **43,** 41-42. (Abstract.)

Dierkens, J.C. (1978). Psychophysiological approach to PK states. In B. Shapin & L. Coly (Eds.), *Psi and states of awareness* (pp. 152-166). New York: Parapsychology Foundation.

Dingwall, E.J. (1961). British investigation of spontaneous cases. *International Journal of Parapsychology,* **3**(1), 89-97.

Dingwall, E.J. (Ed.) (1967-1968). *Abnormal hypnotic phenomena: A survey of nineteenth-century cases* (4 vols.). London: Churchill.

Dommeyer, F.C. (1975). Psychical research at Stanford University. *Journal of Parapsychology,* **39,** 173-205.

Dow, C. (1987, August). *Factors affecting judgments about the occurrence of psi in spontaneous settings.* Paper presented at the 30th Annual Convention of the Parapsychological Association, Edinburgh, Scotland.

Dunne, B.J., Jahn, R.G., & Nelson, R.D. (1983). *Precognitive remote perception. (Technical Note PEAR 83003.)* Princeton, NJ: Engineering Anomalies Research Laboratory, Princeton University.

Dunne, J.W. (1927). *An experiment with time.* London: Macmillan.

Eastman, M. (1962). Out-of-the-body experiences. *Proceedings of the Society for Psychical Research,* **53,** 287-309.

Ebon, M. (1983). *Psychic warfare: Threat or illusion?* New York: McGraw-Hill.

Edge, H.L., Morris, R.L., Palmer, J., & Rush, J.H. (1986). *Foundations of parapsychology: Exploring the boundaries of human capability.* Boston: Routledge & Kegan Paul.

Ehrenwald, J. (1974). Out-of-the-body experiences and the denial of death. *Journal of Nervous and Mental Disease,* **159,** 227–233.

Ehrenwald, J. (1978). *The ESP experience: A psychiatric validation.* New York: Basic Books.

Eilbert, L., & Schmeidler, G.R. (1950). A study of certain psychological factors in relation to ESP performance. *Journal of Parapsychology,* **14,** 53–74.

Eisenbud, J. (1967). *The world of Ted Serios.* New York: Morrow.

Eisenbud, J. (1977). Paranormal photography. In B.B. Wolman (Ed.), *Handbook of parapsychology* (pp. 414–432). New York: Van Nostrand Reinhold.

Eisenbud, J. (1987). Psi in psychotherapy. *ASPR Newsletter,* **13,** 29–30.

Ellis, D.J. (1975). Listening to the "Raudive Voices." *Journal of the Society for Psychical Research,* **48,** 31–42.

Ellwood, G.F. (1971). *Psychic visits to the past: An exploration of retrocognition.* New York: New American Library.

Emmons, C.F. (1982). *Chinese ghosts and ESP: A study of paranormal beliefs and experiences.* Metuchen, NJ: Scarecrow Press.

Estabrooks, G.H. (1961). A contribution to experimental telepathy. *Journal of Parapsychology,* **25,** 190–213. (Original work published 1927.)

Evans, C. (1973). Parapsychology: What the questionnaire revealed. *New Scientist,* **57,** 209.

Eysenck, H.J. (1957). *Sense and nonsense in psychology.* Harmondsworth, England: Penguin.

Faraday, M. (1853). Experimental investigation of table-moving. *The Athenaeum,* No. 1340, 801–803.

Feather, S.R., & Rhine, L.E. (1969). PK experiments with same and different targets. *Journal of Parapsychology,* **33,** 213–227.

Feyerabend, P. (1975). *Against method.* London: Verso.

Finucane, R.C. (1984). *Appearances of the dead: A cultural history of ghosts.* Buffalo, NY: Prometheus Books.

Fisher, R.A. (1929). The statistical method in psychical research. *Proceedings of the Society for Psychical Research,* **39,** 189–192.

Fisk, G.W., & Mitchell, A.M.J. (1953). ESP experiments with clock cards: A new technique with differential scoring. *Journal of the Society for Psychical Research,* **37,** 1–14.

Flew, A. (1953). Coincidence and synchronicity. *Journal of the Society for Psychical Research,* **37,** 198–201.

Flew, A. (1980). Parapsychology: Science or pseudo-science? *Pacific Philosophical Quarterly,* **61,** 100–114.

Flournoy, T. (1900). *From India to the planet Mars: A study of a case of somnambulism with glossolalia.* New York: Harper.

Flynn, C.P. (1986). *After the beyond: Human transformation and the near-death experience.* Englewood Cliffs, NJ: Prentice-Hall.

Fodor, N. (1948). The poltergeist — psychoanalyzed. *Psychiatric Quarterly,* **22,** 195–203.

Forman, J. (1978). *The mask of time: The mystery factor in timeslips, precognition and hindsight.* London: MacDonald & Jane.

Forwald, H. (1961). A PK experiment with die faces as targets. *Journal of Parapsychology,* **25,** 1–12.

Frazier, K. (Ed.) (1981). *Paranormal borderlands of science.* Buffalo, NY: Prometheus Books.

Frazier, K. (Ed.) (1986). *Science confronts the paranormal.* Buffalo, NY: Prometheus Books.

Freeman, J.A. (1970). Sex differences in ESP response as shown by the Freeman picture-figure test. *Journal of Parapsychology,* **34,** 37–46.

Freud, S. (1933). *New introductory lectures on psycho-analysis.* London: Hogarth Press.

Fukurai, T. (1931). *Clairvoyance and thoughtography.* London: Rider.

Fuller, U. (1975). *Confessions of a psychic.* Teaneck, NJ: Fulves.

Furn, B.G. (1987). Adjustment and the near-death experience: A conceptual and therapeutic model. *Journal of Near-Death Studies,* **6,** 4–19.

Gabbard, G.O., & Twemlow, S.W. (1984). *With the eyes of the mind.* New York: Praeger.

Gabbard, G.O., Twemlow, S.W., & Jones, F.C. (1981). Do "near death experiences" occur only near death? *Journal of Nervous and Mental Disease,* **169,** 374–377.

Gackenbach, J.I. (1979). A personality and cognitive style analysis of lucid dreaming. (Doctoral dissertation, Virginia Commonwealth University, 1978.) *Dissertation Abstracts International,* **39-B,** 3487.

Gallup, G., with Proctor, W. (1982). *Adventures in immortality: A look beyond the threshold of death.* New York: McGraw-Hill.

Gardner, M. (1981). *Science—Good, bad and bogus.* Buffalo, NY: Prometheus Books.

Gauld, A. (1961). The "super-ESP" hypothesis. *Proceedings of the Society for Psychical Research,* **53,** 226–246.

Gauld, A. (1977). Discarnate survival. In B.B. Wolman (Ed.), *Handbook of parapsychology* (pp. 577–630). New York: Van Nostrand Reinhold.

Gauld, A. (1982). *Mediumship and survival: A century of investigations.* London: Heinemann.

Gauld, A. (1984). Review of "Appearances of the Dead: A Cultural History of Ghosts" by R.C. Finucane. *Journal of the Society for Psychical Research,* **52,** 330–333.

Gauld, A., & Cornell, A.D. (1979). *Poltergeists.* London: Routledge & Kegan Paul.

Gault, R.H., & Goodfellow, L.D. (1940). Sources of error in psycho-physical measurements. *Journal of General Psychology,* **23,** 197–200.

Gay, K., Salter, W.H., Thouless, R.H., Firebrace, R.H., Phillimore, M., & Sitwell, C. (1955). Report on the Oliver Lodge posthumous test. *Journal of the Society for Psychical Research,* **38,** 121–134.

George, L. (1981). A survey of research into the relationships between imagery and psi. *Journal of Parapsychology,* **45,** 121–146.

Gibson, E.P., & Rhine, J.B. (1943). The PK effect: III. Some introductory series. *Journal of Parapsychology,* **7,** 118–134.

Girden, E. (1962). A review of psychokinesis (PK). *Psychological Bulletin,* **59,** 353–388.

Goodfellow, L.D. (1938). A psychological interpretation of the results of the Zenith radio experiment in telepathy. *Journal of Experimental Psychology,* **23,** 601–632.

Goodfellow, L.D. (1940). The human element in probability. *Journal of General Psychology,* **23,** 201–205.

Grad, B.R. (1976). The biological effects of the "laying on of hands" on animals and plants: Implications for biology. In G.R. Schmeidler (Ed.), *Parapsychology: Its relation to physics, biology, psychology, and psychiatry* (pp. 76–89). Metuchen, NJ: Scarecrow Press.

Green, B.F., & Hall, J.A. (1984). Quantitative methods for literature reviews. *Annual Review of Psychology*, **35**, 37–53.
Green, C. (1960). Analysis of spontaneous cases. *Proceedings of the Society for Psychical Research*, **53**, 97–161.
Green, C. (1968a). *Out-of-the-body experiences*. London: Hamish Hamilton.
Green, C.E. (1968b). *Lucid dreams*. London: Hamish Hamilton.
Green, C., & Leslie, W. (1987). The imagery of totally hallucinatory or "metachoric" experiences. *Journal of Mental Imagery*, **11**, 75–82.
Green, C., & McCreery, C. (1975). *Apparitions*. London: Hamish Hamilton.
Greenwood, J.A. (1938). Analysis of a large chance control series of ESP data. *Journal of Parapsychology*, **2**, 138–146.
Gregory, A. (1982). Ethics and psychical research. In I. Grattan-Guinness (Ed.), *Psychical research: A guide to its history, principles and practices* (pp. 284–291). Wellingborough, England: Aquarian Press.
Grey, M. (1985). *Return from death: An exploration of the near-death experience*. London: Arkana.
Greyson, B. (1977). Telepathy in mental illness: Deluge or delusion? *Journal of Nervous and Mental Disease*, **165**, 184–200.
Greyson, B. (1981). Toward a psychological explanation of near-death experiences: A response to Dr. Grosso's paper. *Anabiosis*, **1**, 88–103.
Greyson, B. (1983). Near-death experiences and personal values. *American Journal of Psychiatry*, **140**, 618–620.
Greyson, B., & Flynn, C.P. (Eds.) (1984). *The near-death experience: Problems, prospects, perspectives*. Springfield, IL: Thomas.
Greyson, B., & Stevenson, I. (1980). The phenomenology of near-death experiences. *American Journal of Psychiatry*, **137**, 1193–1196.
Grosso, M. (1979). The survival of personality in a mind-dependent world. *Journal of the American Society for Psychical Research*, **73**, 367–380.
Grosso, M. (1981). Toward an explanation of near-death phenomena. *Journal of the American Society for Psychical Research*, **75**, 37–60.
Gurney, E., Myers, F.W.H., & Podmore, F. (1886). *Phantasms of the living* (2 vols.). London: Trübner.
Guthrie, M., & Birchall, J. (1883). Record of experiments in thought-transference at Liverpool. *Proceedings of the Society for Psychical Research*, **1**, 263–283.
Haight, J. (1979). Spontaneous psi cases: A survey and preliminary study of ESP, attitude, and personality relationships. *Journal of Parapsychology*, **43**, 179–204.
Hall, T.H. (1962). *The spiritualists: The story of Florence Cook and William Crookes*. London: Duckworth.
Hall, T.H. (1984). *The enigma of Daniel Home: Medium or fraud?* Buffalo, NY: Prometheus Books.
Hanlon, J. (1975). But what about the children? *New Scientist*, **66**, 567.
Hansel, C.E.M. (1966). *ESP: A scientific evaluation*. New York: Scribners.
Hansel, C.E.M. (1980). *ESP and parapsychology: A critical re-evaluation*. Buffalo, NY: Prometheus Books.
Hansen, G.P. (1985). A brief overview of magic for parapsychologists. *Parapsychology Review*, **16**(2), 5–8.
Hansen, G.P. (1987, August). *CSICOP and skepticism: An emerging social movement*. Paper presented at the 30th Annual Convention of the Parapsychological Association, Edinburgh, Scotland.

Haraldsson, E. (1985). Representative national surveys of psychic phenomena: Iceland, Great Britain, Sweden, USA and Gallup's multinational survey. *Journal of the Society for Psychical Research, 53,* 145–158.

Haraldsson, E., Gudmundsdottir, A., Ragnarsson, A., Loftsson, J., & Jonsson, S. (1977). National survey of psychical experiences and attitudes toward the paranormal in Iceland. In J.D. Morris, W.G. Roll, & R.L. Morris (Eds.), *Research in parapsychology 1976* (pp. 182–186). Metuchen, NJ: Scarecrow Press.

Haraldsson, E., Houtkooper, J.M., & Hoeltje, C. (1987). The Defense Mechanism Test as a predictor of ESP performance: Icelandic study VII and meta-analysis of 13 experiments. *Journal of Parapsychology, 51,* 75–90.

Haraldsson, E., & Johnson, M. (1979). ESP and the Defense Mechanism Test (DMT). Icelandic study No. III. A case of experimenter effect? *European Journal of Parapsychology, 3,* 11–20.

Harary, S.B. (1982). The marshmallow ghost: A group-counseling approach to a case of reported apparitions. In W.G. Roll, R.L. Morris, & R.A. White (Eds.), *Research in parapsychology 1981* (pp. 187–189). Metuchen, NJ: Scarecrow Press.

Hardy, A.C. (1950). Telepathy and evolutionary theory. *Journal of the Society for Psychical Research, 35,* 225–238.

Harris, J., & Gregory, R.L. (1981). Tests of the hallucinations of "Ruth." *Perception, 10,* 351–354.

Harris, M. (1986). *Investigating the unexplained.* Buffalo, NY: Prometheus Books.

Hart, H. (1956). Six theories about apparitions. *Proceedings of the Society for Psychical Research, 50,* 153–239.

Hart, H. (1967). Scientific survival research. *International Journal of Parapsychology, 9,* 43–52.

Hasted, J. (1981). *The metal-benders.* London: Routledge & Kegan Paul.

Hasted, J.B., & Robertson, D. (1979). The detail of paranormal metal-bending. *Journal of the Society for Psychical Research, 50,* 9–20.

Hastings, A. (1983). A counseling approach to parapsychological experience. *Journal of Transpersonal Psychology, 15,* 143–167.

Hastings, A. (1987). The study of channeling. In D.H. Weiner & R.D. Nelson (Eds.), *Research in parapsychology 1986* (pp. 152–153). Metuchen, NJ: Scarecrow Press.

Hastings, R.J. (1969). An examination of the Dieppe Raid case. *Journal of the Society for Psychical Research, 45,* 55–63.

Head, J., & Cranston, S.L. (Eds.) (1977). *Reincarnation: The phoenix fire mystery.* New York: Crown.

Hearne, K.M.T. (1984). A survey of reported premonitions and of those who have them. *Journal of the Society for Psychical Research, 52,* 261–270.

Hearnshaw, L.S. (1979). *Cyril Burt, psychologist.* London: Hodder & Stoughton.

Hebb, D.O. (1951). The role of neurological ideas in psychology. *Journal of Personality, 20,* 35–55.

Hitching, F. (1980). *Psi in the laboratory: 12 crucial findings.* London: Society for Psychical Research.

Home, D.D. (ca. 1973). *Incidents in my life* (2nd ed.). Secaucus, NJ: University Books. (Original work published 1864.)

Honegger, B. (1979). Correspondence. *Parapsychology Review, 10*(2), 24–26.

Honorton, C. (1970). Effects of feedback on discrimination between correct and incorrect ESP responses. *Journal of the American Society for Psychical Research, 64,* 404–410.

Honorton, C. (1972). Reported frequency of dream recall and ESP. *Journal of the American Society for Psychical Research,* **66,** 369–374.

Honorton, C. (1975). Objective determination of information rate in psi tasks with pictorial stimuli. *Journal of the American Society for Psychical Research,* **69,** 353–359.

Honorton, C. (1977). Psi and internal attention states. In B.B. Wolman (Ed.), *Handbook of parapsychology* (pp. 435–472). New York: Van Nostrand Reinhold.

Honorton, C. (1978). Psi and internal attention states: Information retrieval in the ganzfeld. In B. Shapin & L. Coly (Eds.), *Psi and states of awareness* (pp. 79–90). New York: Parapsychology Foundation.

Honorton, C. (1985). Meta-analysis of psi ganzfeld research: A response to Hyman. *Journal of Parapsychology,* **49,** 51–91.

Honorton, C., & May, E.C. (1976). Volitional control in a psychokinetic task with auditory and visual feedback. In J.D. Morris, W.G. Roll, & R.L. Morris (Eds.), *Research in parapsychology 1975* (pp. 90–91). Metuchen, NJ: Scarecrow Press.

Honorton, C., Ramsey, M., & Cabibbo, C. (1975). Experimenter effects in extrasensory perception. *Journal of the American Society for Psychical Research,* **69,** 135–149.

Hubbard, G.S., & May, E.C. (1987). Aspects of measurement and application of geomagnetic indices and extremely low frequency electromagnetic radiation for use in parapsychology. In D.H. Weiner & R.D. Nelson (Eds.), *Research in parapsychology 1986* (pp. 79–82). Metuchen, NJ: Scarecrow Press.

Humphrey, B.M. (1946a). Success in ESP as related to form of response drawings: I. Clairvoyance experiments. *Journal of Parapsychology,* **10,** 78–106.

Humphrey, B.M. (1946b). Success in ESP as related to form of response drawings: II. GESP experiments. *Journal of Parapsychology,* **10,** 181–196.

Humphrey, B.M. (1947). Help-hinder comparison in PK tests. *Journal of Parapsychology,* **11,** 4–13.

Humphrey, B.M., & Rhine, J.B. (1945). PK tests with two sizes of dice mechanically thrown. *Journal of Parapsychology,* **9,** 124–132.

Hunter, R., & Derr, J. (1978). Prediction monitoring and evaluation program. *Earthquake Information Bulletin,* **10,** 93–96.

Hutchinson, L. (1940). Variations of time intervals in pre-shuffle card-calling tests. *Journal of Parapsychology,* **4,** 249–270.

Hyman, R. (1977). "Cold reading": How to convince strangers that you know all about them. *The Zetetic,* **1**(2), 18–37.

Hyman, R. (1980). Pathological science: Towards a proper diagnosis and remedy. *Zetetic Scholar,* **6,** 31–39.

Hyman, R. (1985). The ganzfeld psi experiment: A critical appraisal. *Journal of Parapsychology,* **49,** 3–49.

Hyman, R., & Honorton, C. (1986). A joint communiqué: The psi ganzfeld controversy. *Journal of Parapsychology,* **50,** 351–364.

Inglis, B. (1977). *Natural and supernatural: A history of the paranormal from earliest times to 1914.* London: Hodder & Stoughton.

Irwin, H.J. (1978a). ESP and the human information processing system. *Journal of the American Society for Psychical Research,* **72,** 111–126.

Irwin, H.J. (1978b). Psi, attention, and processing capacity. *Journal of the American Society for Psychical Research,* **72,** 301–313.

Irwin, H.J. (1979a). *Psi and the mind: An information processing approach.* Metuchen, NJ: Scarecrow Press.

Irwin, H.J. (1979b). On directional inconsistency in the correlation between ESP and memory. *Journal of Parapsychology,* **43,** 31-39.

Irwin, H.J. (1979c). Coding preferences and the form of spontaneous extrasensory experiences. *Journal of Parapsychology,* **43,** 205-220.

Irwin, H.J. (1980a). Information processing theory and psi phenomena. In B. Shapin & L. Coly (Eds.), *Communication and parapsychology* (pp. 25-43). New York: Parapsychology Foundation.

Irwin, H.J. (1980b). PK and memory: An information-processing model of psychokinetic effects. *Journal of the American Society for Psychical Research,* **74,** 381-394.

Irwin, H.J. (1980c). Out of the body Down Under: Some cognitive characteristics of Australian students reporting OOBEs. *Journal of the Society for Psychical Research,* **50,** 448-459.

Irwin, H.J. (1981a). The psychological function of out-of-body experiences: So who needs the out-of-body experience? *Journal of Nervous and Mental Disease,* **169,** 244-248.

Irwin, H.J. (1981b). Some psychological dimensions of the out-of-body experience. *Parapsychology Review,* **12**(4), 1-6.

Irwin, H.J. (1985a). *Flight of mind: A psychological study of the out-of-body experience.* Metuchen, NJ: Scarecrow Press.

Irwin, H.J. (1985b). Parapsychological phenomena and the absorption domain. *Journal of the American Society for Psychical Research,* **79,** 1-11.

Irwin, H.J. (1985c). Fear of psi and attitude to parapsychological research. *Parapsychology Review,* **16**(6), 1-4.

Irwin, H.J. (1985d). A study of the measurement and the correlates of paranormal belief. *Journal of the American Society for Psychical Research,* **79,** 301-326.

Irwin, H.J. (1985e). Is psi a unitary domain? Analysis in terms of performance patterns. *Parapsychological Journal of South Africa,* **6,** 34-46.

Irwin, H.J. (1986). Perceptual perspective of visual imagery in OBEs, dreams and reminiscence. *Journal of the Society for Psychical Research,* **53,** 210-217.

Irwin, H.J. (1987a). Charles Bailey: A biographical study of the Australian apport medium. *Journal of the Society for Psychical Research,* **54,** 97-118.

Irwin, H.J. (1987b). Images of heaven. *Parapsychology Review,* **18**(1), 1-4.

Irwin, H.J. (1987c). *Extrasensory experiences and the need for absorption.* Paper submitted for publication.

Irwin, H.J. (1987d). Out-of-body experiences in the blind. *Journal of Near-Death Studies,* **6,** 53-60.

Irwin, H.J. (1988a). Out-of-body experiences and dream lucidity: Empirical perspectives. In J. Gackenbach & S. LaBerge (Eds.), *Conscious mind, sleeping brain: Perspectives on lucid dreaming* (pp. 353-371). New York: Plenum Press.

Irwin, H.J. (1988b). Out-of-body experiences and attitudes to life and death. *Journal of the American Society for Psychical Research,* **82,** 237-251.

Isaacs, E. (1983). The Fox sisters and American spiritualism. In H. Kerr & C.L. Crow (Eds.), *The occult in America: New historical perspectives* (pp. 79-110). Urbana, IL: University of Illinois Press.

Isaacs, J. (1983). A twelve-session study of micro-PKMB training. In W.G. Roll, J. Beloff & R.A. White (Eds.), *Research in parapsychology 1982* (pp. 31-35). Metuchen, NJ: Scarecrow Press.

Isaacs, J.D. (1986). PK and conscious awareness. In D.H. Weiner & D.I. Radin (Eds.), *Research in parapsychology 1985* (pp. 162-163). Metuchen, NJ: Scarecrow Press.

Iverson, J. (1976). *More lives than one?* London: Souvenir Press.

Jackson, M., Franzoi, S., & Schmeidler, G.R. (1977). Effects of feedback on ESP: A curious partial replication. *Journal of the American Society for Psychical Research, 71,* 147–155.

Jahn, R.G. (1984). On the representation of psychic research to the community of established science. In R.A. White & R.S. Broughton (Eds.), *Research in parapsychology 1983* (pp. 127–138). Metuchen, NJ: Scarecrow Press.

Jahn, R.G., & Dunne, B.J. (1983). *On the quantum mechanics of consciousness, with application to anomalous phenomena. (Technical Note PEAR 83005.1.)* Princeton, NJ: Engineering Anomalies Research Laboratory, Princeton University.

Jahn, R.G., Nelson, R.D., & Dunne, B.J. (1986). Variance effects in REG series score distributions. In D.H. Weiner & D.I. Radin (Eds.), *Research in parapsychology 1985* (pp. 9–13). Metuchen, NJ: Scarecrow Press.

Jenkins, E. (1982). *The shadow and the light: A defence of Daniel Dunglas Home, the medium.* London: Hamish Hamilton.

Jephson, I. (1928). Evidence for clairvoyance in card-guessing. *Proceedings of the Society for Psychical Research, 38,* 223–268.

Johnson, M., & Nordbeck, B. (1972). Variation in the scoring behavior of a "psychic" subject. *Journal of Parapsychology, 36,* 122–132.

Jones, W.H., & Russell, D. (1980). The selective processing of belief disconfirming information. *European Journal of Social Psychology, 10,* 309–312.

Jung, C.G. (1963). *Memories, dreams, reflections.* London: Collins.

Jung, C.G. (1971). *The archetypes of the collective unconscious.* Princeton, NJ: Princeton University Press. (Original work published 1954.)

Jung, C.G. (1985). *Synchronicity: An acausal connecting principle.* London: Routledge & Kegan Paul. (Original work published 1955.)

Jurgenson, F. (1967). *Sprechfunk mit Verstorbenen.* Freiburg, West Germany: Bauer.

Kampman, R., & Hirvenoja, R. (1978). Dynamic relation of the secondary personality induced by hypnosis to the present personality. In F.H. Frankel & H.S. Zamansky (Eds.), *Hypnosis at its bicentennial* (pp. 183–188). New York: Plenum Press.

Kanthamani, H., & Rao, H.H. (1974). A study of memory–ESP relationships using linguistic forms. *Journal of Parapsychology, 38,* 286–300.

Keene, M.L. (1976). *The psychic Mafia.* New York: Dell.

Keil, J. (1980). The voice on tape phenomena: Limitations and possibilities. *European Journal of Parapsychology, 3,* 297–314.

Keil, H.H.J., Herbert, B., Ullman, M., & Pratt, J.G. (1976). Directly observable voluntary PK effects: A survey and tentative interpretation of available findings from Nina Kulagina and other known related cases of recent date. *Proceedings of the Society for Psychical Research, 56,* 197–235.

Kelly, E.F. (1982). On grouping of hits in some exceptional psi performers. *Journal of the American Society for Psychical Research, 76,* 101–142.

Kelly, E.F., Kanthamani, H., Child, I.L., & Young, F.W. (1975). On the relation between visual and ESP confusion structures in an exceptional ESP subject. *Journal of the American Society for Psychical Research, 69,* 1–31.

Kennedy, J.E. (1978). The role of task complexity in PK: A review. *Journal of Parapsychology, 42,* 89–122.

Kennedy, J.E. (1979). Consistent missing: A type of information-processing error in ESP. *Journal of Parapsychology, 43,* 113–128.

Kennedy, J.E., & Taddonio, J.L. (1976). Experimenter effects in parapsychological research. *Journal of Parapsychology, 40,* 1–33.

Kennedy, J.L. (1939). A methodological review of extra-sensory perception. *Psychological Bulletin, 36,* 59–103.

Kogan, I.M. (1966). Is telepathy possible? *Telecommunication and Radio Engineering, 21* (No. 1, Part 2), 75–81.

Kohn, A. (1987). *False prophets: Fraud and error in science and medicine.* New York: Blackwell.

Kreitler, H., & Kreitler, S. (1973). Subliminal perception and extrasensory perception. *Journal of Parapsychology, 37,* 163–188.

Krieger, J. (1977). Hemispheric specialization in intentional versus nonintentional psi performance. *Journal of Parapsychology, 41,* 40–42. (Abstract.)

Lambert, G.W. (1959). Scottish haunts and poltergeists: A regional study. *Journal of the Society for Psychical Research, 40,* 108–120.

Lambert, G.W. (1976). D.D. Home and the physical world. *Journal of the Society for Psychical Research, 48,* 298–314.

Lambert, G.W., & Gay, K. (1952). The Dieppe Raid case: A collective auditory hallucination. *Journal of the Society for Psychical Research, 36,* 607–618.

Leahey, T.H., & Leahey, G.F. (1983). *Psychology's occult doubles: Psychology and the problem of pseudoscience.* Chicago: Nelson-Hall.

LeShan, L. (1966). Some psychological hypotheses on the non-acceptance of parapsychology as a science. *International Journal of Parapsychology, 8,* 367–385.

Levi, A. (1979). The influence of imagery and feedback on PK effects. *Journal of Parapsychology, 43,* 275–289.

Locke, T.P., & Shontz, F.C. (1983). Personality correlates of the near-death experience: A preliminary study. *Journal of the American Society for Psychical Research, 77,* 311–318.

Lovitts, B.E. (1981). The sheep-goat effect turned upside down. *Journal of Parapsychology, 45,* 293–309.

Lucadou, W. von (1987, August). *The model of pragmatic information (MPI).* Paper presented at the 30th Annual Convention of the Parapsychological Association, Edinburgh, Scotland.

Lucadou, W. von, & Kornwachs, K. (1980). Development of the system theoretic approach to psychokinesis. *European Journal of Parapsychology, 3,* 297–314.

Lundahl, C.R. (Ed.) (1982). *A collection of near-death research readings.* Chicago: Nelson-Hall.

McClenon, J. (1982a). Two experiments in the practical application of psi. *Journal of Parapsychology, 46,* 59. (Abstract.)

McClenon, J. (1982b). A survey of elite scientists: Their attitudes toward ESP and parapsychology. *Journal of Parapsychology, 46,* 127–152.

McClenon, J. (1984). *Deviant science: The case of parapsychology.* Philadelphia, PA: University of Pennsylvania Press.

McConnell, R.A. (1977). The resolution of conflicting beliefs about the ESP evidence. *Journal of Parapsychology, 41,* 198–214.

McConnell, R.A. (1987). *Parapsychology in retrospect: My search for the unicorn.* Pittsburgh, PA: Author.

McConnell, R.A., Snowdon, R.J., & Powell, K.F. (1955). Wishing with dice. *Journal of Experimental Psychology, 50,* 269–275.

McCormick, D.L. (1987). A lawsuit in Hawaii. *ASPR Newsletter, 13,* 14.

McCreery, C. (1986, September). *Spontaneous experiences and the Eysenck Per-*

sonality Questionnaire. Paper presented at the 10th International Conference of the Society for Psychical Research, Trinity College, Cambridge, England.

McElroy, W.A., & Brown, W.R.K. (1950). Electric shocks for errors in ESP card tests. *Journal of Parapsychology, 14,* 257–266.

MacFarland, J.D., & George, R.W. (1937). Extra-sensory perception of normal and distorted symbols. *Journal of Parapsychology, 1,* 93–101.

McHarg, J.F. (1982). The paranormal and the recognition of personal distress. *Journal of the Society for Psychical Research, 51,* 201–209.

MacKenzie, A. (1982). *Hauntings and apparitions.* London: Heinemann.

McMahan, E.A. (1947). A PK experiment under light and dark conditions. *Journal of Parapsychology, 11,* 46–54.

McMullen, T. (1978). A basic confusion in the concept of "psi phenomena." In J.P. Sutcliffe (Ed.), *Conceptual analysis and methods in psychology: Essays in honour of W.M. O'Neil* (pp. 15–20). Sydney: Sydney University Press.

Maher, M., & Schmeidler, G.R. (1977). Cerebral lateralization effects in ESP processing. *Journal of the American Society for Psychical Research, 71,* 261–271.

Mahoney, P.J. (1977). Some observations on the imagery of a group of hallucinating psychiatric patients. (Doctoral dissertation, University of Tennessee, 1976.) *Dissertation Abstracts International, 37*(8-B), 4152–4153.

Marks, D.F. (1986). Investigating the paranormal. *Nature, 320,* 119–124.

Marks, D., & Kammann, R. (1980). *The psychology of the psychic.* Buffalo, NY: Prometheus Books.

Markwick, B. (1978). The Soal-Goldney experiments with Basil Shackleton: New evidence of data manipulation. *Proceedings of the Society for Psychical Research, 56,* 250–277.

Martin, L.J. (1915). Ghosts and the projection of visual images. *American Journal of Psychology, 26,* 251–257.

Martínez-Taboas, A. (1984). An appraisal of the role of aggression and the central nervous system in RSPK agents. *Journal of the American Society for Psychical Research, 78,* 55–69.

Martínez Taboas, A., & Alvarado, C.S. (1981). Poltergeist agents: A review of recent research trends and conceptualizations. *European Journal of Parapsychology, 4,* 99–110.

Mauskopf, S.H., & McVaugh, M.R. (1980). *The elusive science: Origins of experimental psychical research.* Baltimore: Johns Hopkins University Press.

Millar, B. (1978). The observational theories: A primer. *European Journal of Parapsychology, 2,* 304–332.

Mintz, E.E. (1983). *The psychic thread: Paranormal and transpersonal aspects of psychotherapy.* New York: Human Sciences Press.

Mintz, S., & Alpert, M. (1972). Imagery vividness, reality testing, and schizophrenic hallucinations. *Journal of Abnormal Psychology, 79,* 310–316.

Mishlove, J. (1983). *Psi development systems.* Jefferson, NC: McFarland.

Mishlove, J., & Kautz, W.H. (1982). An emerging new discipline! *Applied Psi Newsletter, 1*(1), 1.

Mitchell, J.L., & Drewes, A.A. (1982). The rainbow experiment. *Journal of the American Society for Psychical Research, 76,* 197–215.

Montago, E. de A., & Roll, W.G. (1983). A neurological model for psychokinesis. In W.G. Roll, J. Beloff, & R.A. White (Eds.), *Research in parapsychology 1982* (pp. 272–273). Metuchen, NJ: Scarecrow Press.

Moody, R.A. (1975). *Life after life.* Covington, GA: Mockingbird.

Moody, R.A. (1977). *Reflections on life after life.* Covington, GA: Mockingbird.

Moore, R.L. (1977). *In search of white crows: Spiritualism, parapsychology, and American culture.* New York: Oxford University Press.

Morris, F. (1976). Emotional reactions to psychic experiences. In M. Ebon (Ed.), *The satan trap: Dangers of the occult* (pp. 205-216). Garden City, NY: Doubleday.

Morris, R.L. (1980). Psi functioning within a simple communication model. In B. Shapin & L. Coly (Eds.), *Communication and parapsychology* (pp. 1-24). New York: Parapsychology Foundation.

Morris, R.L. (1981). The case of the Amityville Horror. In K. Frazier (Ed.), *Paranormal borderlines of science* (pp. 170-178). Buffalo, NY: Promctheus Books.

Morris, R.L., & Cohen, D. (1971). A preliminary experiment on the relationships among ESP, alpha rhythm and calling patterns. In W.G. Roll, R.L. Morris, & J.D. Morris (Eds.), *Proceedings of the Parapsychological Association No. 6, 1969* (pp. 22-23). Durham, NC: Parapsychological Association.

Morris, R.L., Nanko, M., & Phillips, D. (1982). A comparison of two popularly advocated visual imagery strategies in a psychokinesis task. *Journal of Parapsychology, 46,* 1-16.

Moss, S., & Butler, D.C. (1978). The scientific credibility of ESP. *Perceptual and Motor Skills, 46,* 1063-1079.

Munson, R.J. (1985, February). *Clinical applications of psi: Three cases.* Paper presented at the 12th annual conference of the Southeastern Regional Parapsychological Association, Duke University, Durham NC.

Murphy, G. (1967). Direct contacts with past and future: Retrocognition and precognition. *Journal of the American Society for Psychical Research, 61,* 3-23.

Myers, F.W.H. (1903). *Human personality and its survival of bodily death.* London: Longmans, Green.

Myers, S.A., & Austrin, H.R. (1985). Distal eidetic technology: Further characteristics of the fantasy-prone personality. *Journal of Mental Imagery, 9,* 57-66.

Myers, S.A., Austrin, H.R., Grisso, J.T., & Nickeson, R.C. (1983). Personality characteristics as related to the out-of-body experience. *Journal of Parapsychology, 47,* 131-144.

Nash, C.B. (1978). Effect of response bias on psi mediation. *Journal of the American Society for Psychical Research, 72,* 333-338.

Nash, C.B. (1983). An extrasensory observational theory. *Journal of the American Society for Psychical Research, 52,* 113-116.

Nash, C.B. (1986). *Parapsychology: The science of psiology.* Springfield, IL: Thomas.

Nash, C.B., & Nash, C.S. (1958). Checking success and the relationship of personality traits to ESP. *Journal of the American Society for Psychical Research, 52,* 98-107.

Nash, C.S., & Nash, C.B. (1968). Effect of target selection, field dependence, and body concept on ESP performance. *Journal of Parapsychology, 32,* 248-257.

Neher, A. (1980). *The psychology of transcendence.* Englewood Cliffs, NJ: Prentice-Hall.

Neppe, V.M. (1983). Temporal lobe symptomatology in subjective paranormal experients. *Journal of the American Society for Psychical Research, 77,* 1-29.

Neppe, V.M. (1984). Subjective paranormal experience psychosis. *Parapsychology Review,* **15**(2), 7-9.

Noyes, R. (1979). Near-death experiences: Their interpretation and significance. In R. Kastenbaum (Ed.), *Between life and death* (pp. 73-88). New York: Springer.

Noyes, R. (1980). Attitude change following near-death experiences. *Psychiatry,* **43**, 234-242.

Noyes, R., & Kletti, R. (1977). Panoramic memory: A response to the threat of death. *Omega,* **8**, 181-194.

Noyes, R., & Slymen, D.J. (1979). The subjective response to life-threatening danger. *Omega,* **9**, 313-321.

Orme, J.E. (1974). Precognition and time. *Journal of the Society for Psychical Research,* **47**, 351-365.

Osis, K. (1974). Out-of-body research at the ASPR. *ASPR Newsletter,* No. 22, 1-3.

Osis, K. (1975). Perceptual experiments on out-of-body experiences. In J.D. Morris, W.G. Roll, & R.L. Morris (Eds.), *Research in parapsychology 1974* (pp. 53-55). Metuchen, NJ: Scarecrow Press.

Osis, K. (1979). Insiders' views of the OBE: A questionnaire survey. In W.G. Roll (Ed.), *Research in parapsychology 1978* (pp. 50-52). Metuchen, NJ: Scarecrow Press.

Osis, K. (1986a). Apparitions old and new. In K.R. Rao (Ed.), *Case studies in parapsychology* (pp. 74-86). Jefferson, NC: McFarland.

Osis, K. (1986b). Characteristics of purposeful action in an apparition case. *Journal of the American Society for Psychical Research,* **80**, 175-193.

Osis, K., & McCormick, D. (1980). Kinetic effects at the ostensible location of an out-of-body projection during perceptual testing. *Journal of the American Society for Psychical Research,* **74**, 319-329.

Osis, K., & McCormick, D. (1982a). A poltergeist case without an identifiable living agent. *Journal of the American Society for Psychical Research,* **76**, 23-51.

Osis, K., & McCormick, D. (1982b). A case of collectively observed apparitions and related phenomena. In W.G. Roll, R.L. Morris, & R.A. White (Eds.), *Research in parapsychology 1981* (pp. 120-123). Metuchen, NJ: Scarecrow Press.

Osis, K., & Perskari, B. (1975). *Perceptual tests of the out-of-body hypothesis.* Unpublished manuscript, American Society for Psychical Research, New York.

Owen, A.R.G. (1964). *Can we explain the poltergeist?* New York: Garrett.

Palmer, J. (1974). A case of RSPK involving a ten-year-old boy: The Powhatan poltergeist. *Journal of the American Society for Psychical Research,* **68**, 1-33.

Palmer, J. (1977). Attitudes and personality traits in experimental ESP research. In B.B. Wolman (Ed.), *Handbook of parapsychology* (pp. 175-201). New York: Van Nostrand Reinhold.

Palmer, J. (1978a). Extrasensory perception: Research findings. In S. Krippner (Ed.), *Advances in parapsychological research, Vol. 2: Extrasensory perception* (pp. 59-243). New York: Plenum Press.

Palmer, J. (1978b). The out-of-body experience: A psychological theory. *Parapsychology Review,* **9**(5), 19-22.

Palmer, J. (1978c). ESP and out-of-body experiences: An experimental approach. In D.S. Rogo (Ed.), *Mind beyond the body* (pp. 193-217). New York: Penguin.

Palmer, J. (1979). A community mail survey of psychic experiences. *Journal of the American Society for Psychical Research,* **73**, 221-251.

Palmer, J. (1982). ESP research findings: 1976-1978. In S. Krippner (Ed.), *Advances in parapsychological research, Vol. 3* (pp. 41-82). New York: Plenum Press.

Palmer, J., & Kramer, W. (1984). Internal state and temporal factors in psychokinesis. *Journal of Parapsychology,* **48,** 1–25.
Palmer, J., & Lieberman, R. (1975). The influence of psychological set on ESP and out-of-body experiences. *Journal of the American Society for Psychical Research,* **69,** 193–213.
Palmer, J., & Lieberman, R. (1976). ESP and out-of-body experiences: A further study. In J.D. Morris, W.G. Roll, & R.L. Morris (Eds.), *Research in parapsychology 1975* (pp. 102–106). Metuchen, NJ: Scarecrow Press.
Palmer, J., & van der Velden, I. (1983). ESP and "hypnotic imagination": A group free-response study. *European Journal of Parapsychology,* **4,** 413–434.
Pamplin, B.R., & Collins, H. (1975). Spoon bending: An experimental approach. *Nature,* **257,** 8.
Parker, A. (1977). Parapsychologists' personality and psi in relation to the experimenter effect. In J.D. Morris, W.G. Roll, & R.L. Morris (Eds.), *Research in parapsychology 1976* (pp. 107–109). Metuchen, NJ: Scarecrow Press.
Parker, A., & Wiklund, N. (1987). The ganzfeld experiments: Toward an assessment. *Journal of the Society for Psychical Research,* **54,** 261–265.
Pasricha, S., & Stevenson, I. (1986). Near-death experiences in India. *Journal of Nervous and Mental Disease,* **174,** 165–170.
Pasricha, S., & Stevenson, I. (1987). Indian cases of the reincarnation type two generations apart. *Journal of the Society for Psychical Research,* **54,** 239–246.
Perry, C., Laurence, J., Nadon, R., & Labelle, L. (1986). Past lives regression. In B. Zilbergeld, M.G. Edelstien, & D.L. Araoz (Eds.), *Hypnosis: Questions and answers* (pp. 50–61). New York: Norton.
Persinger, M.A. (1974). *The paranormal. Part I. Patterns.* New York: MSS Information Corporation.
Persinger, M.A. (1975). ELF waves and ESP. *New Horizons,* **1**(5), 232–235.
Persinger, M.A. (1983). Religious and mystical experiences as artifacts of temporal lobe function: A general hypothesis. *Perceptual and Motor Skills,* **57,** 1255–1262.
Persinger, M.A. (1985). Subjective telepathic experiences, geomagnetic activity and the ELF hypothesis: Part II. Stimulus features and neural detection. *Psi Research,* **4**(2), 4–23.
Persinger, M.A., & Roll, W.G. (1986). The temporal lobe factor in psi phenomena. In D.H. Weiner & D.I. Radin (Eds.), *Research in parapsychology 1985* (p. 119). Metuchen, NJ: Scarecrow Press.
Piddington, J.G. (1908). A series of concordant automatisms. *Proceedings of the Society for Psychical Research,* **22,** 19–416.
Pierce, H.W. (1973). RSPK phenomena observed independently by two families. *Journal of the American Society for Psychical Research,* **67,** 86–101.
Pinch, T.J., & Collins, H.M. (1984). Private science and public knowledge: The Committee for the Scientific Investigation of the Claims of the Paranormal and its use of the literature. *Social Studies of Science,* **14,** 521–546.
Podmore, F. (1896). Poltergeists. *Proceedings of the Society for Psychical Research,* **12,** 45–115.
Podmore, F. (1902). *Modern spiritualism: A history and a criticism. Vol. II.* London: Methuen.
Podmore, F. (1909). *Telepathic hallucinations: The new view of ghosts.* London: Milner.
Podmore, F. (1910). *The newer spiritualism.* London: Fisher Unwin.
Poynton, J.C. (1975). Results of an out-of-body survey. In J.C. Poynton (Ed.),

Parapsychology in South Africa (pp. 109–123). Johannesburg: South African Society for Psychical Research.

Prasad, J., & Stevenson, I. (1968). A survey of spontaneous psychical experiences in school children of Uttar Pradesh, India. *International Journal of Parapsychology,* **10,** 241–261.

Pratt, J.G. (1973). A decade of research with a selected ESP subject: An overview and reappraisal of the work with Pavel Stepanek. *Proceedings of the American Society for Psychical Research,* **30,** 1–78.

Pratt, J.G. (1987). *Gaither Pratt: A life for parapsychology,* ed. J. Keil. Jefferson, NC: McFarland.

Pratt, J.G., Rhine, J.B., Smith, B.M., Stuart, C.E., & Greenwood, J.A. (1940). *Extra-sensory perception after sixty years: A critical appraisal of the research in extra-sensory perception.* New York: Holt.

Pratt, J.G., & Woodruff, J.L. (1946). An exploratory investigation of PK position effects. *Journal of Parapsychology,* **10,** 197–207.

Price, A.D. (1973). Subject's control of imagery, "agent's" mood, and position effects in a dual-target ESP experiment. *Journal of Parapsychology,* **37,** 298–322.

Price, G.R. (1955). Science and the supernatural. *Science,* **122,** 359–367.

Price, G.R. (1956). Where is the definitive experiment? *Science,* **123,** 17–18.

Prince, W.F. (1928). *Noted witnesses for psychic occurrences.* Boston: Boston Society for Psychic Research.

Prince, W.F. (1930). *The enchanted boundary.* Boston: Boston Society for Psychic Research.

Quider, R.F. (1984). The effect of relaxation/suggestion and music on forced-choice ESP scoring. *Journal of the American Society for Psychical Research,* **78,** 241–262.

Radin, D.I. (1987, August). *Precognition of probable versus actual futures: Exploring futures that will never be.* Paper presented at the 30th Annual Convention of the Parapsychological Association, Edinburgh, Scotland.

Radin, D.I., May, E.C., & Thomson, M.J. (1986). Psi experiments with random number generators: Meta-analysis Part 1. In D.H. Weiner & D.I. Radin (Eds.), *Research in parapsychology 1985* (pp. 14–17). Metuchen, NJ: Scarecrow Press.

Randall, J.L. (1982). *Psychokinesis: A study of paranormal forces through the ages.* London: Souvenir Press.

Randall, J.L., & Davis, C.P. (1982). Paranormal deformation of nitinol wire: A confirmatory experiment. *Journal of the Society for Psychical Research,* **51,** 368–373.

Randi, J. (1975). *The magic of Uri Geller.* New York: Ballantine.

Randi, J. (1982). *Flim-flam! Psychics, ESP, unicorns and other delusions.* Buffalo, NY: Prometheus Books.

Randi, J. (1983a). The Project Alpha experiment: Part 1. The first two years. *Skeptical Inquirer,* **7**(4), 24–33.

Randi, J. (1983b). The Project Alpha experiment: Part 2. Beyond the laboratory. *Skeptical Inquirer,* **8**(1), 36–45.

Rank, O. (1971). *The double: A psychoanalytic study.* Chapel Hill, NC: University of North Carolina Press.

Rao, K.R. (1965). The bidirectionality of psi. *Journal of Parapsychology,* **29,** 230–250.

Rao, K.R. (1978). Theories of psi. In S. Krippner (Ed.), *Advances in parapsychological research, Vol. 2: Extrasensory perception* (pp. 245–295). New York: Plenum Press.

Rao, K.R. (1981). Correspondence. *Journal of the Society for Psychical Research,* **51,** 191–193.

Rao, K.R. (Ed.) (1984). *The basic experiments in parapsychology.* Jefferson, NC: McFarland.

Rao, K.R., Kanthamani, H., & Norwood, B. (1983). Sex-related differential scoring in two volitional studies. *Journal of Parapsychology,* **47,** 7–21.

Raudive, K. (1971). *Breakthrough.* New York: Taplinger.

Rawcliffe, D.H. (1959). *Illusions and delusions of the supernatural and the occult.* New York: Dover.

Rawlings, M. (1978, March). *Beyond death's door.* Nashville, TN: Nelson.

Reed, G. (1972). *The psychology of anomalous experience.* London: Hutchinson.

Rein, G. (1978, March). *Healing energy and neurochemistry.* Paper presented at the 2nd International Conference of the Society for Psychical Research, Cambridge, England.

Reiser, M., Ludwig, L., Saxe, S., & Wagner, C. (1979). An evaluation of the use of psychics in the investigation of major crimes. *Journal of Police Science and Administration,* **7,** 18–25.

Rhine, J.B. (1934). *Extra-sensory perception.* Boston: Boston Society for Psychic Research.

Rhine, J.B. (1936). Some selected experiments in extra-sensory perception. *Journal of Abnormal and Social Psychology,* **31,** 216–228.

Rhine, J.B. (1938). Experiments bearing on the precognition hypothesis. *Journal of Parapsychology,* **2,** 38–54.

Rhine, J.B. (1941). Experiments bearing upon the precognition hypothesis: III. Mechanically selected cards. *Journal of Parapsychology,* **5,** 1–58.

Rhine, J.B. (1948). *The reach of the mind.* London: Faber & Faber.

Rhine, J.B. (1969). Position effects in psi test results. *Journal of Parapsychology,* **33,** 136–157.

Rhine, J.B. (1974). Comments: A new case of experimenter unreliability. *Journal of Parapsychology,* **38,** 215–225.

Rhine, J.B. (1975). Comments: Second report on a case of experimenter fraud. *Journal of Parapsychology,* **39,** 306–325.

Rhine, J.B., & Humphrey, B.M. (1944). PK tests with six, twelve, and twenty-four dice per throw. *Journal of Parapsychology,* **8,** 139–157.

Rhine, J.B., & Pratt, J.G. (1954). A review of the Pearce-Pratt distance series of ESP tests. *Journal of Parapsychology,* **18,** 165–177.

Rhine, J.B., Smith, B.M., & Woodruff, J.L. (1938). Experiments bearing on the precognition hypothesis: II. The role of ESP in the shuffling of cards. *Journal of Parapsychology,* **2,** 119–131.

Rhine, L.E. (1937). Some stimulus variations in extra-sensory perception with child subjects. *Journal of Parapsychology,* **1,** 102–113.

Rhine, L.E. (1951). Conviction and associated conditions in spontaneous cases. *Journal of Parapsychology,* **15,** 164–191.

Rhine, L.E. (1953a). Subjective forms of spontaneous psi experiences. *Journal of Parapsychology,* **17,** 77–114.

Rhine, L.E. (1953b). The relation of experience to associated event in spontaneous ESP. *Journal of Parapsychology,* **17,** 187–209.

Rhine, L.E. (1954). Frequency of types of experience in spontaneous precognition. *Journal of Parapsychology,* **18,** 93–123.

Rhine, L.E. (1955). Precognition and intervention. *Journal of Parapsychology,* **19,** 1–34.

Rhine, L.E. (1956). The relationship of agent and percipient in spontaneous telepathy. *Journal of Parapsychology,* **20,** 1–32.

Rhine, L.E. (1957). Hallucinatory psi experiences: II. The initiative of the percipient in hallucinations of the living, the dying, and the dead. *Journal of Parapsychology,* **21,** 13–46.

Rhine, L.E. (1961). *Hidden channels of the mind.* New York: Morrow.

Rhine, L.E. (1962a). Psychological processes in ESP experiences. Part I. Waking experiences. *Journal of Parapsychology,* **26,** 88–111.

Rhine, L.E. (1962b). Psychological processes in ESP experiences. Part II. Dreams. *Journal of Parapsychology,* **26,** 172–199.

Rhine, L.E. (1963). Spontaneous physical effects and the psi process. *Journal of Parapsychology,* **27,** 84–122.

Rhine, L.E. (1970). *Mind over matter: Psychokinesis.* New York: Macmillan.

Rhine, L.E. (1981). *The invisible picture: A study of psychic experiences.* Jefferson, NC: McFarland.

Rhine, L.E., & Rhine, J.B. (1943). The psychokinetic effect. I. The first experiment. *Journal of Parapsychology,* **7,** 20–43.

Richet, C. (1888). Further experiments in hypnotic lucidity or clairvoyance. *Proceedings of the Society for Psychical Research,* **6,** 66–83.

Richet, C. (1923). *Thirty years of psychical research: Being a treatise on metapsychics.* London: Collins.

Ring, K. (1980). *Life at death: A scientific investigation of the near-death experience.* New York: Coward, McCann & Geoghegan.

Ring, K. (1982). Precognitive and prophetic visions in near-death experiences. *Anabiosis,* **2,** 47–74.

Ring, K. (1984). *Heading toward Omega: In search of the meaning of the near-death experience.* New York: Morrow.

Rockwell, T. (1979). Pseudoscience? Or pseudocriticism? *Journal of Parapsychology,* **43,** 221–231.

Rodabough, T. (1985). Near-death experiences: An examination of the supporting data and alternative explanations. *Death Studies,* **9,** 95–113.

Rodin, E.A. (1980). The reality of death experiences: A personal perspective. *Journal of Nervous and Mental Disease,* **168,** 259–263.

Rogo, D.S. (1974). Psychotherapy and the poltergeist. *Journal of the Society for Psychical Research,* **47,** 433–446.

Rogo, D.S. (1975). Psi and psychosis: A review of the experimental evidence. *Journal of Parapsychology,* **39,** 120–128.

Rogo, D.S. (1980). Parapsychology and psychology textbooks. *Research Letter of the University of Utrecht Parapsychology Laboratory,* No. 10, 9–17.

Rogo, D.S. (1982). The poltergeist and family dynamics: A report on a recent investigation. *Journal of the Society for Psychical Research,* **51,** 233–237.

Rogo, D.S. (1983). *Leaving the body: A practical guide to astral projection.* Englewood Cliffs, NJ: Prentice-Hall.

Rogo, D.S. (1985). *The search for yesterday: A critical examination of the evidence for reincarnation.* Englewood Cliffs, NJ: Prentice-Hall.

Roll, W.G. (1966). ESP and memory. *International Journal of Neuropsychiatry,* **2,** 505–521.

Roll, W.G. (1968). Some physical and psychological aspects of a series of poltergeist phenomena. *Journal of the American Society for Psychical Research,* **62,** 263–308.

Roll, W.G. (1976). *The poltergeist.* Metuchen, NJ: Scarecrow Press.

Roll, W.G. (1977). Poltergeists. In B.B. Wolman (Ed.), *Handbook of parapsychology* (pp. 382–413). New York: Van Nostrand Reinhold.

Roll, W.G. (1978a). Understanding the poltergeist. In W.G. Roll (Ed.), *Research in parapsychology 1977* (pp. 183–195). Metuchen, NJ: Scarecrow Press.

Roll, W.G. (1978b). Towards a theory for the poltergeist. *European Journal of Parapsychology, 2,* 167–200.

Romm, E.G. (1977). When you give a closet occultist a Ph.D., what kind of research can you expect? *Humanist, 37*(3), 12–15.

Rose, L. (1955). Some aspects of paranormal healing. *Journal of the Society for Psychical Research, 38,* 105–121.

Rose, L., & Rose, R. (1951). Psi experiments with Australian aborigines. *Journal of Parapsychology, 15,* 122–131.

Rosenblatt, P.C., Walsh, R.P., & Jackson, D.A. (1976). *Grief and mourning in cross-cultural perspective.* New Haven, CT: HRAF Press.

Rubenstein, R., & Newman, R. (1954). The living out of "future" experiences under hypnosis. *Science, 119,* 472–473.

Rush, J.H. (1977). Problems and methods in psychokinesis research. In S. Krippner (Ed.), *Advances in parapsychological research, Vol. 1: Psychokinesis* (pp. 15–78). New York: Plenum Press.

Rush, J.H. (1982). Problems and methods in psychokinesis research. In S. Krippner (Ed.), *Advances in parapsychological research, Vol. 3* (pp. 83–114). New York: Plenum Press.

Sabine, W.H.W. (1950). Is there a case for retrocognition? *Journal of the American Society for Psychical Research, 44,* 43–64.

Sabom, M.B. (1982). *Recollections of death: A medical investigation.* New York: Harper & Row.

Sagan, C. (1979). *Broca's brain: Reflections on the romance of science.* New York: Random House.

St. James-Roberts, I. (1976). Cheating in science. *New Scientist, 72,* 466–469.

Salter, W.H. (1958). F.W.H. Myers' posthumous message. *Proceedings of the Society for Psychical Research, 52,* 1–32.

Saltmarsh, H.F. (1930–1931). A report on the investigation of some sittings with Mrs. Warren Elliot. *Proceedings of the Society for Psychical Research, 39,* 47–184.

Saltmarsh, H.F. (1934). Report on cases of apparent precognition. *Proceedings of the Society for Psychical Research, 42,* 49–103.

Saltmarsh, H.F. (1938). *Evidence of personal survival from cross-correspondences.* London: Bell.

Sandford, J. (1977). Report of three experiments examining the effect of feedback on the direct cognition of an electronic timer. *Journal of Parapsychology, 41,* 36–37. (Abstract.)

Sannwald, G. (1963). On the psychology of spontaneous paranormal phenomena. *International Journal of Parapsychology, 5,* 274–292.

Schacter, D.L. (1976). The hypnagogic state: A critical review of the literature. *Psychological Bulletin, 83,* 452–481.

Schatzman, M. (1980). *The story of Ruth.* New York: Putnam's.

Schechter, E.I. (1977). Nonintentional ESP: A review and replication. *Journal of the American Society for Psychical Research, 71,* 337–374.

Schechter, E.I. (1984). Hypnotic induction vs. control conditions: Illustrating an approach to the evaluation of replicability in parapsychological data. *Journal of the American Society for Psychical Research, 78,* 1–27.

Schmeidler, G.R. (1944). Position effects as psychological phenomena. *Journal of Parapsychology, 8,* 110–123.

Schmeidler, G.R. (1952). Personal values and ESP scores. *Journal of Abnormal and Social Psychology, 47,* 757–761.

Schmeidler, G.R. (Ed.) (1976). *Parapsychology: Its relation to physics, biology, psychology, and psychiatry.* Metuchen, NJ: Scarecrow Press.

Schmeidler, G.R. (1977). Research findings in psychokinesis. In S. Krippner (Ed.), *Advances in parapsychological research, Vol. 1: Psychokinesis* (pp. 79–132). New York: Plenum Press.

Schmeidler, G.R. (1980). Looking ahead: A method for research on survival. *Journal of the Academy of Religion and Psychical Research, 3,* 16–22.

Schmeidler, G.R. (1982). PK research: Findings and theories. In S. Krippner (Ed.), *Advances in parapsychological research, Vol. 3* (pp. 115–146). New York: Plenum Press.

Schmeidler, G.R. (1987). Psychokinesis: Recent studies and a possible paradigm shift. In S. Krippner (Ed.), *Advances in parapsychological research, Vol. 5* (pp. 9–38). Jefferson, NC: McFarland.

Schmeidler, G.R., & Lewis, L. (1968). A search for feedback in ESP: Part II. High ESP scores after two successes on triple-aspect targets. *Journal of the American Society for Psychical Research, 62,* 255–262.

Schmeidler, G.R., & Maher, M. (1981). The nonverbal communications of psi-conducive and psi-inhibitory experimenters. In W.G. Roll & J. Beloff (Eds.), *Research in parapsychology 1980* (pp. 121–124). Metuchen, NJ: Scarecrow Press.

Schmeidler, G.R., & McConnell, R.A. (1958). *ESP and personality patterns.* New Haven, CT: Yale University Press.

Schmidt, H. (1969). Precognition of a quantum process. *Journal of Parapsychology, 33,* 99–108.

Schmidt, H. (1970a). A quantum mechanical random number generator for psi tests. *Journal of Parapsychology, 34,* 219–224.

Schmidt, H. (1970b). PK experiments with animals as subjects. *Journal of Parapsychology, 34,* 255–261.

Schmidt, H. (1973). PK tests with a high-speed random number generator. *Journal of Parapsychology, 37,* 105–118.

Schmidt, H. (1974). Comparison of PK action on two different random number generators. *Journal of Parapsychology, 38,* 47–55.

Schmidt, H. (1975). Toward a mathematical theory of psi. *Journal of the American Society for Psychical Research, 69,* 301–319.

Schmidt, H. (1976). PK effect on pre-recorded targets. *Journal of the American Society for Psychical Research, 70,* 267–291.

Schmidt, H. (1984). Comparison of a teleological model with a quantum collapse model of psi. *Journal of Parapsychology, 48,* 261–276.

Schmidt, H. (1985). Addition effect for PK on prerecorded targets. *Journal of Parapsychology, 49,* 229–244.

Schnaper, N. (1980). Comments germane to the paper entitled "The reality of death experiences" by Ernst Rodin. *Journal of Nervous and Mental Disease, 168,* 268–270.

Schouten, S.A. (1981). Analysing spontaneous cases: A replication based on the Sannwald collection. *European Journal of Parapsychology, 4,* 9–48.

Schouten, S.A. (1982). Analysing spontaneous cases: A replication based on the Rhine collection. *European Journal of Parapsychology, 4,* 113–158.

Schouten, S.A., & Kelly, E.F. (1978). On the experiment of Brugmans, Heymans, and Weinberg. *European Journal of Parapsychology, 2,* 247–290.

Schwarz, B.E. (1980). *Psychic-nexus: Psychic phenomena in psychiatry and every-day life.* New York: Van Nostrand Reinhold.

Scriven, M. (1962). The frontiers of psychology: Psychoanalysis and parapsychology. In R.G. Colodny (Ed.), *Frontiers of science and philosophy* (pp. 79–129). Pittsburgh, PA: University of Pittsburgh Press.

Scutt, D.C. (1981). An investigation into metal bending "Geller Effect" with Ori Svoray. *Journal of the Society for Psychical Research, 51,* 1–6.

Servadio, E. (1956). Transference and thought-transference. *International Journal of Psychoanalysis, 37,* 392–395.

Shadowitz, A., & Walsh, P. (1976). *The dark side of knowledge.* Reading, MA: Addison-Wesley.

Shapiro, T., Sherman, M., & Osowsky, I. (1980). Preschool children's conception of ghosts. *Journal of the American Academy of Child Psychiatry, 19,* 41–55.

Sheils, D. (1978). A cross-cultural study of beliefs in out-of-the-body experiences. *Journal of the Society for Psychical Research, 49,* 697–741.

Sidgwick, Mrs. H. (E.M.) (1888–1889). On the evidence for premonitions. *Proceedings of the Society for Psychical Research, 5,* 288–354.

Sidgwick, Mrs. H. (E.M.) (1891). On the evidence for clairvoyance. *Proceedings of the Society for Psychical Research, 7,* 30–99.

Sidgwick, H., Johnson, A., Myers, F.W.H., Podmore, F., & Sidgwick, E.M. (1894). Report on the Census of Hallucinations. *Proceedings of the Society for Psychical Research, 10,* 25–422.

Siegel, C. (1986). Parapsychological counseling: Six patterns of response to spontaneous psychic experiences. In D.H. Weiner & D.I. Radin (Eds.), *Research in parapsychology 1985* (pp. 172–174). Metuchen, NJ: Scarecrow Press.

Siegel, R.K. (1980). The psychology of life after death. *American Psychologist, 35,* 911–931.

Sigelman, L. (1977). Multi-nation surveys of religious beliefs. *Journal for the Scientific Study of Religion, 16,* 289–294.

Sinclair, U. (1962). *Mental radio* (2nd ed.). Springfield, IL: Thomas. (Original work published 1930.)

Smith, E.L. (1972). The Raudive voices—objective or subjective? A discussion. *Journal of the Society for Psychical Research, 46,* 192–200.

Smith, (M.) J. (1968). Paranormal effects on enzyme activity. *Journal of Parapsychology, 32,* 281. (Abstract.)

Smith, P., & Irwin, H.J. (1981). Out-of-body experiences, needs, and the experimental approach: A laboratory study. *Parapsychology Review, 12*(3), 1–4.

Snoyman, P. (1985). Family therapy in a case of alleged RSPK. *Parapsychological Journal of South Africa, 6,* 75–90.

Soal, S.G., & Bateman, F. (1954). *Modern experiments in telepathy.* London: Faber & Faber.

Solfvin, G.F., & Roll, W.G. (1976). A case of RSPK with an epileptic agent. In J.D. Morris, W.G. Roll, & R.L. Morris (Eds.), *Research in parapsychology 1975* (pp. 115–120). Metuchen, NJ: Scarecrow Press.

Solfvin, J. (1984). Mental healing. In S. Krippner (Ed.), *Advances in parapsychological research, Vol. 4* (pp. 31–63). Jefferson, NC: McFarland.

Sondow, N. (1988). The decline of precognized events with the passage of time: Evidence from spontaneous dreams. *Journal of the American Society for Psychical Research, 82,* 33–51.

Spencer-Brown, G. (1953). *Probability and scientific inference.* New York: Longmans, Green.

Spiritualism exposed: Margaret Fox Kane confesses to fraud. (1985). In P. Kurtz (Ed.), *A skeptic's handbook of parapsychology* (pp. 225–233). Buffalo, NY: Prometheus Books. (Original work published 1888.)

Stanford, R.G. (1967). Response bias and the correctness of ESP test responses. *Journal of Parapsychology, 31,* 280–289.

Stanford, R.G. (1969). "Associative activation of the unconscious" and "visualization" as methods for influencing the PK target. *Journal of the American Society for Psychical Research, 63,* 338–351.

Stanford, R.G. (1975). Response factors in extrasensory performance. *Journal of Communication, 25*(1), 153–161.

Stanford, R.G. (1977). Experimental psychokinesis: A review from diverse perspectives. In B.B. Wolman (Ed.), *Handbook of parapsychology* (pp. 324–381). New York: Van Nostrand Reinhold.

Stanford, R.G. (1978). Toward reinterpreting psi events. *Journal of the American Society for Psychical Research, 72,* 197–214.

Stanford, R.G. (1983). Possible psi-mediated perceptual effects of similarity of REG alternatives to the PK target: A double-blind study. In W.G. Roll, J. Beloff, & R.A. White (Eds.), *Research in parapsychology 1982* (pp. 178–181). Metuchen, NJ: Scarecrow Press.

Stanford, R.G. (1987a). Ganzfeld and hypnotic-induction procedures in ESP research: Toward understanding their success. In S. Krippner (Ed.), *Advances in parapsychological research, Vol. 5* (pp. 39–76). Jefferson, NC: McFarland.

Stanford, R.G. (1987b). The out-of-body experience as an imaginal journey: The developmental perspective. *Journal of Parapsychology, 51,* 137–155.

Stanford, R. (1988). Ethics and professional social responsibility in parapsychological research and publication. *Parapsychology Review, 19*(3), 1–5.

Stanford, R.G., & Angelini, R.F. (1984). Effects of noise and the trait of absorption on ganzfeld ESP performance. *Journal of Parapsychology, 48,* 85–99.

Stanford, R.G., Zenhausern, R., Taylor, A., & Dwyer, M.A. (1975). Psychokinesis as psi-mediated instrumental response. *Journal of the American Society for Psychical Research, 69,* 127–133.

Stanford, T.W. (1903). *Psychic phenomena: A narrative of facts.* Melbourne: Bruce & Davies.

Steilberg, B.J. (1975). "Conscious concentration" versus "visualization" in PK tests. *Journal of Parapsychology, 39,* 12–20.

Stevenson, I. (1960). A review and analysis of paranormal experiences connected with the sinking of the *Titanic. Journal of the American Society for Psychical Research, 54,* 153–171.

Stevenson, I. (1963). A postcognitive dream illustrating some aspects of the pictographic process. *Journal of the American Society for Psychical Research, 57,* 182–202.

Stevenson, I. (1966). Twenty cases suggestive of reincarnation. *Proceedings of the American Society for Psychical Research, 26,* 1–362.

Stevenson, I. (1967). An antagonist's view of parapsychology. A review of Professor Hansel's "ESP: A scientific evaluation." *Journal of the American Society for Psychical Research, 61,* 254–267.

Stevenson, I. (1968). The combination lock test for survival. *Journal of the American Society for Psychical Research, 62,* 246–254.

Stevenson, I. (1970). *Telepathic impressions: A review and report of thirty-five new cases.* Charlottesville, VA: University Press of Virginia.

Stevenson, I. (1971). The substantiality of spontaneous cases. In W.G. Roll, R.L. Morris, & J.D. Morris (Eds.), *Proceedings of the Parapsychological Association No. 5, 1968* (pp. 91–128). Durham, NC: Parapsychological Association.

Stevenson, I. (1972). Are poltergeists living or are they dead? *Journal of the American Society for Psychical Research,* **66,** 233–252.

Stevenson, I. (1974). *Xenoglossy: A review and report of a case.* Charlottesville, VA: University Press of Virginia.

Stevenson, I. (1975). *Cases of the reincarnation type, Vol. I: Ten cases in India.* Charlottesville, VA: University Press of Virginia.

Stevenson, I. (1977a). Reincarnation: Field studies and theoretical issues. In B.B. Wolman (Ed.), *Handbook of parapsychology* (pp. 631–663). New York: Van Nostrand Reinhold.

Stevenson, I. (1977b). The explanatory value of the idea of reincarnation. *Journal of Nervous and Mental Disease,* **164,** 305–326.

Stevenson, I. (1977c). *Cases of the reincarnation type, Vol. II: Ten cases in Sri Lanka.* Charlottesville, VA: University Press of Virginia.

Stevenson, I. (1980). Gaither Pratt: An appreciation. *Journal of the American Society for Psychical Research,* **74,** 277–295.

Stevenson, I. (1982). The contribution of apparitions to the evidence for survival. *Journal of the American Society for Psychical Research,* **76,** 341–358.

Stevenson, I. (1983a). American children who claim to remember previous lives. *Journal of Nervous and Mental Disease,* **171,** 742–748.

Stevenson, I. (1983b). Cryptomnesia and parapsychology. *Journal of the Society for Psychical Research,* **52,** 1–30.

Stevenson, I. (1984). *Unlearned language: New studies in xenoglossy.* Charlottesville, VA: University Press of Virginia.

Stevenson, I. (1987a). *Children who remember previous lives: A question of reincarnation.* Charlottesville, VA: University Press of Virginia.

Stevenson, I. (1987b). Why *investigate* spontaneous cases? *Journal of the American Society for Psychical Research,* **81,** 101–109.

Stevenson, I., Pasricha, S., & Samararatne, G. (1988). Deception and self-deception in cases of the reincarnation type: Seven illustrative cases in Asia. *Journal of the American Society for Psychical Research,* **82,** 1–31.

Stokes, D.M. (1987). Theoretical parapsychology. In S. Krippner (Ed.), *Advances in parapsychological research, Vol. 5* (pp. 77–189). Jefferson, NC: McFarland.

Strauch, I. (1963). Medical aspects of "mental" healing. *International Journal of Parapsychology,* **5,** 135–165.

Struckmeyer, F.R. (1970). Precognition and the "intervention paradox." *Journal of the American Society for Psychical Research,* **64,** 320–326.

Stuart, C.E. (1938). The effect of rate of movement in card matching tests of extrasensory perception. *Journal of Parapsychology,* **2,** 171–183.

Targ, R., & Puthoff, H. (1974). Information transmission under conditions of sensory shielding. *Nature,* **252,** 602–607.

Targ, R., & Puthoff, H. (1978). *Mind-reach.* London: Granada.

Tart, C.T. (1966). Card guessing tests: Learning paradigm or extinction paradigm? *Journal of the American Society for Psychical Research,* **60,** 46–55.

Tart, C.T. (1971). *On being stoned: A psychological study of marijuana intoxication.* Palo Alto, CA: Science & Behavior Books.

Tart, C.T. (1976). *Learning to use extrasensory perception.* Chicago: University of Chicago Press.

Tart, C.T. (1977). Toward conscious control of psi through immediate feedback training: Some considerations of internal processes. *Journal of the American Society for Psychical Research,* **71**, 375–407.

Tart, C.T. (1978). Space, time, and mind. In W.G. Roll (Ed.), *Research in parapsychology 1977* (pp. 197–249). Metuchen, NJ: Scarecrow Press.

Tart, C.T. (1982). The controversy about psi: Two psychological theories. *Journal of Parapsychology,* **46**, 313–320.

Tart, C.T. (1983). Learning to use psychokinesis: Theoretical and methodological notes. In W.G. Roll, J. Beloff, & R.A. White (Eds.), *Research in parapsychology 1982* (pp. 97–99). Metuchen, NJ: Scarecrow Press.

Tart, C.T. (1984). Acknowledging and dealing with the fear of psi. *Journal of the American Society for Psychical Research,* **78**, 133–143.

Tart, C.T. (1988). Effects of electrical shielding on GESP performance. *Journal of the American Society for Psychical Research,* **82**, 129–146.

Tart, C.T., & LaBore, C.M. (1986). Attitudes toward strongly functioning psi: A preliminary survey. *Journal of the American Society for Psychical Research,* **80**, 163–173.

Taylor, J. (1975). *Superminds: An investigation into the paranormal.* London: Macmillan.

Taylor, J.G., & Balanovski, E. (1979). Is there any scientific explanation of the paranormal? *Nature,* **279**, 631–633.

Tellegen, A., & Atkinson, G. (1974). Openness to absorbing and self-altering experiences ("Absorption"), a trait related to hypnotic susceptibility. *Journal of Abnormal Psychology,* **83**, 268–277.

Thalbourne, M.A., & Haraldsson, E. (1980). Personality characteristics of sheep and goats. *Personality and Individual Differences,* **1**, 180–185.

Thomas, C.D. (1932–1933). A consideration of a series of proxy sittings. *Proceedings of the Society for Psychical Research,* **41**, 139–185.

Thomas, K. (1971). *Religion and the decline of magic.* London: Weidenfeld & Nicolson.

Thomson, S. (1986). Ethical dimensions of psi capability. *Applied Psi,* **5**(1), 8–11, 14.

Thouless, R.H. (1946). A test of survival. *Proceedings of the Society for Psychical Research,* **48**, 253–263.

Thouless, R.H. (1979). Theories about survival. *Journal of the Society for Psychical Research,* **50**, 1–8.

Thouless, R.H., & Wiesner, B.P. (1948). The psi processes in normal and "paranormal" psychology. *Proceedings of the Society for Psychical Research,* **48**, 177–196.

Thurston, H. (1953). *Ghosts and poltergeists.* London: Burns Oats & Washbourne.

Tietze, T.R. (1985). The "Margery" affair. *Journal of the American Society for Psychical Research,* **79**, 339–379.

Timm, U. (1969). Mixing-up of symbols in ESP card experiments (so-called consistent missing) as a possible cause for psi-missing. *Journal of Parapsychology,* **33**, 109–124.

Tobacyk, J.J., & Mitchell, T.P. (1987). The out-of-body experience and personality adjustment. *Journal of Nervous and Mental Disease,* **175**, 367–370.

Troland, L.T. (1976). A technique for the experimental study of telepathy and other alleged clairvoyant processes. *Journal of Parapsychology,* **40**, 194–216. (Original work published 1917.)

References 307

Truzzi, M. (1987). Reflections on "Project Alpha": Scientific experiment or conjuror's illusion? *Zetetic Scholar,* **12/13,** 73–98.

Tune, G.S. (1964). A brief survey of variables that influence random-generation. *Perceptual and Motor Skills,* **18,** 705–710.

Twemlow, S.W., & Gabbard, G.O. (1984). The influence of demographic/psychological factors and preexisting conditions on the near-death experience. *Omega,* **15,** 223–235.

Tyrrell, G.N.M. (1963). *Apparitions.* New York: Collier. (Original work published 1942.)

Ullman, M. (1973). Psi and psychiatry: The need for restructuring basic concepts. In W.G. Roll, R.L. Morris, & J.D. Morris (Eds.), *Research in parapsychology 1972* (pp. 110–113). Metuchen, NJ: Scarecrow Press.

Ullman, M., & Krippner, S. (1970). Dream studies and telepathy. *Parapsychological Monographs, No. 12.* New York: Parapsychology Foundation.

Ullman, M., & Krippner, S., with Vaughan, A. (1973). *Dream telepathy.* New York: Macmillan.

Usher, F.L., & Burt, F.P. (1909). Thought transference: Some experiments in long distance thought-transference. *Annals of Psychical Science,* **8,** 561–600.

Van de Castle, R.L. (1958). An exploratory study of some personality correlates associated with PK performance. *Journal of the American Society for Psychical Research,* **52,** 134–150.

Vasiliev, L.L. (1976). *Experiments in distant influence.* New York: Dutton. (Original work published 1963.)

Venn, J. (1986). Hypnosis and the reincarnation hypothesis: A critical review and intensive case study. *Journal of the American Society for Psychical Research,* **80,** 409–425.

Wagenaar, W.A. (1972). Generation of random sequences by human subjects: A critical survey of literature. *Psychological Bulletin,* **77,** 65–72.

Wagner, M.W., & Monnet, M. (1979). Attitudes of college professors toward extrasensory perception. *Zetetic Scholar,* **5,** 7–16.

Walker, E.H. (1975). Foundations of paraphysical and parapsychological phenomena. In L. Oteri (Ed.), *Quantum physics and parapsychology* (pp. 1–53). New York: Parapsychology Foundation.

Walker, E.H. (1984). A review of criticisms of the quantum mechanical theory of psi phenomena. *Journal of Parapsychology,* **48,** 277–332.

Warcollier, R. (1975). *Experimental telepathy.* New York: Arno Press. (Original work published 1938.)

Warner, L. (1952). A second survey of psychological opinion on ESP. *Journal of Parapsychology,* **16,** 284–295.

Warner, L., & Clark, C.C. (1938). A survey of psychological opinion on ESP. *Journal of Parapsychology,* **2,** 296–301.

Wassermann, G.D. (1956). An outline of a field theory of organismic form and behavior. In G.E. Wolstenholme & E.C.P. Millar (Eds.), *Ciba Foundation symposium on extrasensory perception* (pp. 53–72). Boston: Little, Brown.

Watkins, G.K., & Watkins, A.M. (1971). Possible PK influence on the resuscitation of anesthetized mice. *Journal of Parapsychology,* **35,** 257–272.

Weiner, D.H. (1980). Psi counseling: The situation at research laboratories. In W.G. Roll (Ed.), *Research in parapsychology 1979* (pp. 45–46). Metuchen, NJ: Scarecrow Press.

Weiner, D.H. (1982). The effects of preferred cognitive mode and goal conceptualization in an intentional PK task. *Journal of Parapsychology,* **46,** 56–57. (Abstract.)

Weiner, D.H., & Haight, J. (1986). Charting hidden channels: Louisa E. Rhine's case collection project. In K.R. Rao (Ed.), *Case studies in parapsychology* (pp. 14–30). Jefferson, NC: McFarland.

Weiner, D.H., & Zingrone, N.L. (1986). The checker effect revisited. *Journal of Parapsychology,* **50,** 85–121.

West, D.J. (1948). A mass-observation questionnaire on hallucinations. *Journal of the Society for Psychical Research,* **34,** 187–196.

West, D.J. (1982). Thoughts on testimony to the paranormal. *Parapsychology Review,* **13**(5), 1–8.

White, R.A. (1964a). A comparison of old and new methods of response to targets in ESP experiments. *Journal of the American Society for Psychical Research,* **58,** 21–56.

White, R.A. (1964b). Approaches to the study of spontaneous cases. *International Journal of Parapsychology,* **6,** 227–240.

White, R.A. (1976). The limits of experimenter influence on psi test results: Can any be set? *Journal of the American Society for Psychical Research,* **70,** 333–369.

White, R.A. (1977). The influence of experimenter motivation, attitudes, and methods of handling subjects in psi test results. In B.B. Wolman (Ed.), *Handbook of parapsychology* (pp. 273–301). New York: Van Nostrand Reinhold.

Whiteman, J.H.M. (1961). *The mystical life.* London: Faber & Faber.

Whitlock, F.A. (1978). The psychiatry and psychopathology of paranormal phenomena. *Australian and New Zealand Journal of Psychiatry,* **12,** 11–19.

Whitton, J.L. (1975). Qualitative time-domain analysis of acoustic envelopes of psychokinetic table rappings. *New Horizons,* **2**(1), 21–24.

Whitton, J.L. (1976). Paramorphic table rappings: Acoustic analysis. *New Horizons,* **2**(2), 7–11.

Whitton, J.L., & Fisher, J. (1986). *Life between life.* Garden City, NY: Doubleday.

Wilson, I. (1982). *Reincarnation? The claims investigated.* Harmondsworth, England: Penguin.

Wilson, I. (1984). A tragic double act. In P. Brookesmith (Ed.), *Life after death* (pp. 49–51). London: Orbis.

Wilson, S.C., & Barber, T.X. (1983). The fantasy-prone personality: Implications for understanding imagery, hypnosis, and parapsychological phenomena. In A.A. Sheikh (Ed.), *Imagery: Current theory, research, and application* (pp. 340–387). New York: Wiley.

Winkelman, M. (1981). The effect of formal education on extrasensory abilities: The Ozolco study. *Journal of Parapsychology,* **45,** 321–336.

Wolkowski, Z.W. (1977). Reflections on psychokinetic phenomena. In J.D. Morris, W.G. Roll, & R.L. Morris (Eds.), *Research in parapsychology 1976* (pp. 207–209). Metuchen, NJ: Scarecrow Press.

Wooffitt, R.C., & Blackmore, S.J. (1985, September). *Out-of-the-body experiences and young children.* Paper presented at the 9th International Conference of the Society for Psychical Research, Kensington, London.

Wren-Lewis, J. (1974). Resistance to the study of the paranormal. *Journal of Humanistic Psychology,* **14**(2), 41–48.

Wyndham, H. (1937). *Mr. Sludge, the medium: Being the life and adventures of Daniel Dunglas Home.* London: Bles.

Yram. (1974). *Practical astral projection.* New York: Weiser. (Original work published ca. 1926.)

Zenhausern, R., Stanford, R.G., & Esposito, C. (1977). The application of signal detection theory to clairvoyance and precognition tasks. In J.D. Morris, W.G. Roll, & R.L. Morris (Eds.), *Research in parapsychology 1976* (pp. 170–173). Metuchen, NJ: Scarecrow Press.

Zohar, D. (1982). *Through the time barrier: A study in precognition and modern physics.* London: Heinemann.

Zolik, E.S. (1958). An experimental investigation of the psycho-dynamic implications of the hypnotic "previous existence" fantasy. *Journal of Clinical Psychology,* **14,** 179–183.

Zorab, G. (1970). Test sittings with D.D. Home at Amsterdam (1858). *Journal of Parapsychology,* **34,** 47–63.

Zusne, L., & Jones, W.H. (1982). *Anomalistic psychology: A study of extraordinary phenomena of behavior and experience.* Hillsdale, NJ: Lawrence Erlbaum Associates.

Name Index

Subject Index

and beliefs 50
and chance 53–54, 124
and deception 51–53
and inaccurate recall 48–49
limitations 48–55, 124
and misperception 49–50
and subconscious perception 50–51
value 47–48
SPR *see* Society for Psychical Research
Statistical analyses 64–65, 67, 72, 88
Subconscious perception 50–51
Subjects, unselected 59
Super-ESP hypothesis 165, 166, 167, 168–169, 249
Suppression of data 68–69, 72
Surveys 37–38
Survival hypothesis 8, 164–169, 179, 183, 185, 194, 198, 220, 223, 236, 238, 240, 250, 255
cipher test 167–168
combination lock test 168
Synchronicity 157–158
Synesthesia 219–220

Table tipping 19, 23, 33, 139
Teaching 277
Technical precision 134, 268
Teleological view of psi 132, 147, 156, 157, 158–159
Telepathy 6, 14, 36, 44, 58, 59, 60, 61, 63, 64, 93, 120, 236, 237, 257
Temporal displacement 87, 108–110
Temporal lobe 157, 195, 217
Ten-choice trainer 69, 90
Terminal salience 86
Theories of psi 149–162
electromagnetic 150–151
elementary particle 152
energy field 151–152
lack of 149

noncybernetic 157–159
observational 153–155
skeptical 159–162
teleological 158–159
Theories of psi experience 155–157
memory models 156–157
pseudosensory models 155
Therapy *see* Clinical practice
Theta 271
Thoughtography 146
Time 108–118
theories of 115–116
Titanic 112
Training 264; *see also* Learning and ESP
Transcendental realm 187–191, 206
Transference 258
Transtemporal inhibition 87
Tunnel effect 185, 187, 204

Underlying processes *see* Process-oriented research
Unitarian view of psi 157

Variance effects
in ESP 88
in PK 130

Waking ESP 38, 44

Xenoglossy 166, 251–252

Zener cards *see* ESP cards
Zenith Radio study 160